THE WORKS
AND CORRESPONDENCE OF
DAVID RICARDO

EDITED BY
PIERO SRAFFA

WITH THE COLLABORATION OF
M. H. DOBB

VOLUME I

ON THE PRINCIPLES OF
POLITICAL ECONOMY AND
TAXATION

PUBLISHED FOR THE ROYAL ECONOMIC SOCIETY

The right of the
University of Cambridge
to print and sell
all manner of books
was granted by
Henry VIII in 1534.
The University has printed
and published continuously
since 1584.

CAMBRIDGE UNIVERSITY PRESS

CAMBRIDGE
LONDON   NEW YORK   NEW ROCHELLE
MELBOURNE   SYDNEY

Published by the Press Syndicate of the University of Cambridge
The Pitt Building, Trumpington Street, Cambridge CB2 1RP
32 East 57th Street, New York, NY 10022, USA
10 Stamford Road, Oakleigh, Melbourne 3166, Australia

ISBN 0 521 06066 4 hard covers
ISBN 0 521 28505 4 paperback

First published 1951
Reprinted 1953 1962 1966 1970 1975
First paperback edition 1981
Reprinted 1986

Printed in Great Britain at the
University Press, Cambridge

CONTENTS OF VOLUME I

FACSIMILES

GENERAL PREFACE

WHEN Ricardo's *Letters to Trower* were published in 1899 (the last of three similar collections) the editors of that volume remarked in their Introduction: 'Two appreciable *desiderata* still remain—literary evidence of his long and close intimacy with James Mill, and the important "Notes on Malthus"'. They concluded that further knowledge of Ricardo would have to wait 'until some fortunate accident or more successful search' brought these to light. The *Notes on Malthus* have since been found and published; and the last big gap is now filled by the discovery of both sides of the extensive correspondence between Ricardo and James Mill which is here published for the first time.

Moreover, the letters of Malthus to Ricardo have been found and are first published in the present edition. Of these, long believed lost, Professor Foxwell had written in 1907 (when publishing in the *Economic Journal* a solitary letter which had survived): 'The loss of Malthus' share in this correspondence may be ranked by economists next to that other literary disaster, the destruction of David Hume's comments on the "Wealth of Nations."'[1]

It is perhaps unique in economic literature for the writings, letters and speeches of one thinker to have such unity of subject matter (as is the case with Ricardo) that, although his works and correspondence are extant almost complete, they admit of publication virtually in their entirety as being all of them of interest to the economist. A certain amount of repetition is inevitable in the publication in full of this material. Nevertheless, to have the same doctrines presented at successive stages of their development, in varied contexts and to different audiences has evident advantages. At the same time so much of Ricardo's writing consists of discussion with contemporaries as to require the inclusion of much of their contribution in the form of letters and extracts from writings and speeches.

Most of the new material in the present edition will be found in the four volumes of Letters (vols. VI–IX). Besides the correspon-

[1] But see vol. XI, p. xxvii.

dence with Mill and the letters from Malthus and other correspondents, these volumes include a number of new miscellaneous letters of Ricardo. Altogether well over half of the 555 letters have not been previously published. Several new papers and notes are appended to the volumes of Pamphlets and Papers (vols. III–IV): of these the one most likely to attract attention is the unfinished paper on 'Absolute Value and Exchangeable Value' on which Ricardo had been engaged in the last weeks of his life. The speeches in the House of Commons, hitherto scattered over eleven volumes of *Hansard*, have been collected in vol. V, which also contains his speeches on other occasions and his evidence to Parliamentary Committees. The *Notes on Malthus* in vol. II are accompanied by the relevant text of Malthus. For the *Principles* in vol. I the variants of the several editions are given in full in notes and are analysed in the Introduction. In general, editorial Introductions or Notes, which are prefixed to each of Ricardo's works, are confined to an account of the immediate occasion from which that work arose and of the circumstances in which it was written.

When the search for unpublished manuscripts for the present edition started in 1930 a large box labelled 'Papers of the late D. Ricardo, Esq. M.P.' was discovered by Mr Frank Ricardo at Bromesberrow Place, near Ledbury, formerly the residence of Ricardo's eldest son, Osman. This, which had lain untouched for nearly a hundred years, turned out to contain practically all the letters of permanent interest received by Ricardo as well as drafts and other papers of his own. It has been the largest single source of new material and it constitutes the bulk of what in the present edition is referred to as the 'Ricardo Papers' (abbreviated to '*R.P.*'). A bundle of similar papers, which had become separated from the main body, was found earlier by Mr Frank Ricardo and these were published by Professor J. H. Hollander while the present edition was in preparation, so that it was possible to include them as well. Other manuscripts were subsequently traced, among them being smaller groups of letters to John Murray, to Francis Horner and to J.-B. Say.

The result was that all the series of Ricardo's letters to his chief correspondents and theirs to him were to hand, except his letters to

James Mill. Yet it was just these which, having presumably been inherited by John Stuart Mill, one might have expected above all to be preserved. There was, on the other hand, Bain's disquieting statement in the preface to his biography of James Mill (1882) that 'several valuable collections of letters have been destroyed.' Moreover, while the papers of John Stuart Mill, which were dispersed at auction in 1922, included a parcel containing letters addressed to James Mill, none of these when traced to their ultimate buyers proved to be from Ricardo. Years of systematic enquiry among the numerous descendants of Mill and their executors and friends in all parts of the world met with no success; and it looked as though this edition would have to appear with the last gap no more than half-filled.

Then, in July 1943, quite unexpectedly, a locked metal box was found by Mr C. K. Mill in the house of his father-in-law, Mr F. E. Cairnes, at Raheny, Co. Dublin; and on the box being opened by a locksmith the first thing to appear was a brown paper parcel addressed to J. S. Mill, Esq., India House, City, and inscribed 'Mr David Ricardo's Manuscripts'. This parcel proved to contain the whole series of letters to Mill as well as a number of new writings of Ricardo which also had belonged to James Mill. All the papers were promptly and generously placed at the disposal of the editor by the owners, through the good offices of Professor O'Brien and Professor Hayek. Reporting to Lord Keynes on the importance of this discovery, Professor O'Brien wrote from Dublin: 'It can almost be compared with the find of the Boswell manuscripts in the box at Malahide Castle. Curiously enough Malahide Castle and Raheny, where Mr Cairnes lives, are quite close together.'

The remaining contents of the box were papers of John Elliot Cairnes, the economist, who was father of Mr F. E. Cairnes. The Ricardo manuscripts had no doubt come to him from his intimate friend John Stuart Mill, either directly or more probably through the latter's literary executrix, Miss Helen Taylor.

Previous to this, by the summer of 1940, six volumes of the present edition had been set up in page-proof, while the volume of Speeches and Evidence had reached the stage of galley-proofs. The discovery of these 'Mill-Ricardo papers' made it necessary, when work on the edition was resumed after the war, to break up the three volumes of letters (since they were arranged in chronological order) and to expand them to four volumes. At the same time the additions to the volume of Pamphlets and Papers required its division into two volumes. The resultant nine volumes are now in course of publication; and it is hoped to complete the *Works and Correspondence* of Ricardo with a volume of biographical and bibliographical miscellany, and a General Index.

In 1948 Mr Maurice Dobb came in to assist with the editorial work, in particular being associated in the writing of the Introductions to vols. I, II, V and VI.

The fact that such a long time has elapsed since much of the early work on this edition was carried out has resulted in certain anomalies in editorial references. This will be specially noticeable in the case of references to persons who have died in the interim. Moreover, in some cases, manuscripts which are mentioned as being in the possession of a private owner have been transferred to public collections (and others may be before this edition is completed). It is hoped in the tenth volume to bring this type of information up-to-date.

It would be impossible to acknowledge in this Preface all the debts incurred in the preparation of the present edition. Help received in connection with particular points is mentioned in the appropriate places, and acknowledgement here must be confined to those persons to whom the greatest obligations have been incurred or whose help has extended to the edition as a whole.

The initiative in launching this enterprise was due to the late Lord Keynes, who to the end of his life showed the closest interest and lent his active support, particularly in the search for unpublished material and in advising on the planning and annotation of the volumes. His successor as Secretary of the Royal Economic Society, Professor Austin Robinson, has continued his interest and assistance to the progress of the edition. To both of them, as well as to the Council of the Society, a special debt must be acknowledged for their forbearance toward the delays and interruptions in the editing of these volumes.

Thanks are first of all due to the late Lt.-Col. H. G. Ricardo and to Mr Frank Ricardo for their generous cooperation and for permission to publish such of the writings of their ancestor as are copyright; in particular to the former for the loan of books and documents at Gatcombe, and to the latter for his fruitful search for manuscripts, for making available those in his possession and for much trouble taken in securing others. Acknowledgement must also be made to Mr C. K. Mill, to the late Mr F. E. Cairnes and to Mr Robert Malthus for making available important collections of papers in their possession and for waiving any copyright that might belong to them; to Sir John Murray for the loan of letters and for valuable information from the records of his publishing house; to the late Sir Bernard Mallet for permission to quote extensively from the unpublished Diaries of John Lewis Mallet in his possession; to Lady Langman, M. Edgar Raoul-Duval and Professor H. E. Butler for allowing access to letters in their possession; to the Delegates of the Oxford University Press, to The Johns Hopkins Press and to the American Economic Association for permission to reprint writings of Ricardo published by them; and finally, for valuable assistance, advice or information, to the late Dr James Bonar, Professor Jacob Viner, Professor F. A. Hayek, Professor George O'Brien, the late Professor Edwin Cannan, Sir Theodore Gregory, Mr Nicholas Kaldor and Dr R. Mattioli.

Indispensable help of a general nature (apart from what is acknowledged in particular places) has been given at various times in the capacity of editorial assistant by Dr Eduard Rosenbaum, Dr Karl Bode, Mrs Barbara Lowe and, for shorter periods, Miss Margery Seward and Mrs Lucy Munby.

Finally, the editor must record a particular obligation to the printers of the Cambridge University Press for the unfailing patience and sure judgment upon which he has been able to rely throughout the twenty years that this edition has been 'in the press'.

P. S.

TRINITY COLLEGE
CAMBRIDGE
December 1950

INTRODUCTION

I. *The Writing of the Principles*

THE plan from which the *Principles of Political Economy, and Taxation* originated had taken shape soon after the publication of the *Essay on the Influence of a Low Price of Corn on the Profits of Stock* in February 1815. At first Ricardo's intention (at James Mill's suggestion) had been merely to produce an enlarged version of the *Essay*. As he writes to J.-B. Say from his country house, Gatcomb Park, in August 1815: 'Mr. Mill wishes me to write it over again at large', adding immediately, 'I fear the undertaking exceeds my powers'.[1] Mill, however, as he tells Ricardo in the same month, is determined to give him no rest till he is 'plunged over head and ears in political economy.'[2] Six weeks later (on 10 October) the larger book is already being treated by Mill as a definite commitment: 'I expect you are by this time in a condition to give me some account of the progress you have been making in your book. I now consider you as fairly pledged to that task.'[3] On the 29th of the same month Ricardo is writing to Trower of his determination to 'concentrate all the talent' he possesses upon the subject on which his opinions 'differ from the great authority of Adam Smith, Malthus &cᵃ', namely 'the principles of Rent, Profit and Wages'. 'For my own satisfaction I shall certainly make the attempt, and perhaps with repeated revisions during

---

[1] Letter of 18 August 1815, below, VI, 249. Cp. Grenfell's reference in a letter of 1 August 1815 to 'the work which you have in Contemplation on the Corn Trade' (below, VI, 242), which was no doubt an allusion to an enlargement of the *Essay* (whose full title refers to the 'Price of Corn' and 'Restrictions on Importation').

[2] Letter of 23 August 1815, below, VI, 252.

[3] Below, VI, 309.

a year or two I shall at last produce something that may be understood.'[1] On 9 November we find Mill, in reply to a discouraged letter from Ricardo ('Oh that I were capable of writing a book!'[2]), assuming the role of 'schoolmaster' and commanding Ricardo 'to begin to the first of the three heads of your proposed work, rent, profit, wages—viz. *rent*, without an hours delay'.[3]

Throughout this period Ricardo was held back by difficulties of composition. As he later complained to Malthus, 'I make no progress in the difficult art of composition. I believe that ought to be my study'.[4] Trower's help consisted in the not very practical advice to consult Dr Blair's *Lectures on Rhetoric and Belles Lettres*.[5] Mill, however, sent detailed instructions for the writing of the '*opus magnum*';[6] by 22 December 1815 he is waiting 'in anticipation of the MS' which he expects 'soon to receive, as part of the great work'; and in giving further instruction as to the mode of writing he insists always that Ricardo should consider his readers 'as people ignorant of the subject'. Mill also sets him a 'school exercise': to give a proof, step by step, of the proposition which he (Ricardo) had often stated, 'That improvements in agriculture raise the profits of stock, and produce immediately no other effects.' 'For as you are already the best *thinker* on political economy, I am resolved you shall also be the best writer.'[7]

It is remarkable that in these letters of October and November 1815 which give the main headings of the proposed work (Rent, Profit, Wages) there is no reference to Value. This is mentioned for the first time, as a separate subject with which it occurred to Ricardo that he would have to deal, in a letter to Mill of 30 December. 'I know I shall be soon stopped by the word price,' he writes, 'and then I must apply to you for advice and assistance. Before my readers can understand the proof I mean to offer, they must understand the theory of currency and of price.'[8] From this time onwards the problem of Value increasingly troubled him. On 7 February 1816 he

[1] Below, VI, 315–16.
[2] *ib.* 314.
[3] *ib.* 321.
[4] Letter to Malthus, 7 Feb. 1816, below, VII, 19.
[5] Below, VI, 326.
[6] *ib.* 330.
[7] *ib.* 338–40.
[8] *ib.* 348.

writes to Malthus: 'If I could overcome the obstacles in the way of giving a clear insight into the origin and law of relative or exchangeable value I should have gained half the battle.'[1]

In February 1816 he moved to London, whither he brought his papers, some of which he read to Mill while he was there.[2] But in town the work made no progress. 'I may continue to amuse myself with my speculations, but I do not think I shall ever proceed further. Obstacles almost invincible oppose themselves to my progress, and I find the greatest difficulty to avoid confusion in the most simple of my statements.'[3] A month later he is writing: 'My labours have wholly ceased for two months;—whether in the quiet and calm of the country I shall again resume them is very doubtful.'[4]

In July, back at Gatcomb, he resumed work; having (as he writes to Mill) 'little temptation to desert my work for the pleasure of walking or riding, as the weather has been almost uniformly bad', yet not able 'wholly to seclude myself'.[5] But although Ricardo's letters continued 'so much in the old desponding tone',[6] by the middle of August Mill could infer that he must have by that time 'a pretty mass of papers, written first and last upon the subject': papers which Mill asked to have sent to him, arranged by subjects if possible, with 'some indication of what each subdivision is about', or else 'higgledy-piggledy all together'.[7] Despite Mill's insistence, Ricardo delayed sending the manuscript for two months, under the pretext that he must copy it out.[8] Eventually, on 14 October 1816 he sent an extensive draft, covering the ground of the first seven chapters, or the whole of the 'Principles of Political Economy' proper; adding in the letter to Mill in which he announced their despatch, 'I shall now consider the subject of taxation'.[9]

The real reason for the delay was that he had 'been very much impeded by the question of price and value' (as he wrote to Malthus),[10] and that (as he informed Mill) he had 'been beyond measure puzzled

---

[1] Below, VII, 20.
[2] ib. 60.
[3] Letter to Malthus, 24 April 1816, ib. 28.
[4] Letter to Malthus, 28 May 1816, ib. 36.
[5] ib. 54.
[6] ib. 58.
[7] ib. 60.
[8] Ricardo to Mill, 8 September, and Mill to Ricardo, 6 October 1816, ib. 65–6, 73.
[9] ib. 82–4.
[10] ib. 71.

to find out the law of price.' 'I found on a reference to figures that my former opinion could not be correct and I was full a fortnight pondering on my difficulty before I knew how to solve it.'[1] This important change was evidently connected with the 'curious effect' (to which he called Mill's attention in the same letter) of a rise of wages in *lowering* the prices of 'those commodities which are chiefly obtained by the aid of machinery and fixed capital'.[2]

A letter from Mill of 18 November 1816 written immediately after reading the MS and making 'marginal contents' for his own use, enables us to reconstruct the contents of that MS with the help of the text of the first edition; for Mill's comments touch on the main topics in the order in which they were treated under four heads.[3]

1. 'Your explanation of the general principle that quantity of labour is the cause and measure of exchangeable value, excepting in the cases which you except, is both satisfactory, and clear.'

2. 'Your exposition and argumentation to shew, in opposition to A. Smith, that profits of stock do not disturb that law, are luminous. So are the exposition and argumentation to shew that rent also operates no such disturbance.'

Up to this point Mill finds the argument 'clear, and easily understood'. He continues his comments on the MS as follows:

3. 'At page 79 you begin the enquiry concerning the causes of alterations in the state of wages; and from this to p. 105, I think the topics are somewhat mixed together...I consider the inquiry in these pages as an inquiry not into the causes of change in the rate of wages alone, but the causes of changes in the wages, profits, and rent all together.' This is undoubtedly the part which underwent the greatest alteration before publication; and probably included discussion of that 'curious effect' which had cost Ricardo so much time and thought during the summer and which eventually appeared in the chapter On Value in edition 1. Ricardo no doubt had these pages in mind when he wrote to Mill: 'They are worse than they otherwise would be in consequence of my becoming better acquainted

---

[1] Below, VII, 83–4. Cp. Trower's reference to the 'two months' lost by Ricardo in ascertaining the error of his own theory (*ib.* 95).

[2] *ib.* 82.

[3] *ib.* 98–9.

with the subject as I have proceeded. Much of what is said in the beginning should be left out or altered to agree with what I think the more correct views which I afterwards adopted.'[1]

4. Mill goes on to deal with 'the inquiry concerning foreign trade, which commences at p. 106, and continues to the end'. The propositions which he mentions are: 'That foreign trade augments not the value of a nations property: that it may be good for a country to import commodities from a country where the production of those same commodities costs more, than it would cost at home: that a change in manufacturing skill in one country, produces a new distribution of the precious metals'.

Of the four parts of this draft all but the third can easily be identified in the *Principles* in a form which, from its agreement with Mill's description, appears to be substantially unchanged in the first edition.

Thus the first part, consisting of the statement of the law of value, with its exceptions (rare statues, etc.), will be found below, p. 11 to p. 22.

Of the second part, the statement in opposition to Adam Smith that the law is not disturbed either by the payment of profits or by the payment of rent appears in the passage of edition 1 given below, p. 22–3, note 3; the full argument regarding profits is on pages 22 to 26 (first paragraph) in the chapter On Value; that regarding rent is on pages 67 to 78 (first paragraph) in the chapter On Rent.[2]

And of the fourth part (the enquiry into Foreign Trade) the points noted by Mill will be found, in the same order, as follows: (*a*) that Foreign Trade does not add to value, below, p. 128 to p. 133 (second paragraph); (*b*) the theory of comparative costs, below, p. 133 to p. 137 (first paragraph); (*c*) the redistribution of the precious metals following a change of skill in one country, below, p. 137 to p. 141

[1] *ib.* 82.

[2] So much material (the last part of the chapter On Value) was inserted between the two arguments on profits and on rent that the connection between them was obscured. Indeed, in edition 3 the passage establishing that connection (p. 22–3, n. 3) is omitted altogether; while, somewhat incongruously, the opening sentence of the chapter On Rent, which presupposes that connection ('It remains however to be considered'), is preserved in all editions. Cp. also p. 78, n. 1.

(third paragraph). This covers rather more than half of the chapter On Foreign Trade in the *Principles*.

On the other hand, the enquiry into wages (occupying page 79 to page 105 of the MS draft), which Mill considered confused with the enquiries into profits and rent, has no exact counterpart in the published work. No doubt the material which it contained, greatly expanded, was partly embodied in the chapter On Value and for the rest distributed over the chapters On Natural and Market Price, On Wages and On Profits.

Having despatched the first parcel of MS and having set to work on taxation, Ricardo by 17 November 1816 had completed and sent to Mill the 'inquiry into the subject of Taxation' (as Mill described it).[1] This part, Mill thought, would require more work than the first one before it was ready for the press: 'you have followed the order of your own thoughts,' and the matter would need re-arrangement so as 'to facilitate introduction into the minds of your readers'.[2]

Up to this point what Ricardo had done was (as he wrote to Malthus) 'rather a statement of my own opinions, than an attempt at the refutation of the opinions of others'.[3] Having finished taxation, he proceeded 'to read Adam Smith once more, to take note of all passages which very much favor, or are directly opposed to my peculiar opinions';[4] he also re-read Say's *Traité d'Économie politique* and Buchanan's commentary on the *Wealth of Nations* and made notes of his own criticisms.[5] These criticisms formed the basis of the group of controversial chapters which follows the chapters on taxation. Finally, at the end of January he read again Malthus's pamphlets on rent and corn, and early in March, while printing was in progress, he sent to Malthus the MS of his last chapter, which contains his comments upon them.[6]

The printing of the *Principles* began at the end of February 1817. At first it went on briskly at the rate of a sheet a day, as Ricardo wrote to Malthus, and by 9 March eleven sheets, out of a total of thirty-eight, had been corrected.[7] In the *Monthly Literary Advertiser* of

[1] Below, VII, 87–8, 106.
[2] *ib.* 107.
[3] *ib.* 115.
[4] Letter to Mill, 17 Nov. 1816, *ib.* 88.
[5] *ib.* 100–1, 115.
[6] *ib.* 120 and 139–40.
[7] *ib.* 140.

10 March it was included in Murray's list of works 'in the Press'. On 26 March, when Ricardo put the last part of his manuscript into the printer's hands, he complained that the latter did 'not proceed regularly at the same even pace'.[1] But he still hoped that it would be out on Monday, 7 April, which appears to have been the date originally fixed for its appearance.[2] However, publication was delayed, and the final date was announced in *The Day and New Times* of Wednesday, 16 April, where the book was advertised by Murray under the caption, 'On Saturday will be published'. The date was confirmed in the same paper of Saturday, 19 April, with an advertisement opening 'This Day will be published' and giving the price, 14s. Since Trower on 28 April wrote to Ricardo from Godalming thanking him for the book 'which arrived a few days ago',[3] it could not have been sent much later than the 19th. We can therefore take this (19 April 1817) as the date of publication.

II. *James Mill's Contribution*

John Stuart Mill says in his *Autobiography* that Ricardo's *Principles* 'never would have been published or written, but for the entreaty and strong encouragement of my father; for Ricardo, the most modest of men, though firmly convinced of the truth of his doctrines, deemed himself so little capable of doing them justice in exposition and expression, that he shrank from the idea of publicity'.[4] In a similar strain the obituary, probably written by Ricardo's brother, says that he was 'very reluctant, first to write, and afterwards to publish this work; and it was only by the successive urgings of some of his most confidential friends, but particularly through the influence of Mr. Mill, that he was at length prevailed upon to do so.'[5] These statements, if they are taken to refer to James Mill's influence in stimulating and encouraging Ricardo, are fully borne out by the

---

[1] *ib.* 145.
[2] *ib.* 147.
[3] *ib.* 148.
[4] *Autobiography*, 1873, p. 27.
[5] *Annual Biography and Obituary, for the Year 1824*, p. 374. McCulloch makes a similar statement, probably derived from the above, in the numerous versions of his *Life and Writings of Mr. Ricardo* (omitting in the later ones any reference to Mill).

correspondence between Ricardo and Mill.[1] Nevertheless, they are open to misunderstanding. For they have given rise to the view, first advanced by Professor Dunbar, that 'Ricardo's book was written, not for the public eye, but as a statement of opinions made for his own purposes, and that its publication was an after-thought of his friends.'[2] Through its acceptance by Marshall[3] this belief has gained general currency. The Ricardo-Mill correspondence now makes it certain that this opinion is unfounded, and that from the very beginning the idea of publication was present in Ricardo's mind, although from time to time he was beset by doubts as to his ability to achieve his object (as has been shown in several passages quoted above). A typical statement is the following which he made in a letter to Mill when he was in the middle of composition in November 1816: 'I have an anxious desire to produce something worth publishing, but that I unaffectedly fear will not be in my power.'[4]

At the same time it is clear that Mill's contribution to the making of the *Principles* was less than might have been expected from his promises and encouragement. On the theory there is little doubt that his influence was negligible; he had been out of touch with Political Economy for some time[5] and his letters to Ricardo contain little discussion of theoretical issues. Mill's letters of this period are full of advice relating to 'the art of laying down your thoughts, in the way most easy of apprehension'.[6] But despite his repeated as-surances that he would see to the order and arrangement ('if you

[1] His obligations to Mill in this respect are summed up by Ricardo in a letter of 2 Dec. 1816: 'If I am successful in my undertaking it will be to you mainly that my success will be owing, for without your encouragement I do not think that I should have proceeded, and it is to you that I look for assistance of the utmost importance to me—the arranging the different parts, and curtailing what may be superfluous.' (Below, VII, 101.)

[2] C. F. Dunbar, 'Ricardo's Use of Facts', in *Quarterly Journal of Economics*, July 1887, vol. I, p. 475.

[3] 'He was with difficulty induced to publish it; and if in writing it he had in view any readers at all, they were chiefly those statesmen and business men with whom he associated. So he purposely omitted many things which were necessary for the logical completeness of his argument, but which they would regard as obvious.' A. Marshall, *Principles of Economics*, Appendix on 'Ricardo's Theory of Value', 8th ed., p. 813 and cp. p. 761 n.

[4] Below, VII, 88.

[5] Below, VI, 320–1.

[6] ib. 321.

entrust the inspection of it to me'[1]) it seems likely that in the main the sequence of topics was left as Ricardo had originally worked through them. In detail however Mill probably did a good deal of work. Here and there a phrase unmistakeably characteristic of Mill (such as 'It is a truth which admits not a doubt',[2] 'the nature of the evil points out the remedy',[3] or 'none but the prejudiced are ignorant of its true principles'[4]) provides evidence of his hand. His touch can also be recognised in the polished wording of the Preface[5] and in the long passage on the 'pernicious tendency' of the poor laws.[6]

Among Mill's more humble tasks was probably the compilation of the Index, which in method and clarity of expression is strikingly similar to the Index of his *History of British India*, published later in 1817. It is noticeable that several entries exhibit misunderstanding of the text or radical change of emphasis such as to suggest that they cannot be by the author of the book.[7] At any rate contemporary critics of Ricardo seized upon the contrast between the language of the text and that of the Index, to the disadvantage of the former. Thus, one of them says that Ricardo 'relied for a correction of his deficient perspicuity on his Index, which is clear and minute'.[8] Another, Samuel Bailey, notes: 'the only place in Mr. Ricardo's work, where I have been able to find the expression of the general rule properly qualified, is the Index. He there says, "the quantity of

---

[1] *ib.* 321.
[2] Below, p. 106. The old-fashioned use of the negative is a peculiarity of Mill, as Bain points out (*James Mill*, p. 426). Another passage in which it occurs (below, p. 64: 'if wages partook not...') shows also other signs of, at least, revision by Mill.
[3] Below, p. 107.
[4] *ib.* 352.
[5] That the first three paragraphs of the Preface are stamped with Mill's 'tone and style' has been noticed by Simon N. Patten, 'The Interpretation of Ricardo', in *Quarterly Journal of Economics*, April 1893, vol. VII, p. 338.
[6] Below, pp. 105–9.

[7] Compare *e.g.* the following entries with the passages referred to: '*Population*, increase of, no cause of the rise of rent, 410, 411.' '*Labour*, Adam Smith's theory of productive and unproductive labour, considered, 76–77, notes.' '*Value*, Effects of payment of rent on value, 64, 65.' '*Smith*, Strictures on his doctrine relative to labour being the *sole* ultimate standard of the exchangeable value of commodities, 16, 17, 416.' The same applies to additions to the Index made in ed. 3: *e.g.* under *Taxes*, entry stating that a tax on rent 'discourages cultivation, 173–5.' (Page-references are to the present edition.)
[8] 'Ricardo on Political Economy', in *Monthly Review*, Dec. 1820, p. 416.

labour requisite to obtain commodities the *principal* source of their exchangeable value."[1]

The accurate yet free translation of the passages quoted from Say is probably also due to Mill, who had advised against quotation in French.[2]

III. *Arrangement and Subdivision*

Thus Mill's promises that, once Ricardo had set down his thoughts on paper, he himself would attend to their proper arrangement may in the event have fallen short of fulfilment. In any case, the result is not such as to do much credit to Mill's passion for system; and the apparent defects in the arrangement of the work as a whole have often been noted by Ricardo's critics.[3]

This arrangement was the direct result of the manner in which Ricardo proceeded in his work. As his letters show, he wrote according to the sequence of his own ideas, without any more elaborate plan than was implied in the heading, 'Rent, Profit and Wages'. Mill, indeed, had instructed him to 'proceed, without loss of time... thinking nothing of order, thinking nothing of repetitions, thinking nothing of stile—regarding nothing, in short, but to get all the thoughts blurred upon paper some how or another'.[4] 'When we have the whole before us, we will then lay our heads together, to see how it may be sorted and shaped to the best advantage.'[5] The three parts in which Ricardo composed it and which he sent separately to Mill correspond to the three groups into which the chapters of the

[1] *A Critical Dissertation on the Nature, Measures, and Causes of Value,* London, Hunter, 1825, pp. 213–14.
[2] Below, VII, 108.
[3] A number of commentators, from De Quincey to Marx, have suggested ways of rearranging the chapters in a logical order. (See 'Dialogues of Three Templars', in De Quincey's *Works*, ed. Masson, vol. IX, p. 53, and Marx's *Theorien über den Mehrwert*, vol. II, I, pp. 5–6. For several other attempts see J. H. Hollander, *David Ricardo, A Centenary Estimate,* Baltimore, 1910, p. 82.)
[4] Letter from Mill, 14 August 1816, below, VII, 60.

[5] Letter from Mill, 16 Dec. 1816, *ib.* 108–9. It is interesting that it was only at this late stage in the preparation of the book (December 1816) that Mill put to Ricardo the question whether he would 'chuse to include in it a view of the *whole* science': 'Or, whether you will content yourself with those parts of the science which you yourself have improved.' (*ib.* 107.) To which Ricardo replied that it would be easier for him to publish only those parts which had 'particularly engaged' his attention; adding that, if this were favourably received, he might later 'take a view of the whole science.' (*ib.* 112.)

published work naturally fall: the Political Economy, Taxation and the polemical chapters at the end. The arrangement would have been less open to criticism if this division had been made explicitly by means of separate headings. Mill indeed at an early stage had expected such a division to be made, as is shown by a footnote in his *History of British India*, 1817, where he refers to the group of Ricardo's chapters dealing with taxes as 'a Dissertation on the Principles of Taxation'.[1] And Ricardo in a letter to Mill of the same period (December 1816) describes that part of the book to which most of his criticisms of Adam Smith were to be relegated as 'the appendix'.[2]

However, within each of the first two parts the order of the chapters coincides closely with the order in which the topics are treated in the *Wealth of Nations*, as comparison of the chapter-headings shows (see table on the following page).

The only important difference is in the place given to Rent, which was dictated by the necessity for Ricardo of 'getting rid of rent' (as he put it), in order to simplify the problem of the distribution between capitalist and labourer.[3] As a result, unlike Adam Smith, he deals with Rent immediately after Value and before Wages and Profits.

The parallel applies equally to Taxation (see table on p. xxv).

This group of chapters on taxation is followed by Chapter XVII, On Sudden Changes in the Channels of Trade (numbered XIX in ed. 3), the position of which is determined by its arising immediately out of the subject of the removal of capital from one employment to another, discussed at the end of the chapter on Poor Rates.[4] The third, and last, group consists of the chapters commenting upon various doctrines of Adam Smith and other writers, forming 'the

[1] Vol. 1, p. 196, note: 'See a Dissertation on the Principles of Taxation, the most profound, by far, which has yet been given to the world, by David Ricardo, Esq. in his work "On the Principles of Political Economy and Taxation."' This footnote was no doubt inserted in the proofs which Mill was correcting when he received that part of Ricardo's MS (cp. below, VII, 106 and 111).
[2] Below, VII, 100.

[3] Letter to McCulloch, 13 June 1820, below, VIII, 194.
[4] Another question which immediately arises out of this subject (and also lacks any obvious connection with Poor Rates) is that of extending the notion of Rent to include the return on such capital as cannot be withdrawn from the land. This was made the subject of a long footnote attached to the end of the chapter on Poor Rates.

Political Economy

Adam Smith, Book I	Ricardo, Ed. I
Ch. v Of the real and nominal Price of Commodities Ch. vi Of the component Parts of the Price of Commodities	Ch. i On Value
	Ch. ii On Rent Ch. iii On the Rent of Mines
Ch. vii Of the natural and Market Price of Commodities	Ch. iv On Natural and Market Price
Ch. viii Of the Wages of Labour	Ch. v On Wages
Ch. ix Of the Profits of Stock	Ch. v* On Profits
Ch. x Of Wages and Profit in the different Employments of Labour and Stock[1]	
Ch. xi Of the Rent on Land	
	Ch. vi On Foreign Trade

[1] This is treated by Ricardo in the Chapter on Value, in the five paragraphs which were later to constitute Section II of this chapter; below, pp. 20–2.

appendix' or a series of critical excursuses, with little connection each with the other.

It was only after the whole was written that thought was given to the question of subdivision. As late as 16 December 1816, after receiving the MS both of the Political Economy and of Taxation, Mill asks: 'And how would you arrange it in Chapters and Sections? Think of your Chapters and Sections; and when you have made out a list send it to me'.[1] To this Ricardo replies: 'as for the division into chapters, and sections, I am greatly afraid that I shall be unequal to it.'[2]

Thus the process of cutting up the undivided work into chapters began after writing was completed; indeed, it went on while the printing was in progress, and the last cut was made after the book had actually been printed off. As we shall presently see it is by this late subdividing that the puzzling anomaly of ed. 1, namely the

[1] Below, VII, 107.   [2] ib. 112.

Taxation

Adam Smith, Book v, Ch. ii, Part ii	Ricardo, Ed. i
Of Taxes	Ch. vii On Taxes
	Ch. viii Taxes on Raw Produce
Art. 1st Taxes upon Rent Taxes upon Rent of Land	Ch. viii* Taxes on Rent
Taxes which are proportioned, not to the Rent, but to the Produce of Land	Ch. ix Tithes Ch. x Land-Tax
	Ch. xi Taxes on Gold
Taxes upon the Rent of Houses	Ch. xii Taxes on Houses
Art. 2d Taxes upon Profit, or upon the Revenue arising from Stock Taxes upon the Profit of particular Employments	Ch. xiii Taxes on Profits
Art. 3d Taxes upon the Wages of Labour	Ch. xiv Taxes on Wages
Art. 4th Taxes...upon every different Species of Revenue Capitation Taxes	
Taxes upon Consumable Commodities	Ch. xv· Taxes upon other Commodities than Raw Produce
	Ch. xvi Poor Rates

double numbering of chapters, can be explained; and not, as it would be natural to suppose,[1] by the insertion of additional matter as an afterthought. Of this double numbering there are two instances.

The first instance is that of the chapters On Wages and On Profits, both of which are headed 'Chapter V'. In the table of contents, however, while the former is numbered 'V', the latter appears as 'V*'. It is unlikely that this duplication was in the MS which was sent to the printer; since presumably Ricardo had made (as Mill had instructed him to do) a list of his chapters, and in such a list duplica-

[1] See Cannan, *A Review of Economic Theory*, p. 243.

tion could scarcely have been overlooked. It can be conjectured, therefore, that in the MS the matter of what are now Chapter IV, On Natural and Market Price, and Chapter V, On Wages, formed a single Chapter IV (presumably entitled 'On Wages') and that they were then subdivided during the revision of the proofs; the title of Chapter IV being altered and a new chapter-division (Chapter V, On Wages) introduced. The close link between these two chapters (which in the first draft sent to Mill had no doubt been among the topics 'mixed together') is shown by the continuity of the argument which in the chapter On Wages opens (and continues for several pages) in terms of the natural and market price of labour. Moreover, the statement at the end of Chapter III (below, p. 87) that he would continue the supposition of the invariable value of gold '*in the following chapter*', must have been written when the two following chapters were undivided, since the 'supposition' is only relevant to the subject matter of what was to become Chapter V, On Wages. Further, it is a typographical peculiarity of the original edition 1 that the text of the last page of the former of these two chapters and that of the first page of the latter (namely pp. 89 and 90 of ed. 1), if put together, form exactly a normal full page (see facsimile opposite). If we assume that they were so joined together in the first proof, the printer could make the subdivision without disturbing the setting of the subsequent pages[1]—at the expense only of making the opening page of the chapter On Wages two or three lines longer (as turns out to be the case) than the opening page of a chapter would normally be. As Ricardo was receiving a sheet of proofs a day,[2] he could not immediately adjust the numbering of the subsequent chapters; and, as he was presumably returning them at once, he would never have the two chapters numbered V simultaneously before him. Thus the duplication would only be detected when the table of contents came to be compiled, after the body of the book had been printed off.

The explanation in the second instance is based on stronger evidence; and it is, indeed, by analogy with this case that our con-

[1] First proofs were in page galley, not in the long galley which is usual at the present time.

[2] Letter to Malthus of 9 March 1817, below, VII, 140.

CHAPTER IV.

—

ON NATURAL AND MARKET PRICE.

In making labour the foundation of the value of commodities, and the comparative quantity of labour which is necessary to their production, the rule which determines the respective quantities of goods which shall be given in exchange for each other, we must not be supposed to deny the accidental and temporary deviations of the actual or market price of commodities from this, their primary and natural price.

In the ordinary course of events, there is no commodity which continues for any length of time to be supplied precisely in that degree of abundance, which the wants and wishes of mankind require, and therefore

CHAPTER V.

—

ON PROFITS.

The profits of stock in different employments, having been shewn to bear a proportion to each other, and to have a tendency to vary all in the same degree and in the same direction, it remains for us to consider what is the cause of the permanent variations in the rate of profit, and the consequent permanent alterations in the rate of interest.

We have seen that the price of corn is regulated by the quantity of labour necessary to produce it, with that portion of capital which pays no rent. We have seen too that all manufactured commodities rise and fall

* The reader is desired to bear in mind, that for the purpose of making the subject more clear, I consider money to be invariable in value, and therefore every variation of price to be referable to an alteration in the value of the commodity.

89

then of the exchangeable value of commodities, or the power of purchasing possessed by any one commodity, I mean always that power which it would possess, if not disturbed by any temporary or accidental cause, and which is its natural price.

CHAPTER V.

—

ON WAGES.

Labour, like all other things which are purchased and sold, and which may be increased or diminished in quantity, has its natural and its market price. The natural price of labour is that price which is necessary to enable the labourers, one with another, to subsist and to perpetuate their race, without either increase or diminution.

The power of the labourer to support himself, and the family which may be necessary to keep up the number of labourers, does not depend on the quantity of money, which he may receive for wages; but on the quantity of food, necessaries, and conveniences become essential to him from habit, which that money will purchase. The natural price of labour, therefore, depends on the price of the food, necessaries, and conveniences required

Pages of ed. 1 showing double-numbering of Ch. V.

jecture about the first derives support for its own rather slender foundation. This second case concerns the chapters 'Taxes on Raw Produce' and 'Taxes on Rent' which are respectively numbered VIII and VIII*, the asterisk appearing *both* in the chapter-heading and in the table of contents. Our suggestion is that these two at one time formed a single chapter (numbered VIII and entitled 'Taxes on Raw Produce') and that they were separated, not in the revision of the proofs, but at a much later stage—after the Index had been compiled and indeed after the book had been printed off: so that the pages affected had to be reprinted, and substituted by the binder in every one of the 750 copies of the edition.[1]

The existence of these 'cancels', as they are called, becomes apparent on examination of copies bound in paper boards as they were originally published. Three leaves are affected (the 6th, 7th and 8th of the sheet 'signed', or lettered, P); that is to say, six pages, including the last two pages of 'Taxes on Raw Produce' and the four pages of 'Taxes on Rent' (pp. 219–224 of edition 1, corresponding to pp. 171–175 below). These three leaves are visibly pasted in, to replace an equal number cut off, the flaps of which jut out between the pages—in some copies so much as half an inch. That they were printed separately from the sheet is conclusively proved by the fact that the first two of them are 'conjugate', that is to say joined together at the back, thus forming a single piece of paper even after the book has been cut—which otherwise would be impossible for the sixth and seventh leaves of an octavo sheet.

The making of a new Chapter VIII* out of the last four pages of the pre-existing Chapter VIII involved moving forward the text of these four pages to make room for the opening of the new chapter which must be on a fresh page. The repercussion of this displacement would be limited if the last page of the chapter had been partly empty and therefore capable of absorbing it. This appears to have been the case. (See facsimile opposite. As much matter as was removed from p. 220 and p. 221 has been shifted on to p. 224, filling it up

---

[1] This is the case in all the copies examined. It would be of interest if a copy were to be found in which the binder had failed to carry out the replacement.

CHAPTER VIII.

TAXES ON RAW PRODUCE.

HAVING in a former part of this work established, I hope satisfactorily, the principle, that the price of corn is regulated by the cost of its production on that land exclusively, or rather with that capital exclusively, which pays no rent, it will follow that whatever may increase the cost of production will increase the price; whatever may reduce it, will lower the price. The necessity of cultivating poorer land, or of obtaining a less return with a given additional capital on land already in cultivation, will inevitably raise the exchangeable value of raw produce. The discovery of machinery, which will enable the cultivator to obtain his corn at a less cost of production, will necessarily lower its exchangeable value. Any tax which may be

[p. 194]

220

only be of the value of a yard and a quarter, or it might be of the value of a yard and three quarters, and therefore rather a different direction might be given to foreign trade. All these inconveniences would not interfere with the value of the exports and imports; they would only prevent the very best distribution of the capital of the whole world, which is never so well regulated, as when every commodity is freely allowed to settle at its natural price.

Although then the rise in the price of most of our own commodities, would for a time check exportation generally, and might permanently prevent the exportation of a few commodities, it could not materially interfere with foreign trade, and would not place us under any comparative disadvantage as far as regarded competition in foreign markets.

[p. 220]

CHAPTER VIII. *

TAXES ON RENT.

A TAX on rent would affect rent only; it would fall wholly on landlords, and could not be shifted to any class of consumers. The landlord could not raise his rent, because he would leave unaltered the difference between the produce obtained from the least productive land in cultivation, and that obtained from land of every other quality. Three sorts of land, No. 1, 2, and 3, are in cultivation, and yield respectively with the same labour 180, 170, and 160 quarters of wheat; but No. 3 pays no rent, and is therefore untaxed: the rent then of No. 2 cannot be made to exceed the value of ten, nor No. 1, of twenty quarters. Such a tax could not raise the price of raw produce, because as the cultivator of No. 3 pays neither rent nor tax, he would in no way be enabled to raise the price of the commodity produced. A tax on rent would not discourage the cultivation of fresh land, for such land pays no rent, and

[p. 221]

224

furnishing him with the means, either in the shape of a loan, or in the purchase of an annuity for the duration of the lease. Whether distinguished or not, there is a real difference between the nature of the compensations which the landlord receives for these different objects; and it is quite certain, that a tax on the real rent of land falls wholly on the landlord, but that a tax on that remuneration which the landlord receives for the use of his stock expended on the farm, falls on the consumer of raw produce. If a tax were laid on rent, and no means of separating the remuneration now paid by the tenant to the landlord under the name of rent were adopted, the tax, as far as it regarded the rent on the buildings and other fixtures, would never fall for any length of time on the landlord, but on the consumer. The capital expended on these buildings, &c., must afford the usual profits of stock; but it would cease to afford this profit on the land last cultivated, if the expenses of those buildings, &c. did not fall on the tenant; and if they did, the tenant would then cease to make his usual profits of stock, unless he could charge them on the consumer.

[p. 224]

Pages of ed. 1 showing double-numbering of Ch. VIII.

completely; even that was insufficient, with the result that p. 221 is much longer than a normal opening page.)

Thus our hypothesis requires that the discussion of taxes on rent, which now begins on p. 221 (below, p. 173), should originally have begun in the space now blank on p. *220* (below, p. 172). It is in fact verified by an entry in the Index, under *Rent*, 'Tax on rent falls wholly on the landlord' which refers to pp. *220–224* (corresponding to pp. *172–175* below). This, incidentally, shows that the Index had been compiled before Chapter VIII was subdivided.

In the same way we obtain confirmation of the two chapters having been originally one from Index entries which lump them together. (Under *Taxes*, 'Objections against the taxation of the produce of land, considered and refuted, *201–224*'—corresponding to pp. *160–175* below. Similarly under *Produce*.)

While therefore it appears that the first of the two instances of double-numbering was due to an oversight, the second turns out to have been deliberate; and we may suppose that it was the discovery of the first case, by then beyond mending, which suggested the second to Ricardo and made it acceptable to the printer.[1]

The correspondence with Mill and the make-up of the book enable us to follow the process of dividing the work into chapters up to the last moment before publication. This process continued even later, in the form of the subdivision of Chapter I into Sections, which was only done in edition 2, and carried further in edition 3, as is described below, p. lii–liii.

IV. *The Chapter on Value in Edition* 1

By far the most perplexing as well as most extensive changes in successive editions of the *Principles* occur in the first chapter. A necessary preliminary to a study of these changes is a survey of the formation of the new theory of value out of the fragmentary elements of such a theory which are to be found in the *Essay on the Influence of a low Price of Corn on the Profits of Stock*.[2]

---

[1] For helpful criticism of the above arguments concerning chapter-numbers the editor is indebted to the late Professor Cannan to whom they were submitted in 1931.

[2] Generally referred to in these volumes as the *Essay on Profits*.

At first, both in the *Essay* and in Ricardo's letters of 1814 and early 1815, a basic principle had been that 'it is the profits of the farmer that regulate the profits of all other trades'. Malthus opposed him in this view, asserting that 'the profits of the farmer no more regulate the profits of other trades, than the profits of other trades regulate the profits of the farmer'.[1] After the *Essay* this principle disappears from view, and is not to be found in the *Principles*.

The rational foundation of the principle of the determining role of the profits of agriculture, which is never explicitly stated by Ricardo, is that in agriculture the same commodity, namely corn, forms both the capital (conceived as composed of the subsistence necessary for workers) and the product; so that the determination of profit by the difference between total product and capital advanced, and also the determination of the ratio of this profit to the capital, is done directly between quantities of corn without any question of valuation. It is obvious that only one trade can be in the special position of not employing the products of other trades while all the others must employ *its* product as capital. It follows that if there is to be a uniform rate of profit in all trades it is the exchangeable values of the products of *other* trades relatively to their own capitals (*i.e.* relatively to corn) that must be adjusted so as to yield the same rate of profit as has been established in the growing of corn; since in the latter no value changes can alter the ratio of product to capital, both consisting of the same commodity.

Although this argument is never stated by Ricardo in any of his extant letters and papers, he must have formulated it either in his lost 'papers on the profits of Capital' of March 1814[2] or in conversation, since Malthus opposes him in the following terms which are no doubt an echo of Ricardo's own formulation: 'In no case of production, is the produce exactly of the same nature as the capital advanced. Consequently we can never properly refer to a material rate of produce...It is not the particular profits or rate of produce upon the land which determines the general profits of stock and the interest

[1] Ricardo to Trower, 8 March 1814, below, VI, 104. Cp. *Essay on Profits*, below, IV, 23. [2] See below, VI, 102–5.

of money.'[1] The nearest that Ricardo comes to an explicit statement on these lines is in a striking passage in a letter of June 1814: 'The rate of profits and of interest must depend on the proportion of production to the consumption necessary to such production'.[2] The numerical examples in the *Essay* reflect this approach; and particularly in the well-known Table[3] which shows the effects of an increase of capital, both capital and the 'neat produce' are expressed in corn, and thus the profit per cent is calculated without need to mention price.[4]

The advantage of Ricardo's method of approach is that, at the cost of considerable simplification, it makes possible an understanding of how the rate of profit is determined without the need of a method for reducing to a common standard a heterogeneous collection of commodities.

In the *Principles*, however, with the adoption of a general theory of value, it became possible for Ricardo to demonstrate the determination of the rate of profit in society as a whole instead of through the microcosm of one special branch of production. At the same time he was enabled to abandon the simplification that wages consist only of corn, which had been under frequent attack from Malthus, and to treat wages as composed of a variety of products (including manufactures), although food was still predominant among them. It was now labour, instead of corn, that appeared on both sides of the account—in modern terms, both as input and output: as a result, the rate of profits was no longer determined by the ratio of the corn produced to the corn used up in production, but, instead, by the ratio of the total labour of the country to the labour required to produce the necessaries for that labour.[5] (But

---

[1] Letter of 5 Aug. 1814, below, VI, 117–18.

[2] *ib*. 108.

[3] Below, IV, 17.

[4] The feature of calculating the advances of the farmer in corn is singled out by Malthus as 'the fault of Mr. Ricardo's table'; since circulating capital did not consist only of corn, but included 'tea sugar cloaths &c for the labourers'; so that a rise in the relative price of corn would 'afford a greater surplus from the land' (letters of 12 and 14 March 1815, below, VI, 185–7).

[5] See the statement that profits depend upon the 'proportion of the annual labour of the country [which] is devoted to the support of the labourers', below, p. 48–9, and 'the same conclusion' on p. 126 below. Cp. Malthus's reference to Ricardo's criterion of wages as 'the cost in labour of the labourer's wages' and to its connection with the rate of profit, below, II, 249–50.

while the theory that the profits of the farmer determine all other profits disappears in the *Principles*, the more general proposition that the productivity of labour on land which pays no rent is fundamental in determining general profits continues to occupy a central position).

Many years later, an echo of the old corn-ratio theory (which rendered distribution independent of value) can perhaps be recognised when Ricardo in a moment of discouragement with the difficulties of value writes to McCulloch: 'After all, the great questions of Rent, Wages, and Profits must be explained by the proportions in which the whole produce is divided between landlords, capitalists, and labourers, and which are not essentially connected with the doctrine of value.'[1]

Parallel with this ran another theme in the development of Ricardo's thought. At first he had subscribed to the generally accepted view that a rise in corn prices, through its effect upon wages, would be followed by a rise of all other prices.[2] He had not regarded this view as inconsistent with his theory of profit so long as the latter had been expressed in its primitive 'agricultural' form. The conflict between the two however was bound to become apparent in the degree to which he groped towards a more general form of his theory; since the supposed general rise of prices obscured the simple relation of the rise of wages to the fall of profits. Already in the *Essay on Profits*, although his general presentation is still in the 'agricultural' form, he repudiates the accepted view in a footnote: 'It has been thought that the price of corn regulates the prices of all other things. This appears to me to be a mistake.'[3] Elsewhere in the *Essay*, in connection with this question, there are passages which foreshadow his full theory of value and already link it with the theory of profits: 'The exchangeable value of all commodities rises as the

---

[1] Letter of 13 June 1820, below, VIII, 194; cp. also letters to Mill of 16 Nov. 1820, *ib*. 297, and to McCulloch of 17 Jan. 1821, *ib*. 337.
[2] 'The prices of all commodities must increase if the price of corn be increased.' (Letter to Malthus, 25 July 1814, below, VI, 114 and cp. 108.) See also Note 3 on Bentham, below, III, 270.
[3] Below, IV, 21.

difficulties of their production increase. If then new difficulties occur in the production of corn, from more labour being necessary, whilst no more labour is required to produce gold, silver, cloth, linen &c. the exchangeable value of corn will necessarily rise, as compared with those things.'[1] Further on in the *Essay* he states: 'A fall in the price of corn, in consequence of improvements in agriculture or of importation, will lower the exchangeable value of corn only,—the price of no other commodity will be affected. If, then, the price of labour falls, which it must do when the price of corn is lowered, the real profits of all descriptions must rise'.[2]

All these elements of the *Essay* are taken over into the chapter On Value in the *Principles* with the addition of several new ones, some of which have come to be regarded as the most characteristic of Ricardo's theory, and are there built into a systematic theory of Value, on which are now based the theories of Rent, Wages and Profit.

The turning point in this transition from the *Essay* to the *Principles* was reached when, at the end of 1815, having set to work on the *Principles*, he wrote to Mill: 'I know I shall be soon stopped by the word price' (above, p. xiv). This is the first time that he faces the necessity for a general solution of the problem, instead of being content with dealing with the difficulties of price piece-meal as they arise in particular problems. At once a proper understanding of the matter appears to him as involving: (*a*) the distinction between causes which affect the value of money and causes which affect the value of commodities; (*b*) the supposition of the invariability of the precious metals as a standard of value; (*c*) the opposition to the view that the price of corn regulates the prices of all other commodities. These three things, which are so closely connected in his mind as to be almost identified, are what he calls 'the sheet anchor on which all my propositions are built'.[3]

The distinction between the two types of influences upon value (on the side of money and on the side of commodities) is made possible by Ricardo's treatment of money as a commodity like

[1] Below, IV, 19.
[2] *ib.* 35–6.
[3] Letter to Mill of 30 Dec. 1815, below, VI, 348.

any other. Thus a change in wages could not alter the prices of commodities, since (if the gold mine from which money was obtained were in the same country) a rise of wages would affect the owner of the gold mine as much as the other industries.[1] Hence it was the relative conditions of production of gold and of other commodities that determined prices, and not the remuneration of labour.

The attempt to weave into his general theory the proposition which he had established that a rise of wages does not raise prices, led immediately to his discovery of 'the curious effect which the rise of wages produces on the prices of those commodities which are chiefly obtained by the aid of machinery and fixed capital.'[2] It yielded the triumphant conclusion that, not only was it false that a rise of wages would raise the price of every commodity (as 'Adam Smith, and all the writers who have followed him'[3] had maintained that it would do), but on the contrary, it caused the prices of many commodities *to fall*: a result of which he stressed the 'importance to the science of political economy', although it accorded so little 'with some of its received doctrines'.[4]

The importance which Ricardo came to attach to the principle that the value of a thing was regulated by the quantity of labour required for its production, and not by the remuneration of that labour, reflected his recognition that what his new theory was opposed to was not merely the popular view of the effect of wages on prices but another and more general theory of Adam Smith (of which that effect came to appear as a particular case)—what Ricardo referred to in writing to Mill as Adam Smith's 'original error respecting value'.[5] This latter theory, in brief, was that 'as soon as stock has accumulated in the hands of particular persons' and 'as soon as the land of any country has all become private property', the price of commodities is arrived at by a process of *adding up* the wages, profit and rent: 'in every improved society, all the three enter more or less, as component parts, into the price of the far greater part of

---

[1] Below, p. 55; and for the case where gold would have to be imported (which would be impossible in the face of a rise of commodity prices), p. 104–5.

[2] Letter to Mill, 14 Oct. 1816, below, VII, 82.
[3] Below, p. 46.
[4] Below, p. 61.
[5] 2 Dec. 1816, below, VII, 100.

commodities.'[1] In other words, 'wages, profit, and rent, are the three original sources…of all exchangeable value.'[2] Adam Smith speaks also of the natural price varying 'with the natural rate of each of its component parts, of wages, profit, and rent'.[3]

In the chapter On Value, Ricardo criticises Adam Smith for limiting the rule that commodities exchange according to the amount of labour required for their production to 'that early and rude state of society, which precedes both the accumulation of stock and the appropriation of land'; 'as if when profits and rent were to be paid, they would have some influence on the relative value of commodities, independent of the mere quantity of labour that was necessary to their production.' But, Ricardo adds, Adam Smith 'has no where analysed the effects of the accumulation of capital, and the appropriation of land, on relative value.'[4] (The effect of 'the appropriation of land' is left by Ricardo for later consideration in the chapter On Rent, and in the chapter On Value he deals only with the accumulation of capital.) This passage in which he criticises Adam Smith has puzzled readers, since it appears to be 'flatly contradicted' (as Cannan put it)[5] by the following sections of the chapter.

It is not until 1818 in a letter to Mill, now first available, that Ricardo states precisely the nature of his quarrel with Adam Smith's theory and thereby clarifies this passage.

This he does by contrasting his own reading of the matter with that of Torrens. 'He [Torrens] makes it appear that Smith says that after capital accumulates and industrious people are set to work the quantity of labour employed is not the only circumstance that determines the value of commodities, and that I oppose this opinion. Now I want to shew that I do not oppose this opinion in the way that he represents me to do so, but Adam Smith thought, that as in

---

[1] *Wealth of Nations*, Bk. I, ch. vi, 'Of the Component Parts of the Price of Commodities'; Cannan's ed., vol. I, pp. 50, 51, 52. Later however (*ib.* p. 147) this is qualified by the observation that rent enters as an effect, not a cause, of price.

[2] *ib.* p. 54.

[3] *ib.* p. 65.

[4] Below, p. 22–3, note.

[5] *A Review of Economic Theory*, p. 176. The contrast is particularly striking between the headings given in ed. 2 to the respective Sections (II and III–IV) to which Cannan is referring: see the Table of Section-Headings at the end of this Introduction.

the early stages of society, all the produce of labour belonged to the labourer, and as after stock was accumulated, a part went to profits, that accumulation, necessarily, without any regard to the different degrees of durability of capital, or any other circumstance whatever, *raised* the prices or exchangeable value of commodities, and consequently that their value was no longer regulated by the quantity of labour necessary to their production. In opposition to him, I maintain that it is not because of this division into profits and wages,—it is not because capital accumulates, that exchangeable value varies, but it is in all stages of society, owing only to two causes: one the more or less quantity of labour required, the other the greater or less durability of capital:—that the former is never superseded by the latter, but is only modified by it.'[1] The relevance of this statement to certain changes in later editions will become apparent in the next section.

V. *Principal Changes in the Chapter On Value in Editions 2 and 3*

It will be convenient to deal with the main changes in the chapter On Value in editions 2 and 3 before we deal with these editions as a whole.

It has come to be a widely accepted opinion about Ricardo that in subsequent editions he steadily retreated under pressure of his critics from the theory of value presented in edition 1. This was the view disseminated by Professor Hollander in his well-known article on 'The Development of Ricardo's Theory of Value'.[2] In speaking of edition 2 Hollander says that the textual changes in it 'although not vital' could be regarded 'as highly significant' and that it 'showed an appreciable increase of reserve in the advocacy of "embodied labour" as a universal measure of value'.[3] With reference to edition 3 he says that the chapter On Value 'is in content and tendency very different'[4] from that in the first edition; and elsewhere he speaks of 'greater emphasis upon the modifications of the principles which determine relative value' due to the employment of capital.[5] Pro-

[1] Letter to Mill, 28 Dec. 1818, below, VII, 377. Editor's italics.
[2] *Quarterly Journal of Economics,* 1904, vol. XVIII, pp. 455–91.
[3] *ib.* pp. 479 and 481.
[4] *ib.* p. 485.
[5] Editor's note to *Letters to McCulloch,* 1895, p. 72.

fessor Cannan went further and spoke of Ricardo's 'unwilling admission of the influence of interest on capital as a modification of the pure labour-cost theory of value'. Concerning the effect of capital on value, says Cannan, Ricardo 'was weak from the beginning, and he weakened more and more as time went on and criticism multiplied'.[1] Thus the view of a retreat in Ricardo's position over successive editions has become established. But an examination of the changes in the text in the light of the new evidence lends no support to this view: the theory of edition 3 appears to be the same, in essence and in emphasis, as that of edition 1.

The alterations were certainly extensive; little more than half of the final version (edition 3) of the chapter On Value being found in the same form in edition 1. Although the changes made in edition 2 were small and there was little rearrangement of the matter, the subdivision into sections was first introduced in that edition; this only emphasized the repetition and lack of order in the treatment and rendered necessary the complete rearrangement and rewriting of edition 3. Thus the statement of the exceptions to the law of value due to different proportions of capital (or, as Ricardo put it, to the rise or fall of wages), which was repeated in edition 1 in different places[2] (and is still scattered under several sections in edition 2) is mostly collected in edition 3 under Sections IV and V.

All the evidence in favour of a 'weakening' of Ricardo is based on the current misunderstanding of certain changes in the text which the letter to Mill quoted at the end of the last section enables us to rectify. The evidence in question rests mainly upon two changes. First, the dropping in edition 3 of the passage in which Adam Smith was criticised for having limited the application of the principle of value to the 'early and rude state of society',[3] a change which looks at first sight significant; we now know however that this was withdrawn because it had lent itself to misinterpretation, and the letter quoted above shows that Ricardo was not shaken in his position by Torrens's

---

[1] *A Review of Economic Theory*, 1929, p. 185 and p. 176. The opposite and unusual view has been put forward by H. Biaujeaud, *Essai sur la théorie ricardienne de la valeur*, Paris, 1934, p. 125.

[2] Below, pp. 53, 56–63, 66.

[3] Below, p. 22–3, n. 2.

criticism. The second change is the replacement in edition 3 of the statement that exchangeable value 'depends solely' upon the quantity of labour realised in a commodity with 'depends almost exclusively'.[1] But here again the letter to Mill now makes it clear that the background against which the 'solely' of edition 1 is to be understood is that no prices can rise as a result of a rise of wages—they can *only* be raised by an increase in the difficulty of production. On the other hand, in ed. 3 the 'almost exclusively' reflects the change in the choice of standard from ed. 1 to ed. 3 (to be described below, pp. xlii–xlv), the new standard permitting a rise of price, as a result of a rise of wages, in the case of commodities produced without fixed capital.

This phrase thus takes its place as one of a series of modifications which were designed to *minimise* the extent of such price-changes in either direction as, in terms of the newly adopted standard, do occur when wages rise. The other passages introduced in edition 3 to the same effect were as follows: 'it would be...incorrect to attach much importance to it', below, p. 36; 'another, though a minor variation', p. 42; 'comparatively slight in its effects', p. 36 and again p. 45.[2] The implication of these changes is clear enough and Malthus at any rate did not regard edition 3 as showing any weakening: 'The effects of slow or quick returns, and of the different proportions of fixed and circulating capitals, are distinctly allowed by Mr. Ricardo; but in his last edition, (the third, p. [36]) he has much underrated their amount.'[3]

At one moment between edition 2 and edition 3 Ricardo did show signs of weakening. In a much-quoted passage he wrote to McCulloch on 13 June 1820: 'I sometimes think that if I were to write the chapter on value again which is in my book, I should acknowledge that the relative value of commodities was regulated by two causes instead of by one, namely, by the relative quantity of labour necessary to

[1] Below, p. 12, n. 1, and cp. p. 20, n. 3.
[2] See also the reference in *Notes on Malthus* (which belong to the time of the revision for ed. 3) to 'comparatively of very slight effect' (below, II, 59) and 'of no great magnitude' (*ib.* 101), and cp. *ib.* 66,

82. A similar reference to 'insignificant in its effects' is found in a letter to Malthus of 9 Oct. 1820, below, VIII, 279.
[3] *The Measure of Value*, 1823, p. 12, n.

produce the commodities in question, and by the rate of profit for
the time that the capital remained dormant, and until the commodities
were brought to market. Perhaps I should find the difficulties nearly
as great in this view of the subject as in that which I have adopted.'[1]
Within six months he did rewrite the chapter, and evidently found
'the difficulties' of this view even greater than in the case of his
original view, since he now in ed. 3 confirmed it.[2]

Letters written in these intervening months provide evidence
enough that this weakening was no more than a passing mood.
Already on 9 Oct. 1820 he is writing to Malthus: 'You say that my
proposition "that with few exceptions the quantity of labour
employed on commodities determines the rate at which they will
exchange for each other, is not well founded" I acknowledge that it
is not rigidly true, but I say that it is the nearest approximation to
truth, as a rule for measuring relative value, of any I have ever
heard'; and adds: 'My first chapter will not be materially altered—in
principle I think it will not be altered at all.'[3] And on 25 Jan. 1821,
while still wrestling with the problem of a standard of absolute value,
he writes to McCulloch: 'I am fully persuaded that in fixing on the
quantity of labour realised in commodities as the rule which governs
their relative value we are in the right course'.[4]

Although no essential change was made in successive editions
about the rule which determines value, two considerable alterations
were made in connection with the choice of an invariable measure of
value. The search for what has been called 'the chimera of an invariable standard of value'[5] preoccupied Ricardo to the end of his life.
However, the problem which mainly interested him was not that of
finding an actual commodity which would accurately measure the
value of corn or silver at different times and places; but rather that of

---

[1] Below, VIII, 194.
[2] At any rate Professor Hollander's suggestion that Ricardo's failure to carry out a 'thoroughgoing reconstruction' of this chapter in ed. 3 had anything to do with 'the urgency of the printer' (op. cit., p. 484) can be dismissed in view of the ample notice given to the author and the subsequent delays in publishing that edition, described in section VII of this Introduction.
[3] Below, VIII, 279, 280.
[4] ib. 344.
[5] E. Cannan, A Review of Economic Theory, p. 174.

finding the conditions which a commodity would have to satisfy in order to be invariable in value—and this came close to identifying the problem of a measure with that of the law of value: 'Is it not clear then that as soon as we are in possession of the knowledge of the circumstances which determine the value of commodities, we are enabled to say what is necessary to give us an invariable measure of value?'[1]

The first of the alterations of which we have spoken was occasioned by a growing sense of the difficulty of even conceiving of such an invariable commodity. In ed. 1 and ed. 2 the essential quality which a commodity must have to be invariable is that it should require 'at all times, and under all circumstances, precisely the same quantity of labour' to produce it.[2] He admitted that 'of such a commodity we have no knowledge'. But this he regarded as only a practical difficulty; and he expressed no doubts as to what the 'essential qualities' of such a standard were.[3] In ed. 3, however, Ricardo enlarged on the difficulty and stated that, even if a commodity could be found which satisfied that requirement, 'still it would not be a perfect standard or invariable measure of value', since 'it would be subject to relative variations from a rise or fall of wages' on account of different proportions of fixed capital or different durabilities of fixed capital or different times necessary to bring it to market.[4] Thus the same exceptions which he had discovered in the fundamental rule determining value cropped up again in attempting to define the qualities of an invariable standard.

[1] Ricardo to McCulloch, 21 Aug. 1823, below, IX, p. 358 and cp. p. 377. Cp. also below, p. 17, n. 3. This idea that to every theory of value there corresponds an appropriate 'invariable measure' is evidently based on Ricardo's experience with his own theory, where to the determination of value by embodied labour there corresponds an invariable measure in the shape of a commodity produced by a constant quantity of labour; and in so far as there are exceptions to the theory, to the same extent the accuracy of the measure is affected. This correspondence, however, is a peculiar property of Ricardo's theory and does not necessarily apply to other theories. Thus there would not seem to be such a relation between the theory that wages determine prices and the 'labour commanded' standard (see on the other hand below, p. 16–17).

[2] Below, pp. 27, n., and 17, n. 3.

[3] Below, p. 17, n. 3.

[4] Below, p. 44. He adds that such circumstances 'disqualify any commodity that can be thought of from being a perfectly accurate measure of value.'

The second change concerned the conditions of production of the commodity to be adopted as standard. These were defined as follows in ed. 1: 'in this whole argument I am supposing money to be of an invariable value; in other words, to be always the produce of the same quantity of *unassisted* labour'.[1] In that edition Ricardo only acknowledged two forms of variation of capital: different proportions of fixed and circulating capital and different durabilities of fixed capital. He had not yet noticed the 'different times it takes to market' (or durability of circulating capital), to which his attention was to be drawn by Torrens;[2] with the result that in edition 2 this was introduced as a third form of variation of capital.[3] In ed. 1 therefore 'unassisted' meant unassisted by fixed capital, with the tacit assumption that the period which all things took to produce and bring to market (*i.e.* circulating capital to circulate) was a year. As James Mill was to put it in his *Elements*, 'A year is assumed in political economy as the period which includes a revolving circle of production and consumption.'[4]

The qualification 'unassisted' is made explicitly by Ricardo only in the carefully worded passage which we have quoted, and in other places[5] he mentions simply 'the same quantity of labour'. But to the deductions based upon it the qualification is essential; and in ed. 1 it is consistently implied in Ricardo's argument.[6] It is, indeed, from this definition of invariable money that there follows the striking result that 'commodities may be lowered in value in consequence of a real rise of wages, but they never can be raised from that cause'[7] (the reason being that in the production of some commodities

[1] Below, p. 63. The italics are the editor's.
[2] Cp. below, IV, 305–6.
[3] Below, p. 61 n. and cp. p. 31, n. 2, p. 53, n. 1, p. 58, n. 2.
[4] *Elements of Political Economy*, 1821, p. 185. Cp. Ricardo's example, below, p. 61, and his reference on p. 59 to capital 'annually consumed and reproduced, as it is when employed in paying wages'. Malthus also understood it in this way: 'Mr. Ricardo, in order to illustrate his proposition, has placed it, at a venture, among

those commodities where the advances consist solely in the payment of labour, and the returns come in exactly in the year.' (*Principles of Political Economy*; below, II, 64–5.)
[5] Below, pp. 17, n. 3, 27, n., 55, 87, n. 1, 275.
[6] Except where (as in the example on p. 55–6) all commodities, *including money*, are explicitly assumed to be produced with the same proportions of fixed and circulating capitals.
[7] Below, p. 66.

fixed capital enters while it does not enter into the production of gold, or money). Here 'value' clearly refers to 'absolute' value, *i.e.* value measured in the invariable standard. When Ricardo in ed. 1 speaks of 'relative value',[1] he says that, with a rise of wages, some goods will rise compared with others.

In ed. 2 the substance of the argument is unchanged; but a number of alterations in wording, which emphasize this paradox of commodities falling in value when wages rise, tend to obscure the distinction just mentioned between the effect of changes in wages upon 'absolute' and upon 'relative' value. Thus, passages which stated that, with a rise of wages, some commodities *rise* in relative value compared with others, in ed. 2 are turned round so as to say that some commodities *fall* in terms of others.[2] And in the statement of ed. 1 that 'no commodities whatever are raised in absolute price, merely because wages rise', the words 'absolute price' are confusingly replaced by 'exchangeable value'.[3]

Malthus, in his *Principles of Political Economy*, draws attention to the case of commodities where the period of turnover of circulating capital may be *less* than one year.[4] In such a case (covering, as he suggests, 'a large class of commodities') prices will rise 'consequently upon a rise in the price of labour and fall of profits'. Ricardo in his Note[5] upon this passage admits that he has 'inadvertently omitted to consider' this case, and that 'Mr. Malthus is quite right in asserting that many commodities in which labour chiefly enters, and which can be quickly brought to market will rise, with a rise in the value of labour'. The 'correct opinion' as he now states it is that, in consequence of 'a rise in the money price of wages, and a fall of profits, so far from its being true that all other commodities would also rise in price, there will be a large class which will absolutely fall —some which will not vary at all, and another large class which will

---

[1] Below, p. 58.
[2] Below, p. 58, nn. 1 and 4.
[3] Below, p. 63, n. 3. This latter change was the result of summing up in this sentence (which in ed. 2 becomes the conclusion of a Section) the three possible causes of a rise of

commodities. Since one of these causes was a fall in value of the medium itself, this precluded the use of the term 'absolute price' (which presupposes an invariable medium).
[4] Below, II, 62–4.
[5] *ib.* 64.

rise.'[1] This concession in the *Notes on Malthus* marks the transition between ed. 2 and ed. 3.

As an extreme instance of the case to which he had drawn attention Malthus introduced[2] the striking example of silver picked up on the sea-shore with the labour of one day and therefore without either fixed or circulating capital—a standard in terms of which 'no rise in the price of labour could take place'.[3]

At the time when his ed. 3 was already in the press Ricardo wrote to McCulloch: 'when I want to fix a standard of absolute value I am undetermined whether to chuse labour for a year, a month, a week, or a day'.[4] But he had already suggested to McCulloch in a previous letter (in June 1820) that 'perhaps the best adapted to the general mass of commodities' was 'the medium' between the 'two extremes': 'one, where the commodity is produced without delay, and by labour only, without the intervention of capital; the other where it is the result of a great quantity of fixed capital, contains very little labour, and is not produced without considerable delay.' 'Those commodities on one side of this medium, would rise in comparative value with it, with a rise in the price of labour, and a fall in the rate of profits; and those on the other side might fall from the same cause.'[5]

In edition 3, therefore, the standard adopted was money 'produced with such proportions of the two kinds of capital as approach nearest to the average quantity employed in the production of most commodities';[6] and the relevant passages were accordingly altered to the effect that, with a rise of wages, some commodities would fall and others rise in terms of this standard.[7] (If measured in such a

---

[1] Below, II, 62–3. This admission of a rise is made rather grudgingly ('in a trifling degree', and cp. *ib.* n. 7).

[2] First in a letter of 10 Sept. 1819, below, VIII, 64–5, and then in his *Principles of Political Economy*, below, II, 81.

[3] Below, II, 81. As Ricardo later wrote to McCulloch: 'Malthus has supposed a case of a man by a day's labour being enabled to pick up a certain number of grains of gold or silver on the sea shore;—suppose he could pick up as much silver as we coin into a shilling, labour never could fall below a shilling a day, and if corn rose in silver labour could not rise' (below, VIII, 343).

[4] Ricardo to McCulloch, 25 Jan. 1821, *ib.* 344.

[5] *ib.* 193.

[6] Below, p. 45.

[7] Below, p. 35, p. 43, n. 4, p. 48, n. 3.

standard, the average price of all commodities, and their aggregate value, would remain unaffected by a rise or fall of wages.)

Already in one of the letters to McCulloch from which we have just quoted Ricardo had suggested that 'all the exceptions to the general rule' could be reduced to 'one of time':[1] *i.e.* all those deriving from different proportions of fixed and circulating capitals, different durabilities of fixed capital, or differences in the 'time it takes to market' (or durability of circulating capital) could be reduced to terms of labour employed for a longer or a shorter time. This conception was the one to which he finally adhered. In the newly-discovered paper on 'Absolute Value and Exchangeable Value',[2] written at the end of his life, the standard adopted in ed. 3 was in effect equated to that of ed. 1 by the statement that 'a commodity produced by labour employed for a year is a mean between the extremes of commodities produced on one side by labour and advances for much more than a year, and on the other by labour employed for a day only without any advances, and the mean will in most cases give a much less deviation from truth than if either of the extremes were used as a measure.'[3]

Having started, therefore, with 'labour employed for a year', regarded as the 'extreme' of 'unassisted labour', Ricardo became convinced, firstly that this was not really an 'extreme' since many commodities were produced by labour employed for *less* than one year, and secondly that, if he were to take 'labour employed for a day only without any advances', this would be the equivalent of a 'labour commanded' standard and wages could never rise in terms of this standard. He accordingly in edition 3 takes 'a just mean' between the extremes, 'produced with such proportions of the two kinds of capital as approach nearest to the average'.[4] Having done so, he comes finally to the view that this mean can be reduced to 'a commodity produced by labour employed for a year'[5]—the very standard which he had used in edition 1, but which he had at that time treated as being an 'extreme'.

[1] Letter to McCulloch, 13 June 1820, below, VIII, 193.
[2] Below, IV, 357ff.
[3] Below, IV, 405.
[4] Below, p. 45–6.
[5] Below, IV, 405.

The idea of an 'invariable measure' has for Ricardo its necessary complement in that of 'absolute value'. This concept appears in the *Principles* at first (in ed. 1) as 'absolute value'[1] and later (in ed. 3) as 'real value',[2] it comes out from time to time in his letters,[3] and takes more definite shape in his last paper on 'Absolute Value and Exchangeable Value'. In one of his drafts for that paper he writes: 'No one can doubt that it would be a great desideratum in political Economy to have such a measure of absolute value in order to enable us to know[,] when commodities altered in exchangeable value[,] in which the alteration in value had taken place'.[4] In another draft he explains what he means by a test of whether a commodity has altered in value: 'I may be asked what I mean by the word value, and by what criterion I would judge whether a commodity had or had not changed its value. I answer, I know no other criterion of a thing being dear or cheap but by the sacrifices of labour made to obtain it.'[5] And elsewhere he writes: 'To me it appears a contradiction to say a thing has increased in natural[6] value while it continues to be produced under precisely the same circumstances as before.'[7]

Ricardo starts (in ed. 1 of the *Principles*) by applying the concept to the problem of two commodities which have changed in relative value as a result of a change in the difficulty of production: absolute value is then the criterion for deciding in which of the two the real change has occurred. He ends (in his last paper on value) by bringing this criterion to bear upon another problem, namely the distinction between two causes of changes in exchangeable value: for, 'difficulty or facility of production is not absolutely the only cause of variation in value[,] there is one other, the rise or fall of wages', since commodities cannot 'be produced and brought to market in precisely the same time'.[8] Absolute value, however, reflects only the first type of change and is not affected by the latter. As Ricardo says with

---

[1] Below, p. 21 and cp. p. 63.
[2] Below, pp. 42–3.
[3] To Malthus, 9 Oct. 1820, below, VIII, 279; to McCulloch, 25 Jan. 1821, *ib.* 344; to Trower, 4 July (as 'positive value') and 22 Aug. 1821, IX, 1–2 and 38; and frequently in 1823, *ib.* 297–300, 346, 356, 377–8.

[4] Below, IV, 399n. See a similar statement in *Principles*, below, p. 43.
[5] Below, IV, 397.
[6] As the context shows, 'natural' here stands for 'absolute'.
[7] Below, IV, 375.
[8] *ib.* 368.

reference to a commodity which changes in price owing to a rise of wages: 'If the measure was perfect it ought not to vary at all'.[1] After one of the numerical examples with which in a letter of 1823 he illustrates this deviation, he comments as follows: 'The two commodities change in relative value....Can it be said that the proportions of capital we employ are in any way altered? or the proportion of labour? certainly not, nothing has altered but the rate of distribution between employer and employed...—this and this only is the reason why they alter in relative value'; and he concludes: 'The fact is there is not any measure of absolute value which can in any degree be deemed an accurate one.'[2] Accordingly he falls back on his admittedly imperfect standard as giving the least 'deviation from truth'.[3]

In this attempt to extend the application of absolute value to the second problem (that of distinguishing the two sorts of changes in exchangeable values) Ricardo was confronted with this dilemma: whereas the former application presupposes an exact proportionality between relative and absolute value, the latter implies a variable deviation of exchangeable from absolute value for each individual commodity. This contradiction Ricardo never completely succeeded in resolving, as is apparent from his last paper.

There is another respect in which his last paper on value reverts to a position similar to that of edition 1. The effects on value of different proportions or durabilities of capital can be looked upon from two distinct aspects. First, that of occasioning a *difference* in the relative values of two commodities which are produced by equal quantities of labour. Second, that of the effect which a rise of wages has in producing a *change* in their relative value. In edition 1 the second aspect is the one exclusively considered: whenever different proportions or durabilities of capital are mentioned in connection

[1] *ib.* 373.
[2] Draft letter to M{c}Culloch, 15 Aug. 1823, below, IX, 355–6. Cp. the phrase 'It must then be confessed that there is no such thing in nature as a perfect measure of value', below, IV, 404; also a similar expression below, IX, 361, and the closing sentence of his last letter (to Mill, 5 Sept. 1823), *ib.* 387.
[3] Below, IV, 405; quoted more fully above, p. xlv.

with value, Ricardo always speaks in terms of the effect of a rise of wages. The first aspect creeps into the later editions: once into edition 2 and a few times into edition 3, usually as incidental to discussion of variations in value, and probably as a result of argument with his opponents, particularly Torrens and Malthus, who looked at the problem from this angle.[1] But while in edition 3 Ricardo sometimes refers to different proportions or durabilities of capital as causing differences in relative values, the effect of a rise in wages remains in the forefront, and it is upon this aspect that attention is focused in the paper on 'Absolute Value and Exchangeable Value'.

This preoccupation with the effect of a change in wages arose from his approach to the problem of value which, as we have seen, was dominated by his theory of profits. The 'principal problem in Political Economy' was in his view the division of the national product between classes[2] and in the course of that investigation he was troubled by the fact that the size of this product appears to change when the division changes. Even though nothing has occurred to change the magnitude of the aggregate, there may be *apparent* changes due solely to change in measurement, owing to the fact that measurement is in terms of value and relative values have been altered as a result of a change in the division between wages and profits. This is particularly evident in the extreme case where the aggregate is composed of the same commodities in the same quantities, and yet its magnitude will appear to have changed as measured in value.

Thus the problem of value which interested Ricardo was how to find a measure of value which would be invariant to changes in the division of the product; for, if a rise or fall of wages by itself brought about a change in the magnitude of the social product, it would be hard to determine accurately the effect on profits. (This was, of course, the same problem as has been mentioned earlier[3] in connection with

---

[1] In ed. 2 a statement about 'unequal value' is introduced casually below, p. 62, n. In ed. 3 this aspect is considered below, p. 34 and p. 37, second and fourth paragraphs. Cp. also letter to Malthus, 9 Oct. 1820, below, VIII, 279.

[2] See the Preface to the *Principles*, and also the oft-quoted passage on the problem of Political Economy in the letter to Malthus of 9 Oct. 1820, below, VIII, 278.

[3] Above, p. xxxiii.

Ricardo's corn-ratio theory of profits.) On the other hand, Ricardo was not interested for its own sake in the problem of why two commodities produced by the same quantities of labour are not of the same exchangeable value. He was concerned with it only in so far as thereby relative values are affected by changes in wages. The two points of view of difference and of change are closely linked together; yet the search for an invariable measure of value, which is so much at the centre of Ricardo's system, arises exclusively from the second and would have no counterpart in an investigation of the first.

This function of the theory of value of making it possible, in the face of changes in distribution, to measure changes in the magnitude of aggregates of commodities of different kinds or, what is even more important, to ascertain its constancy, appears once more in connection with the measurement of the quantity of capital. With reference to the theory of Torrens ('that commodities are valuable according to the value of the capital employed on their production, and the time for which it is so employed') Ricardo says in the letter to McCulloch of 21 Aug. 1823: 'I would ask what means you have of ascertaining the equal value of capitals?... These capitals are not the same in kind [if they were, he points out in an earlier draft, 'their proportional quantities would indicate their proportional values'[1]]... and if they themselves are produced in unequal times they are subject to the same fluctuations as other commodities. Till you have fixed the criterion by which we are to ascertain value, you can say nothing of equal capitals'; for, as he says in another draft of this letter, 'the means of ascertaining their equality or variation of value is the very thing in dispute.'[2]

VI. *Edition 2*

Only 750 copies of edition 1 of the *Principles* had been printed,[3] and within two months of publication Murray told Ricardo that a second edition would 'most assuredly be required'.[4] Ricardo, however,

[1] Below, IX, 357.
[2] Below, IX, 359–60 and note. Cp. also the paper on value of the same period, below, IV, 393–4.
[3] Of ed. 2 and ed. 3 1000 each were printed. These figures have been kindly supplied by Sir John Murray from the records of his firm.
[4] Ricardo to Trower, 15 June 1817, below, VII, 162.

heard no more of this until after the appearance of McCulloch's review in the number of the *Edinburgh Review* for June 1818 (actually published in August) by which the sale was 'much accelerated'.[1] On 8 November 1818 Ricardo wrote to Mill: 'I hear from various quarters that my book is selling very fast, and that a new edition will soon be required'; adding, 'I think in the last conversation we had together we agreed that there would not be very great advantage in making any new arrangement of the contents, as it appears to have made the impression I could wish on those who have well considered it'.[2] On 17 November 1818 he received a request from Murray to prepare a second edition; and within a week Ricardo had the book ready for the press.[3] In sending the revised copy to Murray, he mentioned that it contained 'a few very trifling alterations' and asked that the proposed division into sections of the first chapter should be sent by messenger to Mill for his approval.[4] However, edition 2 was not published until 27 February 1819.[5]

In the intervening period he received the French translation of his own *Principles*, with Say's notes;[6] and in reply to one of these notes he added a passage referring to the question whether the theory of rent depended upon the existence of land which paid no rent.[7] This point had also been the subject of discussion during a visit of Malthus to Gatcomb in December 1818.[8] At one time he thought of having Say's notes translated and published as an appendix of his own ed. 2; but he referred the matter to Murray, who evidently decided against it.[9]

On the whole, the alterations in edition 2 were unimportant, and Ricardo could say that it contained 'nothing new'.[10] A few changes made to meet criticisms of particular points are of some interest and can be identified as follows. Some passages on taxation had been

[1] Ricardo to McCulloch, 24 Nov. 1818, *ib*. 337. According to Mallet it was this review which 'got off the first edition' (below, VIII, 152, n. 2). In October Malthus wrote: 'I hear the sale of your work goes on swimmingly' (below, VII, 312).
[2] *ib*. 327.
[3] *ib*. 328 and 331.
[4] *ib*. 331.

[5] Advt. in *The Times*. The price was stated as 14s.
[6] Below, VII, 370.
[7] Below, p. 413, note.
[8] Below, VII, 371–2.
[9] Letter to Mill, 22 and 28 Dec. 1818, *ib*. 371, 379.
[10] Letter to Say, 11 Jan. 1820, below VIII, 150.

criticised by McCulloch. When he was revising the book for edition 2 Ricardo wrote to McCulloch that he proposed to alter a passage which might be considered to 'hold out an apology to ministers for taxation', and asked for suggestions 'on all those passages which you would like to see altered'.[1] Two footnotes were added to meet Torrens's complaint that he had not been mentioned.[2] The first of these (p. 96–7) notices a passage from Torrens on the natural price of labour (which is remarkable for its emphasis on the influence of 'habits of living'), for which Torrens had claimed originality.[3] The adoption of Torrens's suggestion about the 'unequal durability' of circulating capitals has been mentioned above. A passage on the causes of the miserable state of the Irish peasantry criticised by George Ensor was omitted;[4] and a note was added to Chapter I in defence of the illustration of a machine producing without human labour which had been ridiculed in the *British Review*.[5] Two changes, one about the effect of improvements in agriculture on rent and the other about corn importation and profits,[6] which appear to have arisen out of correspondence with Malthus, anticipated more extensive alterations in edition 3.

One group of apparently slight corrections may be more significant than at first appears. In ed. 1 Ricardo had frequently employed the curious phrase 'price of wages';[7] in ed. 2 however the expression is removed in several cases,[8] and its elimination is carried further in ed. 3.[9] Although in places he clearly treats this phrase as inter-

---

[1] Ricardo to McCulloch, 24 Nov. 1818, below, VII, 337–8. McCulloch sent a number of suggestions (*ib.* 351–4), several of which were adopted, including: a second passage about taxation which was rewritten in McCulloch's own words (below, p. 152); part of the pamphlet *Economical and Secure Currency* was inserted in Chapter XXVII; and the 'principle of limitation' was enlarged upon in the discussion of paper money (below, p. 353–4).
[2] Below, pp. 96–7, 271. Cp. letter to Mill, below VII, 333.
[3] Preface to *An Essay on the External Corn Trade*, 1815, pp. xiii–xiv.

[4] Below, p. 100.
[5] Below, p. 60, n.
[6] Below, pp. 412 and 428–9. Cp. letters to Malthus, 24 June and 20 Aug. 1818, below, VII, 271, 282–3.
[7] For instances in his earlier writings, see below, IV, 22; letter to Malthus, 30 July 1815, below VI, 241; and in later writings: below, II, 63, n. 5, 231, n. 6 and 411; letter to Malthus, 3 Aug. 1823, below, IX, 325.
[8] Below, p. 95, n. 3, p. 96, notes 1, 3, 4, p. 111, n. 3.
[9] Below, p. 94, n. 1, p. 303, n. 2, p. 334, n. 3. In a few cases the expression was retained in ed. 3: see p. 118, p. 145, and Index, under *Wages*.

changeable with 'price of labour' or simply 'wages',[1] it must originally have been related to the expression 'real value of wages', which he uses in explaining the peculiar sense in which he is to be understood when he speaks of the rise or fall of wages: namely as referring to the *proportion* of the total product going to labour, and not to the absolute quantity of commodities received by the labourers.[2] However, after thus defining the 'real value of wages', he did not use again that expression in the *Principles*, except when in ed. 3 he had to defend himself against Malthus's complaint that he had adopted 'new and unusual language' in connection with wages:[3] —a complaint renewed in later times by Marshall, who deplored Ricardo's failure to invent some new term for the purpose.[4] Perhaps the early use of 'price of wages' was a sign that Ricardo at first felt the need for a special term, whereas later he seems to have come to regard the unqualified term 'wages' as adequate, 'at least among Political Economists',[5] to describe proportional wages.

The only prominent change was the subdivision of the chapter On Value into sections each carrying its own heading. It was on these that he had consulted Mill. The division introduced in edition 2 seems to have been made at first into four sections, and then to have been changed to five before the titles were sent to Mill,[6] in which form it finally appeared. This required the splitting of a section into two, and it was probably Section 1 that was divided, the additional heading being: 'Sect. II. The accumulation of capital makes no difference in the principle stated in the last section'.[7] That the heading of Section 1 was written when that section included the whole of what was published as Section II, is shown by the fact that its statement that value does not depend 'on the greater or less compensation which is paid for that labour' can only refer to the text of

---

[1] See *e.g.* p. 95–6 where all these expressions are used as equivalent.
[2] Cp. below, p. 49–50; and cp. p. 274–5 note.
[3] Below, p. 19.
[4] *Principles of Economics*, 8th ed., p. 550.
[5] As he says in another context, below, IV, 409.

[6] In his letter to Murray of 23 Nov. 1818 Ricardo mentions 4 sections, but in his letter to Mill of the same date (sent through Murray the next day) 'four' is altered to 'five' (below, VII, 331, 333, n. 1).
[7] Below, p. 22, n. 2. See the Table of Section-Headings of Chapter I, below, p. lxiii.

the latter part of Section II.[1] It may be noticed that Section I, thus reduced, was further subdivided in edition 3, without the heading being changed; with the result that the heading of Section I still adequately covers the contents of the whole of the first three sections of the chapter in edition 3.

This subdivision required the rewriting of certain passages which now formed the beginning and the end of sections. But it is surprising how little rearrangement was made: only an obviously misplaced paragraph in the middle of the chapter[2] and the three concluding paragraphs[3] were transferred to more appropriate places.

VII. *Edition 3*

Before Ricardo left London for the country in July 1820 Murray told him that 'he should soon wish to publish a new edition' of the *Principles*;[4] and during the next six months (which, after a few weeks at Brighton, he spent at Gatcomb)[5] he revised his book for edition 3. This was done in the intervals of what was to become his main preoccupation during this period: re-reading, and writing his Notes on, Malthus's *Principles of Political Economy*. At first he had intended to include in edition 3 his defence against Malthus's attacks. But he afterwards gave up this project; Mill (who in August and September was on a visit to Gatcomb) had 'strongly dissuaded' him from it, and advised him not to notice any attacks for fear of 'giving too controversial a character' to the book.[6]

On 4 September 1820 Ricardo writes to Malthus: 'I have been looking over my first chapter, with a view to make a few alterations in it before the work goes to another edition. I find my task very difficult, but I hope I shall make my opinions more clear and

---

[1] Cp. also the heading of Section III: 'The principle stated in the foregoing section...'. This must refer to Section I, which on our supposition originally preceded it immediately. It is also to be noted that the division between Sections I and II is the only one which was effected without a rewriting of the closing and opening passages; by contrast to what Ricardo said to Mill in his letter of 23 Nov. 1818 about a summary 'at the end of each section' (below, VII, 333).

[2] Below, p. 53, n. 1.

[3] Below, p. 66.

[4] Below, VIII, 315.

[5] *ib.* 206, 213.

[6] Ricardo to Trower, 14 Jan. 1821, *ib.* 333.

intelligible.'[1] A month later he could report substantial progress to Mill: 'I have done what I at present think necessary to my first chapter, and have laid it by for fresh inspection after I have forgotten it a little.'[2]

Early in January 1821 Murray included Ricardo's 'Third edition, corrected' in his advertised list of 'works preparing for immediate publication'.[3] In a letter of 14 January Ricardo wrote that he expected his third edition to be printed within a few days;[4] and again on 25 January he wrote that the first chapter was 'now printing' and referred to one of the later chapters of the book as being 'in the printers hands'.[5]

However, it was nearly four months from this time before the new edition was on sale; Murray's advertisement of actual publication appearing for the first time in the *Morning Chronicle* of 18 May 1821, the price being stated as 12s. The reason for the delay is disclosed by a letter of Malthus to Prévost of 26 April 1821: 'Mr. Murray my bookseller seems to be of opinion that the times are not favourable for book-selling and is now keeping back a new edition of Mr. Ricardo's work which is finished, because the former edition has not gone off so soon as he had calculated upon.'[6] This did not prevent Ricardo in the meantime from sending advance copies to his friends. On 25 April he wrote to McCulloch that he had asked Murray to send him a copy 'last week';[7] and on 8 May in sending a copy to Say he wrote: 'Owing to the delay of Bookseller, and Printer, the time has been protracted far beyond my expectation, but at length I am able to send you herewith one of the first published copies of this last edition.'[8]

The changes in this edition were considerably more extensive than those made in edition 2. Yet Ricardo seems to have regarded them, for the most part, as unimportant. We find him writing to Trower on 14 January 1821: 'I have carefully looked over every

[1] Below, VIII, 229.
[2] Letter of 14 Oct. 1820, *ib.* 283–4.
[3] *Monthly Literary Advertiser*, 10 Jan. 1821.
[4] Below, VIII, 333, and cp. 335.
[5] *ib.* 342.

[6] Letter to Professor Prévost of Geneva, published by G. W. Zinke in *Journal of Economic History*, May 1942, vol. II, p. 181.
[7] Below, VIII, 373.
[8] *ib.* 379.

part of it, and with my limited powers of composition I am convinced I can do very little to improve it';[1] and on 25 April to M°Culloch: 'You will not find much of novelty in the new edition'.[2]

The main changes in the first chapter have already been mentioned. As regards arrangement, the five sections of edition 2 were increased to seven by subdividing Section 1 and also adding a new section On an Invariable Measure of Value. The rearrangement of the text of this chapter, begun in edition 2, was continued more extensively; and although a few anomalies remained, the chapter gained greater unity. Passages previously misplaced were transferred to the appropriate sections, and repetitions were avoided either by omitting a passage or by incorporating different passages into one.

Many of the Notes on Malthus's *Principles* are reflected in the alterations made in the new edition. With reference to his old difference with Malthus as to the effect of agricultural improvements upon rent, Ricardo adds a footnote[3] in edition 3 allowing the *ultimate* benefit to landlords, without yielding his contention that the immediate effect of improvements was harmful to them. Malthus had asked in what sense Ricardo could agree with Sismondi and Buchanan in saying that the price of corn 'is like that of a common monopoly, or advantageous only to the landlords, and proportionably *injurious* to the consumers'.[4] Ricardo's reply was that the landlord's interest was 'that the machine which he had for producing corn should be in demand—that in fact his rent depended on it'. Only after cheap corn had increased population would 'the advantage of the improvement' be 'transferred to the landlord'.[5] A similar idea is expressed in two new paragraphs added to Chapter XXIV, in which he states that, when the productivity of the soil is increased, 'all the advantages would, in the first instance, be enjoyed by labourers, capitalists and consumers; but with the progress of population, they would be gradually transferred to the proprietors of the soil.'[6]

On the advantages of free importation of corn Ricardo was even

---

[1] *ib.* 333.
[2] *ib.* 373.
[3] Below, p. 81.
[4] Below, II, 117.
[5] *ib.* 118.

[6] Below, p. 335. However, the statement on the same page that 'the interest of the landlord is always opposed to that of consumer and manufacturer' remains in ed. 3.

more emphatic than he had been in previous editions. In the 'Advertisement to the Third Edition' (below, p. 8) he directs the attention of the reader to the changes which he has introduced into the last chapter, in order to throw into sharper relief the doctrine of the increased ability of a country to pay taxes as a result of a diminished cost of food.

Malthus in his *Principles* had also criticised Ricardo for having applied to rent his measure by '*proportions* or cost in labour',[1] and having suggested as a result that with the extension of cultivation the proportion of rent to the total produce of land would increase. Ricardo devoted one of his Notes[2] to a restatement of his position, and explained in effect that rent would take up an increased proportion of the produce of the *old* lands, or, if additional capitals be employed on the same lands, an increased proportion 'of each quantity before obtained'.[3] In a deleted passage in the *Notes on Malthus* he explains his meaning concisely as follows: 'Rent is not a proportion of the produce obtained—it is not governed like wages or profits by proportions—depending as it does on the difference between the quantity of produce obtained by two equal capitals. If therefore I have anywhere said that rent rises or falls in the proportion that the produce obtained is increased or diminished I have committed an error. I am not however conscious of having so done'.[4] Nevertheless, in edition 3 he modified a number of passages which had laid him open to Malthus's criticism. Typical of these is the change in the phrase of editions 1 and 2, 'In speaking of the rent of the landlord, we have rather considered it as the proportion of the whole produce', the concluding words of which are replaced in edition 3 by: 'as the proportion of the produce obtained with a given capital on any given farm'.[5]

[1] Below, II, 195.
[2] *ib.* 196–7.
[3] *ib.* 197 and 198, n. 2. In the *Essay on Profits* Ricardo, apparently referring to the net, rather than the gross, produce, had made the more sweeping statement: 'The landlord not only obtains a greater produce, but a larger share.' (Below, IV, 18.) This is an instance of a more general change that is noticeable between the *Essay on Profits* and ed. 3 of the *Principles*: namely, a gradual shift of emphasis from the antithesis of rent and profits to that of wages and profits.
[4] Below, II, 196–7, n. 1.
[5] Below, p. 83 and cp. p. 49, n. 1 and pp. 402–3.

The changes in ed. 3 due to Say were occasioned partly by changes in the 4th edition (1819) of Say's *Traité* and partly by Say's *Lettres à M. Malthus* (1820) on which Ricardo had written some notes at the same time as he was writing his *Notes on Malthus*.[1] The main change is the rewriting of several paragraphs in the chapter on Value and Riches[2] and the omission of some paragraphs in the same chapter which cite extensively from the earlier editions of Say's *Traité*,[3] in view of changes made by Say in his 4th edition.[4] There were also a few minor additions in other chapters.[5]

The most revolutionary change in edition 3 is the new chapter On Machinery, in which Ricardo retracts his previous opinion that the introduction of machinery is beneficial to all the different classes of society. 'My mistake', he explains, 'arose from the supposition, that whenever the net income of a society increased, its gross income would also increase; I now, however, see reason to be satisfied that the one fund, from which landlords and capitalists derive their revenue, may increase, while the other, that upon which the labouring class mainly depend, may diminish'.[6] His conclusion must have shocked his friends even more than the change of principle itself: 'That the opinion entertained by the labouring class, that the employment of machinery is frequently detrimental to their interests, is not founded on prejudice and error, but is conformable to the correct principles of political economy.'[7]

Previously Ricardo had held the view that, since machinery made it possible to produce commodities at a lower cost, it must lead to an increase in their quantity and accordingly be beneficial to all classes of society. He had not expressed this view in the earlier editions of the *Principles*, and the only place where he had stated in print an opinion as to the effect of machinery upon labour was an incidental reference in the *Essay on Profits* where he alluded to 'the effects of improved machinery, which it is now no longer questioned, has a decided tendency to raise the real wages of labour.'[8] But as he

---

[1] See below, VIII, 301.
[2] Below, pp. 279–285.
[3] Below, pp. 287–8.
[4] Below, VIII, 315

[5] Below, p. 249, p. 264 and p. 348.
[6] Below, p. 388.
[7] Below, p. 392.
[8] Below, IV, 35.

says at the beginning of the new chapter he had 'in other ways' given support to those doctrines. He probably had in mind a speech in Parliament in 1819 on Robert Owen's plan in which he had declared that 'it could not be denied, on the whole view of the subject, that machinery did not lessen the demand for labour'.[1] Barton's pamphlet of 1817, *Observations on the Condition of the Labouring Classes*, with its view as to the adverse effects of machinery on labour, does not seem to have influenced Ricardo at the time of its publication;[2] although he quotes it with approval in the new chapter in edition 3. When McCulloch, in an article on 'Taxation and the Corn Laws' in the *Edinburgh Review* of January 1820, had approved the ideas of Barton (of whose pamphlet the article was ostensibly a review), Ricardo wrote to McCulloch contesting this opinion. McCulloch had stated that 'the fixed capital invested in a machine, must always displace a considerably greater quantity of circulating capital,—for otherwise there could be no motive to its erection; and hence its first effect is to sink, rather than increase, the rate of wages.'[3] In reply Ricardo had said: 'the employment of machinery I think never diminishes the demand for labour—it is never a cause of a fall in the price of labour, but the effect of its rise.'[4] McCulloch became a convert to this view, and in an article in the *Edinburgh Review* of March 1821 maintained that 'no improvement of machinery can possibly diminish the demand for labour, or reduce the rate of wages.'[5] It is scarcely surprising that he should have taken strong exception to Ricardo's sudden change of front on the matter, and that on seeing the new edition he should have bitterly complained (in a letter now first published) of 'the extreme erroneousness of the principles to which you have incautiously lent the sanction of your name'.[6]

---

[1] 16 Dec. 1819, below, V, 30. That it was generally accepted that Ricardo held these views is shown by Malthus' statement in his *Principles of Political Economy*: 'I quite agree with Mr. Ricardo, however, in approving all saving of labour and inventions in machinery' (below, II, 381).
[2] Cp. Ricardo's letter to Barton of 20 May 1817, which however was prior to the publication of the pamphlet (below, VII, 157–9).
[3] *Edinburgh Review*, Jan. 1820, p. 171.
[4] Letter to McCulloch, 29 March 1820, below, VIII, 171.
[5] *Edinburgh Review*, March 1821, p. 115.
[6] McCulloch to Ricardo, 5 June 1821, below, VIII, 382. He also says that if Ricardo's new opinion is correct 'the laws against the Luddites are a disgrace to the Statute book' (*ib.* 385).

The writing of the *Notes on Malthus* in the autumn of 1820, especially Note 149, marked a transition-stage in Ricardo's thinking on the subject. Malthus in his chapter 'Of the Wages of Labour' had quoted Barton to the effect that 'the demand for labour can only be in proportion to the increase of the circulating, not the fixed capital'; but, while admitting that 'this is no doubt true in individual cases', Malthus had asserted that 'it is not necessary to make the distinction in reference to a whole nation' and that 'in general...the use of fixed capital is extremely favourable to the abundance of circulating capital'.[1] Ricardo commented on this as follows: 'The effective demand for labour must depend upon the increase of that part of capital, in which the wages of labour are paid...—to the capitalist it can be of no importance whether his capital consists of fixed or of circulating capital, but it is of the greatest importance to those who live by the wages of labour; they are greatly interested in increasing the gross revenue, as it is on the gross revenue that must depend the means of providing for the population. If capital is realized in machinery, there will be little demand for an increased quantity of labour'.[2] Another Note (153) seems to approach even closer to the new doctrine: 'It might be possible to do almost all the work performed by men with horses, would the substitution of horses in such case, even if attended with a greater produce, be advantageous to the working classes, would it not on the contrary very materially diminish the demand for labour?'[3]

The final step in his change of opinion came when (as he himself says in the new chapter) he ceased to hold that 'whenever the net income of a society increased, its gross income would also increase',[4] and came to hold instead that machinery could be profitable to introduce and yet result in a smaller total product, and demand for labour.

There is no evidence as to the precise stage at which Ricardo adopted his final view that improved machinery might actually diminish the gross produce. Mallet, in an entry in his diary at the

[1] Below, II, 234–6.
[2] *ib.* 234–6.
[3] *ib.* 239 and cp. footnote. Ricardo, however, in Note 243 states that 'unmixed advantages' are derived from inventions to save labour (*ib.* 365).
[4] Below, p. 388.

time of Ricardo's death in September 1823, stated: 'It accidentally
happened at a dinner at his [Ricardo's] house three years ago, at
which Mr. Grenfell, Mr. Tooke, and other persons were present,
that in consequence of an objection which then occurred to me as
to the prevailing opinions on the subject of the unmixed benefit
resulting from the substitution of machinery for human labour, Mr.
Ricardo was afterwards led (although he then differed from me) to
reconsider the subject and to write the additional chapter on machinery
in his 3rd edition. This he told me himself in the kindest and most
ingenuous manner.'[1] He apparently had not yet changed his views by
29 Nov. 1820;[2] and the first intimation we have is in a letter of Malthus
to Sismondi of 12 March 1821, which mentions that Ricardo has
altered his views on machinery.[3] McCulloch evidently knew nothing
until Ricardo's letter to him of 25 April 1821 with its reference to
'a change in my sentiments respecting the advantages of machinery'.[4]
Having made the change, however, Ricardo stoutly defended his
new position against McCulloch's objections. 'These truths', he
wrote, 'appear to me to be as demonstrable as any of the truths of
geometry, and I am only astonished that I should so long have failed
to see them.'[5]

VIII. *The Present Edition*

The present edition of the *Principles* is based on a complete collation
of the first, second and third editions. The text adopted is that of
edition 3, published in 1821, the last to be revised by Ricardo. All
the variants of editions 1 and 2 are given in the editor's footnotes.

A special method, however, has had to be adopted in the case of
Chapter I, On Value, in some parts of which the changes are so
extensive and so complicated as to make it impossible to convey to
the reader an adequate idea of them by means of footnotes alone.
Accordingly, at the end of that chapter the text of edition 1 for the
last two-thirds of the chapter is printed in smaller type as an Appendix

---

[1] In *Political Economy Club, Centenary Volume*, 1921, pp. 211–12. The occasion referred to may have been the dinner party of 12 Jan. 1820, on which see below, VIII, 152–3, n.

[2] See letter to Malthus of that date, *ib.* 311.
[3] *ib.* 377.
[4] *ib.* 373.
[5] Letter of 18 June 1821, *ib.* 390.

(below, pp. 52–66). The footnotes to the corresponding text of edition 3 (pp. 26–51) indicate all the differences from editions 1 and 2; but while in the case of shorter passages these are quoted in full in the footnotes, for the longer ones reference is merely given to the text in the Appendix. On the other hand, the footnotes to the text of edition 1 in the Appendix give only the changes in edition 2.

In addition, to give a clearer picture of the rearrangement of the matter, a Table of Concordance, exhibiting the relative position of corresponding paragraphs in editions 1 and 3 for this part of the chapter, has been inserted at the end of this Introduction on a folding sheet. The correspondence between the passages shown in this Table is sometimes no more than approximate, and for the precise relation between them the reader should refer to the foot-notes. On the same folding sheet a similar Table has been given for the location in edition 3 of such passages as were newly added in edition 2.

Thus by the combined use of the Tables of Concordance and of the footnotes the reader should be enabled either to read edition 3, tracing back the text to the earlier versions of editions 1 and 2, or alternatively to read edition 1, following out the modifications of the text in the subsequent editions.

A comparative Table of Section-Headings of the chapter On Value in editions 2 and 3 is given at the end of this Introduction.

Ricardo's original Index is reprinted, with the variants of the editions noted, as described on page 430 below.

To facilitate the identification in the present edition of page-references made in terms of the editions of Ricardo's *Principles* most frequently quoted by earlier writers, a Table of Corresponding Pages has been supplied at the end of this volume.

Both in this and in the subsequent volumes of the present edition the author's footnotes are indicated by asterisks and printed right across the page, whereas the editor's footnotes are distinguished by numerals and (when the amount of material allows) by being printed in double column.

The editor's footnotes attempt to indicate Ricardo's sources in particular passages and to complete his references to authorities. The references to Adam Smith have been supplemented with the corresponding pages of Cannan's edition of the *Wealth of Nations* (2 vols., London, Methuen, 1904).

The spelling and punctuation of the original have been retained. Misprints if obvious have been corrected, but those which give a conceivable alternative reading have been left unchanged; in both cases attention has generally been drawn to them in a footnote.

TABLE OF SECTION-HEADINGS
OF CHAPTER I, ON VALUE
IN EDITIONS 2 AND 3

TABLE OF CONCORDANCE

between Editions 1 and 3, by paragraphs, for the latter part of Chapter I, On Value

EDITION 1	page		page	EDITION 3
Economy in the use	52		26	Economy in the use
In every society	52		26	Suppose that in the early
According as capital	52		27	If with the same
Two trades	53		27	If there were any
Again two manufacturers	53		28	Suppose money
Besides the alteration	53		28	No alteration
Suppose that in the early	53		29	Now suppose, that with the same
If with the same	54		29	If we had then
If there were any	54			SECTION IV
Suppose money	54		30	In the former section
No alteration	54		31	The food and clothing
The prices of the commodities	55		31	According as capital
If the gold mine	55		31	It is also to be observed
Now suppose, that with the same	55		32	Two trades
If we had then	56		32	In one trade
If the fixed	56		32	Again two manufacturers
First, when the fixed	56		32	If men employed
Now if wages	57		32	If they employed
Thus we see	58		32	But although commodities
Secondly, suppose	58		33	Suppose two men
Suppose that an engine	59		34	Suppose that for the labour
If the same amount	59		34	But how will
But, as no wages	59		35	There can be no rise
In proportion	60		36	The reader, however
These results	61		36	Not so with the other
A manufacturer of hats	61		37	It is hardly necessary
It appears then, that in proportion	62		37	Suppose I employ
The above statement	63		37	This case appears
Money, from its being	63		37	It appears then that the division
A rise in wages	64			SECTION V
It is according	64		38	In the last section
It is not by the absolute	64		39	If fixed capital be not
The variation	65		39	But a rise in the wages
If, with capital	65		40	I have already said
If at the same time	65		41	The manufacturer, however
It appears then that the accumulation	66		42	It will be seen, then
Commodities	66		43	It appears, too, that in proportion
It appears, too, that commodities	66			SECTION VI
			43	When commodities
			44	If, for example
			44	If we suppose
			46	If, then, I may
			46	To facilitate
			46	Before I quit this subject
			46	It is necessary
				SECTION VII
			47	Although I shall
			48	Money, being a variable
			48	Money, from its being
			48	A rise in wages
			49	It is according
			49	It is not by the absolute
			50	The variation
			51	If, with a capital
			51	If, at the same time

[For a comparable statement in ed. 1 see p. 17, n. 3.]

TABLE OF CONCORDANCE

between Editions 2 and 3 for the paragraphs added in Edition 2
in the latter part of Chapter I, On Value

EDITION 2		EDITION 3	
page		page	
52 n. 1	A division	31 n.	A division
53 n. 1	It is also to be observed	31	It is also to be observed
56 n. 1	It appears then by this section		
58 n. 1	It appears then that the division	37	It appears then that the division
58 n. 2	In the last section	38	In the last section
60 n. 1	To put the principle		
61 n.	The same result	37	It is hardly necessary
		37	Suppose I employ
		37	This case appears
62 n. 1	It will be seen, then	42	It will be seen, then
65 n. 3	If with a capital	51	If, with a capital

ON

THE PRINCIPLES

OF

POLITICAL ECONOMY,

AND

TAXATION.

By DAVID RICARDO, Esq.

LONDON:

JOHN MURRAY, ALBEMARLE-STREET.

—

1817.

ON

THE PRINCIPLES

OF

POLITICAL ECONOMY,

AND

TAXATION.

BY DAVID RICARDO, ESQ.

SECOND EDITION.

LONDON:

JOHN MURRAY, ALBEMARLE-STREET.

1819.

ON

THE PRINCIPLES

OF

POLITICAL ECONOMY,

AND

TAXATION.

BY DAVID RICARDO, ESQ.

THIRD EDITION.

LONDON:

JOHN MURRAY, ALBEMARLE-STREET.

1821.

PREFACE

THE produce of the earth—all that is derived from its surface by the united application of labour, machinery, and capital, is divided among three classes of the community; namely, the proprietor of the land, the owner of the stock or capital necessary for its cultivation, and the labourers by whose industry it is cultivated.

But in different stages of society, the proportions of the whole produce of the earth which will be allotted to each of these classes, under the names of rent, profit, and wages, will be essentially different; depending mainly on the actual fertility of the soil, on the accumulation of capital and population, and on the skill, ingenuity, and instruments employed in agriculture.

To determine the laws which regulate this distribution, is the principal problem in Political Economy: much as the science has been improved by the writings of Turgot, Stuart, Smith, Say, Sismondi, and others, they afford very little satisfactory information respecting the natural course of rent, profit, and wages.

In 1815, Mr. Malthus, in his "Inquiry into the Nature and Progress of Rent," and a Fellow of University College, Oxford,[1] in his "Essay on the Application of Capital to Land," presented to the world, nearly at the same moment, the true doctrine of rent; without a knowledge of which, it is impossible to understand the effect of the progress of wealth on profits and wages, or to trace satisfactorily the influence of taxation on different classes of the community; particularly when the commodities taxed are the productions immediately derived from the surface

[1] Edward West.

of the earth. Adam Smith, and the other able writers to whom I have alluded, not having viewed correctly the principles of rent, have, it appears to me, overlooked many important truths, which can only be discovered after the subject of rent is thoroughly understood.

To supply this deficiency, abilities are required of a far superior cast to any possessed by the writer of the following pages; yet, after having given to this subject his best consideration—after the aid which he has derived from the works of the above-mentioned eminent writers—and after the valuable experience which a few late years, abounding in facts, have yielded to the present generation—it will not, he trusts, be deemed presumptuous in him to state his opinions on the laws of profits and wages, and on the operation of taxes. If the principles which he deems correct, should be found to be so, it will be for others, more able than himself, to trace them to all their important consequences.

The writer, in combating received opinions, has found it necessary to advert more particularly to those passages in the writings of Adam Smith from which he sees reason to differ; but he hopes it will not, on that account, be suspected that he does not, in common with all those who acknowledge the importance of the science of Political Economy, participate in the admiration which the profound work of this celebrated author so justly excites.

The same remark may be applied to the excellent works of M. Say, who not only was the first, or among the first, of continental writers, who justly appreciated and applied the principles of Smith, and who has done more than all other continental writers taken together, to recommend the principles of that enlightened and beneficial system to the nations of Europe; but who has succeeded in placing the science in a more logical, and more instructive order; and has enriched it

by several discussions, original, accurate, and profound.* The
respect, however, which the author entertains for the writings
of this gentleman, has not prevented him from commenting
with that freedom which he thinks the interests of science
require, on such passages of the "Economie Politique," as
appeared at variance with his own ideas.

* Chap. xv. part i. "Des Débouchés," contains, in particular, some
very important principles, which I believe were first explained by this
distinguished writer.[1]

[1] The reference is to the 2nd ed., 1814, of J. B. Say's *Traité d'Économie politique*; the chapter 'Des débouchés' was already in the 1st ed., 1803 (Bk. i, ch. XXII).

ADVERTISEMENT

TO THE

THIRD EDITION

IN this Edition I have endeavoured to explain more fully than in the last, my opinion on the difficult subject of VALUE, and for that purpose have made a few additions to the first chapter. I have also inserted a new chapter on the subject of MACHINERY, and on the effects of its improvement on the interests of the different classes of the State. In the chapter on the DISTINC-TIVE PROPERTIES OF VALUE AND RICHES, I have examined the doctrines of M. Say on that important question, as amended in the fourth and last edition of his work. I have in the last chapter endeavoured to place in a stronger point of view than before, the doctrine of the ability of a country to pay additional money taxes, although the aggregate money value of the mass of its commodities should fall, in consequence either of the diminished quantity of labour required to produce its corn at home, by improvements in its husbandry, or from its obtaining a part of its corn at a cheaper price from abroad, by means of the exportation of its manufactured commodities. This con-sideration is of great importance, as it regards the question of the policy of leaving unrestricted the importation of foreign corn, particularly in a country burthened with a heavy fixed money taxation, the consequence of an immense National Debt. I have endeavoured to shew, that the ability to pay taxes, depends, not on the gross money value of the mass of com-modities, nor on the net money value of the revenues of capitalists and landlords, but on the money value of each man's revenue, compared to the money value of the commodities which he usually consumes.

March 26, 1821.

CONTENTS

[In ed. 1, owing to the duplication in two cases of the chapter numbers, the numbering from Ch. V onwards was as follows: V, On Wages; V*, On Profits; VI, On Foreign Trade; VII, On Taxes; VIII, Taxes on Raw Produce; VIII*, Taxes on Rent; IX, Tithes, and so on. The chapter on Machinery (XXXI) was added in ed. 3; therefore the last chapter (Mr. Malthus's Opinions on Rent) was XXIX in ed. 1, and XXXI in ed. 2.]

CHAPTER I

ON VALUE

SECTION I

The value of a commodity, or the quantity of any other commodity for which it will exchange, depends on the relative quantity of labour which is necessary for its production, and not on the greater or less compensation which is paid for that labour.[1]

IT has been observed by Adam Smith, that "the word Value has two different meanings, and sometimes expresses the utility of some particular object, and sometimes the power of purchasing other goods which the possession of that object conveys. The one may be called *value in use*; the other *value in exchange*. The things," he continues, "which have the greatest value in use, have frequently little or no value in exchange; and, on the contrary, those which have the greatest value in exchange, have little or no value in use."[2] Water and air are abundantly useful; they are indeed indispensable to existence, yet, under ordinary circumstances, nothing can be obtained in exchange for them. Gold, on the contrary, though of little use compared with air or water, will exchange for a great quantity of other goods.

Utility then is not the measure of exchangeable value, although it is absolutely essential to it. If a commodity were in no way useful,—in other words, if it could in no way contribute to our gratification,—it would be destitute of exchangeable value, however scarce it might be, or whatever quantity of labour might be necessary to procure it.

[1] Ed. 1 does not divide this chapter into sections; ed. 2 divides it into five sections and ed. 3 into seven. Section 1 bears the same heading in ed. 2 and in ed. 3.

[2] *Wealth of Nations*, Bk. 1, ch. iv; Cannan's ed., vol. 1, p. 30. The passage continues by contrasting water with diamonds.

Possessing utility, commodities derive their exchangeable value from two sources: from their scarcity, and from the quantity of labour required to obtain them.

There are some commodities, the value of which is determined by their scarcity alone. No labour can increase the quantity of such goods, and therefore their value cannot be lowered by an increased supply. Some rare statues and pictures, scarce books and coins, wines of a peculiar quality, which can be made only from grapes grown on a particular soil, of which there is a very limited quantity, are all of this description. Their value is wholly independent of the quantity of labour originally necessary to produce them, and varies with the varying wealth and inclinations of those who are desirous to possess them.

These commodities, however, form a very small part of the mass of commodities daily exchanged in the market. By far the greatest part of those goods which are the objects of desire, are procured by labour; and they may be multiplied, not in one country alone, but in many, almost without any assignable limit, if we are disposed to bestow the labour necessary to obtain them.

In speaking then of commodities, of their exchangeable value, and of the laws which regulate their relative prices, we mean always such commodities only as can be increased in quantity by the exertion of human industry, and on the production of which competition operates without restraint.

In the early stages of society, the exchangeable value of these commodities, or the rule which determines how much of one shall be given in exchange for another, depends almost exclusively[1] on the comparative quantity of labour expended on each.

"The real price of every thing," says Adam Smith, "what every thing really costs to the man who wants to acquire it,

---

[1] Eds. 1-2 read 'depends solely'.

is the toil and trouble of acquiring it. What every thing is really worth to the man who has acquired it, and who wants to dispose of it, or exchange it for something else, is the toil and trouble which it can save to himself, and which it can impose upon other people." "Labour was the first price—the original purchase-money that was paid for all things." Again, "in that early and rude state of society, which precedes both the accumulation of stock and the appropriation of land, the proportion between the quantities of labour necessary for acquiring different objects seems to be the only circumstance which can afford any rule for exchanging them for one another. If among a nation of hunters, for example, it usually cost twice the labour to kill a beaver which it does to kill a deer, one beaver should naturally exchange for, or be worth two deer. It is natural that what is usually the produce of two days', or two hours' labour, should be worth double of what is usually the produce of one day's, or one hour's labour." *

That this is really the foundation of the exchangeable value of all things, excepting those which cannot be increased by human industry, is a doctrine of the utmost importance in political economy; for from no source do so many errors, and so much difference of opinion in that science proceed, as from the vague ideas which are attached to the word value.

If the quantity of labour realized in commodities, regulate their exchangeable value, every increase of the quantity of labour must augment the value of that commodity on which it is exercised, as every diminution must lower it.

Adam Smith, who so accurately defined the original source of exchangeable value, and who was bound in consistency to maintain, that all things became more or less valuable in proportion as more or less labour was bestowed on their produc-

* Book i. chap. 5.[1]

[1] Ch. v and vi; Cannan's ed. vol. 1, pp. 32 and 49.

tion, has himself erected another standard measure of value, and speaks of things being more or less valuable, in proportion as they will exchange for more or less of this standard measure. Sometimes he speaks of corn, at other times of labour, as a standard measure; not the quantity of labour bestowed on the production of any object, but the quantity which it can command in the market: as if these were two equivalent expressions, and as if because a man's labour had become doubly efficient, and he could therefore produce twice the quantity of a commodity, he would necessarily receive twice the former quantity in exchange for it.

If this indeed were true, if the reward of the labourer were always in proportion to what he produced, the quantity of labour bestowed on a commodity, and the quantity of labour which that commodity would purchase, would be equal, and either might accurately measure the variations of other things: but they are not equal; the first is under many circumstances an invariable standard, indicating correctly the variations of other things; the latter is subject to as many fluctuations as the commodities compared with it. Adam Smith, after most ably showing the insufficiency of a variable medium, such as gold and silver, for the purpose of determining the varying value of other things, has himself, by fixing on corn or labour, chosen a medium no less variable.

Gold and silver are no doubt subject to fluctuations, from the discovery of new and more abundant mines; but such discoveries are rare, and their effects, though powerful, are limited to periods of comparatively short duration. They are subject also to fluctuation, from improvements in the skill and machinery with which the mines may be worked; as in consequence of such improvements, a greater quantity may be obtained with the same labour. They are further subject to fluctuation from the decreasing produce of the mines, after they have yielded a supply to the world, for a succession of ages. But from which of these sources of fluctuation is corn exempted? Does not that also vary, on one hand, from improvements in agriculture, from improved machinery and implements used in husbandry, as well as from the discovery of new tracts of fertile land, which in other countries may be taken into cultivation, and which will affect the value of corn in every market where importation is free? Is it not on the other hand subject to be enhanced in value from prohibitions of importation, from increasing population and wealth, and the greater difficulty of obtaining the increased supplies, on account of the additional quantity of labour which the cultivation of inferior lands requires? Is not the value of labour equally variable; being not only affected, as all other things are, by the proportion between the supply and demand, which uniformly varies with every change in the condition of the community, but also by the varying price of food and other necessaries, on which the wages of labour are expended?

In the same country double the quantity of labour may be required to produce a given quantity of food and necessaries at one time, that may be necessary at another, and a distant time; yet the labourer's reward may possibly be very little diminished. If the labourer's wages at the former period, were a certain quantity of food and necessaries, he probably could not have subsisted if that quantity had been reduced. Food and necessaries in this case will have risen 100 per cent. if estimated by the *quantity* of labour necessary to their production, while they will scarcely have increased in value, if measured by the quantity of labour for which they will *exchange*.

The same remark may be made respecting two or more countries. In America and Poland, on the land last taken into cultivation, a year's labour of any given number of men, will produce much more corn than on land similarly circumstanced in England.[1] Now, supposing all other necessaries to be equally cheap in those three countries, would it not be a great mistake to conclude, that the quantity of corn awarded to the labourer, would in each country be in proportion to the facility of production?

If the shoes and clothing of the labourer, could, by improvements in machinery, be produced by one fourth of the labour now necessary to their production, they would probably fall 75 per cent.; but so far is it from being true, that the labourer would thereby be enabled permanently to consume four coats, or four pair of shoes, instead of one, that it is probable[2] his wages would in no long time be adjusted by the effects of competition, and the stimulus to population, to the new value of the necessaries on which they were expended. If these improvements extended to all the objects of the labourer's consumption, we should find him probably at the end of a very few years, in possession of only a small, if any, addition to his enjoyments, although the exchangeable value of those commodities, compared with any other commodity, in the manufacture of which no such improvement were made, had sustained a very considerable reduction; and though they were the produce of a very considerably diminished quantity of labour.

It cannot then be correct, to say with Adam Smith, "that as labour may sometimes *purchase* a greater, and sometimes a smaller quantity of goods, it is their value which varies, not that of the labour which purchases them;" and therefore, "that labour *alone never varying in its own value*, is alone the ultimate and real standard by which the value of all commodities can

---

[1] In ed. 1 this sentence reads 'In America and Poland, a year's labour will produce much more corn than in England.'

[2] Eds. 1-2 do not contain 'it is probable'.

at all times and places be estimated and compared;"[1]—but it is correct to say, as Adam Smith had previously said, "that the proportion between the quantities of labour necessary for acquiring different objects seems to be the only circumstance which can afford any rule for exchanging them for one another;"[2] or in other words, that it is the comparative quantity of commodities which labour will produce, that determines their present or past relative value, and not the comparative quantities of commodities, which are given to the labourer in exchange for his labour.[3]

Two commodities vary in relative value, and we wish to know in which the variation has really taken place. If we compare the present value of one, with shoes, stockings, hats, iron, sugar, and all other commodities, we find that it will exchange for precisely the same quantity of all these things as before. If we compare the other with the same commodities, we find it has varied with respect to them all: we may then with great

---

[1] Bk. I, ch. v; vol. I, p. 35. The quotations contain some minor inaccuracies and the italics, as in most other cases, are Ricardo's.

[2] Bk. I, ch. vi; vol. I, p. 49. Quoted more fully above, p. 13.

[3] In place of the four paragraphs that follow in the text, and which conclude the section, eds. 1-2 read: 'If any one commodity could be found, which now and at all times required precisely the same quantity of labour to produce it, that commodity would be of an unvarying value, and would be eminently useful as a standard by which the variations of other things might be measured. Of such a commodity we have no knowledge, and consequently are unable to fix on any standard of value. It is,

however, of considerable use towards attaining a correct theory, to ascertain what the essential qualities of a standard are, that we may know the causes of the variation in the relative value of commodities, and that we may be enabled to calculate the degree in which they are likely to operate.' See however a similar passage retained in ed. 3, below, p. 275; and cp. Section VI, p. 43 ff., which is inserted in ed. 3.

In eds. 1-2 the paragraph given in this footnote is followed directly by the paragraph which in ed. 3 opens Section II (p. 20); in ed. 1 the two paragraphs are separated by a printer's rule (the only trace of subdivision of this chapter in ed. 1); in ed. 2 the rule is dropped.

probability infer that the variation has been in this commodity, and not in the commodities with which we have compared it. If on examining still more particularly into all the circumstances connected with the production of these various commodities, we find that precisely the same quantity of labour and capital are necessary to the production of the shoes, stockings, hats, iron, sugar, &c.; but that the same quantity as before is not necessary to produce the single commodity whose relative value is altered, probability is changed into certainty, and we are sure that the variation is in the single commodity: we then discover also the cause of its variation.

If I found that an ounce of gold would exchange for a less quantity of all the commodities above enumerated, and many others; and if, moreover, I found that by the discovery of a new and more fertile mine, or by the employment of machinery to great advantage, a given quantity of gold could be obtained with a less quantity of labour, I should be justified in saying that the cause of the alteration in the value of gold relatively to other commodities, was the greater facility of its production, or the smaller quantity of labour necessary to obtain it. In like manner, if labour fell very considerably in value, relatively to all other things, and if I found that its fall was in consequence of an abundant supply, encouraged by the great facility with which corn, and the other necessaries of the labourer, were produced, it would, I apprehend, be correct for me to say that corn and necessaries had fallen in value in consequence of less quantity of labour being necessary to produce them, and that this facility of providing for the support of the labourer had been followed by a fall in the value of labour. No, say Adam Smith and Mr. Malthus,[1] in the case of the gold you were correct in calling its variation a fall of its value, because corn and labour had not

[1] Malthus's *Principles of Political Economy*, ch. ii, sect. VII; below, II, 95 ff.

then varied; and as gold would command a less quantity of
them, as well as of all other things, than before, it was correct
to say that all things had remained stationary, and that gold
only had varied; but when corn and labour fall, things which
we have selected to be our standard measure of value, notwithstanding all the variations to which we acknowledge they
are subject, it would be highly improper to say so; the correct
language will be to say, that corn and labour have remained
stationary, and all other things have risen in value.

Now it is against this language that I protest. I find that
precisely, as in the case of the gold, the cause of the variation
between corn and other things, is the smaller quantity of labour
necessary to produce it, and therefore, by all just reasoning,
I am bound to call the variation of corn and labour a fall in
their value, and not a rise in the value of the things with which
they are compared. If I have to hire a labourer for a week,
and instead of ten shillings I pay him eight, no variation having
taken place in the value of money, the labourer can probably
obtain more food and necessaries, with his eight shillings, than
he before obtained for ten: but this is owing, not to a rise in
the real value of his wages, as stated by Adam Smith, and more
recently by Mr. Malthus, but to a fall in the value of the things
on which his wages are expended, things perfectly distinct; and
yet for calling this a fall in the real value of wages, I am told
that I adopt new and unusual language, not reconcileable with
the true principles of the science.[1] To me it appears that the
unusual and, indeed, inconsistent language, is that used by my
opponents.

Suppose a labourer to be paid a bushel of corn for a week's
work, when the price of corn is 80s. per quarter, and that he
is paid a bushel and a quarter when the price falls to 40s.
Suppose, too, that he consumes half a bushel of corn a-week

---

[1] Malthus, *op. cit.*, below, II, 190–4.

in his own family, and exchanges the remainder for other things, such as fuel, soap, candles, tea, sugar, salt, &c. &c.; if the three-fourths of a bushel which will remain to him, in one case, cannot procure him as much of the above commodities as half a bushel did in the other, which it will not, will labour have risen or fallen in value? Risen, Adam Smith must say, because his standard is corn, and the labourer receives more corn for a week's labour. Fallen, must the same Adam Smith say, "because the value of a thing depends on the power of purchasing other goods which the possession of that object conveys,"[1] and labour has a less power of purchasing such other goods.

SECTION II

Labour of different qualities differently rewarded. This no cause of variation in the relative value of commodities.[2]

In speaking, however, of labour, as being the foundation of all value, and the relative quantity of labour as almost exclusively[3] determining the relative value of commodities, I must not be supposed to be inattentive to the different qualities of labour, and the difficulty of comparing an hour's or a day's labour, in one employment, with the same duration of labour in another. The estimation[4] in which different qualities of labour are held, comes soon to be adjusted in the market with sufficient precision for all practical purposes, and depends much on the comparative skill of the labourer, and intensity of the labour performed. The scale, when once formed, is liable to little variation. If a day's labour of a working jeweller be more valuable than a day's labour of a common labourer, it has long

---

[1] In substance, Bk. 1, ch. v; vol. 1, p. 33.
[2] Ed. 2 does not contain this heading and continues Section 1 to p. 22.

[3] Eds. 1-2 do not contain 'almost exclusively'.
[4] An echo, as Cannan points out (*Review of Ec. Th.*, p. 175), of Adam Smith's 'esteem' (vol. 1, p. 49).

ago been adjusted, and placed in its proper position in the scale of value.*

In comparing therefore the value of the same commodity, at different periods of time, the consideration of the comparative skill and intensity of labour, required for that particular commodity, needs scarcely to be attended to, as it operates equally at both periods. One description of labour at one time is compared with the same description of labour at another; if a tenth, a fifth, or a fourth, has been added or taken away, an effect proportioned to the cause will be produced on the relative value of the commodity.

If a piece of cloth be now of the value of two pieces of linen, and if, in ten years hence, the ordinary value of a piece of cloth should be four pieces of linen, we may safely conclude, that either more labour is required to make the cloth, or less to make the linen, or that both causes have operated.

As the inquiry to which I wish to draw the reader's attention, relates to the effect of the variations in the relative value of commodities, and not in their absolute value,[1] it will be of little

* "But though labour be the real measure of the exchangeable value of all commodities, it is not that by which their value is commonly estimated. It is often difficult to ascertain the proportion between two different quantities of labour. The time spent in two different sorts of work will not always alone determine this proportion. The different degrees of hardship endured, and of ingenuity exercised, must likewise be taken into account. There may be more labour in an hour's hard work, than in two hours easy business; or, in an hour's application to a trade which it costs ten years' labour to learn, than in a month's industry at an ordinary and obvious employment. But it is not easy to find any accurate measure, either of hardship or ingenuity. In exchanging, indeed, the different productions of different sorts of labour for one another, some allowance is commonly made for both. It is adjusted, however, not by any accurate measure, but by the higgling and bargaining of the market, according to that sort of rough equality, which though not exact, is sufficient for carrying on the business of common life."—*Wealth of Nations*, book i. chap. 10.[2]

[1] Cp. a similar distinction in a letter of 9 Oct. 1820, below, VIII, 279.
[2] This passage actually occurs in Bk. 1, ch. v; vol. 1, p. 33. But Bk. 1, ch. x, pt. i, contains a long discussion of the same subject.

importance to examine into the comparative degree of estimation in which the different kinds of human labour are held. We
may fairly conclude, that whatever inequality there might
originally have been in them, whatever the ingenuity, skill, or
time necessary for the acquirement of one species of manual
dexterity more than another, it continues nearly the same from
one generation to another; or at least, that the variation is very
inconsiderable from year to year, and therefore, can have little
effect, for short periods, on the relative value of commodities.

"The proportion between the different rates both of wages
and profit in the different employments of labour and stock,
seems not to be much affected, as has already been observed,
by the riches or poverty, the advancing, stationary, or declining
state of the society. Such revolutions in the public welfare,
though they affect the general rates both of wages and profit,
must in the end affect them equally in all different employments. The proportion between them therefore must remain
the same, and cannot well be altered, at least for any considerable time, by any such revolutions."*

* Wealth of Nations, book i. chap. 10.[1]

SECTION III

*Not only the labour applied immediately to commodities affect
their value, but the labour also which is bestowed on the implements, tools, and buildings, with which such labour is assisted.*[2]

EVEN[3] in that early state to which Adam Smith refers, some
capital, though possibly made and accumulated by the hunter

[1] Cannan's ed., vol. I, p. 144.
[2] In ed. 2 'SECTION II. *The accumulation of capital makes no
difference in the principle stated in
the last section.*'
[3] Eds. 1-2 prefix to this paragraph
an additional passage, which reads:

'It will be seen by the extract
which I have made in page [13],
from the "Wealth of Nations," that
though Adam Smith fully recog-
nized the principle, that the proportion between the quantities of
labour necessary for acquiring

himself, would be necessary to enable him to kill his game. Without some weapon, neither the beaver nor the deer could be destroyed, and therefore the value of these animals would be regulated, not solely by the time and labour necessary to their destruction, but also by the time and labour necessary for providing the hunter's capital, the weapon, by the aid of which their destruction was effected.

Suppose the weapon necessary to kill the beaver, was[1] constructed with much more labour than that necessary to kill the deer, on account of the greater difficulty of approaching near to the former animal, and the consequent necessity of its being more true to its mark; one beaver would naturally be of more value than two deer, and precisely for this reason, that more labour would, on the whole, be necessary to its destruction. Or suppose that the same quantity of labour was necessary to make both weapons, but that they were of very unequal durability; of the durable implement only a small portion of its value would be transferred to the commodity, a much greater portion of the value of the less durable implement would be realized in the commodity which it contributed to produce.[2]

---

different objects, is the only circumstance which can afford any rule for our exchanging them for one another, yet he limits its application to "that early and rude state of society, which precedes both the accumulation of stock and the appropriation of land;" as if, when profits and rent were to be paid, they would have some influence on the relative value of commodities, independent of the mere quantity of labour that was necessary to their production.

'Adam Smith, however, has no where analyzed the effects of the accumulation of capital, and the appropriation of land, on relative value. It is of importance, therefore, to determine how far the effects which are avowedly produced on the exchangeable value of commodities, by the comparative quantity of labour bestowed on their production, are modified or altered by the accumulation of capital and the payment of rent.

'First, as to the accumulation of capital. Even' etc.

This 'First' is to be related to the phrase 'It remains however to be considered' which opens the chapter on Rent, p. 67; cp. also p. 77–8.

[1] Eds. 1-2 'were'.

[2] Eds. 1-2 do not contain this sentence, beginning 'Or suppose'.

All the implements necessary to kill the beaver and deer might belong to one class of men, and the labour employed in their destruction might be furnished by another class; still, their comparative prices would be in proportion to the actual labour bestowed, both on the formation of the capital, and on the destruction of the animals. Under different circumstances of plenty or scarcity of capital, as compared with labour, under different circumstances of plenty or scarcity of the food and necessaries essential to the support of men, those who furnished an equal value of capital for either one employment or for the other, might have a half, a fourth, or an eighth of the produce obtained, the remainder being paid as wages to those who furnished the labour; yet this division could not affect the relative value of these commodities, since whether the profits of capital were greater or less, whether they were 50, 20, or 10 per cent. or whether the wages of labour were high or low, they would operate equally on both employments.

If we suppose the occupations of the society extended, that some provide canoes and tackle necessary for fishing, others the seed and rude machinery first used in agriculture, still the same principle would hold true, that the exchangeable value of the commodities produced would be in proportion to the labour bestowed on their production; not on their immediate production only, but on all those implements or machines required to give effect to the particular labour to which they were applied.

If we look to a state of society in which greater improvements have been made, and in which arts and commerce flourish, we shall still find that commodities vary in value conformably with this principle: in estimating the exchangeable value of stockings, for example, we shall find that their value, comparatively with other things, depends on the total quantity of labour necessary to manufacture them, and bring them to market. First, there is the labour necessary to cultivate the land on which the raw cotton is grown; secondly, the labour of conveying the cotton to the country where the stockings are to be manufactured, which includes a portion of the labour bestowed in building the ship in which it is conveyed, and which is charged in the freight of the goods; thirdly, the labour of the spinner and weaver; fourthly, a portion of the labour of the engineer, smith, and carpenter, who erected the buildings and machinery, by the help of which they are made; fifthly, the labour of the retail dealer, and of many others, whom it is unnecessary further to particularize. The aggregate sum of these various kinds of labour, determines the quantity of other things for which these stockings will exchange, while the same consideration of the various quantities of labour which have been bestowed on those other things, will equally govern the portion of them which will be given for the stockings.

To convince ourselves that this is the real foundation of exchangeable value, let us suppose any improvement to be made in the means of abridging labour in any one of the various processes through which the raw cotton must pass, before the manufactured stockings come to the market, to be exchanged for other things; and observe the effects which will follow. If fewer men were required to cultivate the raw cotton, or if fewer sailors were employed in navigating, or shipwrights in constructing the ship, in which it was conveyed to us; if fewer hands were employed in raising the buildings and machinery, or if these, when raised, were rendered more efficient, the stockings would inevitably fall in value, and consequently command less of other things. They would fall, because a less quantity of labour was necessary to their production, and would therefore exchange for a smaller quantity of those things in which no such abridgment of labour had been made.

Economy[1] in the use of labour never fails to reduce the relative value of a commodity, whether the saving be in the labour necessary to the manufacture of the commodity itself, or in that necessary to the formation of the capital, by the aid of which it is produced. In either case the price of stockings would fall, whether there were fewer men employed as bleachers, spinners, and weavers, persons immediately necessary to their manufacture; or as sailors, carriers, engineers, and smiths, persons more indirectly concerned. In the one case, the whole saving of labour would fall on the stockings, because that portion of labour was wholly confined to the stockings; in the other, a portion only would fall on the stockings, the remainder being applied to all those other commodities, to the production of which the buildings, machinery, and carriage, were subservient.[2]

Suppose that in the early stages of society, the bows and arrows of the hunter were of equal value, and of equal durability, with the canoe and implements of the fisherman, both being the produce of the same quantity of labour. Under such circumstances the value of the deer, the produce of the hunter's day's labour, would be exactly equal to the value of the fish, the produce of the fisherman's day's labour. The comparative value of the fish and the game, would be entirely regulated by the quantity of labour realized in each; whatever might be the quantity of production, or however high or low general wages or profits might be. If for example the canoes and implements of the fisherman were of the value of 100*l.* and were calculated to last for ten years, and he employed ten men, whose annual labour cost 100*l.* and who in one day obtained

---

[1] The text of ed. 1, with the variants of ed. 2, for the remainder of this chapter is given below, pp. 52–66.
[2] Ed. 1 contains here in addition five paragraphs of which in ed. 3 four occur later in the chapter and the fifth is omitted. Ed. 2 also contains here five paragraphs, all of which occur later in ed. 3, though arranged in a different order. See p. 30, n. 2, and cp. pp. 52–3.

by their labour twenty salmon: If the weapons employed by the hunter were also of 100*l.* value and calculated to last ten years, and if he also employed ten men, whose annual labour cost 100*l.* and who in one day procured him ten deer; then the natural price of a deer would be two salmon, whether the proportion of the whole produce bestowed on the men who obtained it, were large or small. The proportion which might be paid for wages, is of the utmost importance in the question of profits; for it must at once be seen, that profits would be high or low, exactly in proportion as wages were low or high; but it could not in the least affect the relative value of fish and game, as wages would be high or low at the same time in both occupations. If the hunter urged the plea of his paying a large proportion, or the value of a large proportion of his game for wages, as an inducement to the fisherman to give him more fish in exchange for his game, the latter would state that he was equally affected by the same cause; and therefore under all variations of wages and profits, under all the effects of accumulation of capital, as long as they continued by a day's labour to obtain respectively the same quantity of fish, and the same quantity of game, the natural rate of exchange would be one deer for two salmon.

If with the same quantity of labour a less quantity of fish, or a greater quantity of game were obtained, the value of fish would rise in comparison with that of game. If, on the contrary, with the same quantity of labour a less quantity of game, or a greater quantity of fish was obtained, game would rise in comparison with fish.

If there were any other commodity which was invariable in its value,[1] we should be able to ascertain, by comparing the value of fish and game with this commodity, how much of the

---

[1] Eds. 1-2 contain here in addition 'requiring at all times, and under all circumstances, precisely the same quantity of labour to obtain it'. Cp. the discussion of this condition in ed. 3 on p. 44.

variation was to be attributed to a cause which affected the value of fish, and how much to a cause which affected the value of game.

Suppose money to be that commodity. If a salmon were worth 1*l.* and a deer 2*l.* one deer would be worth two salmon. But a deer might become of the value of three salmon, for more labour might be required to obtain the deer, or less to get the salmon, or both these causes might operate at the same time. If we had this invariable standard, we might easily ascertain in what degree either of these causes operated. If salmon continued to sell for 1*l.* whilst deer rose to 3*l.* we might conclude that more labour was required to obtain the deer. If deer continued at the same price of 2*l.* and salmon sold for 13*s.* 4*d.* we might then be sure that less labour was required to obtain the salmon; and if deer rose to 2*l.* 10*s.* and salmon fell to 16*s.* 8*d.* we should be convinced that both causes had operated in producing the alteration of the relative value of these commodities.

No alteration in the wages of labour could produce any alteration in the relative value of these commodities; for suppose them to rise,[1] no greater quantity of labour would be required in any of these occupations, but it would be paid for at a higher price, and the same reasons which should make the hunter and fisherman endeavour to raise the value of their game and fish, would cause the owner of the mine to raise the value of his gold. This inducement acting with the same force on all these three occupations, and the relative situation of those engaged in them being the same before and after the rise of wages, the relative value of game, fish, and gold, would continue unaltered. Wages might rise twenty per cent., and profits

---

[1] In place of the words 'for suppose them to rise' eds. 1-2 contain a passage of twenty-six lines (see pp. 54-5); in the course of this 'the miner' is introduced as a third occupation.

consequently fall in a greater or less proportion, without occasioning the least alteration in the relative value of these commodities.

Now suppose, that with the same labour and fixed capital, more fish could be produced, but no more gold or game, the relative value of fish would fall in comparison with gold or game. If, instead of twenty salmon, twenty-five were the produce of one day's labour, the price of a salmon would be sixteen shillings instead of a pound, and two salmon and a half, instead of two salmon, would be given in exchange for one deer, but the price of deer would continue at 2*l.* as before. In the same manner, if fewer fish could be obtained with the same capital and labour, fish would rise in comparative value. Fish then would rise or fall in exchangeable value, only because more or less labour was required to obtain a given quantity; and it never could rise or fall beyond the proportion of the increased or diminished quantity of labour required.

If we had then an invariable standard, by which we could measure the variation in other commodities, we should find that the utmost limit to which they could permanently rise, if produced under the circumstances supposed,[1] was proportioned to the additional quantity of labour required for their production; and that unless more labour were required for their production, they could not rise in any degree whatever. A rise of wages would not raise them in money value, nor relatively to any other commodities, the production of which required no additional quantity of labour, which employed the same proportion of fixed and circulating capital, and fixed capital of the same durability. If more or less labour were required in the production of the other commodity, we have already stated that this will immediately occasion an alteration in its relative

[1] Eds. 1-2 do not contain 'if produced under the circumstances supposed,'.

value, but such alteration is owing to the altered quantity of requisite labour, and not to the rise of wages.[1]

SECTION IV

The principle that the quantity of labour bestowed on the production of commodities regulates their relative value, considerably modified by the employment of machinery and other fixed and durable capital.[2]

In the former section we have supposed the implements and weapons necessary to kill the deer and salmon, to be equally durable, and to be the result of the same quantity of labour, and we have seen that the variations in the relative value of deer and salmon depended solely on the varying quantities of labour necessary to obtain them,—but in every state of society, the tools, implements, buildings, and machinery employed in different trades may be of various degrees of durability, and may require different portions of labour to produce them. The proportions, too, in which the capital that is to support labour, and the capital that is invested in tools, machinery and buildings, may be variously combined. This difference in the degree of durability of fixed capital, and this variety in the proportions in which the two sorts of capital may be combined, introduce another cause, besides the greater or less quantity of labour necessary to produce commodities, for the variations in their relative value—this cause is the rise or fall in the value of labour.[3]

[1] Ed. 2 contains here an additional paragraph (see p. 56, n. 1), after which it opens 'SECTION III. *The principle stated in the foregoing section considerably modified by the employment of machinery as fixed capital.*'

[2] So much of the first seven paragraphs of this section as is contained in eds. 1-2 occurs in those eds. earlier in the chapter; see p. 26, n. 2 above and cp. pp. 52–3 below.

[3] Eds. 1-2 do not contain this paragraph; but for similar statements in those eds. see p. 53 ('Besides the alteration') and p. 56 ('If the fixed').

The food[1] and clothing consumed by the labourer, the buildings in which he works, the implements with which his labour is assisted, are all of a perishable nature. There is however a vast difference in the time for which these different capitals will endure: a steam-engine will last longer than a ship, a ship than the clothing of the labourer, and the clothing of the labourer longer than the food which he consumes.

According as capital is rapidly perishable, and requires to be frequently reproduced, or is of slow consumption, it is classed under the heads of circulating, or of fixed capital.* A brewer, whose buildings and machinery are valuable and durable, is said to employ a large portion of fixed capital: on the contrary, a shoemaker, whose capital is chiefly employed in the payment of wages, which are expended on food and clothing, commodities more perishable than buildings and machinery, is said to employ a large proportion of his capital as circulating capital.

It is also to be observed that the circulating capital may circulate, or be returned to its employer, in very unequal times. The wheat bought by a farmer to sow is comparatively a fixed capital to the wheat purchased by a baker to make into loaves. One leaves it in the ground, and can obtain no return for a year; the other can get it ground into flour, sell it as bread to his customers, and have his capital free to renew the same, or commence any other employment in a week.[2]

* A division not essential, and in which the line of demarcation cannot be accurately drawn.[3]

[1] Eds. 1-2 prefix to this paragraph an additional sentence which reads: 'In every society the capital which is employed in production, is necessarily of limited durability. The food' etc.

[2] Ed. 1 does not contain this paragraph. Ed. 2 places it three paragraphs below, after the one beginning 'Again two manufacturers'. It was added, like the paragraph quoted on p. 61, note, to meet an objection of Torrens.

[3] Ed. 1 does not contain this footnote; see, however, the passage on the difficulty of demarcation, p. 150.

Two trades then may employ the same amount of capital; but it may be very differently divided with respect to the portion which is fixed, and that which is circulating.

In one trade very little capital may be employed as circulating capital, that is to say in the support of labour—it may be principally invested in machinery, implements, buildings, &c. capital of a comparatively fixed and durable character. In another trade the same amount of capital may be used, but it may be chiefly employed in the support of labour, and very little may be invested in implements, machines, and buildings. A rise in the wages of labour cannot fail to affect unequally, commodities produced under such different circumstances.[1]

Again two manufacturers may employ the same amount of fixed, and the same amount of circulating capital; but the durability of their fixed capitals may be very unequal. One may have steam-engines of the value of 10,000*l.*, the other, ships of the same value.[2]

If men employed no machinery in production but labour only, and were all the same length of time before they brought their commodities to market, the exchangeable value of their goods would be precisely in proportion to the quantity of labour employed.

If they employed fixed capital of the same value and of the same durability, then, too, the value of the commodities produced would be the same, and they would vary with the greater or less quantity of labour employed on their production.

But although commodities produced under similar circumstances, would not vary with respect to each other, from any cause but an addition or diminution of the quantity of labour necessary to produce one or other of them, yet compared with

[1] Eds. 1-2 do not contain this paragraph.
[2] Eds. 1-2 do not contain the re-mainder of this section, except for the passages mentioned in the notes on pp. 35, 37 and 38, n. 2.

others not produced with the same proportionate quantity of
fixed capital, they would vary from the other cause also which
I have before mentioned, namely, a rise in the value of labour,
although neither more nor less labour were employed in the
production of either of them. Barley and oats would continue
to bear the same relation to each other under any variation of
wages. Cotton goods and cloth would do the same, if they
also were produced under circumstances precisely similar to
each other, but yet with a rise or fall of wages, barley might be
more or less valuable compared with cotton goods, and oats
compared with cloth.

Suppose two men employ one hundred men each for a year
in the construction of two machines, and another man employs
the same number of men in cultivating corn, each of the machines
at the end of the year will be of the same value as the corn,
for they will each be produced by the same quantity of labour.
Suppose one of the owners of one of the machines to employ
it, with the assistance of one hundred men, the following year
in making cloth, and the owner of the other machine to employ
his also, with the assistance likewise of one hundred men, in
making cotton goods, while the farmer continues to employ
one hundred men as before in the cultivation of corn. During
the second year they will all have employed the same quantity
of labour, but the goods and machine together of the clothier,
and also of the cotton manufacturer, will be the result of the
labour of two hundred men, employed for a year; or, rather,
of the labour of one hundred men for two years; whereas the
corn will be produced by the labour of one hundred men for
one year, consequently if the corn be of the value of 500*l.* the
machine and cloth of the clothier together, ought to be of the
value of 1000*l.* and the machine and cotton goods of the cotton
manufacturer, ought to be also of twice the value of the corn.
But they will be of more than twice the value of the corn, for

the profit on the clothier's and cotton manufacturer's capital for the first year has been added to their capitals, while that of the farmer has been expended and enjoyed. On account then of the different degrees of durability of their capitals, or, which is the same thing, on account of the time which must elapse before one set of commodities can be brought to market, they will be valuable, not exactly in proportion to the quantity of labour bestowed on them,—they will not be as two to one, but something more, to compensate for the greater length of time which must elapse before the most valuable can be brought to market.

Suppose that for the labour of each workman 50*l*. per annum were paid, or that 5000*l*. capital were employed and profits were 10 per cent., the value of each of the machines as well as of the corn, at the end of the first year, would be 5,500*l*. The second year the manufacturers and farmer will again employ 5000*l*. each in the support of labour, and will therefore again sell their goods for 5,500*l*., but the men using the machines, to be on a par with the farmer, must not only obtain 5,500*l*., for the equal capitals of 5000*l*. employed on labour, but they must obtain a further sum of 550*l*.; for the profit on 5,500*l*. which they have invested in machinery, and consequently their goods must sell for 6,050*l*. Here then are capitalists employing precisely the same quantity of labour annually on the production of their commodities, and yet the goods they produce differ in value on account of the different quantities of fixed capital, or accumulated labour, employed by each respectively. The cloth and cotton goods are of the same value, because they are the produce of equal quantities of labour, and equal quantities of fixed capital; but corn is not of the same value as these commodities, because it is produced, as far as regards fixed capital, under different circumstances.

But how will their relative value be affected by a rise in the value of labour? It is evident that the relative values of cloth and cotton goods will undergo no change, for what affects one must equally affect the other, under the circumstances supposed: neither will the relative values of wheat and barley undergo any change, for they are produced under the same circumstances as far as fixed and circulating capital are concerned; but the relative value of corn to cloth, or to cotton goods, must be altered by a rise of labour.

There can be no rise in the value of labour without a fall of profits. If the corn is to be divided between the farmer and the labourer, the larger the proportion that is given to the latter, the less will remain for the former. So if cloth or cotton goods be divided between the workman and his employer, the larger the proportion given to the former, the less remains for the latter. Suppose then, that owing to a rise of wages, profits fall from 10 to 9 per cent., instead of adding 550*l.* to the common price of their goods (to 5,500*l.*) for the profits on their fixed capital, the manufacturers would add only 9 per cent. on that sum, or 495*l.*, consequently the price would be 5,995*l.* instead of 6,050*l.* As the corn would continue to sell for 5,500*l.*, the manufactured goods in which more fixed capital was employed, would fall relatively to corn or to any other goods in which a less portion of fixed capital entered. The degree of alteration in the relative value of goods, on account of a rise or fall of labour, would depend on the proportion which the fixed capital bore to the whole capital employed. All commodities which are produced by very valuable machinery, or in very valuable buildings, or which require a great length of time before they can be brought to market, would fall in relative value, while all those which were chiefly produced by labour, or which would be speedily brought to market would rise in relative value.[1]

---

[1] Although the last three paragraphs are not contained in eds. 1–2, they correspond in substance to pp. 56 ('First,' etc.) to 58. The text of ed. 3 embodies a correction suggested by Malthus (that some commodities rise with wages); cp. below, p. 43, n. 4.

The reader, however, should remark, that this cause of the variation of commodities is comparatively slight in its effects. With such a rise of wages as should occasion a fall of one per cent. in profits, goods produced under the circumstances I have supposed, vary in relative value only one per cent.; they fall with so great a fall of profits from 6,050*l.* to 5,995*l.* The greatest effects which could be produced on the relative prices of these goods from a rise of wages, could not exceed 6 or 7 per cent.; for profits could not, probably, under any circumstances, admit of a greater general and permanent depression than to that amount.

Not so with the other great cause of the variation in the value of commodities, namely, the increase or diminution in the quantity of labour necessary to produce them. If to produce the corn, eighty, instead of one hundred men, should be required, the value of the corn would fall 20 per cent. or from 5,500*l.* to 4,400*l.* If to produce the cloth, the labour of eighty instead of one hundred men would suffice, cloth would fall from 6,050*l.* to 4,950*l.* An alteration in the permanent rate of profits, to any great amount, is the effect of causes which do not operate but in the course of years; whereas alterations in the quantity of labour necessary to produce commodities, are of daily occurrence. Every improvement in machinery, in tools, in buildings, in raising the raw material, saves labour, and enables us to produce the commodity to which the improvement is applied with more facility, and consequently its value alters. In estimating, then, the causes of the variations in the value of commodities, although it would be wrong wholly to omit the consideration of the effect produced by a rise or fall of labour, it would be equally incorrect to attach much importance to it; and consequently, in the subsequent part of this work, though I shall occasionally refer to this cause of variation, I shall consider all the great variations which take place in the relative value of commodities to be produced by the greater or less quantity of labour which may be required from time to time to produce them.

It is hardly necessary to say, that commodities which have the same quantity of labour bestowed on their production, will differ in exchangeable value, if they cannot be brought to market in the same time.[1]

Suppose I employ twenty men at an expense of 1000*l.* for a year in the production of a commodity, and at the end of the year I employ twenty men again for another year, at a further expense of 1000*l.* in finishing or perfecting the same commodity, and that I bring it to market at the end of two years, if profits be 10 per cent., my commodity must sell for 2,310*l.*; for I have employed 1000*l.* capital for one year, and 2,100*l.* capital for one year more. Another man employs precisely the same quantity of labour, but he employs it all in the first year; he employs forty men at an expense of 2000*l.*, and at the end of the first year he sells it with 10 per cent. profit, or for 2,200*l.* Here then are two commodities having precisely the same quantity of labour bestowed on them, one of which sells for 2,310*l.*—the other for 2,200*l.*

This case appears to differ from the last, but is, in fact, the same. In both cases the superior price of one commodity is owing to the greater length of time which must elapse before it can be brought to market. In the former case the machinery and cloth were more than double the value of the corn, although only double the quantity of labour was bestowed on them. In the second case, one commodity is more valuable than the other, although no more labour was employed on its production. The difference in value arises in both cases from the profits being accumulated as capital, and is only a just compensation for the time that the profits were withheld.

It appears then that the division of capital into different

---

[1] For notice of this case in ed. 2 see p. 61, n. and cp. p. 31, n. 2.

proportions of fixed and circulating capital, employed in different trades, introduces a considerable modification to the rule, which is of universal application when labour is almost exclusively employed in production[1]; namely, that commodities never vary in value, unless a greater or less quantity of labour be bestowed on their production, it being shown in this section that without any variation in the quantity of labour, the rise of its value merely will occasion a fall in the exchangeable value of those goods, in the production of which fixed capital is employed; the larger the amount of fixed capital, the greater will be the fall.[2]

SECTION V

The principle that value does not vary with the rise or fall of wages, modified also by the unequal durability of capital, and by the unequal rapidity with which it is returned to its employer.[3]

IN the last section we have supposed that of two equal capitals in two different occupations, the proportions of fixed and circulating capitals were unequal, now let us suppose them to be in the same proportion but of unequal durability. In proportion as fixed capital is less durable, it approaches to the nature of circulating capital. It will be consumed and its value reproduced in a shorter time, in order to preserve the capital of the manufacturer. We have just seen, that in proportion as fixed capital preponderates in a manufacture, when wages rise, the value of commodities produced in that manufacture, is relatively lower than that of commodities produced in manufactures where circulating capital preponderates. In proportion to the

[1] Eds. 1-2 read 'in the early states [ed. 2 'stages'] of society' in place of 'when labour is almost exclusively employed in production'.

[2] This paragraph appears first in ed. 2 (see p. 58, n. 1); but its opening lines embody a paragraph which in ed. 1 appeared later in the chapter (see p. 66, 'It appears then that the accumulation', etc.).

[3] Section IV of ed. 2; the summary heading is uniform in eds. 2-3.

less durability of fixed capital, and its approach to the nature of circulating capital, the same effect will be produced by the same cause.[1]

If fixed capital be not of a durable nature, it will require a great quantity of labour annually to keep it in its original state of efficiency; but the labour so bestowed may be considered as really expended on the commodity manufactured, which must bear a value in proportion to such labour. If I had a machine worth 20,000*l.* which with very little labour was efficient to the production of commodities, and if the wear and tear of such machine were of trifling amount, and the general rate of profit 10 per cent., I should not require much more than 2000*l.* to be added to the price of the goods, on account of the employment of my machine; but if the wear and tear of the machine were great, if the quantity of labour requisite to keep it in an efficient state were that of fifty men annually, I should require an additional price for my goods, equal to that which would be obtained by any other manufacturer who employed fifty men in the production of other goods, and who used no machinery at all.

But a rise in the wages of labour would not equally affect commodities produced with machinery quickly consumed, and commodities produced with machinery slowly consumed. In the production of the one, a great deal of labour would be continually transferred to the commodity produced—in the other very little would be so transferred. Every rise of wages, therefore, or, which is the same thing, every fall of profits, would lower the relative value of those commodities which were produced with a capital of a durable nature, and would proportionally elevate those which were produced with capital

---

[1] For the differences in this paragraph between ed. 1 and ed. 3 (which in this case is uniform with ed. 2) see the notes to the paragraph beginning 'Secondly', on p. 58 below.

more perishable. A fall of wages would have precisely the contrary effect.[1]

I have already said that fixed capital is of various degrees of durability—suppose now a machine which could in any particular trade be employed to do the work of one hundred men for a year, and that it would last only for one year. Suppose too, the machine to cost 5000*l.*, and the wages annually paid to one hundred men to be 5000*l.*, it is evident that it would be a matter of indifference to the manufacturer whether he bought the machine or employed the men. But suppose labour to rise, and consequently the wages of one hundred men for a year to amount to 5,500*l.*, it is obvious that the manufacturer would now no longer hesitate, it would be for his interest to buy the machine and get his work done for 5000*l.* But will not the machine rise in price, will not that also be worth 5,500*l.* in consequence of the rise of labour?[2] It would rise in price[3] if there were no stock employed on[4] its construction, and no profits to be paid to the maker of it. If for example, the machine were the produce of the labour of one hundred men,[5] working one year upon it with wages of 50*l.* each, and its price were consequently[6] 5000*l.*; should those wages rise to 55*l.*, its price would be 5,500*l.*, but this cannot be the case; less than one hundred men are employed or it could not be sold for 5000*l.*, for out of the 5000*l.* must be paid the profits of stock[7] which employed the men. Suppose then that only

---

[1] The last two paragraphs correspond in substance to the passage of eds. 1-2 which begins on p. 59 ('Suppose that an engine' etc.) and concludes at the end of p. 60.

[2] In eds. 1-2 the first part of this paragraph is contained in substance only (p. 61, 'A manufacturer of hats' etc.).

[3] Eds. 1-2 'It would be increased,'.

[4] Eds. 1-2 'in'.

[5] Eds. 1-2 'were produced by 100 men'.

[6] Eds. 1-2 do not contain 'consequently'.

[7] A misprint for 'of the stock', which is the reading of eds. 1-2. Also the punctuation of this sentence is more correct in the earlier eds.: see below, p. 61.

eighty-five men were employed at an expense of 50*l.* each, or[1] 4,250*l.* per annum, and that the 750*l.* which the sale of the machine would produce over and above the wages advanced to the men, constituted the profits of the engineer's stock. When wages rose 10 per cent. he would be obliged to employ an additional capital of 425*l.* and would therefore employ 4,675*l.* instead of 4,250*l.*, on which capital he would only get a profit of 325*l.* if he continued to sell his machine for 5000*l.*; but this is precisely the case of all manufacturers and capitalists; the rise of wages affects them all. If therefore the maker of the machine should raise the price of it in consequence of a rise of wages, an unusual quantity of capital would be employed in the construction of such machines, till their price afforded only the common rate of profits[2].* We see then that machines would not rise in price, in consequence of a rise of wages.[3]

The manufacturer, however, who in a general rise of wages, can have recourse to a machine which shall not increase the charge of production on his commodity, would enjoy peculiar advantages if he could continue to charge the same price for his goods; but he, as we have already seen, would be obliged to lower the price of his commodities, or capital would flow

---

* We here see why it is that old countries are constantly impelled to employ machinery, and new countries to employ labour. With every difficulty of providing for the maintenance of men, labour necessarily rises, and with every rise in the price of labour, new temptations are offered to the use of machinery. This difficulty of providing for the maintenance of men is in constant operation in old countries, in new ones a very great increase in the population may take place without the least rise in the wages of labour. It may be as easy to provide for the 7th, 8th, and 9th million of men as for the 2d, 3d, and 4th.[4]

---

[1] Eds. 1-2 do not contain '50*l.* each, or'.
[2] Eds. 1-2 'only the usual profits'.
[3] Eds. 1-2 do not contain this sentence and join this paragraph and the next one together.
[4] Eds. 1-2 do not contain this note.

to his trade till his profits had sunk to the general level.[1] Thus then is the public benefited by machinery: these mute agents are always the produce of much less labour than that which they displace, even when they are of the same money value. Through their influence, an increase in the price of provisions which raises wages will affect fewer persons; it will reach, as in the above instance, eighty-five men instead of a hundred, and the saving which is the consequence, shows itself in the reduced price of the commodity manufactured. Neither machines, nor the commodities made by them, rise in real value[2], but all commodities made[3] by machines fall, and fall in proportion to their durability.

It will be seen, then, that in the early stages of society, before much machinery or durable[4] capital is used, the commodities produced by equal capitals will be nearly of equal value, and will rise or fall only relatively to each other[5] on account of more or less labour being required for their production; but after the introduction of these expensive and durable[6] instruments, the commodities produced by the employment of equal capitals will be of very unequal value; and although they will still be liable to rise or fall relatively to each other, as more or less labour becomes necessary to their production, they will be subject to another, though a minor[7] variation, also, from the rise or fall of wages and profits. Since goods which sell for 5000*l.*[8] may be the produce of a capital equal in amount to that from which are produced other goods which sell for 10,000*l.*, the profits on their manufacture will

---

[1] This sentence replaces two sentences of eds. 1-2, in which a similar argument is applied to 'the manufacturer of hats'; for the earlier version see p. 62.

[2] Eds. 1-2 'Neither machines nor any other commodities are raised in price'.

[3] Eds. 1-2 'which are made'.

[4] Ed. 2 contains in addition 'fixed'.

[5] Ed. 2 places the 'only' here.

[6] Ed. 2 does not contain 'and durable'.

[7] Ed. 2 does not contain 'another, though a minor'.

[8] Ed. 2 '2,000*l.*'

be the same; but those profits would be unequal, if the prices of the goods did not vary with a rise or fall in the rate of profits.[1]

It appears, too, that in proportion to the durability of capital[2] employed in any kind of production, the relative prices of those commodities on which such durable[3] capital is employed, will vary inversely as wages; they will fall as wages rise,[4] and rise as wages fall; and, on the contrary, those which are produced chiefly by labour with less fixed capital, or with fixed capital of a less durable character than the medium in which price is estimated, will rise as wages rise, and fall as wages fall.

SECTION VI

On an invariable measure of value.[5]

WHEN commodities varied in relative value, it would be desirable to have the means of ascertaining which of them fell and which rose in real value, and this could be effected only by comparing them one after another with some invariable standard measure of value, which should itself be subject to none of the fluctuations to which other commodities are exposed. Of such a measure it is impossible to be possessed, because there is no commodity which is not itself exposed to

[1] This paragraph is not in ed. 1, but its latter part embodies a paragraph which in ed. 1 appeared later in the chapter (p. 66, 'Commodities, though they continue', etc.).

[2] Ed. 1 'It appears, then, that in proportion to the quantity and durability of the fixed capital'.

[3] Ed. 1 does not contain 'durable'.

[4] For the reading of the remainder of this paragraph in ed. 1 and in ed. 2, see below, p. 63, text and note 3. The essential difference will be found in the statement of the earlier eds. that 'no commodities whatever are raised ['in absolute price', ed. 1; 'in exchangeable value', ed. 2] merely because wages rise'. See Malthus's criticism of ed. 2, accepted by Ricardo, below, II, 64; and cp. above, p. 35, n.

[5] Eds. 1-2 do not contain any part of this Section. For Ricardo's earlier views on an invariable standard of value see above, p. 17, n. 3 and below, p. 63.

the same variations as the things, the value of which is to be ascertained; that is, there is none which is not subject to require more or less labour for its production. But if this cause of variation in the value of a medium could be removed—if it were possible that in the production of our money for instance, the same quantity of labour should at all times be required, still it would not be a perfect standard or invariable measure of value, because, as I have already endeavoured to explain, it would be subject to relative variations from a rise or fall of wages, on account of the different proportions of fixed capital which might be necessary to produce it, and to produce those other commodities whose alteration of value we wished to ascertain. It might be subject to variations too, from the same cause, on account of the different degrees of durability of the fixed capital employed on it, and the commodities to be compared with it—or the time necessary to bring the one to market, might be longer or shorter than the time necessary to bring the other commodities to market, the variations of which were to be determined; all which circumstances disqualify any commodity that can be thought of from being a perfectly accurate measure of value.

If, for example, we were to fix on gold as a standard, it is evident that it is but a commodity obtained under the same contingencies as every other commodity, and requiring labour and fixed capital to produce it. Like every other commodity, improvements in the saving of labour might be applied to its production, and consequently it might fall in relative value to other things merely on account of the greater facility of producing it.

If we suppose this cause of variation to be removed, and the same quantity of labour to be always required to obtain the same quantity of gold, still gold would not be a perfect measure of value, by which we could accurately ascertain the variations in all other things, because it would not be produced with precisely the same combinations of fixed and circulating capital as all other things; nor with fixed capital of the same durability; nor would it require precisely the same length of time, before it could be brought to market. It would be a perfect measure of value for all things produced under the same circumstances precisely as itself, but for no others. If, for example, it were produced under the same circumstances as we have supposed necessary to produce cloth and cotton goods, it would be a perfect measure of value for those things, but not so for corn, for coals, and other commodities produced with either a less or a greater proportion of fixed capital, because, as we have shown, every alteration in the permanent rate of profits would have some effect on the relative value of all these goods, independently of any alteration in the quantity of labour employed on their production. If gold were produced under the same circumstances as corn, even if they never changed, it would not, for the same reasons, be at all times a perfect measure of the value of cloth and cotton goods. Neither gold then, nor any other commodity, can ever be a perfect measure of value for all things; but I have already remarked, that the effect on the relative prices of things, from a variation in profits, is comparatively slight; that by far the most important effects are produced by the varying quantities of labour required for production; and therefore, if we suppose this important cause of variation removed from the production of gold, we shall probably possess as near an approximation to a standard measure of value as can be theoretically conceived. May not gold be considered as a commodity produced with such proportions of the two kinds of capital as approach nearest to the average quantity employed in the production of most commodities? May not these proportions be so nearly equally distant from the two extremes, the one where little fixed capital

is used, the other where little labour is employed, as to form
a just mean between them?

If, then, I may suppose myself to be possessed of a standard
so nearly approaching to an invariable one, the advantage is,
that I shall be enabled to speak of the variations of other things,
without embarrassing myself on every occasion with the consideration of the possible alteration in the value of the medium
in which price and value are estimated.

To facilitate, then, the object of this enquiry, although I
fully allow that money made of gold is subject to most of the
variations of other things, I shall suppose it to be invariable,
and therefore all alterations in price to be occasioned by some
alteration in the value of the commodity of which I may be
speaking.

Before I quit this subject, it may be proper to observe, that
Adam Smith, and all the writers who have followed him, have,
without one exception that I know of, maintained that a rise
in the price of labour would be uniformly followed by a rise
in the price of all commodities.[1] I hope I have succeeded in
showing, that there are no grounds for such an opinion, and
that only those commodities would rise which had less fixed
capital employed upon them than the medium in which price
was estimated, and that all those which had more, would
positively fall in price when wages rose. On the contrary, if
wages fell, those commodities only would fall, which had a
less proportion of fixed capital employed on them, than the
medium in which price was estimated; all those which had
more, would positively rise in price.

It is necessary for me also to remark, that I have not said,
because one commodity has so much labour bestowed upon
it as will cost 1000*l.* and another so much as will cost 2000*l.*

---

[1] See the quotations from some of these writers given below, pp. 302,
307 and 315.

that therefore one would be of the value of 1000*l.* and the
other of the value of 2000*l.* but I have said that their value
will be to each other as two to one, and that in those
proportions they will be exchanged. It is of no importance
to the truth of this doctrine, whether one of these commodities sells for 1,100*l.* and the other for 2,200*l.*, or one for
1,500*l.* and the other for 3000*l.*; into that question I do not
at present enquire; I affirm only, that their relative values will
be governed by the relative quantities of labour bestowed on
their production. *

SECTION VII

*Different effects from the alteration in the value of money, the
medium in which* PRICE *is always expressed, or from the alteration in the value of the commodities which money purchases.*[1]

ALTHOUGH I shall, as I have already explained, have occasion
to consider money as invariable in value, for the purpose of
more distinctly pointing out the causes of relative variations
in the value of other things, it may be useful to notice the
different effects which will follow from the prices of goods
being altered by the causes to which I have already adverted,

* Mr. Malthus remarks on this doctrine, "We have the power indeed,
arbitrarily, to call the labour which has been employed upon a commodity
its real value, but in so doing, we use words in a different sense from that
in which they are customarily used; we confound at once the very important distinction between *cost* and *value*; and render it almost impossible
to explain with clearness, the main stimulus to the production of wealth,
which in fact depends upon this distinction."[2]

Mr. Malthus appears to think that it is a part of my doctrine, that the
cost and value of a thing should be the same;—it is, if he means by cost,
"cost of production" including profits. In the above passage, this is what
he does not mean, and therefore he has not clearly understood me.[3]

[1] Section v of ed. 2; the summary
heading is uniform in eds. 2-3.
[2] Malthus's *Principles*, below, II, 30.

[3] On the issue raised in this note
(which is not contained in eds. 1-2)
see below, II, 34 and 101.

namely, the different quantities of labour required to produce
them, and their being altered by a variation in the value of
money itself.[1]

Money, being a variable commodity, the rise of money-
wages will be[2] frequently occasioned by a fall in the value of
money. A rise of wages from this cause will, indeed, be invariably accompanied by a rise in the price of commodities;
but in such cases, it will be found that labour and all commodities have not varied in regard to each other, and that the variation has been confined to money.

Money, from its being a commodity obtained from a foreign
country, from its being the general medium of exchange between all civilized countries, and from its being also distributed
among those countries in proportions which are ever changing
with every improvement in commerce and machinery, and with
every increasing difficulty of obtaining food and necessaries
for an increasing population, is subject to incessant variations.
In stating the principles which regulate exchangeable value
and price, we should carefully distinguish between those variations which belong to the commodity itself, and those which
are occasioned by a variation in the medium in which value
is estimated, or price expressed.

A rise in wages, from an alteration in the value of money,
produces a general effect on price, and for that reason it produces no real effect whatever on profits. On the contrary, a
rise of wages, from the circumstance of the labourer being
more liberally rewarded, or from a difficulty of procuring the
necessaries on which wages are expended, does not, except in
some instances,[3] produce the effect of raising price, but has a

---

[1] This paragraph is not in eds. 1-2;
but cp. in those eds. the sentence beginning 'It should however be carefully remembered', below, p. 63.
[2] Eds. 1-2 'Money, however, is a
variable commodity; and the rise
of wages as well as of commodities,
is'.
[3] Eds. 1-2 do not contain ', except
in some instances,'.

great effect in lowering profits. In the one case, no greater proportion of the annual labour of the country is devoted to the support of the labourers; in the other case, a larger portion is so devoted.

It is according to the division of the whole produce of the land of any particular farm, between the three classes of land-lord, capitalist, and labourer[1], that we are to judge of the rise or fall of[2] rent, profit, and wages, and not according to the value at which that produce may be estimated in a medium which is confessedly variable.

It is not by the absolute quantity of produce obtained by either class, that we can correctly judge of the rate of profit, rent, and wages, but by the quantity of labour required to obtain that produce. By improvements in machinery and agri-culture, the whole produce may be doubled; but if wages, rent, and profit be also doubled, these three will bear the same pro-portions to one another as before, and neither could be said to have relatively varied. But if wages partook not of the whole of this increase; if they, instead of being doubled, were only increased one-half; if rent, instead of being doubled, were only increased three-fourths, and the remaining increase went to profit, it would, I apprehend, be correct for me to say, that rent and wages had fallen while profits had risen; for if we had an invariable standard by which to measure the value of this produce, we should find that a less value had fallen to the class of labourers and landlords, and a greater to the class of capitalists, than had been given before. We might find, for example, that though the absolute quantity of commodities had been doubled, they were the produce of precisely the former

---

[1] Eds. 1-2 'of the whole produce of the land and labour of the country, between the three classes of land-lords, capitalists, and labourers'. Cp. below, p. 83, n. For what may have been an attempt to redraft this passage for ed. 3, see *Notes on Malthus*, below, II, 195, n. 2.

[2] Ed. 1 does not contain 'the rise or fall of'.

quantity of labour. Of every hundred hats, coats, and quarters of corn produced, if

The labourers had before[1] .	25
The landlords . . .	25
And the capitalists . .	50
	100:

And if, after these commodities were double the[2] quantity, of every 100

The labourers had only .	22
The landlords . . .	22
And the capitalists . .	56
	100:

In that case I should say, that wages and rent had fallen and profits risen; though, in consequence of the abundance of commodities, the quantity paid to the labourer and landlord would have increased in the proportion of 25 to 44. Wages are to be estimated by their real value, viz. by the quantity of labour and capital employed in producing them, and not by their nominal value either in coats, hats, money, or corn. Under the circumstances I have just supposed, commodities would have fallen to half their former value, and if money had not varied, to half their former price also. If then in this medium, which had not varied in value, the wages of the labourer should be found to have fallen, it will not the less be a real fall, because they might furnish him with a greater quantity of cheap commodities than his former wages.

The variation in the value of money, however great, makes no difference in the *rate* of profits; for suppose the goods of the manufacturer to rise from 1000*l.* to 2000*l.*, or 100 per cent., if his capital, on which the variations of money have as much effect as on the value of produce, if his machinery, buildings,

---

[1] Ed. 1 does not contain 'before'.   [2] Eds. 1-2 'were doubled in'.

and stock in trade rise also 100 per cent., his rate of profits
will be the same, and he will have the same quantity, and no
more, of the produce of the labour of the country at his command.

If, with a capital of a given value, he can, by economy in
labour, double the quantity of produce, and it fall to half its
former price, it will bear the same proportion to the capital
that produced it which it did before, and consequently profits
will still be at the same rate.[1]

If, at the same time that he doubles the quantity of produce
by the employment of the same capital, the value of money
is by any accident lowered one half, the produce will sell for
twice the money value that it did before; but the capital employed to produce it will also be of twice its former money
value; and therefore in this case too, the value of the produce
will bear the same proportion to the value of the capital as it
did before; and although the produce be doubled, rent, wages,
and profits will only vary as the proportions vary, in which
this double produce may be divided among the three classes
that share it.[2]

[1] For the differences in the last two
paragraphs between ed. 1 and ed. 3
(which in this case is uniform with
ed. 2) see the notes on p. 65 below.
[2] Ed. 1 has here three additional
paragraphs (see p. 66), which in
eds. 2-3 are partly incorporated
earlier in the chapter (see p. 38,
n. 2 and p. 43, n. 1).

[APPENDIX TO CHAPTER I

Text of edition 1, with variants of edition 2, for the latter part of the Chapter (pp. 26–51)]

Economy in the use of labour never fails to reduce the relative value of a commodity, whether the saving be in the labour necessary to the manufacture of the commodity itself, or in that necessary to the formation of the capital, by the aid of which it is produced. In either case the price of stockings would fall, whether there were fewer men employed as bleachers, spinners, and weavers, persons immediately necessary to their manufacture; or as sailors, carriers, engineers, and smiths, persons more indirectly concerned. In the one case, the whole saving of labour would fall on the stockings, because that portion of labour was wholly confined to the stockings; in the other, a portion only would fall on the stockings, the remainder being applied to all those other commodities, to the production of which the buildings, machinery, and carriage, were subservient.

In every society the capital which is employed in production, is necessarily of limited durability. The food and clothing consumed by the labourer, the buildings in which he works, the implements with which his labour is assisted, are all of a perishable nature. There is however a vast difference in the time for which these different capitals will endure: a steam-engine will last longer than a ship, a ship than the clothing of the labourer, and the clothing of the labourer longer than the food which he consumes.

According as capital is rapidly perishable, and requires to be frequently reproduced, or is of slow consumption, it is classed under the heads of circulating, or of fixed capital.[1] A brewer, whose buildings and machinery are valuable and durable, is said to employ a large portion of fixed capital: on the contrary, a shoe-maker, whose capital is chiefly employed in the payment of wages, which are expended on food and clothing, commodities more perishable than buildings and machinery, is said to employ a large proportion of his capital as circulating capital.

---

[1] Ed. 2 attaches here a footnote: 'A division not essential, and in which the line of demarcation cannot be accurately drawn.' Cp., for ed. 1, p. 150.

Two trades then may employ the same amount of capital; but it may be very differently divided with respect to the portion which is fixed, and that which is circulating.

Again two manufacturers may employ the same amount of fixed, and the same amount of circulating capital; but the durability of their fixed capitals may be very unequal. One may have steam engines of the value of 10,000*l.* the other, ships of the same value.

Besides the alteration in the relative value of commodities, occasioned by more or less labour being required to produce them, they are also subject to fluctuations from a rise of wages, and consequent fall of profits, if the fixed capitals employed be either of unequal value, or of unequal duration.[1]

Suppose that in the early stages of society, the bows and arrows of the hunter were of equal value, and of equal durability, with the canoe and implements of the fisherman, both being the produce of the same quantity of labour. Under such circumstances the value of the deer, the produce of the hunter's day's labour, would be exactly equal to the value of the fish, the produce of the fisherman's day's labour. The comparative value of the fish and the game, would be entirely regulated by the quantity of labour realised in each; whatever might be the quantity of production, or however high or low general wages or profits might be. If for example the canoes and implements of the fisherman were of the value of 100*l.* and were calculated to last for ten years, and he employed ten men, whose annual labour cost 100*l.* and who in one day obtained by their labour twenty salmon: If the weapons employed by the hunter were also of 100*l.* value and calculated to last ten years, and if he also employed ten men, whose annual labour cost 100*l.* and who in one day procured him ten deer; then the natural price of a deer would be two salmon, whether the proportion of the whole produce bestowed on the men who obtained it, were large or small. The proportion which might be paid for wages, is of the utmost importance in the question of profits; for it must at once be seen, that profits would be high

---

[1] Instead of this paragraph, which in ed. 2 is removed to p. 56 below (see *ib.* note 2), ed. 2 has here: 'It is also to be observed that the circulating capital may circulate, or be returned to its employer, in very unequal times. The wheat bought by a farmer to sow is comparatively a fixed capital to the wheat purchased by a baker to make it into loaves. One leaves it in the ground, and can obtain no return for a year; the other can get it ground into flour, sell it as bread to his customers, and have his capital free to renew the same, or commence any other employment in a week.' Cp. the paragraph, also added in ed. 2, below, p. 61, note.

or low, exactly in proportion as wages were low or high; but it could not in the least affect the relative value of fish and game, as wages would be high or low at the same time in both occupations. If the hunter urged the plea of his paying a large proportion, or the value of a large proportion of his game for wages, as an inducement to the fisherman to give him more fish in exchange for his game, the latter would state that he was equally affected by the same cause; and therefore under all variations of wages and profits, under all the effects of accumulation of capital, as long as they continued by a day's labour to obtain respectively the same quantity of fish, and the same quantity of game, the natural rate of exchange would be, one deer for two salmon.

If with the same quantity of labour a less quantity of fish, or a greater quantity of game were obtained, the value of fish would rise in comparison with that of game. If, on the contrary, with the same quantity of labour a less quantity of game, or a greater quantity of fish was obtained, game would rise in comparison with fish.

If there were any other commodity which was invariable in its value, requiring at all times, and under all circumstances, precisely the same quantity of labour to obtain it, we should be able to ascertain, by comparing the value of fish and game with this commodity, how much of the variation was to be attributed to a cause which affected the value of fish, and how much to a cause which affected the value of game.

Suppose money to be that commodity. If a salmon were worth 1*l.* and a deer 2*l.* one deer would be worth two salmon. But a deer might become of the value of three salmon, for more labour might be required to obtain the deer, or less to get the salmon, or both these causes might operate at the same time. If we had this invariable standard, we might easily ascertain in what degree either of these causes operated. If salmon continued to sell for 1*l.* whilst deer rose to 3*l.* we might conclude that more labour was required to obtain the deer. If deer continued at the same price of 2*l.* and salmon sold for 13*s.* 4*d.* we might then be sure that less labour was required to obtain the salmon; and if deer rose to 2*l.* 10*s.* and salmon fell to 16*s.* 8*d.* we should be convinced that both causes had operated in producing the alteration of the relative value of these commodities.

No alteration in the wages of labour could produce any alteration in the relative value of these commodities; for if profits were 10 per cent., then to replace the 100*l.* circulating capital with 10 per cent.

profit, there must be a return of 110*l*: to replace the equal portion
of fixed capital, when profits are at the rate of 10 per cent. there
should be annually received 16.27*l*.; for, the present value of an
annuity of 16.27*l*. for ten years, when money is at 10 per cent., is
100*l*.; consequently all the game of the hunter should annually sell
for 126.27*l*. But the capital of the fisherman being the same in
quantity, and divided in the same proportion into fixed and circulating capital, and being also of the same durability, he, to obtain
the same profits, must sell his goods for the same value. If wages
rose 10 per cent. and consequently 10 per cent. more circulating
capital were required in each trade, it would equally affect both
employments. In both, 210*l*. instead of 200*l*. would be required
in order to produce the former quantity of commodities; and these
would sell precisely for the same money, namely 126.27*l*.: they
would therefore be at the same relative value, and profits would be
equally reduced in both trades.

The prices of the commodities would not rise, because the money
in which they are valued is by the supposition of an invariable value,
always requiring the same quantity of labour to produce it.

If the gold mine from which money was obtained were in the
same country, in that case, after the rise of wages, 210*l*. might be
necessary to be employed, as capital, to obtain the same quantity
of metal that 200*l*. obtained before: for the same reason that the
hunter and fisherman required 10*l*. in addition to their capitals, the
miner would require an equal addition to his. No greater quantity
of labour would be required in any of these occupations, but it
would be paid for at a higher price, and the same reasons which
should make the hunter and fisherman endeavour to raise the value
of their game and fish, would cause the owner of the mine to raise
the value of his gold. This inducement acting with the same force
on all these three occupations, and the relative situation of those
engaged in them being the same before and after the rise of wages,
the relative value of game, fish, and gold, would continue unaltered.
Wages might rise twenty per cent., and profits consequently fall
in a greater or less proportion, without occasioning the least alteration in the relative value of these commodities.

Now suppose, that with the same labour and fixed capital, more
fish could be produced, but no more gold or game, the relative
value of fish would fall in comparison with gold or game. If, instead
of twenty salmon, twenty-five were the produce of one day's labour,

the price of a salmon would be sixteen shillings instead of a pound, and two salmon and a half, instead of two salmon, would be given in exchange for one deer, but the price of deer would continue at 2*l.* as before. In the same manner, if fewer fish could be obtained with the same capital and labour, fish would rise in comparative value. Fish then would rise or fall in exchangeable value, only because more or less labour was required to obtain a given quantity; and it never could rise or fall beyond the proportion of the increased or diminished quantity of labour required.

If we had then an invariable standard, by which we could measure the variation in other commodities, we should find that the utmost limit to which they could permanently rise, was proportioned to the additional quantity of labour required for their production; and that unless more labour were required for their production, they could not rise in any degree whatever. A rise of wages would not raise them in money value, nor relatively to any other commodities, the production of which required no additional quantity of labour, which employed the same proportion of fixed and circulating capital, and fixed capital of the same durability. If more or less labour were required in the production of the other commodity, we have already stated that this will immediately occasion an alteration in its relative value, but such alteration is owing to the altered quantity of requisite labour, and not to the rise of wages.[1]

If the fixed and circulating capitals were in different proportions, or if the fixed capital were of different durability, then the relative value of the commodities produced, would be altered in consequence of a rise of wages.[2]

First, when the fixed and circulating capitals were in different proportions, suppose that instead[3] of 100*l.* fixed capital and 100*l.*

---

[1] Ed. 2 adds here a paragraph which concludes its Section II: 'It appears then by this section, that notwithstanding the accumulation of capital, commodities would not necessarily vary in relative value from a rise in wages, unless it was accompanied by increased facility or difficulty in the production of one or more of them.' (Cp. a draft of this, which showed hesitation whether relative values 'vary' or 'rise', in a letter to Mill, below, VII, 333, n. 2.)

After this, ed. 2 opens 'SECTION III'

under the heading: '*The principle stated in the foregoing section considerably modified by the employment of machinery as fixed capital.*'

[2] Ed. 2 omits this paragraph and places here the paragraph beginning 'Besides the alteration' which in ed. 1 occurs above, p. 53.

[3] Ed. 2 opens the paragraph 'Thus suppose the fixed and circulating capital of the hunter and fisherman to be together equal in amount, but to be in different proportions; suppose that instead' etc.

circulating capital, the hunter should employ 150*l.* fixed capital and 50*l.* circulating capital, and that the fisherman should on the contrary employ only 50*l.* fixed capital and 150*l.* circulating capital.

If profits be 10 per cent., the hunter must sell his goods for 79*l.* 8*s.* For,

To replace his circulating capital of 50*l.* with a profit of 10 per cent. would require a value of . . .	55*l.*
To replace his fixed capital with 10 per cent. profit, the present value of an annuity for ten years of 24.4*l.* at 10 per cent. being 150*l.*	24.4*l.*
	79.4*l.*

If profits be[1] 10 per cent., the fisherman must sell his goods for 173*l.* 2*s.* 7*d.*

To replace his circulating capital of 150*l.* with 10 per cent. profit	165*l.*
To replace his fixed capital with 10 per cent. profit, one-third of the hunter's	8.13
	173.13*l.*

Now if wages rise, although neither of these commodities should require more labour for their production, yet their relative value will be altered. Suppose wages to rise 6 per cent., the hunter would not require more than an increase of 3*l.* to his capital, to employ the same number of men, and obtain the same quantity of game; the fisherman would require three times that sum, or 9*l.* The profits of stock would fall to 4 per cent., the hunter would be obliged to sell his game for 73*l.* 12*s.* 2*d.*

To replace his circulating capital of 53*l.* with a profit of 4 per cent.	55.12*l.*
To replace fixed capital, annually wasted, the present value of an annuity of 18.49*l.* for ten years, when money is at 4 per cent., being 150*l.* . . .	18.49
	£73.61

[1] Ed. 2 'But with the same rate of profits of' in place of 'If profits be'.

The fisherman would sell his fish for 171*l*. 11*s*. 5*d*. viz.

To replace his circulating capital of 159*l*. with a profit
of 4 per cent. £165.360
To replace fixed capital annually wasted, the present
value of an annuity of 6.163*l*., for ten years at 4 per
cent., being 50*l*. 6.163

£171.523

Game was to fish before as 100 to 218.
It would now be . . . as 100 to 233.

Thus we see, that with every rise of wages, in proportion as the
capital employed in any occupation consists of circulating capital,
its produce will be of greater relative value than the goods produced
in another occupation, where a less proportion of circulating, and a
greater proportion of fixed capital are employed.[1]

Secondly, suppose the proportions of fixed capital to be the same;
but of different degrees of durability.[2] In proportion as fixed capital
is less durable, it approaches to the nature of circulating capital.
It will be consumed in a shorter time, and its value reproduced[3] in
order to preserve the capital of the manufacturer. We have just seen,
that in proportion as circulating[4] capital preponderates in a manufacture, when wages rise, the value of commodities produced in that

[1] In place of this paragraph ed. 2
reads: 'It appears then that the division
of capital into different proportions
of fixed and circulating capital, employed in different trades, introduces
a considerable modification to the
rule, which is of universal application
in the early stages of society, namely,
that commodities never vary in value,
unless a greater or less quantity of
labour be bestowed on their production, it being shewn in this section
that without any variation in the
quantity of labour, the rise of its
value merely will occasion a fall in
the exchangeable value of those
goods, in the production of which
fixed capital is employed; the larger
the amount of fixed capital, the
greater will be the fall.' This in-
corporates a paragraph which in ed. 1
occurs on p. 66 (see *ib*. note 2).

After this, ed. 2 opens 'SECTION IV'
under the heading: '*The principle that
value does not vary with the rise or fall
of wages, modified also by the unequal
durability of capital, and by the unequal
rapidity with which it is returned to its
employer*.'
[2] Ed. 2 replaces this sentence by: 'In
the last section we have supposed
that of two equal capitals in two
different occupations, the proportions
of fixed and circulating capitals were
unequal, now let us suppose them to
be in the same proportion but of unequal durability.' Cp. below, p. 61, n.
[3] Ed. 2 places 'in a shorter time,'
here instead of five words earlier.
[4] Ed. 2 reads 'fixed' in place of
'circulating'; and accordingly, farther
down in the sentence, 'relatively
lower' in place of 'relatively higher'
and 'circulating' in place of 'fixed'.

manufacture, is relatively higher than that of commodities produced
in manufactures where fixed capital preponderates. In proportion
to the less durability of fixed capital, and its approach to the nature
of circulating capital, the same effect will be produced by the same
cause.

Suppose that an engine is made, which will last for a hundred years,
and that its value is 20,000*l.* Suppose too, that this machine, without
any labour whatever, could produce a certain quantity of commodities annually, and that profits were 10 per cent.: the whole value
of the goods produced would be annually 2,000*l.* 2*s.* 11*d.*; for the
profit of 20,000*l.* at 10 per cent. per annum, is   .   £2,000
And an annuity of 2*s.* 11*d.* for 100 years, at 10 per
cent. will, at the end of that period, replace a
capital of 20,000*l.* 2 11
                                                      ————————
Consequently the goods must sell for   .   .   .   £2000 2 11

If the same amount of capital, viz. 20,000*l.*, be employed in supporting productive labour, and be annually consumed and reproduced, as it is when employed in paying wages, then to give an
equal profit of 10 per cent. on 20,000*l.* the commodities produced
must sell for 22,000*l.* Now suppose labour so to rise, that instead
of 20,000*l.* being sufficient to pay the wages of those employed in
producing the latter commodities, 20,952*l.* is required; then profits
will fall to 5 per cent.: for as these commodities would sell for no
more than before, viz.   .   .   .   £22,000 and to produce
them   .   .   .   .   .   .   £20,952 would be requisite, there would remain no more   ————————
than   .   .   .   .   .   .   £1048[1] on a capital of

20,952*l.* If labour so rose, that 21,153*l.* were required, profits would
fall to 4 per cent. and if it rose, so that 21,359*l.* was employed,
profits would fall to 3 per cent.

But, as no wages would be paid by the owner of the machine,
which would last 100 years, when profits fell to 5 per cent. the price
of his goods must fall to 1007*l.* 13*s.* 8*d.* viz. 1000*l.* to pay his profits,
and 7*l.* 13*s.* 8*d.* to accumulate for 100 years at 5 per cent. to replace
his capital of 20,000*l.* When profits fell to 4 per cent. his goods must
sell for 816*l.* 3*s.* 2*d.*, and when at 3 per cent. for 632*l.* 16*s.* 7*d.* By
a rise in the price of labour then, under 7 per cent., which has no

———————
[1] Ed. 2 adds 'or 5 per cent. profit,'.

effect on the prices of commodities wholly produced by labour, a fall of no less than 68 per cent. is effected on those commodities wholly produced by machinery. If the proprietor of the machine sold his goods for more than 632*l.* 16*s.* 7*d.*, he would get more than 3 per cent., the general profit of stock; and as others could furnish themselves with machines at the same price of 20,000*l.* they would be so multiplied, that he would be inevitably obliged to sink the price of his goods, till they afforded only the usual and general profits of stock.

In proportion as this machine were less durable, prices would be less affected by the fall of profit, and the rise of wages. If, for example, the machine would last only ten years, when profits were at 10 per cent. the goods should sell for . . . £3254

when at	5 per cent.	2590
	4 per cent.	2465
	3 per cent.	2344

for such are the sums requisite to place his profits on a par with others, and to replace his capital at the end of ten years; or, which is the same thing, such are the annuities which 20,000*l.* would purchase for ten years at those rates. If the machine would last only three years, when profits were 10 per cent. the price of the goods would be £8042

at 5 per cent.	7344
4 per cent.	7206
3 per cent.	7070

If it would last only one year, when profits were 10 per cent. the goods would sell for £22,000

at 5 per cent.	21,000
4 per cent.	20,800
3 per cent.	20,600: therefore

when profits fell from 10 to 3 per cent. the goods, which were produced with equal capitals, would fall

68 per cent. if the machine would last	100 years.
28 per cent. if the machine would last	10 years.
13 per cent. if it would last	3 years.
And little more than 6 per cent. if it would last only	1 year.[1]

[1] Ed. 2 attaches here a footnote and adds a paragraph in the text.

The footnote reads: 'To put the principle in a strong point of view, I have supposed a machine to do work without any assistance from human labour, which is evidently impossible. A writer in the British Review has absurdly argued as if this supposition was essential to the

These results are of such importance to the science of political economy, yet accord so little with some of its received doctrines, which maintain that every rise in wages is necessarily transferred to the price of commodities, that it may not be superfluous to elucidate the subject still further.

A manufacturer of hats employs a hundred men at an annual expense of 50*l.* each, who produce him commodities of the value of 8000*l.* A machine calculated to last precisely a year, and to do equally well the same work as the 100 men, is offered to him for 5000*l.*, the sum, exactly, that he is expending on wages. It will be a matter of indifference to the manufacturer, whether he purchase the machine, or continue to employ the men. Now if the wages of labour rise 10 per cent. and an additional capital of 500*l.* be consequently required to enable him to employ the same labour, whilst his commodities continue to sell for 8000*l.*, he will no longer hesitate, but will at once purchase the machine, and will do the same annually, while wages continue above the original 5000*l.* But will he be able now to purchase the machine at the former price? will not its value be increased, in consequence of the rise of labour? It would be increased, if there were no stock employed in its construction, and no profits to be paid to the maker of it. If, for example, the machine were produced by 100 men working one year upon it with wages of 50*l.* each, and its price were 5000*l.*, should those wages rise to 55*l.* its price would be 5500*l.*: but this cannot be the case; less than 100 men are employed, or it could not be sold for 5000*l.*; for out of the 5000*l.* must be paid the profits of the stock which employed the men. Suppose then that only eighty-five men were employed

truth of the principle. But it is obvious that similar results, though not equal in degree, will take place when both manufacturers employ labour, and machinery or other capital, if the latter be of unequal durability.' (See *British Review*, Nov. 1817, Art. xv, 'Political Economy and Taxation'; cp. letter to Trower, below, VII, 219.)

The new paragraph reads: 'The same result will take place if the circulating capitals be of unequal durability. If from the nature of two different trades, in which equal capitals are employed, one manufacturer could not bring the commodity he produced to market in less than one year, while the other could bring his there in three months, the commodity of the first would fall in relative value to the second with every rise of wages and fall of profits. It must be unnecessary to go into further calculations to prove this to be true, as it rests precisely on the same principle as the case already considered, namely, the different degree of durability of two equal capitals.' This was intended to meet an objection raised by Torrens; see letter to McCulloch, below, VII, 338. Cp. similar changes above, p. 31, n. 2, p. 53, n. 1 and p. 58, n. 1 (heading of Section iv) and n. 2.

at an expense of 4250*l.* per annum, and that the 750*l.*, which the
sale of the machine would produce over and above the wages advanced to the men, constituted the profits of the engineer's stock.
When wages rose 10 per cent., he would be obliged to employ an
additional capital of 425*l.*, and would therefore employ 4675*l.*, instead
of 4250*l.*, on which capital he would only get a profit of 325*l.* if
he continued to sell his machine for 5000*l.*; but this is precisely the
case of all manufacturers and capitalists; the rise of wages affects
them all. If therefore the maker of the machine should raise the
price of his machine in consequence of a rise of wages, an unusual
quantity of capital would be employed in the construction of such
machines, till their price afforded only the usual profits. The manufacturer of hats, by the employment of the machine, if he sells his
hats for 8000*l.*, is precisely in the same situation as before; he employs no more capital, and obtains the same profits. The competition
of trade would not long allow this; for as capital would flow to
the most profitable employment, he would be obliged to lower the
price of hats, till his profits had sunk to the general level. Thus
then is the public benefited by machinery: these mute agents are
always the produce of much less labour than that which they displace, even when they are of the same money value. Through their
influence, an increase in the price of provisions which raises wages,
will affect fewer persons: it will reach, as in the above instance,
eighty-five men instead of a hundred; and the saving which is the
consequence, shews itself in the reduced price of the commodity
manufactured. Neither machines nor any other commodities are
raised in price, but all commodities which are made by machines
fall, and fall in proportion to their durability.[1]

It appears, then, that in proportion to the quantity and the

[1] Ed. 2 adds here a paragraph
embodying one which in ed. 1 appears on p. 66 (see *ib.* note 3). The
new paragraph reads: 'It will be
seen, then, that in the early stages of
society, before much machinery or
durable fixed capital is used, the commodities produced by equal capitals
will be nearly of equal value, and will
rise or fall relatively to each other
only on account of more or less labour
being required for their production;
but after the introduction of these
expensive instruments, the commodities produced by the employment of equal capitals will be of very
unequal value; and although they
will still be liable to rise or fall
relatively to each other, as more or
less labour becomes necessary to their
production, they will be subject to
variation also from the rise or fall
of wages and profits. Since goods
which sell for 2,000*l.* may be the
produce of a capital equal in amount
to that from which are produced
other goods which sell for 10,000*l.*
the profits on their manufacture will
be the same; but those profits would
be unequal, if the prices of the goods
did not vary with a rise or fall in the
rate of profits.'

durability of the fixed capital[1] employed in any kind of production, the relative prices of those commodities on which such[2] capital is employed, will vary inversely as wages; they will fall as wages rise[3]. It appears too that no commodities whatever are raised in absolute price, merely because wages rise; that they never rise unless additional labour be bestowed on them; but that all commodities in the production of which fixed capital enters, not only do not rise with a rise of wages, but absolutely fall; fall too as much as 68 per cent., with a rise of seven per cent. in wages, if fixed capital be exclusively employed, and be of the duration of 100 years.

The above[4] statement, which asserts the compatibility of a rise of wages, with a fall of prices, has, I know, the disadvantage of novelty, and must trust to its own merits for advocates; whilst it has for its opponents, writers of distinguished and deserved reputation.[5] It should however be carefully remembered, that in this whole argument I am supposing money to be of an invariable value; in other words, to be always the produce of the same quantity of unassisted labour. Money, however, is a variable commodity; and the rise of wages as well as of commodities, is frequently occasioned by a fall in the value of money. A rise of wages from this cause will indeed be invariably accompanied by a rise in the price of commodities: but in such cases, it will be found that labour and all commodities have not varied in regard to each other, and that the variation has been confined to money.

Money, from its being a commodity obtained from a foreign country, from its being the general medium of exchange between all civilized countries, and from its being also distributed among those countries in proportions which are ever changing with every improvement in commerce and machinery, and with every increasing difficulty of obtaining food and necessaries for an increasing population, is subject to incessant variations. In stating the principles which regulate exchangeable value and price, we should carefully

---

[1] Ed. 2 'It appears, too, that in proportion to the durability of capital'.
[2] Ed. 2 adds 'durable'.
[3] The remainder of the paragraph in ed. 2 reads ', and rise as wages fall; and that no commodities whatever are raised in exchangeable value merely because wages rise; they are only so raised when more labour is bestowed on their production, *when wages fall*, or when the medium in which they are estimated falls in value.'

After this, ed. 2 opens 'SECTION V' under the heading: *Different effects from the alteration in the value of money, the medium in which* PRICE *is always expressed, or from the alteration in the value of the commodities which money purchases.*'
[4] Ed. 2 'The foregoing'.
[5] Cp. above, p. 46.

distinguish between those variations which belong to the commodity itself, and those which are occasioned by a variation in the medium in which value is estimated, or price expressed.

A rise in wages, from an alteration in the value of money, produces a general effect on price, and for that reason it produces no real effect whatever on profits. On the contrary, a rise of wages, from the circumstance of the labourer being more liberally rewarded, or from a difficulty of procuring the necessaries on which wages are expended, does not produce the effect of raising price, but has a great effect in lowering profits. In the one case, no greater proportion of the annual labour of the country is devoted to the support of the labourers, in the other case, a larger portion is so devoted.

It is according to the division of the whole produce of the land and labour of the country, between the three classes of landlords, capitalists, and labourers, that we are to judge of[1] rent, profit, and wages, and not according to the value at which that produce may be estimated in a medium which is confessedly variable.

It is not by the absolute quantity of produce obtained by either class, that we can correctly judge of the rate of profit, rent, and wages, but by the quantity of labour required to obtain that produce. By improvements in machinery and agriculture, the whole produce may be doubled; but if wages, rent, and profit, be also doubled, these three will bear the same proportions to one another, and neither could be said to have relatively varied. But if wages partook not of the whole of this increase; if they, instead of being doubled, were only increased one half, if rent, instead of being doubled, were only increased three-fourths, and the remaining increase went to profit, it would, I apprehend, be correct for me to say, that rent and wages had fallen, while profits had risen; for if we had an invariable standard, by which to measure the value of this produce, we should find that a less value had fallen to the class of labourers and landlords, and a greater to the class of capitalists, than had been given before. We might find for example, that though the absolute quantity of commodities had been doubled, they were the produce of precisely the former quantity of labour. Of every hundred hats, coats and quarters of corn produced, if the labourers had[2]   25

The landlords   25

And the capitalists 50
───
100

───

[1] Ed. 2 adds 'the rise or fall of'.   [2] Ed. 2 adds 'before'.

And if, after these commodities were doubled in quantity, of every 100

The labourers had only	.	.	.	.	22
The landlords	.	.	.	.	22
And the capitalists	.	.	.	.	56
					100[1]

In that case I should say, that wages and rent had fallen, and profits risen; though in consequence of the abundance of commodities, the quantity paid to the labourer and landlord would have increased in the proportion of 25 to 44. Wages are to be estimated by their real value, viz. by the quantity of labour and capital employed in producing them, and not by their nominal value either in coats, hats, money, or corn. Under the circumstances I have just supposed, commodities would have fallen to half their former value; and, if money had not varied, to half their former price also. If then in this medium, which had not varied in value, the wages of the labourer should be found to have fallen, it will not the less be a real fall, because they might furnish him with a greater quantity of cheap commodities, than his former wages.

The variation in the value of money, however great, makes no difference in the *rate* of profits; for suppose the goods of the manufacturer to rise from 1000*l.* to 2000*l.*, or 100 per cent., if his capital, on which the variations of money have as much effect as on the value of produce, if his machinery, buildings, and stock in trade[2] rise more than 100 per cent., his rate of profits has fallen, and he has a proportionably less quantity of the produce of the labour of the country at his command.

If, with capital of a given value, he double the quantity of produce, its value falls one half, and then it will bear the same proportion to the capital which produced it, as it did before.[3]

If at the same time that he doubles the quantity of produce by

---

[1] There is a full stop here in ed. 1, which seems uncalled for.

[2] Ed. 2 from here reads 'rise also 100 per cent., his rate of profits will be the same, and he will have the same quantity and no more of the produce of the labour of the country at his command.'

[3] In ed. 2 this paragraph reads 'If with a capital of a given value, he can by economy in labour double the quantity of produce, and it fall to half its former price, it will bear the same proportion to the capital that produced it which it did before, and consequently profits will still be at the same rate.'

the employment of the same capital, the value of money is by any accident lowered one half, the produce will sell for twice the money value that it did before; but the capital employed to produce it, will also be of twice its former money value; and therefore in this case too, the value of the produce will bear the same proportion to the value of the capital as it did before; and although the produce be doubled, rent, wages, and profits will only vary as the proportions vary, in which this double produce may be divided among the three classes that share it.[1]

It appears then that the accumulation of capital, by occasioning different proportions of fixed and circulating capital to be employed in different trades, and by giving different degrees of durability to such fixed capital, introduces a considerable modification to the rule, which is of universal application in the early states of society.[2]

Commodities, though they continue to rise and fall, in proportion as more or less labour is necessary to their production, are also affected in their relative value by a rise or fall of profits, since equal profits may be derived from goods which sell for 2,000*l.* and from those which sell for 10,000*l.*; and consequently the variations of those profits, independently of any increased or diminished quantity of labour required for the goods in question, must affect their prices in different proportions.[3]

It appears too, that commodities may be lowered in value in consequence of a real rise of wages, but they never can be raised from that cause. On the other hand, they may rise from a fall of wages, as they then lose the peculiar advantages of production, which high wages afforded them.[4]

[1] Ed. 2 concludes the chapter here.
[2] In ed. 2 this paragraph is incorporated above, p. 58 (see *ib.* n. 1).
[3] In ed. 2 this paragraph is incorporated above, p. 62 (see *ib.* n. 1).

[4] Ed. 2 omits this paragraph. See however, for a similar passage carried over into ed. 2, above, p. 63, first paragraph and n. 3.

CHAPTER II

ON RENT

It remains[1] however to be considered, whether the appropriation of land, and the consequent creation of rent, will occasion any variation in the relative value of commodities, independently of the quantity of labour necessary to production. In order to understand this part of the subject, we must enquire into the nature of rent, and the laws by which its rise or fall is regulated.[2]

Rent is that portion of the produce of the earth, which is paid to the landlord for the use of the original and indestructible powers of the soil. It is often, however, confounded with the interest and profit of capital, and, in popular language, the term is applied to whatever is annually paid by a farmer to his landlord. If, of two adjoining farms of the same extent, and of the same natural fertility, one had all the conveniences of farming buildings, and, besides, were[3] properly drained and manured, and advantageously divided by hedges, fences and walls, while the other had none of these advantages, more remuneration would naturally be paid for the use of one, than for the use of the other; yet in both cases this remuneration would be called rent. But it is evident, that a portion only of the money annually to be paid for the improved farm, would be given for the original and indestructible powers of the soil; the other portion would be paid for the use of the capital which had been employed in ameliorating the quality of the land, and in erecting such buildings as were necessary to secure and preserve the produce. Adam Smith sometimes speaks of rent, in the strict sense to which I am desirous of confining it, but more often

[1] Cp. above, p. 22–3, end of n. 3.
[2] In ed. 1 this and the next paragraph are not separated.
[3] Eds. 1-2 'buildings, were, besides,'.

in the popular sense, in which the term is usually employed. He tells us, that the demand for timber, and its consequent high price, in the more southern countries of Europe, caused a rent to be paid for forests in Norway, which could before afford no rent.[1] Is it not, however, evident, that the person who paid what he thus calls rent, paid it in consideration of the valuable commodity which was then standing on the land, and that he actually repaid himself with a profit, by the sale of the timber? If, indeed, after the timber was removed, any compensation were paid to the landlord for the use of the land, for the purpose of growing timber or any other produce, with a view to future demand, such compensation might justly be called rent, because it would be paid for the productive powers of the land; but in the case stated by Adam Smith, the compensation was paid for the liberty of removing and selling the timber, and not for the liberty of growing it. He speaks also of the rent of coal mines, and of stone quarries,[2] to which the same observation applies—that the compensation given for the mine or quarry, is paid for the value of the coal or stone which can be removed from them, and has no connection with the original and indestructible powers of the land. This is a distinction of great importance, in an enquiry concerning rent and profits; for it is found, that the laws which regulate the progress of rent, are widely different from those which regulate the progress of profits, and seldom operate in the same direction. In all improved countries, that which is annually paid to the landlord, partaking of both characters, rent and profit, is sometimes kept stationary by the effects of opposing causes; at other times advances or recedes, as one or the[3] other of these causes preponderates. In the future pages of this work, then, whenever I speak of the rent of land, I wish to be understood as speaking

---

[1] Bk. I, ch. xi, pt. ii; vol. I, p. 164.   [3] Eds. 1-2 do not contain 'the'.
[2] ib. vol. I, pp. 163, 167.

of that compensation, which is paid to the owner of land for the use of its original and indestructible powers.[1]

On the first settling of a country, in which there is an abundance of rich and fertile land, a very small proportion of which is required to be cultivated for the support of the actual population, or indeed can be cultivated with the capital which the population can command, there will be no rent; for no one would pay for the use of land, when there was an abundant quantity not yet appropriated, and, therefore, at the disposal of whosoever might choose to cultivate it.

On the common principles of supply and demand, no rent could be paid for such land, for the reason stated why nothing is given for the use of air and water, or for any other of the gifts of nature which exist in boundless quantity. With a given quantity of materials, and with the assistance of the pressure of the atmosphere, and the elasticity of steam, engines may perform work, and abridge human labour to a very great extent; but no charge is made for the use of these natural aids, because they are inexhaustible, and at every man's disposal. In the same manner the brewer, the distiller, the dyer, make incessant use of the air and water for the production of their commodities; but as the supply is boundless, they bear[2] no price.*

* "The earth, as we have already seen, is not the only agent of nature which has a productive power; but it is the only one, or nearly so, that one set of men take to themselves, to the exclusion of others; and of which, consequently, they can appropriate the benefits. The waters of rivers, and of the sea, by the power which they have of giving movement to our machines, carrying our boats, nourishing our fish, have also a productive power; the wind which turns our mills, and even the heat of the sun, work for us; but happily no one has yet been able to say, the 'wind and the sun are mine, and the service which they render must be paid for.'"—*Economie Politique, par J. B. Say*, vol. ii. p. 124.

[1] Cp. the 'original and inherent power of the land' in *Essay on Profits*, below, IV, 18, n. The definition of rent is extended below, p. 261, n., to include the remuneration paid to the landlord for the use of all 'indestructible powers' of land, whether original or not.

[2] Ed. 1 'it bears'.

If all land had the same properties, if it were unlimited in quantity[1], and uniform in quality, no charge could be made for its use, unless where it possessed peculiar advantages of situation. It is only, then, because land is not unlimited in quantity and uniform in quality,[2] and because in the progress of population, land of an inferior quality, or less advantageously situated, is called into cultivation, that rent is ever paid for the use of it. When in the progress of society, land of the second degree of fertility is taken into cultivation, rent immediately commences on that of the first quality, and the amount of that rent will depend on the difference in the quality of these two portions of land.

When land of the third quality is taken into cultivation, rent immediately commences on the second, and it is regulated as before, by the difference in their productive powers. At the same time, the rent of the first quality will rise, for that must always be above the rent of the second, by the difference between the produce which they yield with a given quantity of capital and labour. With every step in the progress of population, which shall oblige a country to have recourse to land of a worse quality, to enable it to raise its supply of food, rent, on all the more fertile land, will rise.

Thus suppose land—No. 1, 2, 3,—to yield, with an equal employment of capital and labour, a net produce of 100, 90, and 80 quarters of corn. In a new country, where there is an abundance of fertile land compared with the population, and where therefore it is only necessary to cultivate No. 1, the whole net produce will belong to the cultivator, and will be the profits of the stock which he advances. As soon as population had so far increased as to make it necessary to cultivate

---

[1] Eds. 1-2 'boundless in quantity'.
[2] Ed. 1 'It is only then because land is of different qualities with respect to its productive powers'.

Ed. 2 is uniform with ed. 3, except that it has 'boundless' in place of 'unlimited'.

No. 2, from which ninety quarters only can be obtained after supporting the labourers, rent would commence on No. 1; for either there must be two rates of profit on agricultural capital, or ten quarters, or the value of ten quarters must be withdrawn from the produce of No. 1, for some other purpose. Whether the proprietor of the land, or any other person, cultivated No. 1, these ten quarters would equally constitute rent; for the cultivator of No. 2 would get the same result with his capital, whether he cultivated No. 1, paying ten quarters for rent, or continued to cultivate No. 2, paying no rent. In the same manner it might be shown that when No. 3 is brought into cultivation, the rent of No. 2 must be ten quarters, or the value of ten quarters, whilst the rent of No. 1 would rise to twenty quarters; for the cultivator of No. 3 would have the same profits whether he paid twenty quarters for the rent of No. 1, ten quarters for the rent of No. 2, or cultivated No. 3 free of all rent.

It often, and, indeed, commonly happens, that before No. 2, 3, 4, or 5, or the inferior lands are cultivated, capital can be employed more productively on those lands which are already in cultivation. It may perhaps be found, that by doubling the original capital employed on No. 1, though the produce will not be doubled, will not be increased by 100 quarters, it may be increased by eighty-five quarters, and that this quantity exceeds what could be obtained by employing the same capital, on land No. 3.

In such case, capital will be preferably employed on the old land, and will equally create a rent; for rent is always the difference between the produce obtained by the employment of two equal quantities of capital and labour. If, with a capital of 1000*l.*, a tenant obtain 100 quarters of wheat from his land, and by the employment of a second capital of 1000*l.*, he obtain a further return of eighty-five, his landlord would have the power at the expiration of his lease, of obliging him to pay fifteen quarters, or an equivalent value, for additional rent; for there cannot be two rates of profit. If he is satisfied with a diminution of fifteen quarters in the return for his second 1000*l*., it is because no employment more profitable can be found for it. The common rate of profit would be in that proportion, and if the original tenant refused, some other person would be found willing to give all which exceeded that rate of profit to the owner of the land from which he derived it.

In this case, as well as in the other, the capital last employed pays no rent. For the greater productive powers of the first 1000*l*., fifteen quarters is paid for rent, for the employment of the second 1000*l*. no rent whatever is paid. If a third 1000*l*. be employed on the same land, with a return of seventy-five quarters, rent will then be paid for the second 1000*l*., and will be equal to the difference between the produce of these two, or ten quarters; and at the same time the rent of the first 1000*l*. will rise from fifteen to twenty-five quarters; while the last 1000*l*. will pay no rent whatever.

If, then, good land existed in a quantity much more abundant than the production of food for an increasing population required, or if capital could be indefinitely employed without a diminished return on the old land, there could be no rise of rent; for rent invariably proceeds from the employment of an additional quantity of labour with a proportionally less return.

The most fertile, and most favorably situated, land will be first cultivated, and the exchangeable value of its produce will be adjusted in the same manner as the exchangeable value of all other commodities, by the total quantity of labour necessary in various forms, from first to last, to produce it, and bring it to market. When land of an inferior quality is taken into cultivation, the exchangeable value of raw produce will rise, because more labour is required to produce it.

The exchangeable value of all commodities, whether they be manufactured, or the produce of the mines, or the produce of land, is always regulated, not by the less quantity of labour that will suffice for their production under circumstances highly favorable, and exclusively enjoyed by those who have peculiar facilities of production; but by the greater quantity of labour necessarily bestowed on their production by those who have no such facilities; by those who continue to produce them under the most unfavorable circumstances; meaning—by the most unfavorable circumstances, the most unfavorable under which the quantity of produce required, renders it necessary to carry on the production.

Thus, in a charitable institution, where the poor are set to work with the funds of benefactors, the general prices of the commodities, which are the produce of such work, will not be governed by the peculiar facilities afforded to these work-men, but by the common, usual, and natural difficulties, which every other manufacturer will have to encounter. The manu-facturer enjoying none of these facilities might indeed be driven altogether from the market, if the supply afforded by these favored workmen were equal to all the wants of the com-munity; but if he continued the trade, it would be only on condition that he should derive from it the usual and general rate of profits on stock; and that could only happen when his commodity sold for a price proportioned to the quantity of labour bestowed on its production.*

---

* Has not M. Say forgotten, in the following passage, that it is the cost of production which ultimately regulates price? "The produce of labour employed on the land has this peculiar property, that it does not become more dear by becoming more scarce, because population always diminishes at the same time that food diminishes, and consequently the quantity of these products *demanded*, diminishes at the same time as the quantity sup-plied. Besides, it is not observed that corn is more dear in those places where there is plenty of uncultivated land, than in completely cultivated countries. England and France were much more imperfectly cultivated

It is true, that on the best land, the same produce would still be obtained with the same labour as before, but its value would be enhanced in consequence of the diminished returns obtained by those who employed fresh labour and stock on the less fertile land. Notwithstanding, then, that the advantages of fertile over inferior lands are in no case lost, but only transferred from the cultivator, or consumer, to the landlord, yet, since more labour is required on the inferior lands, and since it is from such land only that we are enabled to furnish ourselves with the additional supply of raw produce, the comparative value of that produce will continue permanently above its former level, and make it exchange for more hats, cloth, shoes, &c. &c. in the production of which no such additional quantity of labour is required.

The reason then, why raw produce rises in comparative value, is because more labour is employed in the production of the last portion obtained, and not because a rent is paid to the landlord. The value of corn is regulated by the quantity of labour bestowed on its production on that quality of land, or with that portion of capital, which pays no rent. Corn is not high because a rent is paid, but a rent is paid because corn is high; and it has been justly observed, [1] that no reduction

in the middle ages than they are now; they produced much less raw produce: nevertheless from all that we can judge by a comparison with the value of other things, corn was not sold at a dearer price. If the produce was less, so was the population; the weakness of the demand compensated the feebleness of the supply." Vol. ii. 338. M. Say being impressed with the opinion that the price of commodities is regulated by the price of labour, and justly supposing that charitable institutions of all sorts tend to increase the population beyond what it otherwise would be, and therefore to lower wages, says, "I suspect that the cheapness of the goods, which come from England, is partly caused by the numerous charitable institutions which exist in that country." vol. ii. 277. This is a consistent opinion in one who maintains that wages regulate price.

[1] See Malthus's *Inquiry into the Nature and Progress of Rent*, 1815, p. 57.

would take place in the price of corn, although landlords should forego the whole of their rent. Such a measure would only enable some farmers to live like gentlemen, but would not diminish the quantity of labour necessary to raise raw produce on the least productive land in cultivation.

Nothing is more common than to hear of the advantages which the land possesses over every other source of useful produce, on account of the surplus which it yields in the form of rent. Yet when land is most abundant, when most productive, and most fertile, it yields no rent; and it is only when its powers decay, and less is yielded in return for labour, that a share of the original produce of the more fertile portions is set apart for rent. It is singular that this quality in the land, which should have been noticed as an imperfection, compared with the natural agents by which manufacturers are assisted, should have been pointed out as constituting its peculiar pre-eminence. If air, water, the elasticity of steam, and the pressure of the atmosphere, were of various qualities; if they could be appropriated, and each quality existed only in moderate abundance, they, as well as the land, would afford a rent, as the successive qualities were brought into use. With every worse quality employed, the value of the commodities in the manufacture of which they were used, would rise, because equal quantities of labour would be less productive. Man would do more by the sweat of his brow, and nature perform less; and the land would be no longer pre-eminent for its limited powers.

If the surplus produce which land affords in the form of rent be an advantage, it is desirable that, every year, the machinery newly constructed should be less efficient than the old, as that would undoubtedly give a greater exchangeable value to the goods manufactured, not only by that machinery but by all the other machinery in the kingdom; and a rent would be paid to all those who possessed the most productive machinery.*

* "In agriculture too," says Adam Smith, "nature labours along with man; and though her labour costs no expense, its produce has its value, as well as that of the most expensive workman." The labour of nature is paid, not because she does much, but because she does little. In proportion as she becomes niggardly in her gifts, she exacts a greater price for her work. Where she is munificently beneficent, she always works gratis. "The[1] labouring cattle employed in agriculture, not only occasion, like the workmen in manufactures, the reproduction of a value equal to their own consumption, or to the capital which employs them, together with its owner's profits, but of a much greater value. Over and above the capital of the farmer and all its profits, they regularly occasion the reproduction of the rent of the landlord. This rent may be considered as the produce of those powers of nature, the use of which the landlord lends to the farmer. It is greater or smaller according to the supposed extent of those powers, or in other words, according to the supposed natural or improved fertility of the land. It is the work of nature which remains, after deducting or compensating every thing which can be regarded as the work of man. It is seldom less than a fourth, and frequently more than a third of the whole produce. No equal quantity of productive labour employed in manufactures, can ever occasion so great a reproduction. *In them nature does nothing, man does all;* and the reproduction must always be in proportion to the strength of the agents that occasion it. The capital employed in agriculture, therefore, not only puts into motion a greater quantity of productive labour than any equal capital employed in manufactures, but in proportion too, to the quantity of the productive labour which it employs, it adds a much greater value to the annual produce of the land and labour of the country, to the *real* wealth and revenue of its inhabitants. Of all the ways in which a capital can be employed, it is by far the most advantageous to the society."—Book II. chap. v. p. 15.[2]

Does nature nothing for man in manufactures? Are the powers of wind and water, which move our machinery, and assist navigation, nothing? The pressure of the atmosphere and the elasticity of steam, which enable us to work the most stupendous engines—are they not the gifts of nature? to say nothing of the effects of the matter of heat in softening and melting metals, of the decomposition of the atmosphere in the process of dyeing[3] and fermentation. There is not a manufacture which can be mentioned, in which nature does not give her assistance to man, and give it too, generously and gratuitously.

In remarking on the passage which I have copied from Adam Smith,

[1] Adam Smith actually says 'The labourers and'. There are other minor inaccuracies in the quotation.

[2] Cannan's ed., vol. I, pp. 343–4. The italics are Ricardo's.

[3] Ed. 3 misprints 'dying'.

The rise of rent is always the effect of the increasing wealth of the country, and of the difficulty of providing food for its augmented population. It is a symptom, but it is never a cause of wealth; for wealth often increases most rapidly while rent is either stationary, or even falling. Rent increases most rapidly, as the disposable land decreases in its productive powers. Wealth increases most rapidly in those countries where the disposable land is most fertile, where importation is least restricted, and where through agricultural improvements, productions can be multiplied without any increase in the proportional quantity of labour, and where consequently the progress of rent is slow.

If the high price of corn were the effect, and not the cause of rent, price would be proportionally influenced as rents were high or low, and rent would be a component part of price. But that corn which is produced by the greatest quantity of labour is the regulator of the price of corn; and rent does not and cannot enter in the least degree as a component part of its price.* Adam Smith, therefore, cannot be correct in supposing that the original rule which regulated the exchangeable

Mr. Buchanan observes, "I have endeavoured to show, in the observations on productive and unproductive labour, contained in the fourth volume, that agriculture adds no more to the national stock than any other sort of industry. In dwelling on the reproduction of rent as so great an advantage to society, Dr. Smith does not reflect that rent is the effect of high price, and that what the landlord gains in this way, he gains at the expense of the community at large. There is no absolute gain to the society by the reproduction of rent; it is only one class profiting at the expense of another class. The notion[1] of agriculture yielding a produce, and a rent in consequence, because nature concurs with human industry in the process of cultivation, is a mere fancy. It is not from the produce, but from the price at which the produce is sold, that the rent is derived; and this price is got not because nature assists in the production, but because it is the price which suits the consumption to the supply."[2]

* The clearly understanding this principle is, I am persuaded, of the utmost importance to the science of political economy.[3]

[1] Misprinted 'motion' in all eds. of Ricardo.

[2] Buchanan's ed. of the *Wealth of Nations*, vol. II, p. 55, note.

[3] Ed. 1 does not contain this note.

value of commodities, namely, the comparative quantity of labour by which they were produced, can be at all altered by the appropriation of land and the payment of rent.[1] Raw material enters into the composition of most commodities, but the value of that raw material, as well as corn, is regulated by the productiveness of the portion of capital last employed on the land, and paying no rent; and therefore rent is not a component part of the price of commodities.

We have been hitherto considering the effects of the natural progress of wealth and population on rent, in a country in which the land is of variously productive powers; and we have seen, that with every portion of additional capital which it becomes necessary to employ on the land with a less productive return, rent would rise. It follows from the same principles, that any circumstances in the society which should make it unnecessary to employ the same amount of capital on the land, and which should therefore make the portion last employed more productive, would lower rent. Any great reduction in the capital of a country, which should materially diminish the funds destined for the maintenance of labour, would naturally have this effect. Population regulates itself by the funds which are to employ it, and therefore always increases or diminishes with the increase or diminution of capital. Every reduction of capital is therefore necessarily followed by a less effective demand for corn, by a fall of price, and by diminished cultivation. In the reverse order to that in which the accumulation of capital raises rent, will the diminution of it lower rent. Land of a less[2] unproductive quality will be in succession relinquished, the

---

[1] For Adam Smith's 'supposition' (not previously referred to in ed. 3), see p. 22–3, n. 3.

[2] Should probably read 'a less and less', as the sense requires. This may indeed have been the reading in the copy sent to the printer, as an abnormally wide spacing of the next line in ed. 1 indicates that some letters were removed after the type had been set.

exchangeable value of produce will fall, and land of a superior quality will be the land last cultivated, and that which will then pay no rent.

The same effects may however be produced, when the wealth and population of a country are increased, if that increase is accompanied by such marked improvements in agriculture, as shall have the same effect of diminishing the necessity of cultivating the poorer lands, or of expending the same amount of capital on the cultivation of the more fertile portions.

If a million of quarters of corn be necessary for the support of a given population, and it be raised on land of the qualities of No. 1, 2, 3; and if an improvement be afterwards discovered by which it can be raised on No. 1 and 2, without employing No. 3, it is evident that the immediate effect must be a fall of rent; for No. 2, instead of No. 3, will then be cultivated without paying any rent; and the rent of No. 1, instead of being the difference between the produce of No. 3 and No. 1, will be the difference only between No. 2 and 1. With the same population, and no more, there can be no demand for any additional quantity of corn; the capital and labour employed on No. 3 will be devoted to the production of other commodities desirable to the community, and can have no effect in raising rent, unless the raw material from which they are made cannot be obtained without employing capital less advantageously on the land, in which case No. 3 must again be cultivated.

It is undoubtedly true, that the fall in the relative price of raw produce, in consequence of the improvement in agriculture, or rather in consequence of less labour being bestowed on its production, would naturally lead to increased accumulation; for the profits of stock would be greatly augmented. This accumulation would lead to an increased demand for labour, to higher wages, to an increased population, to a further demand for raw produce, and to an increased cultivation. It is only, however, after the increase in the population, that rent would be as high as before; that is to say, after No. 3 was taken into cultivation. A considerable period would have elapsed, attended with a positive diminution of rent.

But improvements in agriculture are of two kinds: those which increase the productive powers of the land, and those which enable us, by improving our machinery,[1] to obtain its produce with less labour. They both lead to a fall in the price of raw produce; they both affect rent, but they do not affect[2] it equally. If they did not occasion a fall in the price of raw produce, they would not be improvements; for it is the essential quality of an improvement to diminish the quantity of labour before required to produce a commodity; and this diminution cannot take place without a fall of its price or relative value.

The improvements which increase[3] the productive powers of the land, are such as the more skilful rotation of crops, or the better choice of manure. These improvements absolutely enable us to obtain the same produce from a smaller quantity of land. If, by the introduction of a course of turnips, I can feed my sheep besides raising my corn, the land on which the sheep were before fed becomes unnecessary, and the same quantity of raw produce is raised by the employment of a less quantity of land. If I discover a manure which will enable me to make a piece of land produce 20 per cent. more corn, I may withdraw at least a portion of my capital from the most unproductive part of my farm. But, as I[4] before observed, it is not necessary that land should be thrown out of cultivation, in order to reduce rent: to produce this effect, it is sufficient that successive portions of capital are employed on the same land with different results, and that the portion which gives the least result should be withdrawn. If, by the introduction of the

---

[1] Ed. 1 does not contain ', by improving our machinery,'.
[2] Misprinted 'effect' in ed. 3.

[3] Misprinted 'increased' in eds. 2-3.
[4] Ed. 1 'as I have'.

turnip husbandry, or by the use of a more invigorating manure, I can obtain the same produce with less capital, and without disturbing the difference between the productive powers of the successive portions of capital, I shall lower rent; for a different and more productive portion will be that which will form the standard from which every other will be reckoned. If, for example, the successive portions of capital yielded 100, 90, 80, 70; whilst I employed these four portions, my rent would be 60, or the difference between

$$
\left.\begin{array}{l}
70 \text{ and } 100 = 30 \\
70 \text{ and } 90 = 20 \\
70 \text{ and } 80 = 10 \\
\overline{} \\
60
\end{array}\right\} \text{whilst the produce would be 340} \quad \left\{\begin{array}{l}
100 \\
90 \\
80 \\
70 \\
\overline{340}
\end{array}\right.
$$

and while I employed these portions, the rent would remain the same, although the produce of each should have an equal augmentation. If, instead of 100, 90, 80, 70, the produce should be increased to 125, 115, 105, 95, the rent would still be 60, or the difference between

$$
\left.\begin{array}{l}
95 \text{ and } 125 = 30 \\
95 \text{ and } 115 = 20 \\
95 \text{ and } 105 = 10 \\
\overline{} \\
60
\end{array}\right\} \text{whilst the produce would be increased to 440} \quad \left\{\begin{array}{l}
125 \\
115 \\
105 \\
95 \\
\overline{440}
\end{array}\right.
$$

But with such an increase of produce, without an increase of demand,* there could be no motive for employing so much

---

* I hope I am not understood as undervaluing the importance of all sorts of improvements in agriculture to landlords—their immediate effect is to lower rent; but as they give a great stimulus to population, and at the same time enable us to cultivate poorer lands, with less labour, they are ultimately of immense advantage to landlords. A period however must elapse, during which they are positively injurious to him.[1]

[1] Eds. 1-2 do not contain this note; it was added, with other similar passages elsewhere, as a reply to Malthus's criticisms (below, II, 118), but Ricardo had already stated in the *Essay on Profits* (below, IV, 19), that the fall of rent would be temporary; cp. also, for ed. 1, above, pp. 79–80 and for ed. 2, below, p. 412.

capital on the land; one portion would be withdrawn, and consequently the last portion of capital would yield 105 instead of 95, and rent would fall to 30, or the difference between

$$
\left.\begin{array}{l}
105 \text{ and } 125 = 20 \\
105 \text{ and } 115 = 10 \\
\overline{} \\
30
\end{array}\right\}
\begin{array}{l}
\text{whilst the produce will[1] be still} \\
\text{adequate to the wants of the} \\
\text{population, for it would be 345} \\
\text{quarters, or}
\end{array}
\left\{\begin{array}{l}
125 \\
115 \\
105 \\
\overline{} \\
345
\end{array}\right.
$$

the demand being only for 340 quarters.—But there are improvements which may lower the relative value of produce without lowering the corn rent, though they will lower the money rent of land. Such improvements do not increase the productive powers of the land; but they enable us to obtain its produce with less labour. They are rather directed to the formation of the capital applied to the land, than to the cultivation of the land itself. Improvements in agricultural implements, such as the plough and the thrashing machine, economy in the use of horses employed in husbandry, and a better knowledge of the veterinary art, are of this nature. Less capital, which is the same thing as less labour, will be employed on the land; but to obtain the same produce, less land cannot be cultivated. Whether improvements of this kind, however, affect corn rent, must depend on the question, whether the difference between the produce obtained by the employment of different portions of capital be increased, stationary, or diminished. If four portions of capital, 50, 60, 70, 80, be employed on the land, giving each the same results, and any improvement in the formation of such capital should enable me to withdraw 5 from each, so that they should be 45, 55, 65, and 75, no alteration would take place in the corn rent; but if the improvements were such as to enable me to make the whole saving on that portion of capital,[2] which is least productively employed,

[1] Ed. 1 'would'.

[2] Ed. 1 'on the largest portion of capital, that portion'.

corn rent would immediately fall, because the difference between the capital most productive, and the capital least productive, would be diminished; and it is this difference which
constitutes rent.

Without multiplying instances, I hope enough has been said
to show, that whatever diminishes the inequality in the produce
obtained from successive portions of capital employed on the
same or on new land, tends to lower rent; and that whatever
increases that inequality, necessarily produces an opposite effect,
and tends to raise it.

In speaking of the rent of the landlord, we have rather considered it as the proportion of the produce,[1] obtained with a
given capital on any given farm, without any reference to its
exchangeable value; but since the same cause, the difficulty of
production, raises the exchangeable value of raw produce, and
raises also the proportion of raw produce paid to the landlord
for rent, it is obvious that the landlord is doubly benefited by
difficulty of production. First he obtains a greater share, and
secondly the commodity in which he is paid is of greater value.*

* To make this obvious, and to show the degrees in which corn and
money rent will vary, let us suppose that the labour of ten men will,
on land of a certain quality, obtain 180 quarters of wheat, and its value
to be $4l.$ per quarter, or $720l.$; and that the labour of ten additional men
will, on the same or any other land, produce only 170 quarters in addition;
wheat would rise from $4l.$ to $4l.$ $4s.$ $8d.$ for $170 : 180 : : 4l. : 4l.$ $4s.$ $8d.$; or,
as in the production of 170 quarters, the labour of 10 men is necessary
in one case, and only of 9.44 in the other, the rise would be as 9.44 to
10, or as $4l.$ to $4l.$ $4s.$ $8d.$ If 10 men be further employed, and the return be

$$160, \text{ the price will rise to } £4 \quad 10 \quad 0$$
$$150, \quad . \quad . \quad . \quad . \quad . \quad . \quad 4 \quad 16 \quad 0$$
$$140, \quad . \quad . \quad . \quad . \quad . \quad . \quad 5 \quad 2 \quad 10$$

Now if no rent was paid for the land which yielded 180 quarters, when
corn was at $4l.$ per quarter, the value of 10 quarters would be paid as

[1] Eds. 1-2 read 'of the whole produce,' and do not contain 'obtained
with a given capital on any given
farm,'. On the question of rent as
a proportion (with which this correction and those on p. 49, n. 1
above and p. 402, n. 4 below are
concerned) see *Notes on Malthus*,
below, II, 196–8.

rent when only 170 could be procured, which, at 4*l.* 4*s.* 8*d.* would be 42*l.* 7*s.* 6*d.*

20 qrs. when 160 were produced, which at £4 10   0 would be £90   0   0

30 qrs. ...... 150 .... 4 16   0 144   0   0

40 qrs. ...... 140 5   2 10 .... 205 13   4

$$\text{Corn rent}^1 \text{ would increase in the proportion of } \begin{cases} 100 \\ 200 \\ 300 \\ 400 \end{cases} \text{ and money rent in the proportion of } \begin{cases} 100 \\ 212 \\ 340 \\ 485 \end{cases}$$

---

¹ Ed. 1 has here in addition 'then'.

CHAPTER III

ON THE RENT OF MINES

THE metals, like other things, are obtained by labour. Nature, indeed, produces them; but it is the labour of man which extracts them from the bowels of the earth, and prepares them for our service.

Mines, as well as land, generally pay a rent to their owner; and this rent, as well as the rent of land, is the effect, and never the cause of the high value of their produce.

If there were abundance of equally fertile mines, which any one might appropriate, they could yield no rent; the value of their produce would depend on the quantity of labour necessary to extract the metal from the mine and bring it to market.

But there are mines of various qualities, affording very different results, with equal quantities of labour. The metal produced from the poorest mine that is worked, must at least have an exchangeable value, not only sufficient to procure all the clothes, food, and other necessaries consumed by those employed in working it, and bringing the produce to market, but also to afford the common and ordinary profits to him who advances the stock necessary to carry on the undertaking. The return for capital from the poorest mine paying no rent, would regulate the rent of all the other more productive mines. This mine is supposed to yield the usual profits of stock. All that the other mines produce more than this, will necessarily be paid to the owners for rent. Since this principle is precisely the same as that which we have already laid down respecting land, it will not be necessary further to enlarge on it.

It will be sufficient to remark, that the same general rule which regulates the value of raw produce and manufactured commodities, is applicable also to the metals; their value depending not on the rate of profits, nor on the rate of wages, nor on the rent paid for mines, but on the total quantity of labour necessary to obtain the metal, and to bring it to market.

Like every other commodity, the value of the metals is subject to variation. Improvements may be made in the implements and machinery used in mining, which may considerably abridge labour; new and more productive mines may be discovered, in which, with the same labour, more metal may be obtained; or the facilities of bringing it to market may be increased. In either of these cases the metals would fall in value, and would therefore exchange for a less quantity of other things. On the other hand, from the increasing difficulty of obtaining the metal, occasioned by the greater depth at which the mine must be worked, and the accumulation of water, or any other contingency, its value compared with that of other things, might be considerably increased.

It has therefore been justly observed, that however honestly the coin of a country may conform to its standard, money made of gold and silver is still liable to fluctuations in value, not only to accidental and temporary, but to permanent and natural variations, in the same manner as other commodities.

By the discovery of America and the rich mines in which it abounds, a very great effect was produced on the natural price of the precious metals. This effect is by many supposed not yet to have terminated. It is probable, however, that all the effects on the value of the metals, resulting from the discovery of America, have long ceased; and if any fall has of late years taken place in their value, it is to be attributed to improvements in the mode of working the mines.

From whatever cause it may have proceeded, the effect has been so slow and gradual, that little practical inconvenience has been felt from gold and silver being the general medium in

which the value of all other things is estimated. Though undoubtedly a variable measure of value, there is probably no
commodity subject to fewer variations. This and the other
advantages which these metals possess, such as their hardness,
their malleability, their divisibility, and many more, have justly
secured the preference every where given to them, as a standard
for the money of civilized countries.

If equal quantities of labour, with equal quantities of fixed
capital, could at all times obtain, from that mine which paid
no rent, equal quantities of gold, gold would be as nearly an
invariable measure of value, as we could in the nature of things
possess.[1] The quantity indeed would enlarge with the demand,
but its value would be invariable, and it would be eminently
well calculated to measure the varying value of all other things.
I have already in a former part of this work considered gold as
endowed with this uniformity, and in the following chapter[2]
I shall continue the supposition. In speaking therefore of
varying price, the variation will be always considered as being
in the commodity, and never in the medium in which it is
estimated.

[1] In place of this sentence eds. 1-2
read: 'Having acknowledged the
imperfections to which money made
of gold and silver is liable as a
measure of value, from the greater
or less quantity of labour which
may, under varying circumstances,
be necessary for the production of
those metals, we may be permitted
to make the supposition that all
these imperfections were removed,
and that equal quantities of labour

could at all times obtain, from that
mine which paid no rent, equal
quantities of gold. Gold would
then be an invariable measure of
value.' (Cp. *Notes on Malthus*,
below, II, 83.)

[2] When this was written, 'the
following chapter' probably included what is now the chapter
'On Wages'. See Introduction,
section III.

CHAPTER IV

ON NATURAL AND MARKET PRICE

In making labour the foundation of the value of commodities, and the comparative quantity of labour which is necessary to their production, the rule which determines the respective quantities of goods which shall be given in exchange for each other, we must not be supposed to deny the accidental and temporary deviations of the actual or market price of commodities from this, their primary and natural price.

In the ordinary course of events, there is no commodity which continues for any length of time to be supplied precisely in that degree of abundance, which the wants and wishes of mankind require, and therefore there is none which is not subject to accidental and temporary variations of price.

It is only in consequence of such variations, that capital is apportioned precisely, in the requisite abundance and no more, to the production of the different commodities which happen to be in demand. With the rise or fall of price, profits are elevated above, or depressed below their general level, and capital is either encouraged to enter into, or is warned to depart from the particular employment in which the variation has taken place.

Whilst every man is free to employ his capital where he pleases, he will naturally seek for it that employment which is most advantageous; he will naturally be dissatisfied with a profit of 10 per cent., if by removing his capital he can obtain a profit of 15 per cent. This restless desire on the part of all the employers of stock, to quit a less profitable for a more advantageous business, has a strong tendency to equalize the rate of profits of all, or to fix them in such proportions, as may

in the estimation of the parties, compensate for any advantage
which one may have, or may appear to have over the other.
It is perhaps very difficult to trace the steps by which this change
is effected: it is probably effected, by a manufacturer not absolutely changing his employment, but only lessening the quantity
of capital he has in that employment. In all rich countries, there
is a number of men forming what is called the monied class;
these men are engaged in no trade, but live on the interest of
their money, which is employed in discounting bills, or in loans
to the more industrious part of the community. The bankers
too employ a large capital on the same objects. The capital so
employed forms a circulating capital of a large amount, and is
employed, in larger or smaller proportions, by all the different
trades of a country. There is perhaps no manufacturer, however rich, who limits his business to the extent that his own
funds alone will allow: he has always some portion of this
floating capital, increasing or diminishing according to the
activity of the demand for his commodities. When the demand
for silks increases, and that for cloth diminishes, the clothier
does not remove with his capital to the silk trade, but he dis-
misses some of his workmen, he discontinues his demand for
the loan from bankers and monied men; while the case of the
silk manufacturer is the reverse: he wishes to employ more
workmen, and thus his motive for borrowing is increased: he
borrows more, and thus capital is transferred from one employment to another, without the necessity of a manufacturer dis-
continuing his usual occupation. When we look to the markets
of a large town, and observe how regularly they are supplied
both with home and foreign commodities, in the quantity in
which they are required, under all the circumstances of varying
demand, arising from the caprice of taste, or a change in the
amount of population, without often producing either the
effects of a glut from a too abundant supply, or an enormously

high price from the supply being unequal to the demand, we must confess that the principle which apportions capital to each trade in the precise amount that it is required, is more active than is generally supposed.

A capitalist, in seeking profitable employment for his funds, will naturally take into consideration all the advantages which one occupation possesses over another. He may therefore be willing to forego a part of his money profit, in consideration of the security, cleanliness, ease, or any other real or fancied advantage which one employment may possess over another.

If from a consideration of these circumstances, the profits of stock should be so adjusted, that in one trade they were 20, in another 25, and in another 30 per cent., they would probably continue permanently with that relative difference, and with that difference only; for if any cause should elevate the profits of one of these trades 10 per cent. either these profits would be temporary, and would soon again fall back to their usual station, or the profits of the others would be elevated in the same proportion.

The present time appears to be one of the exceptions to the justness of this remark. The termination of the war has so deranged the division which before existed of employments in Europe, that every capitalist has not yet found his place in the new division which has now become necessary.[1]

Let us suppose that all commodities are at their natural price, and consequently that the profits of capital in all employments are exactly at the same rate, or differ only so much as, in the estimation of the parties, is equivalent to any real or fancied advantage which they possess or forego. Suppose now that a change of fashion should increase the demand for silks, and lessen that for woollens; their natural price, the quantity of labour necessary to their production, would continue un-

---

[1] Eds. 1-2 do not contain this paragraph.

altered, but the market price of silks would rise, and that of
woollens would fall; and consequently the profits of the silk
manufacturer would be above, whilst those of the woollen
manufacturer would be below, the general and adjusted rate
of profits. Not only the profits, but the wages of the workmen,
would be affected in these employments. This increased demand
for silks would however soon be supplied, by the transference
of capital and labour from the woollen to the silk manufacture;
when the market prices of silks and woollens would again
approach their natural prices, and then the usual profits would
be obtained by the respective manufacturers of those commodities.

It is then the desire, which every capitalist has, of diverting
his funds from a less to a more profitable employment, that
prevents the market price of commodities from continuing
for any length of time either much above, or much below
their natural price. It is this competition which so adjusts the
exchangeable[1] value of commodities, that after paying the
wages for the labour necessary to their production, and all other
expenses required to put the capital employed in its original
state of efficiency, the remaining value or overplus will in each
trade be in proportion to the value of the capital employed.

In the 7th chap. of the Wealth of Nations,[2] all that concerns
this question is most ably treated. Having fully acknowledged
the temporary effects which, in particular employments of
capital, may be produced on the prices of commodities, as well
as on the wages of labour, and the profits of stock, by accidental
causes, without influencing the general price of commodities,
wages, or profits, since these effects are equally operative in all
stages of society, we will[3] leave them entirely out of our con-

[1] Misprinted 'changeable' in ed. 3.   [3] Ed. 1 'we may be permitted to'.
[2] Bk. 1, ch. vii, 'Of the natural and
market Price of Commodities.'

sideration, whilst we are treating of the laws which regulate natural prices, natural wages and natural profits, effects totally independent of these accidental causes. In speaking then of the exchangeable value of commodities, or the power of purchasing possessed by any one commodity, I mean always that power which it would possess, if not disturbed by any temporary or accidental cause, and which is its natural price.

CHAPTER V

ON WAGES

LABOUR, like all other things which are purchased and sold, and which may be increased or diminished in quantity, has its natural and its market price. The natural price of labour is that price which is necessary to enable the labourers, one with another, to subsist and to perpetuate their race, without either increase or diminution.

The power of the labourer to support himself, and the family which may be necessary to keep up the number of labourers, does not depend on the quantity of money which he may receive for wages, but on the quantity of food, necessaries, and conveniences become essential to him from habit, which that money will purchase. The natural price of labour, therefore, depends on the price of the food, necessaries, and conveniences required for the support of the labourer and his family. With a rise in the price of food and necessaries, the natural price of labour will rise; with the fall in their price, the natural price of labour will fall.[1]

With the progress of society the natural price of labour has always a tendency to rise, because one of the principal commodities by which its natural price is regulated, has a tendency to become dearer, from the greater difficulty of producing it. As, however, the improvements in agriculture, the discovery of new markets, whence provisions may be imported, may for a time counteract the tendency to a rise in the price of necessaries, and may even occasion their natural price to fall, so will the same causes produce the correspondent effects on the natural price of labour.

The natural price of all commodities, excepting raw produce

[1] These opening passages appear to be derived from Torrens's *Essay* *on the External Corn Trade*, 1815, p. 62; cp. below, p. 96-7, n.

and labour, has a tendency to fall, in the progress of wealth and population; for though, on one hand, they are enhanced in real value, from the rise in the natural price of the raw material of which they are made, this is more than counterbalanced by the improvements in machinery, by the better division and distribution of labour, and by the increasing skill, both in science and art, of the producers.

The market price of labour is the price which is really paid for it, from the natural operation of the proportion of the supply to the demand; labour is dear when it is scarce, and cheap when it is plentiful. However much the market price of labour may deviate from its natural price, it has, like commodities, a tendency to conform to it.

It is when the market price of labour exceeds its natural price, that the condition of the labourer is flourishing and happy, that he has it in his power to command a greater proportion of the necessaries and enjoyments of life, and therefore to rear a healthy and numerous family. When, however, by the encouragement which high wages give to the increase of population, the number of labourers is increased, wages again fall to their natural price, and indeed from a re-action sometimes fall below it.

When the market price of labour is below its natural price, the condition of the labourers is most wretched: then poverty deprives them of those comforts which custom renders absolute necessaries. It is only after their privations have reduced their number, or the demand for labour has increased, that the market price of labour will rise to its natural price, and that the labourer will have the moderate comforts which the natural rate of wages[1] will afford.

Notwithstanding the tendency of wages to conform to their natural rate, their market rate may, in an improving society,

[1] Eds. 1-2 'natural price of wages'.

for an indefinite period, be constantly above it; for no sooner
may the impulse, which an increased capital gives to a new
demand for labour be obeyed, than another increase of capital
may produce the same effect; and thus, if the increase of capital
be gradual and constant, the demand for labour may give a
continued stimulus to an increase of people.

Capital is that part of the wealth of a country which is
employed in production, and consists of food, clothing, tools,
raw materials[1], machinery, &c. necessary to give effect to labour.

Capital may increase in quantity at the same time that its
value rises. An addition may be made to the food and clothing
of a country, at the same time that more labour may be required to produce the additional quantity than before; in that
case not only the quantity, but the value of capital will rise.

Or capital may increase without its value increasing, and
even while its value is actually diminishing; not only may an
addition be made to the food and clothing of a country, but
the addition may be made by the aid of machinery, without any
increase, and even with an absolute diminution in the proportional quantity of labour required to produce them. The
quantity of capital may increase, while neither the whole
together, nor any part of it singly, will have a greater value than
before, but may actually have a less[2].

In the first case, the natural price of labour[3], which always
depends on the price of food, clothing, and other necessaries,
will rise; in the second, it will remain stationary, or fall; but
in both cases the market rate of wages will rise, for in proportion to the increase of capital will be the increase in the demand
for labour; in proportion to the work to be done will be the
demand for those who are to do it.

---

[1] Ed. 1 'raw material'.   [3] Ed. 1 'natural price of wages'.
[2] Ed. 1 does not contain ', but may
actually have a less'.

In both cases too the market price of labour will rise above its natural price; and in both cases it will have a tendency to conform to its natural price, but in the first case this agreement will be most speedily effected. The situation of the labourer will be improved, but not much improved; for the increased price of food and necessaries will absorb a large portion of his increased wages; consequently a small supply of labour, or a trifling increase in the population, will soon reduce the market price to the then increased natural price of labour.

In the second case, the condition of the labourer will be very greatly improved; he will receive increased money wages, without having to pay any increased price, and perhaps even a diminished price for the commodities which he and his family consume; and it will not be till after a great addition has been made to the population, that the market price of labour[1] will again sink to its[2] then low and reduced natural price.

Thus, then, with every improvement of society, with every increase in its capital, the market wages of labour will rise; but the permanence of their rise will depend on the question, whether the natural price of labour[3] has also risen; and this again will depend on the rise in the natural price of those necessaries on which the wages of labour are expended.

It is not to be understood that the natural price of labour[4], estimated even in food and necessaries, is absolutely fixed and constant. It varies at different times in the same country, and very materially differs in different countries.* It essentially

* "The shelter and the clothing which are indispensable in one country may be no way necessary in another; and a labourer in Hindostan may continue to work with perfect vigour, though receiving, as his natural wages, only such a supply of covering as would be insufficient to preserve a labourer in Russia from perishing. Even in countries situated in the same climate, different habits of living will often occasion variations in

[1] Ed. 1 'market price of wages'. [3] Ed. 1 'natural price of wages'.
[2] Eds. 1-2 'their'.   [4] Ed. 1 'natural price of wages'.

depends on the habits and customs of the people. An English labourer would consider his wages under their natural rate, and too scanty to support a family, if they enabled him to purchase no other food than potatoes, and to live in no better habitation than a mud cabin; yet these moderate demands of nature are often deemed sufficient in countries where "man's life is cheap", and his wants easily satisfied. Many of the conveniences now enjoyed in an English cottage, would have been thought luxuries at an earlier[1] period of our history.

From manufactured commodities always falling, and raw produce always rising, with the progress of society, such a disproportion in their relative value is at length created, that in rich countries a labourer, by the sacrifice of a very small quantity only of his food, is able to provide liberally for all his other wants.

Independently of the variations in the value of money, which necessarily affect money[2] wages, but which we have here supposed to have no operation, as we have considered money to be uniformly of the same value, it appears then that[3] wages are subject to a rise or fall from two causes:

1st. The supply and demand of labourers.

2dly. The price of the commodities on which the wages of labour are expended.

the natural price of labour, as considerable as those which are produced by natural causes."—p. 68. *An Essay on the External Corn Trade, by R. Torrens, Esq.*[4]

The whole of this subject is most ably illustrated by Colonel[5] Torrens.[6]

---

[1] Ed. 1 'early'.
[2] Eds. 1-2 do not contain 'money'.
[3] Ed. 1 does not contain 'it appears then that'.
[4] London, Hatchard, 1815. The reference should be to p. 63.
[5] Ed. 2 'Major'.

[6] Ed. 1 does not contain this note. It was inserted, with another on p. 271 below, because of Torrens's complaint that he had not been mentioned in ed. 1; see letter to Trower, below, VII, 179–80, and to Mill, *ib.* p. 333.

In different stages of society, the accumulation of capital, or of the means of employing labour, is more or less rapid, and must in all cases depend on the productive powers of labour. The productive powers of labour are generally greatest when there is an abundance of fertile land: at such periods accumulation is often so rapid, that labourers cannot be supplied with the same rapidity as capital.

It has been calculated, that under favourable circumstances population may be doubled in twenty-five years;[1] but under the same favourable circumstances, the whole capital of a country might possibly be doubled in a shorter period. In that case, wages during the whole period would have a tendency to rise, because the demand for labour would increase still faster than the supply.

In new settlements, where the arts and knowledge of countries far advanced in refinement are introduced, it is probable that capital has a tendency to increase faster than mankind: and if the deficiency of labourers were not supplied by more populous countries, this tendency would very much raise the price of labour. In proportion as these countries become populous, and land of a worse quality is taken into cultivation, the tendency to an increase of capital diminishes; for the surplus produce remaining, after satisfying the wants of the existing population, must necessarily be in proportion to the facility of production, viz. to the smaller number of persons employed in production. Although, then, it is probable, that under the most favourable circumstances, the power of production is still greater than that of population, it will not long continue so; for the land being limited in quantity, and differing in quality, with every increased portion of capital employed on it, there will be a decreased rate of production, whilst the power of population continues always the same.

[1] Malthus's *Essay on Population*, Bk. i, ch. i.

In those countries where there is abundance of fertile land, but where, from the ignorance, indolence, and barbarism of the inhabitants, they are exposed to all the evils of want and famine, and where it has been said that population presses against the means of subsistence, a very different remedy should be applied from that which is necessary in long settled countries, where, from the diminishing rate of the supply of raw produce, all the evils of a crowded population are experienced. In the one case, the evil proceeds from bad government, from the insecurity of property, and from a want of education in all ranks of the people. To be made happier they require only to be better governed and instructed, as the augmentation of capital, beyond the augmentation of people, would be the inevitable result. No increase[1] in the population can be too great, as the powers of production are still greater. In the other case, the population increases faster than the funds required for its support. Every exertion of industry, unless accompanied by a diminished rate of increase in the population, will add to the evil, for production cannot keep pace with it.[2]

With a population pressing against the means of subsistence, the only remedies are either a reduction of people, or a more rapid accumulation of capital. In rich countries, where all the fertile land is already cultivated, the latter remedy is neither very practicable nor very desirable, because its effect would be, if pushed very far, to render all classes equally poor. But in poor countries, where there are abundant means of production in store, from fertile land not yet brought into cultivation, it

[1] Ed. 1 in place of the last two sentences reads 'In the one case, the misery proceeds from the in- activity of the people. To be made happier, they need only to be stimu- lated to exertion; with such ex- ertion, no increase'. Cp. below, p. 100, n.

[2] The argument in this paragraph is derived from John Weyland (*The Principles of Population and Production*, 1815, pp. 25–30). Cp. letter to Trower of 15 July 1816, below, VII, 48.

is the only safe and efficacious means of removing the evil, particularly as its effect would be to elevate all classes of the people.

The friends of humanity cannot but wish that in all countries the labouring classes should have a taste for comforts and enjoyments, and that they should be stimulated by all legal means in their exertions to procure them. There cannot be a better security against a superabundant population.[1] In those coun-

---

[1] In place of these last two sentences and the preceding paragraph, ed. 1 reads: 'In some countries of Europe, and many of Asia, as well as in the islands in the South Seas, the people are miserable, either from a vicious government or from habits of indolence, which make them prefer present ease and inactivity, though without security against want, to a moderate degree of exertion, with plenty of food and necessaries. By diminishing their population, no relief would be afforded, for productions would diminish in as great, or even in a greater, proportion. The remedy for the evils under which Poland and Ireland suffer, which are similar to those experienced in the South Seas, is to stimulate exertion, to create new wants, and to implant new tastes; for those countries must accumulate a much larger amount of capital, before the diminished rate of production will render the progress of capital necessarily less rapid than the progress of population. The facility with which the wants of the Irish are supplied, permits that people to pass a great part of their time in idleness: if the population were diminished, this evil would increase, because wages would rise, and therefore the labourer would be enabled, in exchange for a still less portion of his labour, to obtain all that his moderate wants require.

'Give to the Irish labourer a taste for the comforts and enjoyments which habit has made essential to the English labourer, and he would be then content to devote a further portion of his time to industry, that he might be enabled to obtain them. Not only would all the food now produced be obtained, but a vast additional value in those other commodities, to the production of which the now unemployed labour of the country might be directed.'

These passages were rewritten as a result of criticisms by George Ensor in his *Inquiry concerning the Population of Nations: containing a Refutation of Mr. Malthus's Essay on Population*, London, E. Wilson, 1818, pp. 264–5. After pointing out that Ricardo's own account of an English labourer (below, p. 106) 'is no object of admiration', Ensor asked: 'But how are these tastes to be excited in Irish labourers? Is it supposed that they are not like other human creatures? but that they make choice of privations?' (See Ricardo's letter to Mill of 23 Nov. 1818, below, VII, 334.)

tries, where the labouring classes have the fewest wants, and are contented with the cheapest food, the people are exposed to the greatest vicissitudes and miseries. They have no place of refuge from calamity; they cannot seek safety in a lower station; they are already so low, that they can fall no lower. On any deficiency of the chief article of their subsistence, there are few substitutes of which they can avail themselves, and dearth to them is attended with almost all the evils of famine.

In the natural advance of society, the wages of labour will have a tendency to fall, as far as they are regulated by supply and demand; for the supply of labourers will continue to increase at the same rate, whilst the demand for them will increase at a slower rate. If, for instance, wages were regulated by a yearly increase of capital, at the rate of 2 per cent., they would fall when it accumulated only at the rate of $1\frac{1}{2}$ per cent. They would fall still lower when it increased only at the rate of 1, or $\frac{1}{2}$ per cent., and would continue to do so until the capital became stationary, when wages also would become stationary, and be only sufficient to keep up the numbers of the actual population. I say that, under these circumstances, wages would fall, if they were regulated only by the supply and demand of labourers; but we must not forget, that wages are also regulated by the prices of the commodities on which they are expended.

As population increases, these necessaries will be constantly rising in price, because more labour will be necessary to produce them. If, then, the money wages of labour should fall, whilst every commodity on which the wages of labour were expended rose, the labourer would be doubly affected, and would be soon totally deprived of subsistence. Instead, therefore, of the money wages of labour falling, they would rise; but they would not rise sufficiently to enable the labourer to purchase as many comforts and necessaries as he did before the rise in the price of those commodities. If his annual wages were before 24*l.*, or six quarters of corn when the price was 4*l.* per quarter, he would probably receive only the value of five quarters when corn rose to 5*l.* per quarter. But five quarters would cost 25*l.*; he would therefore receive an addition in his money wages, though with that addition he would be unable to furnish himself with the same quantity of corn and other commodities, which he had before consumed in his family.

Notwithstanding, then, that the labourer would be really worse paid, yet this increase in his wages would necessarily diminish the profits of the manufacturer; for his goods would sell at no higher price, and yet the expense of producing them would be increased. This, however, will be considered in our examination into the principles which regulate profits.

It appears, then, that the same cause which raises rent, namely, the increasing difficulty of providing an additional quantity of food with the same proportional quantity of labour, will also raise wages; and therefore if money be of an unvarying value, both rent and wages will have a tendency to rise with the progress of wealth and population.

But there is this essential difference between the rise of rent and the rise of wages. The rise in the money value of rent is accompanied by an increased share of the produce; not only is the landlord's money rent greater, but his corn rent also; he will have more corn, and each defined measure of that corn will exchange for a greater quantity of all other goods which have not been raised in value. The fate of the labourer will be less happy; he will receive more money wages, it is true, but his corn wages will be reduced; and not only his command of corn, but his general condition will be deteriorated, by his finding it more difficult to maintain the market rate of wages above their natural rate. While the price of corn rises 10 per cent., wages will always rise less than 10 per cent., but rent will always rise more; the condition of the labourer will generally decline, and that of the landlord will always be improved.

When wheat was at 4*l*. per quarter, suppose the labourer's wages to be 24*l*. per annum, or the value of six quarters of wheat, and suppose half his wages to be expended on wheat, and the other half, or 12*l*., on other things. He would receive

$$
\left.\begin{array}{l}
24l.\ 14s.\\
25l.\ 10s.\\
26l.\ 8s.\\
27l.\ 8s.\ 6d.
\end{array}\right\}
\begin{array}{l}
\text{when wheat}\\
\text{was at}
\end{array}
\left\{\begin{array}{l}
4l.\ 4s.\ 8d.\\
4l.\ 10s.\\
4l.\ 16s.\\
5l.\ 2s.\ 10d.
\end{array}\right\}
\begin{array}{l}
\text{or the}\\
\text{value of}
\end{array}
\left\{\begin{array}{l}
5.83\ \text{qrs.}\\
5.66\ \text{qrs.}\\
5.50\ \text{qrs.}\\
5.33\ \text{qrs.}
\end{array}\right.
$$

He would receive these wages to enable him to live just as well, and no better, than before; for when corn was at 4*l*. per quarter, he would expend for three quarters of corn, at 4*l*. per

quarter . . . . 12*l*.
and on other things . . . . . 12*l*.
_____
24*l*.

When wheat was 4*l*. 4*s*. 8*d*., three quarters, which he and his family consumed, would cost him . . . . . . 12*l*. 14*s*.
other things not altered in price . . . . . . 12*l*.
_____
24*l*. 14*s*.

When at 4*l*. 10*s*., three quarters of wheat would cost   13*l*. 10*s*.
and other things . . . . 12*l*.
_____
25*l*. 10*s*.

When at 4*l*. 16*s*., three qrs. of wheat . . . . .   14*l*. 8*s*.
Other things . . . . 12*l*.
_____
26*l*. 8*s*.

When at 5*l*. 2*s*. 10*d*. three quarters of wheat would
cost . . . .   15*l*. 8*s*. 6*d*.
Other things . . . . 12*l*.
_____
27*l*. 8*s*. 6*d*.

In proportion as corn became dear, he would receive less corn wages, but his money wages would always increase, whilst his enjoyments, on the above supposition, would be precisely the same. But as other commodities would be raised in price in proportion as raw produce entered into their composition, he would have more to pay for some of them. Although his tea, sugar, soap, candles, and house rent, would probably be no dearer, he would pay more for his bacon, cheese, butter, linen, shoes, and cloth; and therefore, even with the above increase of wages, his situation would be comparatively worse. But it may be said that I have been considering the effect of wages on price, on the supposition that gold, or the metal from which money is made, is the produce of the country in which wages varied; and that the consequences which I have deduced agree little with the actual state of things, because gold is a metal of foreign production. The circumstance, however, of gold being a foreign production, will not invalidate the truth of the argument, because it may be shewn, that whether it were found at home, or were imported from abroad, the effects ultimately and, indeed, immediately would be the same.

When wages rise, it is generally because the increase of wealth and capital have occasioned a new demand for labour, which will infallibly be attended with an increased production of commodities. To circulate these additional commodities, even at the same prices as before, more money is required, more of this foreign commodity from which money is made, and which can only be obtained by importation. Whenever a commodity is required in greater abundance than before, its relative value rises comparatively with those commodities with which its purchase is made. If more hats were wanted, their price would rise, and more gold would be given for them. If more gold were required, gold would rise, and hats would fall in price, as a greater quantity of hats and of all other things would then be necessary to purchase the same quantity of gold. But in the case supposed, to say that commodities will rise, because wages rise, is to affirm a positive contradiction; for we first say that gold will rise in relative value in consequence of demand, and secondly, that it will fall in relative value because prices will rise, two effects which are totally incompatible with each other. To say that commodities are raised in price, is the same thing as to say that money is lowered in relative value; for it is by commodities that the relative value of gold is estimated. If then all commodities rose in price, gold could not come from abroad to purchase those dear commodities, but it would go from home to be employed with advantage in purchasing the comparatively cheaper foreign commodities. It appears, then, that the rise of wages will not raise the prices of commodities, whether the metal from which money is made be produced at home or in a foreign country. All commodities cannot rise at the same time without an addition to the quantity of money. This addition could not be obtained at home, as we have already shewn; nor could it be imported from abroad. To purchase any additional quantity of gold from abroad, commodities at home must be cheap, not dear. The importation of gold, and a rise in the price of all home-made commodities with which gold is purchased or paid for, are effects absolutely incompatible. The extensive use of paper money does not alter this question, for paper money conforms, or ought to conform, to the value of gold, and therefore its value is influenced by such causes only as influence the value of that metal.

These then are the laws by which wages are regulated, and by which the happiness of far the greatest part of every community is governed. Like all other contracts, wages should be left to the fair and free competition of the market, and should never be controlled by the interference of the legislature.

The clear and direct tendency of the poor laws, is in direct opposition to these obvious principles: it is not, as the legislature benevolently intended, to amend the condition of the poor, but to deteriorate the condition of both poor and rich; instead of making the poor rich, they are calculated to make the rich poor; and whilst the present laws are in force, it is quite in the natural order of things that the fund for the maintenance of the poor should progressively increase, till it has absorbed all the net[1] revenue of the country, or at least so much of it as the state shall leave to us, after satisfying its own never failing demands for the public expenditure.*

This pernicious tendency of these laws is no longer a mystery, since it has been fully developed by the able hand of Mr. Malthus;[2] and every friend to the poor must ardently wish for their abolition. Unfortunately, however, they have been so long established, and the habits of the poor have been so formed upon their operation, that to eradicate them with safety from our political system, requires the most cautious and skilful management. It is agreed by all who are most friendly to a repeal of these laws, that if it be desirable to prevent the most overwhelming distress to those for whose benefit they were erroneously enacted, their abolition should be effected by the most gradual steps.

It is a truth which admits not a doubt, that the comforts and well-being of the poor cannot be permanently secured without some regard on their part, or some effort on the part of the

---

* With Mr. Buchanan in the following passage, if it refers to temporary states of misery, I so far agree, that "the great evil of the labourer's condition is poverty, arising either from a scarcity of food or of work; and in all countries, laws without number have been enacted for his relief. But there are miseries in the social state which legislation cannot relieve; and it is useful therefore to know its limits, that we may not, by aiming at what is impracticable, miss the good which is really in our power."— *Buchanan*, page 61.[3]

[1] Ed. 1 'neat'.
[2] *Essay on Population*, 4th ed., London, 1807; vol. II, Bk. III, chs. v, vi.

[3] Buchanan's ed. of the *Wealth of Nations*, vol. IV, *Observations*.

legislature, to regulate the increase of their numbers, and to render less frequent among them early and improvident marriages. The operation of the system of poor laws has been directly contrary to this. They have rendered restraint superfluous, and have invited imprudence, by offering it a portion of the wages of prudence and industry. *

The nature of the evil points out the remedy. By gradually contracting the sphere of the poor laws; by impressing on the poor the value of independence, by teaching them that they must look not to systematic or casual charity, but to their own exertions for support, that prudence and forethought are neither unnecessary nor unprofitable virtues, we shall by degrees approach a sounder and more healthful state.

No scheme for the amendment of the poor laws merits the least attention, which has not their abolition for its ultimate object; and he is the best friend to the poor, and to the cause of humanity, who can point out how this end can be attained with the most security, and at the same time with the least violence. It is not by raising in any manner different from the present, the fund from which the poor are supported, that the evil can be mitigated. It would not only be no improvement,

---

* The progress of knowledge manifested upon this subject in the House of Commons since 1796, has happily not been very small, as may be seen by contrasting the late report of the committee on the poor laws,[1] and the following sentiments of Mr. Pitt, in that year.

"Let us," said he, "make relief in cases where there are a number of children a matter of right and honour, instead of a ground of opprobrium and contempt. This will make a large family a blessing, and not a curse; and this will draw a proper line of distinction between those who are able to provide for themselves by their labour, and those who after having enriched their country with a number of children, have a claim upon its assistance for support."—*Hansard's Parliamentary History*, vol. 32, page 710.[2]

---

[1] See the 'Report from the Select Committee on the Poor Laws' dated 4 July 1817 (*Parliamentary Papers*, 1817, vol. VI) and cp. letter to Trower of 10 Dec. 1817, below, VII, 219.

[2] Ed. 1 does not contain this note.

but it would be an aggravation of the distress which we wish to see removed, if the fund were increased in amount, or were levied according to some late proposals,[1] as a general fund from the country at large. The present mode of its collection and application has served to mitigate its pernicious effects. Each parish raises a separate fund for the support of its own poor. Hence it becomes an object of more interest and more practicability to keep the rates low, than if one general fund were raised for the relief of the poor of the whole kingdom. A parish is much more interested in an economical collection of the rate, and a sparing distribution of relief, when the whole saving will be for its own benefit, than if hundreds of other parishes were to partake of it.

It is to this cause, that we must ascribe the fact of the poor laws not having yet absorbed all the net revenue of the country; it is to the rigour with which they are applied, that we are indebted for their not having become overwhelmingly oppressive. If by law every human being wanting support could be sure to obtain it, and obtain it in such a degree as to make life tolerably[2] comfortable, theory would lead us to expect that all other taxes together would be light compared with the single one of poor rates. The principle of gravitation is not more certain than the tendency of such laws to change wealth and power into misery and weakness; to call away the exertions of labour from every object, except that of providing mere subsistence; to confound all intellectual distinction; to busy the mind continually in supplying the body's wants; until at last all classes should be infected with the plague of universal poverty. Happily these laws have been in operation during a period of progressive prosperity, when the funds for the main-

[1] See Curwen's speech on the Poor Laws, 21 Feb. 1817, *Hansard*, XXXV, 520-1.

[2] Misprinted 'tolerable' in ed. 3.

tenance of labour have regularly increased, and when an increase of population would be naturally called for. But if our progress should become more slow; if we should attain the stationary state, from which I trust we are yet far distant, then will the pernicious nature of these laws become more manifest and alarming; and then, too, will their removal be obstructed by many additional difficulties.

CHAPTER VI

ON PROFITS[1]

THE profits of stock, in different employments, having been shewn[2] to bear a proportion to each other, and to have a tendency to vary all in the same degree and in the same direction, it remains for us to consider what is the cause of the permanent variations in the rate of profit, and the consequent permanent alterations in the rate of interest.

We have seen that the price* of corn is regulated by the quantity of labour necessary to produce it, with that portion of capital which pays no rent. We have seen, too, that all manufactured commodities rise and fall in price, in proportion as more or less labour becomes necessary to their production. Neither the farmer who cultivates that quantity[3] of land, which regulates price, nor the manufacturer, who manufactures goods, sacrifice any portion of the produce for rent. The whole value of their commodities is divided into two portions only: one constitutes the profits of stock, the other the wages of labour.

Supposing corn and manufactured goods always to sell at the same price, profits would be high or low in proportion as wages were low or high. But suppose corn to rise in price because more labour is necessary to produce it; that cause will not raise the price of manufactured goods in the production of which no additional quantity of labour is required. If, then,

---

* The reader is desired to bear in mind, that for the purpose of making the subject more clear, I consider money to be invariable in value, and therefore every variation of price to be referable to an alteration in the value of the commodity.

[1] In ed. 1 this chapter is numbered 'V' in the chapter-heading and 'V*' in the Contents. See above, p. 10, n.

[2] Above, p. 90.

[3] Eds. 1-2 read 'quality', which seems more appropriate.

wages continued the same, the profits of manufacturers[1] would remain the same; but if, as is absolutely certain, wages should rise with the rise of corn, then their[2] profits would necessarily fall.

If a manufacturer always sold his goods for the same money, for 1000*l.*, for example, his profits would depend on the price of the labour necessary to manufacture those goods. His profits would be less when wages amounted to 800*l.* than when he paid only 600*l.* In proportion then as wages rose, would profits fall. But if the price of raw produce would increase, it may be asked, whether the farmer at least would not have the same rate of profits, although he should pay an additional sum for wages[3]? Certainly not: for he will not only have to pay, in common with the manufacturer, an increase of wages to each labourer he employs, but he will be obliged either to pay rent, or to employ an additional number of labourers to obtain the same produce; and the rise in the price of raw produce will be proportioned only to that rent, or that additional number, and will not compensate him for the rise of wages.

If both the manufacturer and farmer employed ten men, on wages rising from 24*l.* to 25*l.* per annum per man, the whole sum paid by each would be 250*l.* instead of 240*l.* This is, however, the whole addition that would be paid by the manufacturer to obtain the same quantity of commodities; but the farmer on new land would probably be obliged to employ an additional man, and therefore to pay an additional sum of 25*l.* for wages; and the farmer on the old land would be obliged to pay precisely the same additional sum of 25*l.* for rent; without which additional labour, corn would not have risen, nor

[1] Ed. 1 does not contain 'of manufacturers'.

[2] Ed. 1 does not contain 'their'.

[3] Ed. 1 'an additional price for wages'.

rent have been increased[1]. One will therefore have to pay 275*l.*
for wages alone, the other, for wages and rent together; each
25*l.* more than the manufacturer: for this latter 25*l.* the farmer
is[2] compensated by the addition to the price of raw produce,
and therefore his[3] profits still conform to the profits of the
manufacturer. As this proposition is important, I will endeavour still further to elucidate it.

We have shewn that in early stages of society, both the landlord's and the labourer's share of the *value* of the produce of
the earth, would be but small; and that it would increase in
proportion to the progress of wealth, and the difficulty of procuring food. We have shewn, too, that although the value of
the labourer's portion will be increased by the high value of
food, his real share will be diminished; whilst that of the landlord will not only be raised in value, but will also be increased
in quantity.

The remaining quantity of the produce of the land, after the
landlord and labourer are paid, necessarily belongs to the
farmer, and constitutes the profits of his stock. But it may be
alleged, that though as society advances, his proportion of the
whole produce will be diminished, yet as it will rise in value,
he, as well as the landlord and labourer, may, notwithstanding,
receive a greater value.

It may be said for example, that when corn rose from 4*l.* to
10*l.*, the 180 quarters obtained from the best land would sell
for 1800*l.* instead of 720*l.*; and, therefore, though the landlord
and labourer be proved to have a greater value for rent and
wages, still the value of the farmer's profit might also be
augmented. This, however, is impossible, as I shall now endeavour to shew.

---

[1] Ed. 1 does not contain ', nor rent
have been increased'.

[2] Ed. 1 'they are' in place of 'the
farmer is'.

[3] Ed. 1 'their'.

In the first place, the price of corn would rise only in proportion to the increased difficulty of growing it on land of a worse quality.

It has been already remarked,[1] that if the labour of ten men will, on land of a certain quality, obtain 180 quarters of wheat, and its value be 4*l.* per quarter, or 720*l.*; and if the labour of ten additional men, will on the same or any other land produce only 170 quarters in addition, wheat would rise from 4*l.* to 4*l.* 4*s.* 8*d.*; for 170 : 180 :: 4*l.* : 4*l.* 4*s.* 8*d.* In other words, as for the production of 170 quarters, the labour of ten men is necessary, in the one case, and only that of 9.44 in the other, the rise would be as 9.44 to 10, or, as 4*l.* to 4*l.* 4*s.* 8*d.* In the same manner it might be shewn, that if the labour of ten additional men would only produce 160 quarters, the price would further rise to 4*l.* 10*s.*; if 150, to 4*l.* 16*s.* &c. &c.

But when 180 quarters were produced on the land
   paying no rent, and its price was 4*l.* per quarter, it
   is sold[2] for £720
And when 170 quarters were produced on the land
   paying no rent, and the price rose to 4*l.* 4*s.* 8*d.* it
   still sold for 720
So 160 quarters at 4*l.* 10*s.* produce 720
And 150 quarters at 4*l.* 16*s.* produce the same sum of . 720

Now it is evident, that if out of these equal values, the farmer is at one time obliged to pay wages regulated by the price of wheat at 4*l.*, and at other times at higher prices, the rate of his profits will diminish in proportion to the rise in the price of corn.

In this case, therefore, I think it is clearly demonstrated that a rise in the price of corn, which increases the money wages

---

[1] Above, p. 83, n.   [2] Ed. 1 'it sold', which seems correct.

of the labourer, diminishes the money value of the farmer's profits.

But the case of the farmer of the old and better land will be in no way different; he also will have increased wages to pay, and will never retain more of the value of the produce, however high may be its price, than 720*l.* to be divided between himself and his always equal number of labourers; in proportion therefore as they get more, he must retain less.

When the price of corn was at 4*l.* the whole 180 quarters belonged to the cultivator, and he sold it for 720*l.* When corn rose to 4*l.* 4*s.* 8*d.* he was obliged to pay the value of ten quarters out of his 180 for rent, consequently the remaining 170 yielded him no more than 720*l.*: when it rose further to 4*l.* 10*s.* he paid twenty quarters, or their value, for rent, and consequently only retained 160 quarters, which yielded the same sum of 720*l.*

It will be seen, then, that whatever rise may take place in the price of corn, in consequence of the necessity of employing more labour and capital to obtain a given additional quantity of produce, such rise will always be equalled in value by the additional rent, or additional labour employed; so that whether corn sells for 4*l.*, 4*l.* 10*s.* or 5*l.* 2*s.* 10*d.* the farmer will obtain for that which remains to him, after paying rent, the same real value. Thus we see, that whether the produce belonging to the farmer be 180, 170, 160, or 150 quarters, he always obtains the same sum of 720*l.* for it; the price increasing in an inverse proportion to the quantity.

Rent then, it appears, always falls on the consumer, and never on the farmer; for if the produce of his farm should uniformly be 180 quarters, with the rise of price, he would retain the value of a less quantity for himself, and give the value of a larger quantity to his landlord; but the deduction would be such as to leave him always the same sum of 720*l.*

It will be seen too, that, in all cases, the same sum of 720*l.*
must be divided between wages and profits. If the value of
the raw produce from the land exceed this value, it belongs to
rent, whatever may be its amount. If there be no excess, there
will be no rent. Whether wages or profits rise or fall, it is this
sum of 720*l.* from which they must both be provided. On the
one hand, profits can never rise so high as to absorb so much
of this 720*l.* that enough will not be left to furnish the labourers
with absolute necessaries; on the other hand, wages can never
rise so high as to leave no portion of this sum for profits.

Thus in every case, agricultural, as well as manufacturing
profits are lowered by a rise in the price of raw produce, if it
be accompanied by a rise of wages.* If the farmer gets no
additional value for the corn which remains to him after paying
rent, if the manufacturer gets no additional value for the goods
which he manufactures, and if both are obliged to pay a greater
value in wages, can any point be more clearly established than
that profits must fall, with a rise of wages?

The farmer then, although he pays no part of his landlord's
rent, that being always regulated by the price of produce, and
invariably falling on the consumers, has however a very
decided interest in keeping rent low, or rather in keeping the
natural price of produce low. As a consumer of raw produce,
and of those things into which raw produce enters as a component part, he will, in common with all other consumers, be
interested in keeping the price low. But he is most materially
concerned with the high price of corn as it affects wages. With
every rise in the price of corn, he will have to pay out of an
equal and unvarying sum of 720*l.* an additional sum for wages

---

* The reader is aware, that we are leaving out of our consideration
the accidental variations arising from bad and good seasons, or from
the demand increasing or diminishing by any sudden effect on the state
of population. We are speaking of the natural and constant, not of the
accidental and fluctuating price of corn.

to the ten men whom he is supposed constantly to employ. We have seen in treating on wages that they invariably rise with the rise in the price of raw produce. On a basis assumed for the purpose of calculation, page 103, it will be seen that if when wheat is at 4*l.* per quarter, wages should be 24*l.* per annum[1]

When Wheat is at	£. s. d.		£. s. d.
	4 4 8		24 14 0
	4 10 0	wages would be	25 10 0
	4 16 0		26 8 0
	5 2 10		27 8 6

Now, of the unvarying fund of 720*l.* to be distributed between labourers and farmers,

When the price of Wheat is at	£. s. d.		£. s.		£. s. d.
	4 0 0		240 0		480 0 0
	4 4 8	the labourers[2]	247 0	the farmer	473 0 0
	4 10 0	will receive	255 0	will receive	465 0 0
	4 16 0		264 0		456 0 0
	5 2 10		274 5		455[3] 15 *

* The 180 quarters of corn would be divided in the following proportions between landlords, farmers, and labourers, with the above-named variations in the value of corn.

Price per qr. £. s. d.	Rent. In Wheat.	Profit. In Wheat.	Wages. In Wheat.	Total.
4 0 0	None.	120 qrs.	60 qrs.	
4 4 8	10 qrs.	111.7	58.3	
4 10 0	20	103.4	56.6	180
4 16 0	30	95	55	
5 2 10	40	86.7	53.3	

and, under the same circumstances, money rent, wages, and profit, would be as follows:

Price per qr. £. s. d.	Rent. £. s. d.	Profit. £. s. d.	Wages. £. s. d.	Total. £. s. d.
4 0 0	None.	480 0 0	240 0 0	720 0 0
4 4 8	42 7 6	473 0 0	247 0 0	762 7 6
4 10 0	90 0 0	465 0 0	255 0 0	810 0 0
4 16 0	144 0 0	456 0 0	264 0 0	864 0 0
5 2 10	205 13 4	445 15 0	274 5 0	925 13 4

[1] All eds. have a full stop here, where it seems out of place.   [2] Ed. 1 'labourer'.   [3] Should be '445'.

And supposing that the original capital of the farmer was
3000*l.*, the profits of his stock being in the first instance 480*l.*
would be at the rate of 16 per cent. When his profits fell to
473*l.* they would be at the rate of 15.7 per cent.

465*l.*	.	.	.	.	15.5
456*l.*	.	.	.	.	15.2
445*l.*	.	.	.	.	14.8

But the *rate* of profits will fall still more, because the capital
of the farmer, it must be recollected, consists in a great measure
of raw produce, such as his corn and hay-ricks, his unthreshed
wheat and barley, his horses and cows, which would all rise
in price in consequence of the rise of produce. His absolute
profits would fall from 480*l.* to 445*l.* 15*s.*; but if from the cause
which I have just stated, his capital should rise from 3000*l.*
to 3200*l.* the rate of his profits would, when corn was at
5*l.* 2*s.* 10*d.* be under 14 per cent.

If a manufacturer had also employed 3000*l.* in his business,
he would be obliged in consequence of the rise of wages, to
increase his capital, in order to be enabled to carry on the same
business. If his commodities sold before for 720*l.* they would
continue to sell at the same price; but the wages of labour,
which were before 240*l.* would rise when corn was at 5*l.* 2*s.* 10*d.*
to 274*l.* 5*s.* In the first case he would have a balance of 480*l.* as
profit on 3000*l.*, in the second he would have a profit only
of 445*l.* 15*s.*, on an increased capital, and therefore his profits
would conform to the altered rate of those of the farmer.

There are few commodities which are not more or less
affected in their price by the rise of raw produce, because some
raw material from the land enters into the composition of most
commodities. Cotton goods, linen, and cloth, will all rise in
price with the rise of wheat; but they rise on account of the
greater quantity of labour expended on the raw material from
which they are made, and not because more was paid by the

manufacturer to the labourers whom he employed on those commodities.

In all cases, commodities rise because more labour is expended on them, and not because the labour which is expended on them is at a higher value. Articles of jewellery, of iron, of plate, and of copper, would not rise, because none of the raw produce from the surface of the earth enters into their composition.

It may be said that I have taken it for granted, that money wages would rise with a rise in the price of raw produce, but that this is by no means a necessary consequence, as the labourer may be contented with fewer enjoyments. It is true that the wages of labour may previously have been at a high level, and that they may bear some reduction. If so, the fall of profits will be checked; but it is impossible to conceive that the money price of wages should fall, or remain stationary with a gradually increasing price of necessaries; and therefore it may be taken for granted that, under ordinary circumstances, no permanent rise takes place in the price of necessaries, without occasioning, or having been preceded by a rise in wages.

The effects produced on profits would have been the same, or nearly the same, if there had been any rise in the price of those other necessaries, besides food, on which the wages of labour are expended. The necessity which the labourer would be under of paying an increased price for such necessaries, would oblige him to demand more wages; and whatever increases wages, necessarily reduces profits. But suppose the price of silks, velvets, furniture, and any other commodities, not required by the labourer, to rise in consequence of more labour being expended on them, would not that affect profits? Certainly not: for nothing can affect profits but a rise in wages; silks and velvets are not consumed by the labourer, and therefore cannot raise wages.

It is to be understood that I am speaking of profits generally. I have already remarked, that the market price of a commodity may exceed its natural or necessary price, as it may be produced in less abundance than the new demand for it requires. This, however, is but a temporary effect. The high profits on capital employed in producing that commodity, will naturally attract capital to that trade; and as soon as the requisite funds are supplied, and the quantity of the commodity is duly increased, its price will fall, and the profits of the trade will conform to the general level. A fall in the general rate of profits is by no means incompatible with a partial rise of profits in particular employments. It is through the inequality of profits, that capital is moved from one employment to another. Whilst then general profits are falling, and gradually settling at a lower level in consequence of the rise of wages, and the increasing difficulty of supplying the increasing population with necessaries, the profits of the farmer may, for an interval of some little duration, be above the former level. An extraordinary stimulus may be also given for a certain time, to a particular branch of foreign and colonial trade; but the admission of this fact by no means invalidates the theory, that profits depend on high or low wages, wages on the price of necessaries, and the price of necessaries chiefly on the price of food, because all other requisites may be increased almost without limit.

It should be recollected that prices always vary in the market, and in the first instance, through the comparative state of demand and supply. Although cloth could be furnished at 40s. per yard, and give the usual profits of stock, it may rise to 60 or 80s. from a general change of fashion, or from any other cause which should suddenly and unexpectedly increase the demand, or diminish the supply of it. The makers of cloth will for a time have unusual profits, but capital will naturally flow to that manufacture, till the supply and demand are again at their fair level, when the price of cloth will again sink to 40s., its natural or necessary price. In the same manner, with every increased demand for corn, it may rise so high as to afford more than the general profits to the farmer. If there be plenty of fertile land, the price of corn will again fall to its former standard, after the requisite quantity of capital has been employed in producing it, and profits will be as before; but if there be not plenty of fertile land, if, to produce this additional quantity, more than the usual quantity of capital and labour be required, corn will not fall to its former level. Its natural price will be raised, and the farmer, instead of obtaining permanently larger profits, will find himself obliged to be satisfied with the diminished rate which is the inevitable consequence of the rise of wages, produced by the rise of necessaries.

The natural tendency of profits then is to fall; for, in the progress of society and wealth, the additional quantity of food required is obtained by the sacrifice of more and more labour. This tendency, this gravitation as it were of profits, is happily checked at repeated intervals by the improvements in machinery, connected with the production of necessaries, as well as by discoveries in the science of agriculture which enable us to relinquish a portion of labour before required, and therefore to lower the price of the prime necessary of the labourer. The rise in the price of necessaries and in the wages of labour is however limited; for as soon as wages should be equal (as in the case formerly stated) to 720l., the whole receipts of the farmer, there must be an end of accumulation; for no capital can then yield any profit whatever, and no additional labour can be demanded, and consequently population will have reached its highest point. Long indeed before this period, the very low rate of profits will have arrested all accumulation, and almost the whole produce of the country, after paying the labourers, will be the property of the owners of land and the receivers of tithes and taxes.

Thus, taking the former very imperfect basis as the grounds of my calculation, it would appear that when corn was at 20*l.* per quarter, the whole net income of the country would belong to the landlords, for then the same quantity of labour that was originally necessary to produce 180 quarters, would be necessary to produce 36; since 20*l.* : 4*l.* : : 180 : 36. The farmer then, who[1] produced 180 quarters, (if any such there were, for the old and new capital employed on the land would be so blended, that it could in no way be distinguished,) would sell the

180 qrs. at 20*l.* per qr. or	£3600
the value of 144 qrs. { to landlord for rent, being the difference } { between 36 and 180 qrs. }	2880
36 qrs.	720
the value of 36 qrs. to labourers ten in number	720

leaving nothing whatever for profit.

I have supposed that[2] at this price of 20*l.* the labourers would continue
  to consume three quarters each per annum or £60
And that on the other[3] commodities they would
  expend   12
                                        —
                              72 for each labourer.
        And therefore ten labourers would cost 720*l.* per annum.

In all these calculations I have been desirous only to elucidate the principle, and it is scarcely necessary to observe, that my whole basis is assumed at random, and merely for the purpose of exemplification. The results though different in degree, would have been the same in principle, however accurately I might have set out in stating the difference in the number of labourers necessary to obtain the successive quantities of corn required by an increasing population, the quantity consumed by the labourer's family, &c. &c. My object has been to simplify the

---

[1] Eds. 1-2 have here in addition 'originally'.

[2] Ed. 1 does not contain 'I have supposed that'.

[3] Eds. 1-2 'And on other'.

subject, and I have therefore made no allowance for the increasing price of the other necessaries, besides food, of the labourer; an increase which would be the consequence of the increased value of the raw materials from which they are made, and which would of course further increase wages, and lower profits.

I have already said, that long before this state of prices was become permanent, there would be no motive for accumulation; for no one accumulates but with a view to make his accumulation productive, and it is only when so employed that it operates on profits. Without a motive there could be no accumulation, and consequently such a state of prices never could take place. The farmer and manufacturer can no more live without profit, than the labourer without wages. Their motive for accumulation will diminish with every diminution of profit, and will cease altogether when their profits are so low as not to afford them an adequate compensation for their trouble, and the risk which they must necessarily encounter in employing their capital productively.

I must again observe, that the rate of profits would fall much more rapidly than I have estimated in my calculation: for the value of the produce being what I have stated it under the circumstances supposed, the value of the farmer's stock would be greatly increased from its necessarily consisting of many of the commodities which had risen in value. Before corn could rise from 4*l*. to 12*l*. his capital would probably be doubled in exchangeable value, and be worth 6000*l*. instead of 3000*l*. If then his profit were 180*l*., or 6 per cent. on his original capital, profits would not at that time be really at a higher *rate* than 3 per cent.; for 6000*l*. at 3 per cent. gives 180*l*.; and on those terms only could a new farmer with 6000*l*. money in his pocket enter into the farming business.

Many trades would derive some advantage, more or less,

from the same source. The brewer, the distiller, the clothier, the linen manufacturer, would be partly compensated for the diminution of their profits, by the rise in the value of their stock of raw and finished materials; but a manufacturer of hardware, of jewellery, and of many other commodities, as well as those whose capitals uniformly consisted of money, would be subject to the whole fall in the rate of profits, without any compensation whatever.

We should also expect that, however the rate of the profits of stock might diminish in consequence of the accumulation of capital on the land, and the rise of wages, yet that[1] the aggregate amount of profits would increase. Thus supposing that, with repeated accumulations of 100,000*l.*, the rate of profit should fall from 20 to 19, to 18, to 17 per cent., a constantly diminishing rate, we should expect that the whole amount of profits received by those successive owners of capital would be always progressive; that it would be greater when the capital was 200,000*l.*, than when 100,000*l.*; still greater when 300,000*l.*; and so on, increasing, though at a diminishing rate, with every increase of capital. This progression however is only true for a certain time: thus 19 per cent. on 200,000*l.* is more than 20 on 100,000*l.*; again 18 per cent. on 300,000*l.* is more than 19 per cent. on 200,000*l.*; but after capital has accumulated to a large amount, and profits have fallen, the further accumulation diminishes the aggregate of profits. Thus suppose the accumulation should be 1,000,000*l.*, and the profits 7 per cent. the whole amount of profits will be 70,000*l.*; now if an addition of 100,000*l.* capital be made to the million, and profits should fall to 6 per cent., 66,000*l.* or a diminution of 4,000*l.* will be received by the owners of stock, although the whole amount of stock will be increased from 1,000,000*l.* to 1,100,000*l.*

There can, however, be no accumulation of capital, so long

[1] Ed. 1 does not contain 'that'.

as stock yields any profit at all, without its yielding not only
an increase of produce, but an increase of value. By employing
100,000*l.* additional capital, no part of the former capital will
be rendered less productive. The produce of the land and labour
of the country must increase, and its value will be raised, not
only by the value of the addition which is made to the former
quantity of productions, but by the new value which is given
to the whole produce of the land, by the increased difficulty
of producing the last portion of it[1]. When the accumulation
of capital, however, becomes very great, notwithstanding this
increased value, it will be so distributed that a less value than
before will be appropriated to profits, while that which is
devoted to rent and wages will be increased. Thus with successive additions of 100,000*l.* to capital, with a fall in the rate
of profits, from 20 to 19, to 18, to 17 per cent. &c. the productions annually obtained will increase in quantity, and be of
more than the whole additional value, which the additional
capital is calculated to produce. From 20,000*l.* it will rise to
more than 39,000*l.* and then to more than 57,000*l.* and when
the capital employed is a million, as we before supposed, if
100,000*l.* more be added to it, and the aggregate of profits is
actually lower than before, more than 6,000*l.* will nevertheless
be added to the revenue of the country, but it will be to the
revenue of the landlords and labourers[2]; they will obtain more
than the additional produce, and will from their situation be
enabled to encroach even on the former gains of the capitalist.
Thus, suppose the price of corn to be 4*l.* per quarter, and that
therefore, as we before calculated, of every 720*l.* remaining to
the farmer after payment of his rent, 480*l.* were retained by
him, and 240*l.* were paid to his labourers; when the price rose
to 6*l.* per quarter, he would be obliged to pay his labourers

---

[1] **Ed. 1** has here in addition ', which
new value always goes to rent'.

[2] Ed. 1 does not contain 'and
labourers'.

300*l*. and retain only 420*l*. for profits: he would be obliged
to pay them 300*l*. to enable them to consume the same quantity
of necessaries as before, and no more[1]. Now if the capital
employed were so large as to yield a hundred thousand
times 720*l*. or 72,000,000*l*. the aggregate of profits would be
48,000,000*l*. when wheat was at 4*l*. per quarter; and if by employing a larger capital, 105,000 times 720*l*. were obtained
when wheat was at 6*l*., or 75,600,000*l*., profits would actually
fall from 48,000,000*l*. to 44,100,000*l*. or 105,000 times 420*l*.,
and wages would rise from 24,000,000*l*. to 31,500,000*l*. Wages
would rise because more labourers would be employed, in proportion to capital; and each labourer would receive more
money wages; but the condition of the labourer, as we have
already shewn, would be worse, inasmuch as he would be able
to command a less quantity of the produce of the country. The
only real gainers would be the landlords; they would receive
higher rents, first, because produce would be of a higher value,
and secondly, because they would have a greatly increased proportion of that produce[2].

Although a greater value is produced, a greater proportion
of what remains of that value, after paying rent, is consumed
by the producers, and it is this, and this alone, which regulates
profits. Whilst the land yields abundantly, wages may temporarily rise, and the producers may consume more than their
accustomed proportion; but the stimulus which will thus be
given to population, will speedily reduce the labourers to their
usual consumption. But when poor lands are taken into cultivation, or when more capital and labour are expended on the old
land, with a less return of produce, the effect must be permanent.
A greater proportion of that part of the produce which remains

---

[1] Ed. 1 does not contain the last two
lines, beginning ': he would be
obliged'.

[2] Eds. 1-2 do not contain 'of that
produce'.

to be divided, after paying rent, between the owners of stock
and the labourers, will be apportioned to the latter. Each man
may, and probably will, have a less absolute quantity; but as
more labourers are employed in proportion to the whole produce retained by the farmer, the value of a greater proportion
of the whole produce will be absorbed by wages, and consequently the value of a smaller proportion will be devoted
to profits. This will necessarily be rendered permanent by the
laws of nature, which have limited the productive powers of
the land.

Thus we again arrive at the same conclusion which we have
before [1] attempted to establish:—that in all countries, and all
times [2], profits depend on the quantity of labour requisite to
provide necessaries for the labourers, on that land or with that
capital which yields no rent. The effects then of accumulation
will be different in different countries, and will depend chiefly
on the fertility of the land. However extensive a country may
be where the land is of a poor quality, and where the importation of food is prohibited, the most moderate accumulations
of capital will be attended with great reductions in the rate of
profit, and a rapid rise in rent; and on the contrary a small but
fertile country, particularly if it freely permits the importation
of food, may accumulate a large stock of capital without any
great diminution in the rate of profits, or any great increase
in the rent of land. In the Chapter on Wages, we have endeavoured to shew [3] that the money price of commodities would
not be raised by a rise of wages, either on the supposition that
gold, the standard of money, was the produce of this country,
or that it was imported from abroad. But if it were otherwise,
if the prices of commodities were permanently raised by high
wages, the proposition would not be less true, which asserts

---

[1] Above, p. 48–9.   [2] Eds. 1–2 'and at all times'.
[3] Above, p. 105.

that high wages invariably affect the employers of labour, by
depriving them of a portion of their real profits. Supposing
the hatter, the hosier, and the shoemaker, each paid 10*l.* more
wages in the manufacture of a particular quantity of their commodities, and that the price of hats, stockings, and shoes, rose
by a sum sufficient to repay the manufacturer the 10*l.*; their
situation would be no better than if no such rise took place.
If the hosier sold his stockings for 110*l.* instead of 100*l.*, his
profits would be precisely the same money amount as before;
but as he would obtain in exchange for this equal sum, one
tenth less of hats, shoes, and every other commodity, and as
he could with his former amount of savings employ fewer
labourers at the increased wages, and purchase fewer raw
materials at the increased prices, he would be in no better
situation than if his money profits had been really diminished
in amount, and every thing had remained at its former price.
Thus then I have endeavoured to shew, first, that a rise of wages
would not raise the price of commodities, but would invariably
lower profits; and secondly, that if the prices of all[1] commodities
could be raised, still the effect on profits would be the same;
and that in fact the value of the medium only in which prices
and profits are estimated would be lowered.

[1] Eds. 1-2 do not contain 'all'.

CHAPTER VII

ON FOREIGN TRADE

No extension of foreign trade will immediately increase the amount of value in a country, although it will very powerfully contribute to increase the mass of commodities, and therefore the sum of enjoyments. As the value of all foreign goods is measured by the quantity of the produce of our land and labour, which is given in exchange for them, we should have no greater value, if by the discovery of new markets, we obtained double the quantity of foreign goods in exchange for a given quantity of our's. If by the purchase of English goods to the amount of 1000*l.*, a merchant can obtain a quantity of foreign goods, which he can sell in the English market for 1,200*l.*, he will obtain 20 per cent. profit by such an employment of his capital; but neither his gains, nor the value of the commodities imported, will be increased or diminished by the greater or smaller quantity of foreign goods obtained. Whether, for example, he imports twenty-five or fifty pipes of wine, his interest can be no way affected, if at one time the twenty-five pipes, and at another the fifty pipes, equally sell for 1,200*l.* In either case his profit will be limited to 200*l.*, or 20 per cent. on his capital; and in either case the same value will be imported into England. If the fifty pipes sold for more than 1,200*l.*, the profits of this individual merchant would exceed the general rate of profits, and capital would naturally flow into this advantageous trade, till the fall of the price of wine had brought every thing to the former level.

It has indeed been contended, that the great profits which are sometimes made by particular merchants in foreign trade, will elevate the general rate of profits in the country, and that the abstraction of capital from other employments, to partake of the new and beneficial foreign commerce, will raise prices generally, and thereby increase profits. It has been said, by high authority, that less capital being necessarily devoted to the growth of corn, to the manufacture of cloth, hats, shoes, &c. while the demand continues the same, the price of these commodities will be so increased, that the farmer, hatter, clothier, and shoemaker, will have an increase of profits, as well as the foreign merchant.*

They who hold this argument agree with me, that the profits of different employments have a tendency to conform to one another; to advance and recede together. Our variance consists in this: They contend, that the equality of profits will be brought about by the general rise of profits; and I am of opinion, that the profits of the favoured trade will speedily subside to the general level.

For, first, I deny that less capital will necessarily be devoted to the growth of corn, to the manufacture of cloth, hats, shoes, &c. unless the demand for these commodities be diminished; and if so, their price will not rise. In the purchase of foreign commodities, either the same, a larger, or a less portion of the produce of the land and labour of England will be employed. If the same portion be so employed, then will the same demand exist for cloth, shoes, corn, and hats, as before, and the same portion of capital will be devoted to their production. If, in consequence of the price of foreign commodities being cheaper, a less portion of the annual produce of the land and labour of England is employed in the purchase of foreign commodities, more will remain for the purchase of other things. If there be a greater demand for hats, shoes, corn, &c. than before, which there may be, the consumers of foreign commodities having an

* See Adam Smith, book i. chap. 9.[1]

[1] Cannan's ed., vol. I, p. 95.

additional portion of their revenue disposable, the capital is
also disposable with which the greater value of foreign commodities was before purchased; so that with the increased
demand for corn, shoes, &c. there exists also the means of
procuring an increased supply, and therefore neither prices nor
profits can permanently rise. If more of the produce of the
land and labour of England be employed in the purchase of
foreign commodities, less can be employed in the purchase of
other things, and therefore fewer hats, shoes, &c. will be required. At the same time that capital is liberated from the
production of shoes, hats, &c. more must be employed in
manufacturing those commodities with which foreign commodities are purchased; and consequently in all cases the demand for foreign and home commodities together, as far as
regards value, is limited by the revenue and capital of the
country. If one increases, the other must diminish. If the
quantity of wine, imported[1] in exchange for the same quantity
of English commodities, be doubled, the people of England
can either consume double the quantity of wine that they did
before, or the same quantity of wine and a greater quantity of
English commodities. If my revenue had been 1000*l*., with
which I purchased annually one pipe of wine for 100*l*. and
a certain quantity of English commodities for 900*l*.; when wine
fell to 50*l*. per pipe, I might lay out the 50*l*. saved, either in the
purchase of an additional pipe of wine, or in the purchase of
more English commodities. If I bought more wine, and every
wine-drinker did the same, the foreign trade would not be in
the least disturbed; the same quantity of English commodities
would be exported in exchange for wine, and we should receive double the quantity, though not double the value of wine.
But if I, and others, contented ourselves with the same quantity
of wine as before, fewer English commodities would be ex-

[1] Ed. 1 'If the importation of wine, given'.

ported, and the wine-drinkers might either consume the commodities which were before exported, or any others for which they had an inclination. The capital required for their production would be supplied by the capital liberated from the foreign trade.

There are two ways in which capital may be accumulated: it may be saved either in consequence of increased revenue, or of diminished consumption. If my profits are raised from 1000*l*. to 1200*l*. while my expenditure continues the same, I accumulate annually 200*l*. more than I did before. If I save 200*l*. out of my expenditure, while my profits continue the same, the same effect will be produced; 200*l*. per annum will be added to my capital. The merchant who imported wine after profits had been raised from 20 per cent. to 40 per cent., instead of purchasing his English goods for 1000*l*. must purchase them for 857*l*. 2*s*. 10*d*., still selling the wine which he imports in return for those goods for 1200*l*.; or, if he continued to purchase his English goods for 1000*l*. must raise the price of his wine to 1400*l*.; he would thus obtain 40 instead of 20 per cent. profit on his capital; but if, in consequence of the cheapness of all the commodities on which his revenue was expended, he and all other consumers could save the value of 200*l*. out of every 1000*l*. they before expended, they would more effectually add to the real wealth of the country; in one case, the savings would be made in consequence of an increase of revenue, in the other, in consequence of diminished expenditure.

If, by the introduction of machinery, the generality of the commodities on which revenue was expended fell 20 per cent. in value, I should be enabled to save as effectually as if my revenue had been raised 20 per cent.; but in one case the rate of profits is stationary, in the other it is raised 20 per cent.— If, by the introduction of cheap foreign goods, I can save 20 per cent. from my expenditure, the effect will be precisely the same as if machinery had lowered the expense of their production, but profits would not be raised.

It is not, therefore, in consequence of the extension of the market that the rate of profit[1] is raised, although such extension may be equally efficacious in increasing the mass of commodities, and may thereby enable us to augment the funds destined for the maintenance of labour, and the materials on which labour may be employed. It is quite as important to the happiness of mankind, that our enjoyments should be increased by the better distribution of labour, by each country producing those commodities for which by its situation, its climate, and its other natural or artificial advantages, it is adapted, and by their exchanging them for the commodities of other countries, as that they should be augmented by a rise in the rate of profits.

It has been my endeavour to shew throughout this work, that the rate of profits can never be increased but by a fall in wages, and that there can be no permanent fall of wages but in consequence of a fall of the necessaries on which wages are expended. If, therefore, by the extension of foreign trade, or by improvements in machinery, the food and necessaries of the labourer can be brought to market at a reduced price, profits will rise. If, instead of growing our own corn, or manufacturing the clothing and other necessaries of the labourer, we discover a new market from which we can supply ourselves with these commodities at a cheaper price, wages will fall and profits rise; but if the commodities obtained at a cheaper rate, by the extension of foreign commerce, or by the improvement of machinery, be exclusively the commodities consumed by the rich, no alteration will take place in the rate of profits. The rate of wages would not be affected, although wine, velvets, silks, and other expensive commodities should fall 50 per cent., and consequently profits would continue unaltered.

[1] Ed. 1 'profits' in place of 'profit'.

Foreign trade, then, though highly beneficial to a country, as it increases the amount and variety of the objects on which revenue may be expended, and affords, by the abundance and cheapness of commodities, incentives to saving, and to the accumulation of capital, has no tendency to raise the profits of stock, unless the commodities imported be of that description on which the wages of labour are expended.

The remarks which have been made respecting foreign trade, apply equally to home trade. The rate of profits is never increased by a better distribution of labour, by the invention of machinery, by the establishment of roads and canals, or by any means of abridging labour either in the manufacture or in the conveyance of goods. These are causes which operate on price, and never fail to be highly beneficial to consumers; since they enable them with the same labour, or with the value of the produce of the same labour, to obtain in exchange a greater quantity of the commodity to which the improvement is applied; but they have no effect whatever on profit. On the other hand, every diminution in the wages of labour raises profits, but produces no effect on the price of commodities. One is advantageous to all classes, for all classes are consumers; the other is beneficial only to producers; they gain more, but every thing remains at its former price. In the first case they get the same as before; but every thing on which their gains are expended, is diminished in exchangeable value.

The same rule which regulates the relative value of commodities in one country, does not regulate the relative value of the commodities exchanged between two or more countries.

Under a system of perfectly free commerce, each country naturally devotes its capital and labour to such employments as are most beneficial to each. This pursuit of individual advantage is admirably connected with the universal good of the whole. By stimulating industry, by rewarding ingenuity, and by using most efficaciously the peculiar powers bestowed by nature, it distributes labour most effectively and most economically: while, by increasing the general mass of productions, it diffuses general benefit, and binds together by one common tie of interest and intercourse, the universal society of nations throughout the civilized world. It is this principle which determines that wine shall be made in France and Portugal, that corn shall be grown in America and Poland, and that hardware and other goods shall be manufactured in England.

In one and the same country, profits are, generally speaking, always on the same level; or differ only as the employment of capital may be more or less secure and agreeable. It is not so between different countries. If the profits of capital employed in Yorkshire, should exceed those of capital employed in London, capital would speedily move from London to Yorkshire, and an equality of profits would be effected; but if in consequence of the diminished rate of production in the lands of England, from the increase of capital and population, wages should rise, and profits fall, it would not follow that capital and population would necessarily move from England to Holland, or Spain, or Russia, where profits might be higher.

If Portugal had no commercial connexion with other countries, instead of employing a great part of her capital and industry in the production of wines, with which she purchases for her own use the cloth and hardware of other countries, she would be obliged to devote a part of that capital to the manufacture of those commodities, which she would thus obtain probably inferior in quality as well as quantity.

The quantity of wine which she shall give in exchange for the cloth of England, is not determined by the respective quantities of labour devoted to the production of each, as it would be, if both commodities were manufactured in England, or both in Portugal.

England may be so circumstanced, that to produce the cloth may require the labour of 100 men for one year; and if she attempted to make the wine, it might require the labour of 120 men for the same time. England would therefore find it her interest to import wine, and to purchase it by the exportation of cloth.

To produce the wine in Portugal, might require only the labour of 80 men for one year, and to produce the cloth in the same country, might require the labour of 90 men for the same time. It would therefore be advantageous for her to export wine in exchange for cloth. This exchange might even take place, notwithstanding that the commodity imported by Portugal could be produced there with less labour than in England. Though she could make the cloth with the labour of 90 men, she would import it from a country where it required the labour of 100 men to produce it, because it would be advantageous to her rather to employ her capital in the production of wine, for which she would obtain more cloth from England, than she could produce by diverting a portion of her capital from the cultivation of vines to the manufacture of cloth.

Thus England would give the produce of the labour of 100 men, for the produce of the labour of 80. Such an exchange could not take place between the individuals of the same country. The labour of 100 Englishmen cannot be given for that of 80 Englishmen, but the produce of the labour of 100 Englishmen may be given for the produce of the labour of 80 Portuguese, 60 Russians, or 120 East Indians. The difference in this respect, between a single country and many, is easily accounted for, by considering the difficulty with which capital moves from one country to another, to seek a more profitable employment, and the activity with which it invariably passes from one province to another in the same country.*

It would undoubtedly be advantageous to the capitalists of England, and to the consumers in both countries, that under such circumstances, the wine and the cloth should both be made in Portugal, and therefore that the capital and labour of England employed in making cloth, should be removed to Portugal for that purpose. In that case, the relative value of these commodities would be regulated by the same principle, as if one were the produce of Yorkshire, and the other of London: and in every other case, if capital freely flowed towards those countries where it could be most profitably employed, there could be no difference in the rate of profit, and no other difference in the real or labour price of commodities, than the additional quantity of labour required to convey them to the various markets where they were to be sold.

Experience, however, shews, that the fancied or real insecurity of capital, when not under the immediate control of its owner, together with the natural disinclination which every man has to quit the country of his birth and connexions, and intrust himself with all his habits fixed, to a strange government and new laws, check the emigration of capital. These feelings, which I should be sorry to see weakened, induce most

* It will appear then, that a country possessing very considerable advantages in machinery and skill, and which may therefore be enabled to manufacture commodities with much less labour than her neighbours, may, in return for such commodities, import a portion of the corn required for its consumption, even if its land were more fertile, and corn could be grown with less labour than in the country from which it was imported. Two men can both make shoes and hats, and one is superior to the other in both employments; but in making hats, he can only exceed his competitor by one-fifth or 20 per cent., and in making shoes he can excel him by one-third or 33 per cent.;—will it not be for the interest of both, that the superior man should employ himself exclusively in making shoes, and the inferior man in making hats?[1]

[1] Cp. A. Smith's taylor and shoemaker, Bk. IV, ch. ii; vol. I, p. 422.

men of property to be satisfied with a low rate of profits in their own country, rather than seek a more advantageous employment for their wealth in foreign nations.

Gold and silver having been chosen for the general medium of circulation, they are, by the competition of commerce, distributed in such proportions amongst the different countries of the world, as to accommodate themselves to the natural traffic which would take place if no such metals existed, and the trade between countries were purely a trade of barter.

Thus, cloth cannot be imported into Portugal, unless it sell there for more gold than it cost in the country from which it was imported; and wine cannot be imported into England, unless it will sell for more there than it cost in Portugal. If the trade were purely a trade of barter, it could only continue whilst England could make cloth so cheap as to obtain a greater quantity of wine with a given quantity of labour, by manufacturing cloth than by growing vines; and also whilst the industry of Portugal were attended by the reverse effects. Now suppose England to discover a process for making wine, so that it should become her interest rather to grow it than import it; she would naturally divert a portion of her capital from the foreign trade to the home trade; she would cease to manufacture cloth for exportation, and would grow wine for herself. The money price of these commodities would be regulated accordingly; wine would fall here while cloth continued at its former price, and in Portugal no alteration would take place in the price of either commodity. Cloth would continue for some time to be exported from this country, because its price would continue to be higher in Portugal than here; but money instead of wine would be given in exchange for it, till the accumulation of money here, and its diminution abroad, should so operate on the relative value of cloth in the two countries, that it would cease to be profitable to export it. If the improvement in making wine were of a very important description, it might become profitable for the two countries to exchange employments; for England to make all the wine, and Portugal all the cloth consumed by them; but this could be effected only by a new distribution of the precious metals, which should raise the price of cloth in England, and lower it in Portugal. The relative price of wine would fall in England in consequence of the real advantage from the improvement of its manufacture; that is to say, its natural price would fall; the relative price of cloth would rise there from the accumulation of money.

Thus, suppose before the improvement in making wine in England, the price of wine here were 50*l.* per pipe, and the price of a certain quantity of cloth were 45*l.*, whilst in Portugal the price of the same quantity of wine was 45*l.*, and that of the same quantity of cloth 50*l.*; wine would be exported from Portugal with a profit of 5*l.* and cloth from England with a profit of the same amount.

Suppose that, after the improvement, wine falls to 45*l.* in England, the cloth continuing at the same price. Every transaction in commerce is an independent transaction. Whilst a merchant can buy cloth in England for 45*l.* and sell it with the usual profit in Portugal, he will continue to export it from England. His business is simply to purchase English cloth, and to pay for it by a bill of exchange, which he purchases with Portuguese money. It is to him of no importance what becomes of this money: he has discharged his debt by the remittance of the bill. His transaction is undoubtedly regulated by the terms on which he can obtain this bill, but they are known to him at the time; and the causes which may influence the market price of bills, or the rate of exchange, is no consideration of his.

If the markets be favourable for the exportation of wine from

Portugal to England, the exporter of the wine will be a seller of a bill, which will be purchased either by the importer of the cloth, or by the person who sold him his bill; and thus without the necessity of money passing from either country, the exporters in each country will be paid for their goods. Without having any direct transaction with each other, the money paid in Portugal by the importer of cloth will be paid to the Portuguese exporter of wine; and in England by the negotiation of the same bill, the exporter of the cloth will be authorized to receive its value from the importer of wine.

But if the prices of wine were such that no wine could be exported to England, the importer of cloth would equally purchase a bill; but the price of that bill would be higher, from the knowledge which the seller of it would possess, that there was no counter bill in the market by which he could ultimately settle the transactions between the two countries; he might know that the gold or silver money which he received in exchange for his bill, must be actually exported to his correspondent in England, to enable him to pay the demand which he had authorized to be made upon him, and he might therefore charge in the price of his bill all the expenses to be incurred, together with his fair and usual profit.

If then this premium for a bill on England should be equal to the profit on importing cloth, the importation would of course cease; but if the premium on the bill were only 2 per cent., if to be enabled to pay a debt in England of 100*l.*, 102*l.* should be paid in Portugal, whilst cloth which cost 45*l.* would sell for 50*l.*, cloth would be imported, bills would be bought, and money would be exported, till the diminution of money in Portugal, and its accumulation in England, had produced such a state of prices as would make it no longer profitable to continue these transactions.

But the diminution of money in one country, and its increase in another, do not operate on the price of one commodity only, but on the prices of all, and therefore the price of wine and cloth will be both raised in England, and both lowered in Portugal. The price of cloth, from being 45*l.* in one country and 50*l.* in the other, would probably fall to 49*l.* or 48*l.* in Portugal, and rise to 46*l.* or 47*l.* in England, and not afford a sufficient profit after paying a premium for a bill to induce any merchant to import that commodity.

It is thus that the money of each country is apportioned to it in such quantities only as may be necessary to regulate a profitable trade of barter. England exported cloth in exchange for wine, because, by so doing, her industry was rendered more productive to her; she had more cloth and wine than if she had manufactured both for herself; and Portugal imported cloth and exported wine, because the industry of Portugal could be more beneficially employed for both countries in producing wine. Let there be more difficulty in England in producing cloth, or in Portugal in producing wine, or let there be more facility in England in producing wine, or in Portugal in producing cloth, and the trade must immediately cease.

No change whatever takes place in the circumstances of Portugal; but England finds that she can employ her labour more productively in the manufacture of wine, and instantly the trade of barter between the two countries changes. Not only is the exportation of wine from Portugal stopped, but a new distribution of the precious metals takes place, and her importation of cloth is also prevented.

Both countries would probably find it their interest to make their own wine and their own cloth; but this singular result would take place: in England, though wine would be cheaper, cloth would be elevated in price, more would be paid for it by the consumer; while in Portugal the consumers, both of cloth and of wine, would be able to purchase those commodities cheaper. In the country where the improvement was made, prices would be enhanced; in that where no change had taken place, but where they had been deprived of a profitable branch of foreign trade, prices would fall.

This, however, is only a seeming advantage to Portugal, for the quantity of cloth and wine together produced in that country would be diminished, while the quantity produced in England would be increased. Money would in some degree have changed its value in the two countries, it would be lowered in England and raised in Portugal. Estimated in money, the whole revenue of Portugal would be diminished; estimated in the same medium, the whole revenue of England would be increased.

Thus then it appears, that the improvement of a manufacture in any country tends to alter the distribution of the precious metals amongst the nations of the world: it tends to increase the quantity of commodities, at the same time that it raises general prices in the country where the improvement takes place.

To simplify the question, I have been supposing the trade between two countries to be confined to two commodities—to wine and cloth; but it is well known that many and various articles enter into the list of exports and imports. By the abstraction of money from one country, and the accumulation of it in another, all commodities are affected in price, and consequently encouragement is given to the exportation of many more commodities besides money, which will therefore prevent so great an effect from taking place on the value of money in the two countries as might otherwise be expected.

Beside the improvements in arts and machinery, there are various other causes which are constantly operating on the natural course of trade, and which interfere with the equili-

brium, and the relative value of money. Bounties on exportation or importation, new taxes on commodities, sometimes by
their direct, and at other times by their indirect operation,
disturb the natural trade of barter, and produce a consequent
necessity of importing or exporting money, in order that prices
may be accommodated to the natural course of commerce; and
this effect is produced not only in the country where the
disturbing cause takes place, but, in a greater or less degree,
in every country of the commercial world.

This will in some measure account for the different value
of money in different countries; it will explain to us why the
prices of home commodities, and those of great bulk, though
of comparatively small value,[1] are, independently of other
causes, higher in those countries where manufactures flourish.
Of two countries having precisely the same population, and
the same quantity of land of equal fertility in cultivation, with
the same knowledge too of agriculture, the prices of raw produce will be highest in that where the greater skill, and the
better machinery is used in the manufacture of exportable commodities. The rate of profits will probably differ but little; for
wages, or the real reward of the labourer, may be the same in
both; but those wages, as well as raw produce, will be rated
higher in money in that country, into which, from the advantages attending their skill and machinery, an abundance of
money is imported in exchange for their goods.

Of these two countries, if one had the advantage in the manufacture of goods of one quality, and the other in the manufacture
of goods of another quality, there would be no decided influx
of the precious metals into either; but if the advantage very
heavily preponderated in favour of either, that effect would
be inevitable.

In the former part of this work, we have assumed, for the

[1] Ed. 1 does not contain 'though of comparatively small value,'.

purpose of argument, that money always continued of the same value; we are now endeavouring to shew that besides the ordinary variations in the value of money, and those which are common to the whole commercial world, there are also partial variations to which money is subject in particular countries; and in fact[1], that the value of money is never the same in any two countries, depending as it does on relative taxation, on manufacturing skill, on the advantages of climate, natural productions, and many other causes.

Although, however, money is subject to such perpetual variations, and consequently the prices of the commodities which are common to most countries, are also subject to considerable difference, yet no effect will be produced on the rate of profits, either from the influx or efflux of money. Capital will not be increased, because the circulating medium is augmented. If the rent paid by the farmer to his landlord, and the wages to his labourers, be 20 per cent. higher in one country than another, and if at the same time the nominal value of the farmer's capital be 20 per cent. more, he will receive precisely the same rate of profits, although he should sell his raw produce 20 per cent. higher.

Profits, it cannot be too often repeated, depend on wages; not on nominal, but real wages; not on the number of pounds that may be annually paid to the labourer, but on the number of days' work, necessary to obtain those pounds. Wages may therefore be precisely the same in two countries; they may bear too the same proportion to rent, and to the whole produce obtained from the land, although in one of those countries the labourer should receive ten shillings per week, and in the other twelve.

In the early states of society, when manufactures have made little progress, and the produce of all countries is nearly similar,

[1] 'in fact' is the reading of eds. 1-2; ed. 3 misprints 'to fact'.

consisting of the bulky and most useful commodities, the value of money in different countries will be chiefly regulated by their distance from the mines which supply the precious metals; but as the arts and improvements of society advance, and different nations excel in particular manufactures, although distance will still enter into the calculation, the value of the precious metals will be chiefly regulated by the superiority of those manufactures.

Suppose all nations to produce corn, cattle, and coarse clothing only, and that it was by the exportation of such commodities that gold could be obtained from the countries which produced them, or from those who held them in subjection; gold would naturally be of greater exchangeable value in Poland than in England, on account of the greater expense of sending such a bulky commodity as corn the more distant voyage, and also the greater expense attending the conveying of gold to Poland.

This difference in the value of gold, or which is the same thing, this difference in the price of corn in the two countries, would exist, although the facilities of producing corn in England should far exceed those of Poland, from the greater fertility of the land, and the superiority in the skill and implements of the labourer.

If however Poland should be the first to improve her manufactures, if she should succeed in making a commodity which was generally desirable, including great value in little bulk, or if she should be exclusively blessed with some natural production, generally desirable, and not possessed by other countries, she would obtain an additional quantity of gold in exchange for this commodity, which would operate on the price of her corn, cattle, and coarse clothing. The disadvantage of distance would probably be more than compensated by the advantage of having an exportable commodity of great value, and money would be permanently of lower value in Poland than in England. If, on the contrary, the advantage of skill and machinery were possessed by England, another reason would be added to that which before existed, why gold should be less valuable in England than in Poland, and why corn, cattle, and clothing, should be at a higher price in the former country.

These I believe to be the only two causes which regulate the comparative value of money in the different countries of the world; for although taxation occasions a disturbance of the equilibrium of money, it does so by depriving the country in which it is imposed of some of the advantages attending skill, industry, and climate.

It has been my endeavour carefully to distinguish between a low value of money, and a high value of corn, or any other commodity with which money may be compared. These have been generally considered as meaning the same thing; but it is evident, that when corn rises from five to ten shillings a bushel, it may be owing either to a fall in the value of money, or to a rise in the value of corn. Thus we have seen, that from the necessity of having recourse successively to land of a worse and worse quality, in order to feed an increasing population, corn must rise in relative value to other things. If therefore money continue permanently of the same value, corn will exchange for more of such money, that is to say, it will rise in price. The same rise in the price of corn will be produced by such improvement of machinery in manufactures, as shall enable us to manufacture commodities with peculiar advantages: for the influx of money will be the consequence; it will fall in value, and therefore exchange for less corn. But the effects resulting from a high price of corn when produced by the rise in the value of corn, and when caused by a fall in the value of money, are totally different. In both cases the money price of wages will rise, but if it be in consequence of the fall in the

value of money, not only wages and corn, but all other commodities will rise. If the manufacturer has more to pay for
wages, he will receive more for his manufactured goods, and
the rate of profits will remain unaffected. But when the rise
in the price of corn is the effect of the difficulty of production,
profits will fall; for the manufacturer will be obliged to pay
more wages, and will not be enabled to remunerate himself by
raising the price of his manufactured commodity.

Any improvement in the facility of working the mines, by
which the precious metals may be produced with a less quantity
of labour, will sink the value of money generally. It will then
exchange for fewer commodities in all countries; but when any
particular country excels in manufactures, so as to occasion an
influx of money towards it, the value of money will be lower,
and the prices of corn and labour will be relatively higher in
that country, than in any other.

This higher value of money will not be indicated by the
exchange; bills may continue to be negociated at par, although
the prices of corn and labour should be 10, 20, or 30 per cent.
higher in one country than another. Under the circumstances
supposed, such a difference of prices is the natural order of
things, and the exchange can only be at par, when a sufficient
quantity of money is introduced into the country excelling in
manufactures, so as to raise the price of its corn and labour.
If foreign countries should prohibit the exportation of money,
and could successfully enforce obedience to such a law, they
might indeed prevent the rise in the prices of the corn and
labour of the manufacturing country; for such rise can only
take place after the influx of the precious metals, supposing
paper money not to be used; but they could not prevent the
exchange from being very unfavourable to them. If England
were the manufacturing country, and it were possible to prevent the importation of money, the exchange with France,

Holland, and Spain, might be 5, 10, or 20 per cent. against those countries.

Whenever the current of money is forcibly stopped, and when money is prevented from settling at its just level, there are no limits to the possible variations of the exchange. The effects are similar to those which follow, when a paper money, not exchangeable for specie at the will of the holder, is forced into circulation. Such a currency is necessarily confined to the country where it is issued: it cannot, when too abundant, diffuse itself generally amongst other countries. The level of circulation is destroyed, and the exchange will inevitably be unfavourable to the country where it is excessive in quantity: just so would be the effects of a metallic circulation, if by forcible means, by laws which could not be evaded, money should be detained in a country, when the stream of trade gave it an impetus towards other countries.

When each country has precisely the quantity of money which it ought to have, money will not indeed be of the same value in each, for with respect to many commodities it may differ 5, 10, or even 20 per cent., but the exchange will be at par. One hundred pounds in England, or the silver which is in 100*l*., will purchase a bill of 100*l*., or an equal quantity of silver in France, Spain, or Holland.

In speaking of the exchange and the comparative value of money in different countries, we must not in the least refer to the value of money estimated in commodities, in either country. The exchange is never ascertained by estimating the comparative value of money in corn, cloth, or any commodity whatever, but by estimating the value of the currency of one country, in the currency of another.

It may also be ascertained by comparing it with some standard common to both countries. If a bill on England for 100*l*. will purchase the same quantity of goods in France or Spain, that a bill on Hamburgh for the same sum will do, the exchange between Hamburgh and England is at par; but if a bill on England for 130*l.*, will purchase no more than a bill on Hamburgh for 100*l.*, the exchange is 30 per cent. against England.

In England 100*l.* may purchase a bill, or the right of receiving 101*l.* in Holland, 102*l.* in France, and 105*l.* in Spain. The exchange with England is, in that case, said to be 1 per cent. against Holland, 2 per cent. against France, and 5 per cent. against Spain. It indicates that the level of currency is higher than it should be in those countries, and the comparative value of their currencies, and that of England, would be immediately restored to par, by abstracting from theirs, or by adding to that of England.

Those who maintained that our currency was depreciated during the last ten years, when the exchange varied from 20 to 30 per cent. against this country, have never contended, as they have been accused of doing, that money could not be more valuable in one country than another, as compared with various commodities; but they did contend, that 130*l.* could not be detained in England, unless it was depreciated,[1] when it was of no more value, estimated in the money of Hamburgh, or of Holland, than the bullion in[2] 100*l.*

By sending 130*l.* good English pounds sterling to Hamburgh, even at an expense of 5*l.*, I should be possessed there of 125*l.*; what then could make me consent to give 130*l.* for a bill which would give me 100*l.* in Hamburgh, but that my pounds were not good pounds sterling?—they were deteriorated, were degraded in intrinsic value below the pounds sterling of Hamburgh, and if actually sent there, at an expense of 5*l.*, would sell only for 100*l.* With metallic pounds sterling, it is not denied that my 130*l.* would procure me 125*l.* in Hamburgh, but with paper pounds sterling I can only obtain 100*l.*;

[1] Eds. 1-2 do not contain 'unless it was depreciated,'.

[2] Eds. 1-2 do not contain 'the bullion in'.

and yet it was[1] maintained that 130*l.* in paper, was of equal value with 130*l.* in silver or gold.

Some indeed more reasonably maintained, that 130*l.* in paper was not of equal value with 130*l.* in metallic money; but they said that it was the metallic money which had changed its value, and not the paper money. They wished to confine the meaning of the word depreciation to an actual fall of value, and not to a comparative difference between the value of money, and the standard by which by law it is regulated. One hundred pounds of English money was formerly of equal value with, and could purchase 100*l.* of Hamburgh money: in any other country a bill of 100*l.* on England, or on Hamburgh, could purchase precisely the same quantity of commodities. To obtain the same things, I was lately obliged to give 130*l.* English money, when Hamburgh could obtain them for 100*l.* Hamburgh money. If English money was of the same value then as before, Hamburgh money must have risen in value. But where is the proof of this? How is it to be ascertained whether English money has fallen, or Hamburgh money has risen? there is no standard by which this can be determined. It is a plea which admits of no proof, and can neither be positively affirmed, nor positively contradicted. The nations of the world must have been early convinced, that there was no standard of value in nature, to which they[2] might unerringly refer, and therefore chose a medium, which on the whole appeared to them less variable than any other commodity.

To this standard we must conform till the law is changed, and till some other commodity is discovered, by the use of which we shall obtain a more perfect standard, than that which we have established. While gold is exclusively the standard in this country, money will be depreciated, when a pound sterling is not of equal value with 5 dwts. and 3 grs. of standard gold, and that, whether gold rises or falls in general value.

---

[1] Eds. 1-2 'is', here and six words below.   [2] Ed. 1 'we'.

CHAPTER VIII

ON TAXES

TAXES are a portion of the produce of the land and labour of a country, placed at the disposal of the government; and are always ultimately paid, either from the capital, or from the revenue of the country.

We have already shewn how the capital of a country is either fixed or circulating, according as it is of a more or of a less durable nature.[1] It is difficult to define strictly, where the distinction between circulating and fixed capital begins; for there are almost infinite degrees in the durability of capital. The food of a country is consumed and reproduced at least once in every year; the clothing of the labourer is probably not consumed and reproduced in less than two years; whilst his house and furniture are calculated to endure for a period of ten or twenty years.

When the annual productions of a country more than replace[2] its annual consumption, it is said to increase its capital; when its annual consumption is not at least[3] replaced by its annual production, it is said to diminish its capital. Capital may therefore be increased by an increased production, or by a diminished unproductive[4] consumption.

If the consumption of the government, when increased by the levy of additional taxes, be met either by an increased production, or by a diminished consumption on the part of the people, the taxes will fall upon revenue, and the national capital will remain unimpaired; but if there be no increased

---

[1] Above p. 31.
[2] Eds. 1-2 read 'exceed' instead of 'more than replace'.
[3] Eds. 1-2 'at least is not'.
[4] Eds. 1-2 do not contain 'unproductive'.

production or diminished unproductive[1] consumption on the part of the people, the taxes will necessarily fall on capital[2], that is to say, they will impair the fund allotted to productive consumption.*

In proportion as the capital of a country is diminished, its productions will be necessarily diminished; and, therefore, if the same unproductive[3] expenditure on the part of the people and of the government continue, with a constantly diminishing annual reproduction, the resources of the people and the state will fall away with increasing rapidity, and distress and ruin will follow.

Notwithstanding the immense expenditure of the English government during the last twenty years, there can be little doubt but that the increased production on the part of the people has more than compensated for it. The national capital has not merely been unimpaired, it has been greatly increased, and the annual revenue of the people, even after the payment of their taxes, is probably greater at the present time than at any former period of our history.

For the proof of this we might refer to the increase of population—to the extension of agriculture—to the increase

* It must be understood that all the productions of a country are consumed; but it makes the greatest difference imaginable whether they are consumed by those who reproduce, or by those who do not reproduce another value. When we say that revenue is saved, and added to capital, what we mean is, that the portion of revenue, so said to be added to capital, is consumed by productive instead of unproductive labourers.[4] There can be no greater error than in supposing that capital is increased by non-consumption. If the price of labour should rise so high, that notwithstanding the increase of capital, no more could be employed, I should say that such increase of capital would be still unproductively consumed.[5]

[1] Eds. 1-2 do not contain 'unproductive'.
[2] Eds. 1-2 do not contain the remainder of this sentence.

[3] Eds. 1-2 do not contain 'unproductive'.
[4] Cp. *Wealth of Nations*, Bk. II, ch. iii; vol. I, p. 320.
[5] Eds. 1-2 do not contain this note.

of shipping and manufactures—to the building of docks—to the opening of numerous canals, as well as to many other expensive undertakings; all denoting an increase both of capital and of annual production.

Still, however, it is certain that but for taxation this increase of capital would have been much greater. There are no taxes which have not a tendency to lessen the power to accumulate. All taxes must either fall on capital or revenue. If they encroach on capital, they must proportionably diminish that fund by whose extent the extent of the productive industry of the country must always be regulated; and if they fall on revenue, they must either lessen accumulation, or force the contributors to save the amount of the tax, by making a corresponding diminution of their former unproductive[1] consumption of the necessaries and luxuries of life. Some taxes will produce these effects in a much greater degree than others; but the great evil of taxation is to be found,[2] not so much in any selection of its objects, as in the general amount of its effects taken collectively.

Taxes are not necessarily taxes on capital, because they are laid on capital; nor on income, because they are laid on income. If from my income of 1000*l.* per annum, I am required to pay 100*l.*, it will really be a tax on my income, should I be content with the expenditure of the remaining 900*l.*; but it will be a tax on capital, if I continue to spend 1000*l.*

[1] Ed. 2 does not contain 'unproductive'.

[2] In ed. 1 this paragraph does not contain the first sentence and reads: 'There are no taxes which have not a tendency to impede accumulation, because there are none which may not be considered as checking production, and as causing the same effects as a bad soil or climate, a diminution of skill or industry, a worse distribution of labour, or the loss of some useful machinery; and although some taxes will produce these effects in a much greater degree than others, it must be confessed that the great evil of taxation is to be found,' etc. The alteration, and the actual wording of it, were suggested by McCulloch; see his letter, below, VII, 353.

The capital from which my income of 1000*l.* is derived, may be of the value of 10,000*l.*; a tax of one per cent. on such capital would be 100*l.*; but my capital would be unaffected, if after paying this tax, I in like manner contented myself with the expenditure of 900*l.*

The desire which every man has to keep his station in life, and to maintain his wealth at the height which it has once attained[1], occasions most taxes, whether laid on capital or on income, to be paid from income; and therefore as taxation proceeds, or as government increases its expenditure, the annual enjoyments[2] of the people must be diminished, unless they are enabled proportionally to increase their capitals and income. It should be the policy of governments to encourage a disposition to do this in the people, and never to lay such taxes as will inevitably fall on capital; since by so doing, they impair the funds for the maintenance of labour, and thereby diminish the future production of the country.

In England this policy has been neglected, in taxing the probates of wills, in the legacy duty, and in all taxes affecting the transference of property from the dead to the living. If a legacy of 1000*l.* be subject to a tax of 100*l.*, the legatee considers his legacy as only 900*l.* and feels no particular motive to save the 100*l.* duty from his expenditure, and thus the capital of the country is diminished; but if he had really received 1000*l.*, and had been required to pay 100*l.* as a tax on income, on wine, on horses, or on servants, he would probably have diminished, or rather not increased his expenditure by that sum, and the capital of the country would have been unimpaired.

"Taxes upon the transference of property from the dead to the living," says Adam Smith, "fall finally, as well as immediately, upon the persons to whom the property is transferred.

---

[1] Ed. 1 'obtained', corrected in *Errata*.

[2] Eds. 1-2 'expenditure' in place of 'enjoyments'.

Taxes on the sale of land fall altogether upon the seller. The seller is almost always under the necessity of selling, and must, therefore, take such a price as he can get. The buyer is scarce ever under the necessity of buying, and will, therefore, only give such a price as he likes. He considers what the land will cost him in tax and price together. The more he is obliged to pay in the way of tax, the less he will be disposed to give in the way of price. Such taxes, therefore, fall almost always upon a necessitous person, and must, therefore, be very cruel [1] and oppressive." "Stamp duties, and duties upon the registration of bonds and contracts for borrowed money, fall altogether upon the borrower, and in fact are always paid by him. Duties of the same kind upon law proceedings fall upon the suitors. They reduce to both the capital value of the subject in dispute. The more it costs to acquire any property, the less must be the neat value of it when acquired. All taxes upon the transference of property of every kind, so far as they diminish the capital value of that property, tend to diminish the funds destined for the maintenance of labour [2]. They are all more or less unthrifty taxes, that increase the revenue of the sovereign, which seldom maintains any but unproductive labourers, at the expense of the capital of the people, which maintains none but productive." [3]

But this is not the only objection to taxes on the transference of property; they prevent the national capital from being distributed in the way most beneficial to the community. For the general prosperity, there cannot be too much facility given to the conveyance and exchange of all kinds of property, as it is by such means that capital of every species is likely to find its way into the hands of those, who will best employ it

[1] Adam Smith says 'very frequently cruel'.
[2] Adam Smith says 'of productive labour'.
[3] Bk. v, ch. ii, Appendix to articles i and ii; vol. ii, pp. 346–7.

in increasing the productions of the country. "Why," asks
M. Say, "does an individual wish to sell his land? it is because
he has another employment in view in which his funds will
be more productive. Why does another wish to purchase this
same land? it is to employ a capital which brings him in too
little, which was unemployed, or the use of which he thinks
susceptible of improvement. This exchange will increase the
general income, since it increases the income of these parties.
But if the charges are so exorbitant as to prevent the exchange,
they are an obstacle to this increase of the general income."[1]
Those taxes, however, are easily collected; and this by many
may be thought to afford some compensation for their injurious
effects.

[1] *Traité d'Économie politique,* 2nd ed., 1814, vol. II, p. 312.

CHAPTER IX

TAXES ON RAW PRODUCE

HAVING in a former part of this work established, I hope satisfactorily, the principle, that the price of corn is regulated by the cost of its production on that land exclusively, or rather with that capital exclusively, which pays no rent, it will follow that whatever may increase the cost of production will increase the price; whatever may reduce it, will lower the price. The necessity of cultivating poorer land, or of obtaining a less return with a given additional capital on land already in cultivation, will inevitably raise the exchangeable value of raw produce. The discovery of machinery, which will enable the cultivator to obtain his corn at a less cost of production, will necessarily lower its exchangeable value. Any tax which may be imposed on the cultivator, whether in the shape of land-tax, tithes, or a tax on the produce when obtained, will increase the cost of production, and will therefore raise the price of raw produce.

If the price of raw produce did not rise so as to compensate the cultivator for the tax, he would naturally quit a trade where his profits were reduced below the general level of profits; this would occasion a diminution of supply, until the unabated demand should have produced such a rise in the price of raw produce, as to make the cultivation of it equally profitable with the investment of capital in any other trade.

A rise of price is the only means by which he could pay the tax, and continue to derive the usual and general profits from this employment of his capital. He could not deduct the tax from his rent, and oblige his landlord to pay it, for he pays no rent. He would not deduct it from his profits, for there is no reason why he should continue in an employment which yields small profits, when all other employments are yielding greater. There can then be no question, but that he will have the power of raising the price of raw produce by a sum equal to the tax.

A tax on raw produce would not be paid by the landlord; it would not be paid by the farmer; but it would be paid, in an increased price, by the consumer.

Rent, it should be remembered, is the difference between the produce obtained by equal portions of labour and capital employed on land of the same or different qualities. It should be remembered too, that the money rent of land, and the corn rent of land, do not vary in the same proportion.

In the case of a tax on raw produce, of a land-tax, or tithes, the corn rent of land will vary, while the money rent will remain as before.

If, as we have before supposed,[1] the land in cultivation were of three qualities, and that with an equal amount of capital,

> 180 qrs. of corn were obtained from land No. 1.
> 170 . . . . . from . . . . . . 2.
> 160 . . . . . from . . . . . 3.

the rent of No. 1 would be 20 quarters, the difference between that of No. 3 and No. 1; and of No. 2, 10 quarters, the difference between that of No. 3 and No. 2; while No. 3 would pay no rent whatever.

Now if the price of corn were 4*l.* per quarter, the money rent of No. 1 would be 80*l.*, and that of No. 2, 40*l.*

Suppose a tax of 8*s.* per quarter to be imposed on corn; then the price would rise to 4*l.* 8*s.*; and if the landlords obtained the same corn rent as before, the rent of No. 1 would be 88*l.* and that of No. 2, 44*l.* But they would not obtain the

---

[1] Above, p. 83, n. and p. 113.

same corn rent; the tax would fall heavier on No. 1 than on No. 2, and on No. 2 than on No. 3, because it would be levied on a greater quantity of corn. It is the difficulty of production on No. 3 which regulates price; and corn rises to 4*l*. 8*s*., that the profits of the capital employed on No. 3 may be on a level with the general profits of stock.

The produce and tax on the three qualities of land will be as follows:

No. 1, yielding	180 qrs. at 4*l*. 8*s*. per qr. . . .	£792
Deduct the value of	16.3 or 8*s*. per qr. on 180 qrs.[1] .	72
Net corn produce	163.7	Net money produce £720

No. 2, yielding	170 qrs. at 4*l*. 8*s*. per qr. . . .	£748
Deduct the value of	15.4 { qrs. at 4*l*. 8*s*. or 8*s*. per qr. on 170 qrs. . . . . }	68
Net corn produce	154.6	Net money produce £680

No. 3, yielding[2]	160 qrs. at 4*l*. 8*s*.	£704
Deduct the value of	14.5 { qrs. at 4*l*. 8*s*. or 8*s*. per qr. on 160 . . . . . }	64
Net corn produce	145.5	Net money produce £640

The money rent of No. 1 would continue to be 80*l*., or the difference between 640*l*. and 720*l*.; and that of No. 2, 40*l*., or the difference between 640*l*. and 680*l*., precisely the same as before; but the corn rent will be reduced from 20 quarters on No. 1, to 18.2 quarters, the difference between 145.5 and 163.7 quarters,[3] and that on No. 2 from 10 to 9.1 quarters, the difference between 145.5 and 154.6 quarters.

---

[1] Should read 'Deduct the value of 16.3 qrs. at 4*l*. 8*s*. or 8*s*. per qr. on 180 qrs.'; cp. under Nos. 2 and 3.

[2] Eds. 1-2 do not contain 'yielding'.

[3] Ed. 1 does not contain 'the difference between 145.5 and 163.7 quarters,' nor the similar phrase at the end of the paragraph.

A tax on corn, then, would fall on the consumers of corn, and would raise its value as compared with all other commodities, in a degree proportioned to the tax. In proportion as raw produce entered into the composition of other commodities, would their value also be raised, unless the tax were countervailed by other causes. They would in fact be indirectly taxed, and their value would rise in proportion to the tax.

A tax, however, on raw produce, and on the necessaries of the labourer, would have another effect—it would raise wages. From the effect of the principle of population on the increase of mankind, wages of the lowest kind never continue much above that rate which nature and habit demand for the support of the labourers. This class is never able to bear any considerable proportion[1] of taxation; and, consequently, if they had to pay 8s. per quarter in addition for wheat and in some smaller proportion for other necessaries, they would not be able to subsist on the same wages as before, and to keep up the race of labourers. Wages would inevitably and necessarily rise; and in proportion as they rose, profits would fall. Government would receive a tax of 8s. per quarter on all the corn consumed in the country, a part of which would be paid directly by the consumers of corn; the other part would be paid indirectly by those who employed labour, and would affect profits in the same manner as if wages had been raised from the increased demand for labour compared with the supply, or from an increasing difficulty of obtaining the food and necessaries required by the labourer.

In as far as the tax might affect consumers, it would be an equal tax, but in as far as it would affect profits, it would be a partial tax; for it would neither operate on the landlord nor on the stockholder, since they would continue to receive, the one the same money rent, the other the same money dividends

---

[1] Eds. 1-2 'portion'.

as before. A tax on the produce of the land then would operate as follows:

    1st. It would raise the price of raw produce by a sum equal to the tax, and would therefore fall on each consumer in proportion to his consumption.

2dly. It would raise the wages of labour, and lower profits.

It may then be objected against such a tax,

    1st. That by raising the wages of labour, and lowering profits, it is an unequal tax, as it affects the income of the farmer, trader, and manufacturer, and leaves untaxed the income of the landlord, stockholder, and others enjoying fixed incomes.

    2dly. That there would be a considerable interval between the rise in the price of corn and the rise of wages, during which much distress would be experienced by the labourer.

    3dly. That raising wages and lowering profits is a discouragement to accumulation, and acts in the same way as a natural poverty of soil.

    4thly. That by raising the price of raw produce, the prices of all commodities into which raw produce enters, would be raised, and that therefore we should not meet the foreign manufacturer[1] on equal terms in the general market.

With respect to the first objection, that by raising the wages of labour and lowering profits it acts unequally, as it affects the income of the farmer, trader, and manufacturer, and leaves untaxed the income of the landlord, stockholder, and others enjoying fixed incomes,—it may be answered, that if the operation of the tax be unequal, it is for the legislature to make it equal, by taxing directly the rent of land, and the dividends

---

[1] Eds. 1-2 'manufacture'.

from stock. By so doing, all the objects of an income tax would be obtained, without the inconvenience of having recourse to the obnoxious measure of prying into every man's concerns, and arming commissioners with powers repugnant to the habits and feelings of a free country.

With respect to the second objection, that there would be a considerable interval between the rise of the price of corn and the rise of wages, during which much distress would be experienced by the lower classes,—I answer, that under different circumstances, wages follow the price of raw produce with very different degrees of celerity; that in some cases no effect whatever is produced on wages by a rise of corn; in others, the rise of wages precedes the rise in the price of corn; again, in some the effect on wages is slow, and in others rapid.[1]

Those who maintain that it is the price of necessaries which regulates the price of labour, always allowing for the particular state of progression in which the society may be, seem to have conceded too readily, that a rise or fall in the price of necessaries will be very slowly succeeded by a rise or fall of wages. A high price of provisions may arise from very different causes, and may accordingly produce very different effects. It may arise from

1st. A deficient supply.

2nd. From a gradually increasing demand, which may be ultimately attended with an increased cost of production.

3rdly. From a fall in the value of money.

4thly. From taxes on necessaries.

These four causes have not been sufficiently distinguished and separated by those who have inquired into the influence of a high price of necessaries on wages. We will examine them severally.

---

[1] Ed. 1 'again, in some the effect is slow, and in others the interval must be very short.'

A bad harvest will produce a high price of provisions, and the high price is the only means by which the consumption is compelled to conform to the state of the supply. If all the purchasers of corn were rich, the price might rise to any degree, but the result would remain unaltered; the price would at last be so high, that the least rich would be obliged to forego the use of a part of the quantity which they usually consumed, as by diminished consumption alone the demand could be brought down to the limits of the supply. Under such circumstances no policy can be more absurd, than that of forcibly regulating money wages by the price of food, as is frequently done, by misapplication of the poor laws. Such a measure affords no real relief to the labourer, because its effect is to raise still higher the price of corn, and at last he must be obliged to limit his consumption in proportion to the limited supply. In the natural course of affairs a deficient supply from bad seasons, without any pernicious and unwise interference, would not be followed by a rise of wages. The raising of wages is merely nominal to those who receive them; it increases the competition in the corn market, and its ultimate effect is to raise the profits of the growers and dealers in corn. The wages of labour are really regulated by the proportion between the supply and demand of necessaries, and the supply and demand of labour; and money is merely the medium, or measure, in which wages are expressed. In this case then the distress of the labourer is unavoidable, and no legislation can afford a remedy, except by the importation of additional food, or by adopting the most useful substitutes[1].

When a high price of corn is the effect of an increasing demand, it is always preceded by an increase of wages, for

[1] Eds. 1-2 do not contain ', or by adopting the most useful sub- stitutes'.

The argument in this paragraph is derived from Malthus, *Essay on Population*, 4th ed., 1807, vol. II, pp. 79-82.

demand cannot increase, without an increase of means in the people to pay for that which they desire. An accumulation of capital naturally produces an increased competition among the employers of labour, and a consequent rise in its price. The increased wages are not always[1] immediately expended on food, but are first made to contribute to the other enjoyments of the labourer. His improved condition however induces, and enables him to marry, and then the demand for food for the support of his family naturally supersedes that of those other enjoyments on which his wages were temporarily expended. Corn rises then because the demand for it increases, because there are those in the society who have improved means of paying for it; and the profits of the farmer will be raised above the general level of profits, till the requisite quantity of capital has been employed on its production. Whether, after this has taken place, corn shall again fall to its former price, or shall continue permanently higher, will depend on the quality of the land from which the increased quantity of corn has been supplied. If it be obtained from land of the same fertility, as that which was last in cultivation, and with no greater cost of labour, the price will fall to its former state; if from poorer land, it will continue permanently higher. The high wages in the first instance proceeded from an increase in the demand for labour: inasmuch as it encouraged marriage, and supported children, it produced the effect of increasing the supply of labour. But when the supply is obtained, wages will again fall to their former price, if corn has fallen to its former price: to a higher than the former price, if the increased supply of corn has been produced from land of an inferior quality. A high price is by no means incompatible with an abundant supply: the price is permanently high, not because the quantity is deficient, but because there has been an increased cost in

---

[1] Eds. 1-2 do not contain 'always'.

producing it. It generally happens indeed, that when a stimulus has been given to population, an effect is produced beyond what the case requires; the population may be, and generally is so much increased as, notwithstanding the increased demand for labour, to bear a greater proportion to the funds for maintaining labourers than before the increase of capital. In this case a re-action will take place, wages will be below their natural level, and will continue so, till the usual proportion between the supply and demand has been restored. In this case then, the rise in the price of corn is preceded by a rise of wages, and therefore entails no distress on the labourer.

A fall in the value of money, in consequence of an influx of the precious metals from the mines, or from the abuse of the privileges of banking, is another cause for the rise of the price of food; but it will make no alteration in the quantity produced. It leaves undisturbed too the number of labourers, as well as the demand for them; for there will be neither an increase nor a diminution of capital. The quantity of necessaries to be allotted to the labourer, depends on the comparative demand and supply of necessaries, with the comparative demand and supply of labour; money being only the medium in which the quantity is expressed; and as neither of these is altered, the real reward of the labourer will not alter. Money wages will rise, but they will only enable him to furnish himself with the same quantity of necessaries as before. Those who dispute this principle, are bound to shew why an increase of money should not have the same effect in raising the price of labour, the quantity of which has not been increased, as they acknowledge it would have on the price of shoes, of hats, and of corn, if the quantity of those commodities were not increased. The relative market value of hats and shoes is regulated by the demand and supply of hats, compared with the demand and supply of shoes, and money is but the medium in which their value is expressed. If shoes be doubled in price, hats will also be doubled in price, and they will retain the same comparative value. So if corn and all the necessaries of the labourer be doubled in price, labour will be doubled in price also, and while there is no interruption to the usual demand and supply of necessaries and of labour, there can be no reason why they should not preserve their relative value.

Neither a fall in the value of money, nor a tax on raw produce, though each will raise the price, will *necessarily* interfere with the quantity of raw produce; or with the number of people, who are both able to purchase, and willing to consume it. It is very easy to perceive why, when the capital of a country increases irregularly, wages should rise, whilst the price of corn remains stationary, or rises in a less proportion; and why, when the capital of a country diminishes, wages should fall whilst corn remains stationary, or falls in a much less proportion, and this too for a considerable time; the reason is, because labour is a commodity which cannot be increased and diminished at pleasure. If there are too few hats in the market for the demand, the price will rise, but only for a short time; for in the course of one year, by employing more capital in that trade, any reasonable addition may be made to the quantity of hats, and therefore their market price cannot long very much exceed their natural price; but it is not so with men; you cannot increase their number in one or two years when there is an increase of capital, nor can you rapidly diminish their number when capital is in a retrograde state; and, therefore, the number of hands increasing or diminishing slowly, whilst the funds for the maintenance of labour increase or diminish rapidly, there must be a considerable interval before the price of labour is exactly regulated by the price of corn and necessaries; but in the case of a fall in the value of money, or of a tax on corn, there is not necessarily any excess in the supply of labour, nor any abatement of demand, and therefore there can be no reason why the labourer should sustain a real diminution of wages.

A tax on corn does not necessarily diminish the quantity of corn, it only raises its money price; it does not necessarily diminish the demand compared with the supply of labour; why then should it diminish the portion paid to the labourer? Suppose it true that it did diminish the quantity given to the labourer, in other words, that it did not raise his money wages in the same proportion as the tax raised the price of the corn which he consumed; would not the supply of corn exceed the demand?—would it not fall in price? and would not the labourer thus obtain his usual portion? In such case, indeed, capital would be withdrawn from agriculture; for if the price were not increased by the whole amount of the tax, agricultural profits would be lower than the general level of profits, and capital would seek a[1] more advantageous employment. In regard then to a tax on raw produce, which is the point under discussion, it appears to me that no interval which could bear oppressively on the labourer, would elapse between the rise in the price of raw produce, and the rise in the wages of the labourer; and that therefore no other inconvenience would be suffered by this class, than that which they would suffer from any other mode of taxation, namely, the risk that the tax might infringe on the funds destined for the maintenance of labour, and might therefore check or abate the demand for it.

With respect to the third objection against taxes on raw produce, namely, that the raising wages, and lowering profits, is a discouragement to accumulation, and acts in the same way as a natural poverty of soil; I have endeavoured to shew in another part of this work[2] that savings may be as effectually made from expenditure as from production; from a reduction

----

[1] Eds. 1-2 do not contain 'a'.   [2] Above, p. 131.

in the value of commodities, as from a rise in the rate of profits. By increasing my profits from 1000*l*. to 1200*l*., whilst prices continue the same, my power of increasing my capital by savings is increased, but it is not increased so much as it would be if my profits continued as before, whilst commodities were so lowered in price, that 800*l*. would procure me as much as 1000*l*. purchased before.

Now the sum required by the tax must be raised, and the question simply is, whether the same amount shall be taken from individuals by diminishing their profits, or by raising the prices of the commodities on which their profits will be expended.[1]

Taxation under every form presents but a choice of evils; if it do not act on profit, or other sources of income,[2] it must act on expenditure; and provided the burthen[3] be equally borne, and do not repress reproduction, it is indifferent on which it is laid. Taxes on production, or on the profits of stock, whether applied immediately to profits, or indirectly, by taxing the land or its produce, have this advantage over other taxes; that provided all other income be taxed,[4] no class of the community can escape them, and each contributes according to his means.

From taxes on expenditure a miser may escape; he may have an income of 10,000*l*. per annum, and expend only 300*l*.; but from taxes on profits, whether direct or indirect, he cannot escape; he will contribute to them either by giving up a part or the value of a part of his produce; or by the advanced prices of the necessaries essential to production, he will be unable to continue to accumulate at the same rate. He may, indeed, have an income of the same value, but he will not have the same

---

[1] Ed. 1 does not contain this paragraph.
[2] Eds. 1-2 do not contain 'or other sources of income,'.

[3] Ed. 1 'burden'.
[4] Eds. 1-2 do not contain 'that provided all other income be taxed,'.

command of labour, nor of an equal quantity of materials on which such labour can be exercised.

If a country is insulated from all others, having no commerce with any of its neighbours, it can in no way shift any portion of its taxes from itself. A portion of the produce of its land and labour will be devoted to the service of the State; and I cannot but think that, unless it presses unequally on that class which accumulates and saves, it will be of little importance whether the taxes be levied on profits, on agricultural, or on manufactured commodities. If my revenue be 1000*l.* per annum, and I must pay taxes to the amount of 100*l.*, it is of little importance whether I pay it from my revenue, leaving myself only 900*l.*, or pay 100*l.* in addition for my agricultural commodities, or for my manufactured goods. If 100*l.* is my fair proportion of the expenses of the country, the virtue of taxation consists[1] in making sure that I shall pay that 100*l.*, neither more nor less; and that cannot be effected in any manner so securely as by taxes on wages, profits, or raw produce.

The fourth and last objection which remains to be noticed is: That by raising the price of raw produce, the prices of all commodities into which raw produce enters, will be raised, and that, therefore, we shall not meet the foreign manufacturer on equal terms in the general market.

In the first place, corn and *all* home commodities could not be materially raised in price without an influx of the precious metals; for the same quantity of money could not circulate the same quantity of commodities, at high as at low prices, and the precious metals never could be purchased with dear commodities. When more gold is required, it must be obtained by giving more, and not fewer commodities in exchange for it. Neither could the want of money be supplied by paper, for it is not paper that regulates the value of gold as a commodity,

---

[1] Eds. 2-3 misprint 'consist'.

but gold that regulates the value of paper. Unless then the value of gold could be lowered, no paper could be added to the circulation without being depreciated. And that the value of gold could not be lowered, appears clear, when we consider that the value of gold as a commodity must be regulated by the quantity of goods which must be given to foreigners in exchange for it. When gold is cheap, commodities are dear; and when gold is dear, commodities are cheap, and fall in price. Now as no cause is shewn why foreigners should sell their gold cheaper than usual, it does not appear probable that there would be any influx of gold. Without such an influx there can be no increase of quantity, no fall in its value, no rise in the general price of goods. *

The probable effect of a tax on raw produce, would be to raise[1] the price of raw produce, and[2] of all commodities in which raw produce entered, but not in any degree proportioned to the tax; while other commodities in which no raw produce entered, such as articles made of the metals and the earths, would fall in price: so that the same quantity of money as before would be adequate to the whole circulation.

A tax which should have the effect of raising the price of all home productions, would not discourage exportation, except during a very limited time. If they were raised in price at home, they could not indeed immediately be profitably exported, because they would be subject to a burthen here from which abroad they were free. The tax would produce the same effect as an alteration in the value of money, which was not general and common to all countries, but confined to a single

* It may be doubted whether commodities raised in price, merely by taxation, would require any more money for their circulation. I believe they would not.[3]

[1] Ed. 2 misprints 'rise'.
[2] Ed. 1 does not contain 'of raw produce, and'.

[3] Eds. 1-2 do not contain this note. Cp. below, p. 213–14, n.

one. If England were that country, she might not be able to sell, but she would be able to buy, because importable commodities would not be raised in price. Under these circumstances nothing but money could be exported in return for foreign commodities, but this is a trade which could not long continue; a nation cannot be exhausted of its money, for after a certain quantity has left it, the value of the remainder will rise, and such a price of commodities will be the consequence, that they will again be capable of being profitably exported. When money had risen, therefore, we should no longer export it in return for goods[1], but we should export those manufactures which had first been raised in price, by the rise in the price of the raw produce from which they were made, and then again lowered by the exportation of money.

But it may be objected, that when money so rose in value, it would rise with respect to foreign as well as home commodities, and therefore that all encouragement to import foreign goods would cease. Thus, suppose we imported goods which cost 100*l*. abroad, and which sold for 120*l*. here, we should cease to import them, when the value of money had so risen in England, that they would only sell for 100*l*. here: this, however, could never happen. The motive which determines us to import a commodity, is the discovery of its relative cheapness abroad: it is the comparison of its price abroad with its price at home[2]. If a country exports[3] hats, and imports cloth, it does so because it can obtain more cloth by making hats, and exchanging them for cloth, than if it made the cloth itself. If the rise of raw produce occasions any increased cost of production in making hats, it would occasion also an increased cost in making cloth. If, therefore, both commodities were made at

---

[1] Eds. 1–2 'for goods imported'.   [3] Ed. 3 misprints 'export'.
[2] Eds. 1–2 'its natural price abroad with its natural price at home'.

home, they would both rise. One, however, being a commodity which we import, would not rise, neither would it fall, when the value of money rose; for by not falling, it would regain its natural relation to the exported commodity. The rise of raw produce makes a hat rise from 30 to 33 shillings, or 10 per cent.: the same cause if we manufactured cloth, would make it rise from 20s. to 22s. per yard. This rise does not destroy the relation between cloth and hats; a hat was, and continues to be, worth one yard and a half of cloth. But if we import cloth, its price will continue uniformly at 20s. per yard, unaffected first by the fall, and then by the rise in the value of money; whilst hats, which had risen from 30s. to 33s., will again fall from 33s. to 30s., at which point the relation between cloth and hats will be restored.

To simplify the consideration of this subject, I have been supposing that a rise in the value of raw materials would affect, in an equal proportion, all home commodities; that if the effect on one were to raise it 10 per cent., it would raise all 10 per cent.; but as the value of commodities is very differently made up of raw material and labour; as some commodities, for instance, all those made from the metals, would be unaffected by the rise of raw produce from the surface of the earth, it is evident that there would be the greatest variety in the effects produced on the value of commodities, by a tax on raw produce. As far as this effect was produced, it would stimulate or retard the exportation of particular commodities, and would undoubtedly be attended with the same inconvenience that attends the taxing of commodities; it would destroy the natural relation between the value of each. Thus the natural price of a hat, instead of being the same as a yard and a half of cloth, might only be of the value of a yard and a quarter, or it might be of the value of a yard and three quarters, and therefore rather a different direction might be given to foreign trade.

All these inconveniences would probably[1] not interfere with the value of the exports and imports; they would only prevent the very best distribution of the capital of the whole world, which is never so well regulated, as when every commodity is freely allowed to settle at its natural price, unfettered by artificial restraints[2].

Although then the rise in the price of most of our own commodities, would for a time check exportation generally, and might permanently prevent the exportation of a few commodities, it could not materially interfere with foreign trade, and would not place us under any comparative disadvantage as far as regarded competition in foreign markets.

[1] Ed. 1 does not contain 'probably'. [2] Ed. 1 does not contain ', unfettered by artificial restraints'.

CHAPTER X

TAXES ON RENT[1]

A TAX on rent would affect rent only; it would fall wholly on landlords, and could not be shifted to any class of consumers. The landlord could not raise his rent, because he would leave unaltered the difference between the produce obtained from the least productive land in cultivation, and that obtained from land of every other quality. Three sorts of land, No. 1, 2, and 3, are in cultivation, and yield respectively with the same labour, 180, 170, and 160 quarters of wheat; but No. 3 pays no rent, and is therefore untaxed: the rent then of No. 2 cannot be made to exceed the value of ten, nor No. 1, of twenty quarters. Such a tax could not raise the price of raw produce, because as the cultivator of No. 3 pays neither rent nor tax, he would in no way be enabled to raise the price of the commodity produced. A tax on rent would not discourage the cultivation of fresh land, for such land pays no rent, and would be untaxed. If No. 4 were taken into cultivation, and yielded 150 quarters, no tax would be paid for such land; but it would create a rent of ten quarters on No. 3, which would then commence paying the tax.

A tax on rent, as rent is constituted, would discourage cultivation, because it would be a tax on the profits of the landlord. The term rent of land, as I have elsewhere observed,[2] is applied to the whole amount of the value paid by the farmer to his landlord, a part only of which is strictly rent. The buildings and fixtures, and other expenses paid for by the landlord, form strictly a part of the stock of the farm, and must have been

---

[1] In ed. 1 this chapter is numbered 'VIII*' both here and in the Contents. See above, p. 10, n.
[2] Above, p. 67.

furnished by the tenant, if not provided by the landlord. Rent
is the sum paid to the landlord for the use of the land, and for
the use of the land only. The further sum that is paid to him
under the name of rent, is for the use of the buildings, &c.,
and is really the profits of the landlord's stock. In taxing rent,
as no distinction would be made between that part paid for
the use of the land, and that paid for the use of the landlord's
stock, a portion of the tax would fall on the landlord's profits,
and would, therefore, discourage cultivation, unless the price
of raw produce rose. On that land, for the use of which no
rent was paid, a compensation under that name might be given
to the landlord for the use of his buildings. These buildings
would not be erected, nor would raw produce be grown on
such land, till the price at which it sold would not only pay
for all the usual outgoings, but also this[1] additional one of the
tax. This part of the tax does not fall on the landlord, nor on
the farmer, but on the consumer of raw produce.

There can be little doubt but that if a tax were laid on rent,
landlords would soon find a way to discriminate between that
which is[2] paid to them for the use of the land, and that which
is[3] paid for the use of the buildings, and the improvements
which are[4] made by the landlord's stock. The latter would
either be called the rent of house and buildings, or on[5] all new
land taken into cultivation, such buildings would be erected,[6]
and improvements would be made by the tenant, and not by
the landlord. The landlord's capital might indeed be really
employed for that purpose; it might be nominally expended
by the tenant, the landlord furnishing him with the means,
either in the shape of a loan, or in the purchase of an annuity
for the duration of the lease. Whether distinguished or not,

[1] Ed. 1 'but also for this'.
[2] Ed. 1 'was'.
[3] Ed. 1 'was'.
[4] Ed. 1 'were'.
[5] Ed. 1 'in'.
[6] Ed. 1 does not contain 'would be erected,'.

there is a real difference between the nature of the compensations which the landlord receives for these different objects;
and it is quite certain, that a tax on the real rent of land falls
wholly on the landlord, but that a tax on that remuneration
which the landlord receives for the use of his stock expended
on the farm, falls, in a progressive country,[1] on the consumer
of raw produce. If a tax were laid on rent, and no means of
separating the remuneration now paid by the tenant to the
landlord under the name of rent were adopted, the tax, as far
as it regarded the rent on the buildings and other fixtures,
would never fall for any length of time on the landlord, but
on the consumer. The capital expended on these buildings, &c.,
must afford the usual profit[2] of stock; but it would cease to
afford this profit on the land last cultivated, if the expenses of
those buildings, &c., did not fall on the tenant; and if they
did, the tenant would then cease to make his usual profits of
stock, unless he could charge them on the consumer.

[1] Eds. 1-2 do not contain ', in a   [2] Eds. 1-2 'profits'.
progressive country,'.

CHAPTER XI

TITHES

TITHES are a tax on the gross produce of the land, and, like taxes on raw produce, fall wholly on the consumer. They differ from a tax on rent, inasmuch as they affect land which such a tax would not reach; and raise the price of raw produce, which that tax would not alter. Lands of the worst quality, as well as of the best, pay tithes, and exactly in proportion to the quantity of produce obtained from them; tithes are therefore an equal tax.

If land of the last quality, or that which pays no rent, and which regulates the price of corn, yield a sufficient quantity to give the farmer the usual profits of stock, when the price of wheat is 4*l.* per quarter, the price must rise to 4*l.* 8*s.* before the same profits can be obtained after the tithes are imposed, because for every quarter of wheat the cultivator must pay eight shillings to the church[1], and if he does not obtain the same profits, there is no reason why he should not quit his employment, when he can get them in other trades.

The only difference between tithes and taxes on raw produce, is, that one is a variable money tax, the other a fixed money tax. In a stationary state of society, where there is neither increased nor diminished facility of producing corn, they will be precisely the same in their effects; for, in such a state, corn will be at an invariable price, and the tax will therefore be also invariable. In either a retrograde state, or in a state in which great improvements are made in agriculture, and where consequently raw produce will fall in value comparatively with other things, tithes will be a lighter tax than a permanent

[1] Ed. 1 does not contain the remainder of this paragraph.

money tax; for if the price of corn should fall from 4*l.* to 3*l.*, the tax would fall from eight to six shillings. In a progressive state of society, yet without any marked improvements in agriculture, the price of corn would rise, and tithes would be a heavier tax than a permanent money tax. If corn rose from 4*l.* to 5*l.*, the tithes on the same land would advance from eight to ten shillings.

Neither tithes nor a money tax will affect the money rent of landlords, but both will materially affect corn rents. We have already observed[1] how a money tax operates on corn rents, and it is equally evident that a similar effect would be produced by tithes. If the lands, No. 1, 2, 3, respectively produced 180, 170, and 160 quarters, the rents might be on No. 1, twenty quarters, and on No. 2, ten quarters; but they would no longer preserve that proportion after the payment of tithes: for if a tenth be taken from each, the remaining produce will be 162, 153, 144, and consequently the corn rent of No. 1 will be reduced to eighteen, and that of No. 2 to nine quarters. But the price of corn would rise from 4*l.* to 4*l.* 8*s.* 10$\frac{2}{3}$*d.*; for 144[2] quarters are to 4*l.* as 160[3] quarters to 4*l.* 8*s.* 10$\frac{2}{3}$*d.*, and consequently the money rent would continue unaltered; for on No. 1 it would be 80*l.*,[*] and on No. 2, 40*l.*[†]

The chief objection against tithes is, that they are not a permanent and fixed tax, but increase in value, in proportion as the difficulty of producing corn increases. If those difficulties should make the price of corn 4*l.*, the tax is 8*s.*, if they should increase it to 5*l.*, the tax is 10*s.*, and at 6*l.*, it is 12*s.* They not only rise in value, but they increase in amount: thus,

---

[*] 18 Quarters at 4*l.* 8*s.* 10$\frac{2}{3}$*d.*[4]
[†] 9 Quarters at 4*l.* 8*s.* 10$\frac{2}{3}$*d.*

[1] Above, p. 157 ff.
[2] Ed. 1 'nine' in place of '144'.
[3] Ed. 1 'ten' in place of '160'.
[4] Eds. 1-2 do not contain this or the next note.

when No. 1 was cultivated, the tax was only levied on 180 quarters; when No. 2 was cultivated, it was levied on 180 + 170, or 350 quarters; and when No. 3 was cultivated, on 180 + 170 + 160 = 510 quarters. Not only is the amount of tax[1] increased from 100,000 quarters, to 200,000 quarters, when the produce is increased from one to two millions of quarters; but, owing to the increased labour necessary to produce the second million, the relative value of raw produce is so advanced, that the 200,000 quarters may be, though only twice in quantity, yet in value three times that of the 100,000 quarters which were paid before.

If an equal value were raised for the church by any other means, increasing in the same manner as tithes increase, proportionably with the difficulty of cultivation, the effect would be the same[2], and therefore it is a mistake to suppose that, because they are raised on the land, they discourage cultivation more than an equal amount would do if raised in any other manner. The church would in both cases[3] be constantly obtaining an increased portion of the net produce of the land and labour of the country. In an improving state of society, the net produce of land is always diminishing in proportion to its gross produce; but it is from the net income of a country that all taxes are ultimately paid, either in a progressive or in a stationary country. A tax increasing with the gross income, and falling on the net income, must necessarily be a very burdensome, and a very intolerable tax. Tithes are a tenth of the gross, and not of the net produce of the land, and therefore as society improves in wealth, they must, though the same proportion of the gross produce, become a larger and larger proportion[4] of the net produce.

[1] Eds. 1-2 'of the tax'.
[2] Ed. 1 does not contain the remainder of this sentence.
[3] Ed. 1 does not contain 'in both cases'.
[4] Eds. 1-2 'portion'.

Tithes, however, may be considered as injurious to land-lords, inasmuch as they act as a bounty on importation, by taxing the growth of home corn, while the importation of foreign corn remains unfettered. And if, in order to relieve the landlords from the effects of the diminished demand for land, which such a bounty must encourage, imported corn were also taxed, in an equal degree with corn grown at home[1], and the produce paid to the State, no measure could be more fair and equitable; since whatever were paid to the State by this tax, would go to diminish the other taxes which the expenses of Government make necessary: but if such a tax were devoted only to increase the fund paid to the church, it might indeed on the whole increase the general mass of production, but it would diminish the portion of that mass allotted to the pro-ductive classes.

If the trade of cloth were left perfectly free, our manu-facturers might be able to sell cloth cheaper than we could import it. If a tax were laid on the home manufacturer, and not on the importer of cloth, capital might be injuriously driven from the manufacture of cloth to the manufacture of some other commodity, as cloth[2] might then be imported cheaper than it could be made at home. If imported cloth should also be taxed, cloth would again be manufactured at home. The consumer first bought cloth at home, because it was cheaper than foreign cloth; he then bought foreign cloth, be-cause it was cheaper untaxed than home cloth taxed: he lastly bought it again at home, because it was cheaper when both home and foreign cloth were taxed. It is in the last case that he pays the greatest price for his cloth, but all his additional payment is gained by the state. In the second case, he pays

---

[1] Ed. 1 reads 'taxed one tenth' in place of 'taxed, in an equal degree with corn grown at home'.

[2] Eds. 1-2 'it' in place of 'cloth'.

more than in the first, but all he pays in addition is not received by the State, it is an increased price caused by difficulty of production, which is incurred, because the easiest means of production are taken away from us, by being fettered with a tax.

CHAPTER XII

LAND-TAX

A LAND-TAX, levied in proportion to the rent of land, and varying with every variation of rent, is in effect a tax on rent; and as such a tax will not apply to that land which yields no rent, nor to the produce of that capital which is employed on the land with a view to profit merely, and which never pays rent, it will not in any way affect the price of raw produce, but will fall wholly on the landlords. In no respect would such a tax differ from a tax on rent. But if a land-tax be imposed on all cultivated land, however moderate that tax may be, it will be a tax on produce, and will therefore raise the price of produce. If No. 3 be the land last cultivated, although it should pay no rent, it cannot, after the tax, be cultivated, and afford the general rate of profit, unless the price of produce rise to meet the tax. Either capital will be withheld from that employment until the price of corn shall have risen, in consequence of demand, sufficiently to afford the usual profit; or if already employed on such land, it will quit it, to seek a more advantageous employment. The tax cannot be removed to the landlord, for by the supposition he receives no rent. Such a tax may be proportioned to the quality of the land and the abundance of its produce, and then it differs in no respect from tithes; or it may be a fixed tax per acre on all land cultivated, whatever its quality may be.

A land-tax of this latter description would be a very unequal tax, and would be contrary to one of the four maxims with regard to taxes in general, to which, according to Adam Smith,[1] all taxes should conform. The four maxims are as follow:

[1] Bk. v, ch. ii; vol. II, pp. 310–12.

1. "The subjects of every state ought to contribute towards the support of the government, as nearly as possible in proportion to their respective abilities.

2. "The tax which each individual is bound to pay ought to be certain and not arbitrary.

3. "Every tax ought to be levied at the time, or in the manner in which it is most likely to be convenient for the contributor to pay it.

4. "Every tax ought to be so contrived as both to take out and to keep out of the pockets of the people as little as possible, over and above what it brings into the public treasury of the State."

An equal land-tax, imposed indiscriminately and without any regard to the distinction of its quality, on all land cultivated, will raise the price of corn in proportion to the tax paid by the cultivator of the land of the worst quality. Lands of different quality, with the employment of the same capital, will yield very different quantities of raw produce. If on the land which yields a thousand quarters of corn with a given capital, a tax of 100*l.* be laid, corn will rise 2*s.* per quarter to compensate the farmer for the tax. But with the same capital on land of a better quality, 2,000 quarters may be produced, which at 2*s.* a quarter advance, would give 200*l.*; the tax, however, bearing equally on both lands will be 100*l.* on the better as well as on the inferior, and consequently the consumer of corn will be taxed, not only to pay the exigencies of the State, but also to give to the cultivator of the better land, 100*l.* per annum during the period of his lease, and afterwards to raise the rent of the landlord to that amount. A tax of this description then would be contrary to the fourth maxim of Adam Smith, it would take out and keep out of the pockets of the people more than what it brought into the treasury of the State. The taille in France before the Revolution, was a tax of this description; those lands only were taxed, which were held by an ignoble tenure, the price of raw produce rose in proportion to the tax, and therefore they whose lands were not taxed, were benefited by the increase of their rent. Taxes on raw produce, as well as tithes, are free from this objection: they raise the price of raw produce, but they take from each quality of land a contribution in proportion to its actual produce, and not in proportion to the produce of that which is the least productive.

From the peculiar view which Adam Smith took of rent, from his not having observed that much capital is expended in every country, on the land for which no rent is paid, he concluded that all taxes on the land, whether they were laid on the land itself in the form of land-tax or tithes, or on the produce of the land, or were taken from the profits of the farmer, were all invariably paid by the landlord, and that he was in all cases the real contributor, although the tax was, in general, nominally advanced by the tenant. "Taxes upon the produce of the land," he says, "are in reality taxes upon the rent; and though they may be originally advanced by the farmer, are finally paid by the landlord. When a certain portion of the produce is to be paid away for a tax, the farmer computes as well as he can, what the value of this portion is, one year with another, likely to amount to, and he makes a proportionable abatement in the rent which he agrees to pay to the landlord. There is no farmer who does not compute beforehand what the church-tithe, which is a land-tax of this kind is, one year with another, likely to amount to."[1] It is undoubtedly true, that the farmer does calculate his probable outgoings of all descriptions, when agreeing with his landlord for[2] the rent of his farm; and if for the tithe paid to the church, or for the

---

[1] Bk. v, ch. ii; vol. II, p. 321. [2] Ed. 1 'concerning' in place of 'for'.

tax on the produce of the land, he were not compensated by a rise in the relative value of the produce of his farm, he would naturally endeavour to[1] deduct them from his rent. But this is precisely the question in dispute: whether he will eventually deduct them from his rent, or be compensated by a higher price of produce. For the reasons which have been already given, I cannot have the least doubt but that they would raise the price of produce, and consequently that Adam Smith has taken an incorrect view of this important question.

Dr. Smith's view of this subject is probably the reason why he has described "the tithe, and every other land-tax of this kind, under the appearance of perfect equality, as very un-equal taxes; a certain portion of the produce being, in different situations, equivalent to a very different portion of the rent."[2] I have endeavoured to shew that such taxes do not fall with unequal weight on the different classes of farmers or landlords, as they are both compensated by the rise of raw produce, and only contribute to the tax in proportion as they are consumers of raw produce. Inasmuch indeed as wages, and through wages, the rate of profits are affected, landlords, instead of contributing their full share to such a tax, are the class peculiarly exempted. It is the profits of stock, from which that portion of the tax is derived which falls on those labourers, who, from the in-sufficiency of their funds, are incapable of paying taxes; this portion is exclusively borne by all those whose income is derived from the employment of stock, and therefore it in no degree affects landlords.

It is not to be inferred from this view of tithes, and taxes on the land and its produce, that they do not discourage cultivation. Every thing which raises the exchangeable value of commodities of any kind, which are in very general demand,

---

[1] Eds. 1-2 do not contain 'en-deavour to'.   [2] Bk. v, ch. ii; vol. II, p. 321.

tends to discourage both cultivation and production; but this is an evil inseparable from all taxation, and is not confined to the particular taxes of which we are now speaking.

This may be considered, indeed, as the unavoidable disadvantage attending all taxes received and expended by the State. Every new tax becomes a new charge on production, and raises natural price. A portion of the labour of the country which was before at the disposal of the contributor to the tax, is placed at the disposal of the State, and cannot therefore be employed productively[1]. This portion may become so large, that sufficient surplus produce may not be left to stimulate the exertions of those who usually augment by their savings the capital of the State. Taxation has happily never yet in any free country been carried so far as constantly from year to year to diminish its capital. Such a state of taxation could not be long endured; or if endured, it would be constantly absorbing so much of the annual produce of the country as to occasion the most extensive scene of misery, famine, and depopulation.

"A land-tax," says Adam Smith, "which, like that of Great Britain, is assessed upon each district according to a certain invariable canon, though it should be equal at the time of its first establishment, necessarily becomes unequal in process of time, according to the unequal degrees of improvement or neglect in the cultivation of the different parts of the country. In England the valuation according to which the different counties and parishes were assessed to the land-tax by the 4th, William and Mary, was very unequal, even at its first establishment. This tax, therefore, so far offends against the first of the four maxims above mentioned. It is perfectly agreeable to the other three. It is perfectly certain. The time of payment for

---

[1] Eds. 1-2 do not contain ', and cannot therefore be employed productively'.

the tax being the same as that for the rent, is as convenient as it can be to the contributor. Though the landlord is in all cases the real contributor, the tax is commonly advanced by the tenant, to whom the landlord is obliged to allow it in the payment of the rent."[1]

If the tax be shifted by the tenant not on the landlord but on the consumer, then if it be not unequal at first, it can never become so; for the price of produce has been at once raised in proportion to the tax, and will afterwards vary no more on that account. It may offend, if unequal, as I have attempted to shew that it will, against the fourth maxim above mentioned, but it will not offend against the first. It may take more out of the pockets of the people than it brings into the public treasury of the State, but it will not fall unequally on any particular class of contributors. M. Say appears to me to have mistaken the nature and effects of the English land-tax, when he says, "Many persons attribute to this fixed valuation, the great prosperity of English agriculture. That it has very much contributed to it there can be no doubt. But what should we say to a Government, which, addressing itself to a small trader, should hold this language: 'With a small capital you are carrying on a limited trade, and your direct contribution is in consequence very small. Borrow and accumulate capital; extend your trade, so that it may procure you immense profits; yet you shall never pay a greater contribution. Moreover, when your successors shall inherit your profits, and shall have further increased them, they shall not be valued higher to them than they are to you; and your successors shall not bear a greater portion of the public burdens.'

"Without doubt this would be a great encouragement given to manufactures and trade; but would it be just? Could not their advancement be obtained at any other price? In England

[1] Bk. v, ch. ii; vol. II, p. 313.

itself, has not manufacturing and commercial industry made even greater progress, since the same period, without being distinguished with so much partiality? A landlord by his assiduity, economy, and skill, increases his annual revenue by 5000 francs. If the State claim of him the fifth part of his augmented income, will there not remain 4000 francs of increase to stimulate his further exertions?"[1]

M. Say supposes, "A landlord by his assiduity, economy and skill, to increase his annual revenue by 5000 francs;" but a landlord has no means of employing his assiduity, economy and skill on his land, unless he farms it himself; and then it is in quality of capitalist and farmer that he makes the improvement, and not in quality of landlord. It is not conceivable that he could so augment the produce of his farm by any *peculiar* skill on his part, without first increasing the quantity of capital employed upon it. If he increased the capital, his larger revenue might bear the same proportion to his increased capital, as the revenue of all other farmers to their capitals.[2]

If M.[3] Say's suggestion were followed, and the State were to claim the fifth part of the augmented income of the farmer, it would be[4] a partial tax on farmers, acting on their profits, and not affecting the profits of those in other employments. The tax would be paid by all lands, by those which yielded scantily as well as by those which yielded abundantly; and on some lands there could be no compensation for it by deduction from rent, for no rent is paid. A partial tax on profits never falls on the trade on which it is laid, for the trader will either quit his employment, or remunerate himself for the tax. Now those who pay no rent could be recompensed only by a rise

---

[1] *Traité d'Économie politique*, 2nd ed., 1814, vol. II, pp. 353-4.
[2] Eds. 1-2 do not contain this paragraph.
[3] Ed. 1 'Mr.'

[4] In eds. 1-2 the remainder of this sentence reads 'a partial tax, acting on the farmer's profits, and not affecting the profits of other employments.'

in the price of produce, and thus would M. Say's proposed tax fall on the consumer, and not either on the landlord or farmer.

If the proposed tax were increased in proportion to the increased quantity, or value, of the gross produce obtained from the land, it would differ in nothing from tithes, and would equally be transferred to the consumer. Whether then it fell on the gross or on the net produce of land, it would be equally a tax on consumption, and would only affect the landlord and farmer in the same way as other taxes on raw produce.

If no tax whatever had been laid on the land, and the same sum had been raised by any other means, agriculture would have flourished at least as well as it has done; for it is impossible that any tax on land can be an *encouragement*[1] to agriculture; a moderate tax may not, and probably does not, greatly prevent, but it cannot encourage production. The English Government has held no such language as M. Say has supposed. It did not promise to exempt the agricultural class and their successors from all future taxation, and to raise the further supplies which the State might require, from the other classes of society; it said only, "in this mode we will no further burthen the land; but we retain to ourselves the most perfect liberty of making you pay, under some other form, your full quota to the future exigencies of the State."

Speaking of taxes in kind, or a tax of a certain proportion of the produce, which is precisely the same as tithes, M. Say says, "This mode of taxation appears to be the most equitable; there is, however, none which is less so: it totally leaves out of consideration the advances made by the producer; it is proportioned to the gross, and not to the net revenue. Two agriculturists cultivate different kinds of raw produce: one cultivates corn on middling land, his expenses amounting an-

---

[1] Eds. 1-2 'encouragement', not in italics.

nually on an average to 8000 francs: the raw produce from his lands sells for 12,000 francs; he has then a net revenue of 4000 francs.

"His neighbour has pasture or wood land, which brings in every year a like sum of 12,000 francs, but his expenses amount only to 2000 francs. He has therefore on an average a net revenue of 10,000 francs.

"A law ordains that a twelfth of the produce of all the fruits of the earth be levied in kind, whatever they may be. From the first is taken in consequence of this law, corn of the value of 1000 francs; and from the second, hay, cattle, or wood, of the same value of 1000 francs. What has happened? From the one, a quarter of his net income, 4000 francs, has been taken; from the other, whose income was 10,000 francs, a tenth only has been taken. Income is the net profit which remains after replacing the capital exactly in its former state. Has a merchant an income equal to all the sales which he makes in the course of a year? certainly not; his income only amounts to the excess of his sales above his advances, and it is on this excess only that taxes on income should fall."[1]

M. Say's error in the above passage lies in supposing that because the value of the produce of one of these two farms, after reinstating the capital, is greater than the value of the produce of the other, on that account the net income of the cultivators will differ by the same amount. The net income of the landlords and tenants together of the wood land, may be much greater than the net income of the landlords and tenants of the corn land; but it is on account of the difference of rent, and not on account of the difference in the rate of profit.[2] M. Say has wholly omitted the consideration of the different amount of rent, which these cultivators would have to pay.

---

[1] *Traité d'Économie politique*, 1814, vol. II, pp. 349–50.

[2] Eds. 1–2 do not contain this sentence, beginning 'The net income'.

There cannot be two rates of profit in the same employment, and therefore when the value of[1] produce is in different proportions to capital, it is the rent which will differ, and not the profit. Upon what pretence would one man with a capital of 2000 francs, be allowed to obtain a net profit of 10,000 francs from its employment, whilst another, with a capital of 8000 francs, would only obtain 4000 francs? Let M. Say make a due allowance for rent; let him further allow for the effect which such a tax would have on the prices of these different kinds of raw produce, and he will then perceive that it is not an unequal tax, and further that the producers themselves will no otherwise contribute to it, than any other class of consumers.

[1] Eds. 1-2 do not contain 'the value of'.

CHAPTER XIII

TAXES ON GOLD

THE rise in the price of commodities, in consequence of taxation or of difficulty of production, will in all cases ultimately ensue; but the duration of the interval, before the market price will conform to the[1] natural price, must depend on the nature of the commodity, and on the facility with which it can be reduced in quantity. If the quantity of the commodity taxed could not be diminished, if the capital of the farmer or of the hatter for instance, could not be withdrawn to other employments, it would be of no consequence that their profits were reduced below the general level by means of a tax; unless the demand for their commodities should increase, they would never be able to elevate the market price of corn and of hats up to their[2] increased natural price. Their threats to leave their employments, and remove their capitals to more favoured trades, would be treated as an idle menace which could not be carried into effect; and consequently the price would not be raised by diminished production. Commodities, however, of all descriptions can be reduced in quantity, and capital can be removed from trades which are less profitable to those which are more so, but with different degrees of rapidity. In proportion as the supply of a particular commodity can be more easily reduced, without inconvenience to the producer,[3] the price of it will more quickly rise after the difficulty of its production has been increased by taxation, or by any other means. Corn being a commodity indispensably necessary to every one,

---

[1] Eds. 1-2 read 'before the market price of commodities conforms to their'.

[2] Eds. 1-2 'and hats up to the'.

[3] Eds. 1-2 do not contain 'without inconvenience to the producer,'.

little effect will be produced on the demand for it in consequence of a tax, and therefore the supply would not probably be[1] long excessive, even if the producers had great difficulty in removing their capitals from the land. For this reason, the price of corn[2] will speedily be raised by taxation, and the farmer will be enabled to transfer the tax from himself to the consumer.

If the mines which supply us with gold were in this country, and if gold were taxed, it could not rise in relative value to other things, till its quantity were reduced. This would be more particularly the case, if gold were used exclusively[3] for money. It is true that the least productive mines, those which paid no rent, could no longer be worked, as they could not afford the general rate of profits till the relative value of gold rose, by a sum equal to the tax. The quantity of gold, and, therefore, the quantity of money would be slowly reduced: it would be a little diminished in one year, a little more in another, and finally its value would be raised in proportion to the tax; but in the interval, the proprietors or holders, as they would pay the tax, would be the sufferers, and not those who used money. If out of every 1,000 quarters of wheat in the country, and every 1000 produced in future, Government should exact 100 quarters as a tax, the remaining 900 quarters would exchange for the same quantity of other commodities that 1000 did before; but if the same thing took place with respect to gold, if of every 1000*l.* money now in the country, or in future to be brought into it, Government could exact 100*l.* as a tax, the remaining 900*l.* would purchase very little more than 900*l.* purchased before. The tax would fall upon him, whose property consisted of money, and would continue to do so till its quantity

---

[1] Eds. 1-2 'could not be'.
[2] Eds. 1-2 read 'from the land; the price of corn therefore,'.

[3] Eds. 1-2 'exclusively used'.

were reduced in proportion to the increased cost of its production caused by the tax.

This, perhaps, would be more particularly the case with respect to a metal used for money, than any other commodity; because the demand for money is not for a definite quantity, as is the demand for clothes, or for food. The demand for money is regulated entirely by its value, and its value by its quantity. If gold were of double the value, half the quantity would perform the same functions in circulation, and if it were of half the value, double the quantity would be required. If the market value of corn be increased one tenth by taxation, or by difficulty of production, it is doubtful whether any effect whatever would be produced on the quantity consumed, because every man's want is for a definite quantity, and, therefore, if he has the means of purchasing, he will continue to consume as before: but for money, the demand is exactly proportioned to its value. No man could consume twice the quantity of corn, which is usually necessary for his support, but every man purchasing and selling only the same quantity of goods, may be obliged to employ twice, thrice, or any number of times the same quantity of money.

The argument which I have just been using, applies only to those states of society in which the precious metals are used for money, and where paper credit is not established. The metal gold, like all other commodities, has its value in the market ultimately regulated by the comparative facility or difficulty of producing it; and although from its durable nature, and from the difficulty of reducing its quantity, it does not readily bend to variations in its market value, yet that difficulty is much increased from the circumstance of its being used as money. If the quantity of gold in the market for the purpose of commerce only, were 10,000 ounces, and the consumption in our manufactures were 2000 ounces annually, it might be raised one fourth, or 25 per cent. in its value, in one year, by with-holding the annual supply; but if in consequence of its being used as money, the quantity employed were 100,000 ounces, it would not be raised one fourth in value in less than ten years. As money made of paper may be readily reduced in quantity, its value, though its standard were gold, would be increased as rapidly as that of the metal itself would be increased,[1] if the metal, by forming a very small part of the circulation, had a very slight connexion with money.

If gold were the produce of one country only, and it were used universally for money, a very considerable tax might be imposed on it, which would not fall on any country, except in proportion as they used it in manufactures, and for utensils; upon that portion which was used for money, though a large tax might be received, nobody would pay it. This is a quality peculiar to money. All other commodities of which there exists a limited quantity, and which cannot be increased by competition, are dependent for their value, on the tastes, the caprice, and the power of purchasers; but money is a com-modity which no country has any wish or necessity to increase: no more advantage results from using twenty millions, than from using ten millions of currency. A country might have a monopoly of silk, or of wine, and yet the prices of silks and wine might fall, because from caprice or fashion, or taste, cloth and brandy might be preferred, and substituted; the same effect might in a degree take place with gold, as far as its use is con-fined to manufactures: but while money is the general medium of exchange, the demand for it is never a matter of choice, but always of necessity: you must take it in exchange for your goods, and, therefore, there are no limits to the quantity which

---

[1] The remainder of this sentence in ed. 1 reads 'if it had no connexion whatever with money'; in ed. 2 'if by forming a very small part, it had a very slight connection with money'.

may be forced on you by foreign trade, if it fall in value; and
no reduction to which you must not submit, if it rise. You
may, indeed, substitute paper money, but by this you do not,
and cannot lessen the quantity of money, for that is regulated
by the value of the standard for which it is exchangeable[1];
it is only by the rise of the price of commodities, that you can
prevent them from being exported from a country where they
are purchased with little money, to a country where they can
be sold for more, and this rise can only be effected by an
importation of metallic money from abroad, or by the creation
or addition of paper money at home. If then the King of
Spain, supposing him to be in exclusive possession of the mines,
and gold alone to be used for money, were to lay a considerable
tax on gold, he would very much raise its natural value; and
as its market value in Europe is ultimately regulated by its
natural value in Spanish America, more commodities would be
given by Europe for a given quantity of gold. But the same
quantity of gold would not be produced in America, as its
value would only be increased in proportion to the diminution
of quantity consequent on its increased cost of production.
No more goods then would be obtained in America, in exchange for all their gold exported, than before; and it may be
asked, where then would be the benefit to Spain and her
Colonies? The benefit would be this, that if less gold were
produced, less capital would be employed in producing it; the
same value of goods from Europe would be imported by the
employment of the smaller capital, that was before obtained
by the employment of the larger; and, therefore, all the productions obtained by the employment of the capital withdrawn
from the mines, would be a benefit which Spain would derive
from the imposition of the tax, and which she could not obtain

---

[1] Ed. 1 does not contain ', for that   standard for which it is exchange-
is regulated by the value of the   able'.

in such abundance, or with such certainty, by possessing the monopoly of any other commodity whatever. From such a tax, as far as money was concerned, the nations of Europe would suffer no injury whatever; they would have the same quantity of goods, and consequently the same means of enjoyment as before, but these goods would be circulated with a less quantity, because a more valuable money.[1]

If in consequence of the tax, only one tenth of the present quantity of gold were obtained from the mines, that tenth would be of equal value with the ten tenths now produced. But the King of Spain is not exclusively in possession of the mines of the precious metals; and if he were, his advantage from their possession, and the power of taxation, would be very much reduced by the limitation of demand and consumption in Europe, in consequence of the universal substitution, in a greater or less degree, of paper money. The agreement of the market and natural prices of all commodities, depends at all times on the facility with which the supply can be increased or diminished. In the case of gold, houses, and labour, as well as many other things, this effect cannot, under some circumstances, be speedily produced. But it is different with those commodities which are consumed and reproduced from year to year, such as hats, shoes, corn, and cloth; they may be reduced, if necessary, and the interval cannot be long before the supply is contracted in proportion to the increased charge of producing them.

A tax on raw produce from the surface of the earth, will, as we have seen, fall on the consumer, and will in no way affect rent; unless, by diminishing the funds for the maintenance of labour, it lowers wages, reduces the population, and diminishes the demand for corn. But a tax on the produce of gold mines must, by enhancing the value of that metal,

---

[1] Ed. 1 reads simply 'a less quantity of money.'

necessarily reduce the demand for it, and must therefore necessarily displace capital from the employment to which it was
applied. Notwithstanding then, that Spain would derive all
the benefits which I have stated from a tax on gold, the proprietors of those mines from which capital was withdrawn
would lose all their rent. This would be a loss to individuals,
but not a national loss; rent being not a creation, but merely
a transfer of wealth: the King of Spain, and the proprietors
of the mines which continued to be worked, would together
receive not only all that the liberated capital produced, but all
that the other proprietors lost.

Suppose the mines of the 1st, 2nd, and 3rd quality to be
worked, and to produce respectively 100, 80, and 70 pounds
weight of gold, and therefore the rent of No. 1 to be thirty
pounds, and that of No. 2 ten pounds. Suppose now the tax
to be seventy pounds of gold per annum on each mine worked;
and consequently that No. 1 alone could be profitably worked;
it is evident that all rent would immediately disappear. Before
the imposition of the tax, out of the 100 pounds produced
on No. 1, a rent was paid of thirty pounds, and the worker of
the mine[1] retained seventy, a sum equal to the produce of the
least productive mine. The value, then, of what remains to the
capitalist of the mine No. 1, must be the same as before, or
he would not obtain the common profits of stock; and, consequently, after paying seventy out of his 100 pounds for tax,
the value of the remaining thirty must be as great as the value
of seventy was before[2], and therefore the value of the whole
hundred as great as 233 pounds before. Its value might be
higher, but it could not be lower, or even this mine would
cease to be worked. Being a monopolised commodity, it could

---

[1] *i.e.* 'the capitalist of the mine'
mentioned two lines below; cp.
'deprive the worker of the mine

of the common profits of stock',
below, p. 199.
[2] Eds. 1-2 'must be as great as
seventy were before'.

exceed its natural value, and then it would pay a rent equal to that excess; but no funds would be employed in the mine, if it were below this value. In return for one third of the labour and capital employed in the mines, Spain would obtain as much gold as would exchange for the same, or very nearly the same quantity of commodities as before. She would be richer by the produce of the two thirds liberated from the mines. If the value of the 100 pounds of gold should be equal to that of the 250 pounds extracted before; the King of Spain's portion, his seventy pounds, would be equal to 175 at the former value: a small part of the King's tax only would fall on his own subjects, the greater part being obtained by the better distribution of capital.

The account of Spain would stand thus:

Formerly produced:

Gold 250 pounds, of the value of (suppose) .   10,000 yards of cloth.

Now produced:

By the two capitalists who quitted the mines, the same value as 140 pounds of gold formerly exchanged for; equal to[1]	5,600 yards of cloth.
By the capitalist who works the mine, No. 1, thirty pounds of gold, increased in value, as 1 to 2½, and therefore now of the value of . .	3,000 yards of cloth.
Tax to the King[2] seventy pounds, increased also in value as 1 to 2½, and therefore[3] now of the value of	7,000 yards of cloth.

15,600

Of the 7000 received by the King, the people of Spain would

---

[1] Ed. 1 reads 'the value of 140 pounds of gold, or'.
[2] Eds. 1-2 'king', here and four lines below.

[3] Ed. 1 does not contain 'increased also in value as 1 to 2½, and therefore'.

contribute only 1400, and 5600 would be pure gain, effected by the liberated capital.

If the tax, instead of being a fixed sum per mine worked, were a certain portion of its produce, the quantity would not be immediately[1] reduced in consequence. If a half, a fourth, or a third of each mine were taken for the tax, it would nevertheless be the interest of the proprietors to make their mines yield as abundantly as before; but if the quantity were not reduced, but only a part of it transferred from the proprietor to the king, its value would not rise; the tax would fall on the people of the colonies, and no advantage would be gained. A tax of this kind would have the effect that Adam Smith supposes taxes on raw produce would have on the rent of land—it would fall entirely on the rent of the mine. If pushed a little further, indeed,[2] the tax would not only absorb the whole rent, but would deprive the worker of the mine of the common profits of stock, and he would consequently withdraw his capital from the production of gold. If still further extended, the rent of still better mines would be absorbed, and capital would be further withdrawn; and thus the quantity would be continually reduced, and its value raised, and the same effects would take place as we have already pointed out; a part of the tax would be paid by the people of the Spanish colonies, and the other part would be a new creation of produce, by increasing the power of the instrument used as a medium of exchange.[3]

Taxes on gold are of two kinds, one on the actual quantity of gold in circulation, the other on the quantity that is annually produced from the mines. Both have a tendency to reduce the quantity, and to raise the value of gold; but by neither will

---

[1] Ed. 1 does not contain 'immediately'.

[2] Ed. 1 does not contain 'indeed,'.

[3] In ed. 1 this and the following paragraph are not separated.

its value be raised till the quantity is reduced, and therefore such taxes will fall for a time, until the supply is diminished, on the proprietors of money, but ultimately that part which will permanently fall on the community,[1] will be paid by the owner of the mine in the reduction of rent, and by the purchasers of that portion of gold, which is used as a commodity contributing to the enjoyments of mankind, and not set apart exclusively for a circulating medium.

[1] Ed. 1 reads 'they' in place of 'that part which will permanently fall on the community,'.

CHAPTER XIV

TAXES ON HOUSES

THERE are also other commodities besides gold which cannot be speedily reduced in quantity; any tax on which will therefore fall on the proprietor, if the increase of price should lessen the demand.

Taxes on houses are of this description; though laid on the occupier, they will frequently fall by a diminution of rent on the landlord. The produce of the land is consumed and re-produced from year to year, and so are many other commodities; as they may therefore be speedily brought to a level with the demand, they cannot long exceed their natural price. But as a tax on houses may be considered in the light of an additional rent paid by the tenant, its tendency will be to diminish the demand for houses of the same annual rent, without diminishing their supply. Rent will therefore fall, and a part of the tax[1] will be paid indirectly by the landlord.

"The rent of a house," says Adam Smith, "may be distinguished into two parts, of which the one may very properly be called the building rent, the other is commonly called the ground rent. The building rent is the interest or profit of the capital expended in building the house. In order to put the trade of a builder upon a level with other trades, it is necessary that this rent should be sufficient first to pay the same interest which he would have got for his capital, if he had lent it upon good security; and, secondly, to keep the house in constant repair, or what comes to the same thing, to replace within a certain term of years the capital which had been employed in

---

[1] Ed. 3 inserts here 'that' (perhaps a misprint for 'then'); it is not contained in eds. 1-2.

building it." "If in proportion to the interest of money, the trade of the builder affords at any time a much greater profit than this, it will soon draw so much capital from other trades, as will reduce the profit to its proper level. If it affords at any time much less than this, other trades will soon draw so much capital from it as will again raise that profit. Whatever part of the whole rent of a house is over and above what is sufficient for affording this reasonable profit, naturally goes to the ground rent; and where the owner of the ground, and the owner of the building, are two different persons, it is in most cases completely paid to the former.[1] In country houses, at a distance from any great town, where there is a plentiful choice of ground, the ground rent is scarcely any thing, or no more than what the space upon which the house stands, would pay employed in agriculture. In country villas, in the neighbourhood of some great town, it is sometimes a good deal higher, and the peculiar conveniency, or beauty of situation, is there frequently very highly paid for. Ground rents are generally highest in the capital, and in those particular parts of it, where there happens to be the greatest demand for houses, whatever be the reason for that demand, whether for trade and business, for pleasure and society, or for mere vanity and fashion."[2] A tax on the rent of houses may either fall on the occupier, on the ground landlord, or on the building landlord. In ordinary cases it may be presumed, that the whole tax would be paid both immediately and finally by the occupier.

If the tax be moderate, and the circumstances of the country such, that it is either stationary or advancing, there would be little motive for the occupier of a house to content himself with one of a worse description. But if the tax be high, or any

---

[1] Ricardo here omits a sentence of Adam Smith; the following sentence is inaccurately quoted.

[2] Bk. v, ch. ii, pt. ii, art. i; vol. II, pp. 324–5.

other circumstances should diminish the demand for houses, the landlord's income would fall, for the occupier would be partly compensated for the tax by a diminution of rent. It is, however, difficult to say, in what proportions that part of the tax, which was saved by the occupier by a fall of rent, would fall on the building rent and the ground rent. It is probable that, in the first instance, both would be affected; but as houses are, though slowly, yet certainly perishable, and as no more would be built, till the profits of the builder were restored to the general level, building rent would, after an interval, be restored to its natural price. As the builder receives rent only whilst the building endures, he could pay no part of the tax, under the most disastrous circumstances, for any longer period.

The payment of this tax, then, would ultimately fall on the occupier and ground landlord, but, "in what proportion, this final payment would be divided between them," says Adam Smith, "it is not perhaps very easy to ascertain. The division would probably be very different in different circumstances, and a tax of this kind might, according to those different circumstances, affect very unequally both the inhabitant of the house, and the owner of the ground."*

Adam Smith considers ground rents as peculiarly fit subjects for taxation. "Both ground rents, and the ordinary rent of land," he says, "are a species of revenue, which the owner in many cases enjoys, without any care or attention of his own. Though a part of this revenue should be taken from him, in order to defray the expenses of the State, no discouragement will thereby be given to any sort of industry. The annual produce of the land and labour of the society, the real wealth and revenue of the great body of the people, might be the same

* Book v. chap. ii.[1]

[1] Cannan's ed., vol II, p. 326.

after such a tax as before. Ground rents, and the ordinary rent of land are, therefore, perhaps, the species of revenue, which can best bear to have a peculiar tax imposed upon them."[1] It must be admitted that the effects of these taxes would be such as Adam Smith has described; but it would surely be very unjust, to tax exclusively the revenue of any particular class of a community. The burdens of the State should be borne by all in proportion to their means: this is one of the four maxims mentioned by Adam Smith, which should govern all taxation. Rent often belongs to those who, after many years of toil, have realised their gains, and expended their fortunes in the purchase of land or houses[2]; and it certainly would be an infringement of that principle which should ever be held sacred, the security of property, to subject it to unequal taxation. It is to be lamented, that the duty by stamps, with which the transfer of landed property is loaded, materially impedes the conveyance of it into those hands, where it would probably be made most productive. And if it be considered, that land, regarded as a fit subject for exclusive taxation, would not only be reduced in price, to compensate for the risk of that taxation, but in proportion to the indefinite nature and uncertain value of the risk, would become a fit subject for speculations, partaking more of the nature of gambling, than of sober trade, it will appear probable, that the hands into which land would in that case be most apt to fall, would be the hands of those, who possess more of the qualities of the gambler, than of the qualities of the sober-minded proprietor, who is likely to employ his land to the greatest advantage.

[1] Bk. v, ch. ii; vol. II, p. 328.   [2] Ed. I does not contain 'or houses'.

CHAPTER XV

TAXES ON PROFITS

TAXES on those commodities, which are generally denominated luxuries, fall on those only who make use of them. A tax on wine is paid by the consumer of wine. A tax on pleasure horses, or on coaches, is paid by those who provide for themselves such enjoyments, and in exact proportion as they provide them. But taxes on necessaries do not affect the consumers of necessaries, in proportion to the quantity that may be consumed by them, but often in a much higher proportion. A tax on corn, we have observed,[1] not only affects a manufacturer in the proportion that he and his family may consume corn, but it alters the rate of profits of stock, and therefore also affects his income. Whatever raises the wages of labour, lowers the profits of stock; therefore every tax on any commodity consumed by the labourer, has a tendency to lower the rate of profits.

A tax on hats will raise the price of hats; a tax on shoes, the price of shoes; if this were not the case, the tax would be finally paid by the manufacturer; his profits would be reduced below the general level, and he would quit his trade. A partial tax on profits will raise the price of the commodity on which it falls: a tax, for example, on the profits of the hatter, would raise the price of hats; for if his profits were taxed, and not those of any other trade, his profits, unless he raised the price of his hats, would be below the general rate of profits, and he would quit his employment for another.

In the same manner, a tax on the profits of the farmer would raise the price of corn; a tax on the profits of the clothier, the price of cloth; and if a tax in proportion to profits were laid on all trades, every commodity would be raised in price. But

[1] Above, p. 159.

if the mine, which supplied us with the standard of our money, were in this country, and the profits of the miner were also taxed, the price of no commodity would rise, each man would give an equal proportion of his income, and every thing would be as before.

If money be not taxed, and therefore be permitted to preserve its value, whilst every thing else is taxed, and is raised in value, the hatter, the farmer, and clothier, each employing the same capitals, and obtaining the same profits, will pay the same amount of tax. If the tax be 100*l.*, the hats, the cloth, and the corn, will each be increased in value 100*l.* If the hatter gains[1] by his hats 1100*l.*, instead of 1000*l.*, he will pay 100*l.* to Government for the tax; and therefore will still have 1000*l.* to lay out on goods for his own consumption. But as the cloth, corn, and all other commodities, will be raised in price from the same cause, he will not obtain more for his 1000*l.* than he before obtained for 910*l.*, and thus will he contribute by his diminished expenditure to the exigencies of the State; he will, by the payment of the tax, have placed a portion of the produce of the land and labour of the country at the disposal of Government, instead of using that portion himself. If instead of expending his 1000*l.*, he adds it to his capital, he will find in the rise of wages, and in the increased cost of the raw material and machinery, that his saving of 1000*l.* does not amount to more than a saving of 910*l.* amounted to before.

If money be taxed,[2] or if by any other cause its value be altered, and all commodities remain precisely at the same price as before, the profits of the manufacturer and farmer will also be the same as before, they will continue to be 1000*l.*; and as they will each have to pay 100*l.* to Government, they will retain only 900*l.*, which will give them a less command over

---

[1] Eds. 1-2 'gain'.

[2] 'every thing else is taxed' is to be assumed, as in the preceding paragraph.

the produce of the land and labour of the country, whether they expend it in productive or unproductive labour. Precisely what they lose, Government will gain. In the first case the contributor to the tax would, for 1000*l.*, have as great a quantity of goods as he before had for 910*l.*; in the second, he would have only as much as he before had for 900*l.*, for the price of goods would remain unaltered, and he would have only 900*l.* to expend[1]. This proceeds from the difference in the amount of the tax; in the first case it is only an eleventh of his income, in the second it is a tenth; money in the two cases being of a different value.

But although, if money be not taxed, and do not alter in value, all commodities will rise in price, they will not rise in the same proportion; they will not after the tax bear the same relative value to each other which they did before the tax. In a former part of this work,[2] we discussed the effects of the division of capital into fixed and circulating, or rather into durable and perishable capital, on the prices of commodities. We shewed that two manufacturers might employ precisely the same amount of capital, and might derive from it precisely the same amount of profits, but that they would sell their commodities for very different sums of money, according as the capitals they employed were rapidly, or slowly, consumed and reproduced. The one might sell his goods for 4000*l.*, the other for 10,000*l.*, and they might both employ 10,000*l.* of capital, and obtain 20 per cent. profit or 2000*l.* The capital of one might consist, for example, of 2000*l.* circulating capital, to be reproduced, and 8000*l.* fixed, in buildings and machinery; the capital of the other, on the contrary, might consist of 8000*l.* of circulating, and of only 2000*l.* fixed capital in machinery and

---

[1] Ed. 1 does not contain ', for the price of goods would remain unaltered, and he would have only 900*l.* to expend'.

[2] Above, pp. 30–38 and 52–3.

buildings. Now, if each of these persons were to be taxed ten per cent. on his income, or 200*l.*, the one, to make his business yield him the general rate of profit, must raise his goods from 10,000*l.* to 10,200*l.*; the other would also be obliged to raise the price of his goods from 4000*l.* to 4200*l.* Before the tax, the goods sold by one of these manufacturers were 2½ times more valuable than the goods of the other; after the tax they will be 2.42 times more valuable: the one kind will have risen two per cent.; the other five per cent.: consequently a tax upon income, whilst money continued unaltered in value, would alter the relative prices and value of commodities. This would be true also[1], if the tax instead of being laid on the profits, were laid on the commodities themselves: provided they were taxed in proportion to the value of the capital employed on their production, they would rise equally, whatever might be their value, and therefore they would not preserve the same proportion as before. A commodity, which rose from ten to eleven thousand pounds, would not bear the same relation as before, to another which rose from 2 to 3000*l.* If under these circumstances, money rose in value, from whatever cause it might proceed, it would not affect the prices of commodities in the same proportion. The same cause which would lower the price of one from 10,200*l.* to 10,000*l.* or less than two per cent. would lower the price of the other from 4200*l.* to 4000*l.* or 4¾ per cent. If they fell in any different proportion, profits would not be equal; for to make them equal, when the price of the first commodity was 10,000*l.*, the price of the second should be 4000*l.*; and when the price of the first was 10,200*l.*, the price of the other should be 4200*l.*

The consideration of this fact will lead to the understanding of a very important principle, which, I believe, has never been adverted to. It is this; that in a country where no taxation

[1] Ed. 1 'This is true'.

subsists, the alteration in the value of money arising from scarcity or abundance will operate in an equal proportion on the prices of all commodities; that if a commodity of 1000*l.* value rise to 1200*l.*, or fall to 800*l.*, a commodity of 10,000*l.* value will rise to 12,000*l.* or fall to 8000*l.*; but in a country where prices are artificially raised by taxation, the abundance of money from an influx, or the exportation and consequent scarcity of it from foreign demand, will not operate in the same proportion on the prices of all commodities; some it will raise or lower 5, 6, or 12 per cent., others 3, 4, or 7 per cent. If a country were not taxed, and money should fall in value, its abundance in every market would produce similar effects in each. If meat rose 20 per cent., bread, beer, shoes, labour, and every commodity, would also rise 20 per cent.; it is necessary they should do so, to secure to each trade the same rate of profits. But this is no longer true when any of these commodities is taxed; if in that case they should all rise in proportion to the fall in the value of money, profits would be rendered unequal; in the case of the commodities taxed, profits would be raised above the general level, and capital would be removed from one employment to another, till an equilibrium of profits was restored, which could only be, after the relative prices were altered.

Will not this principle account for the different effects, which it was remarked were produced on the prices of commodities, from the altered value of money during the Bank-restriction? It was objected to those who contended that the currency was at[1] that period depreciated, from the too great abundance of the paper circulation, that, if that were the fact, all commodities ought to have risen in the same proportion; but it was found that many had varied considerably more than others, and thence it was inferred that the rise of prices was owing to something

[1] Misprinted 'as' in ed. 3.

affecting the value of commodities, and not to any alteration in the value of the currency. It appears, however, as we have just seen, that in a country where commodities are taxed, they will not all vary in price in the same proportion, either in consequence of a rise or of a fall in the value of currency.[1]

If the profits of all trades were taxed, excepting the profits of the farmer, all goods would rise in money value, excepting raw produce. The farmer would have the same corn income as before, and would sell his corn also for the same money price; but as he would be obliged to pay an additional price for all the commodities, except corn, which he consumed, it would be to him a tax on expenditure. Nor would he be relieved from this tax by an alteration in the value of money, for an alteration in the value of money might sink all the taxed commodities to their former price, but the untaxed one would sink below its former level; and, therefore, though the farmer would purchase his commodities at the same price as before, he would have less money with which to purchase them.

The landlord, too, would be precisely in the same situation, he would have the same corn, and the same money-rent as before, if all commodities rose in price, and money remained at the same value; and he would have the same corn, but a less money-rent, if all commodities remained at the same price: so that in either case, though his income were not directly taxed, he would indirectly contribute towards the money raised.

But suppose the profits of the farmer to be also taxed, he then would be in the same situation as other traders: his raw produce would rise, so that he would have the same money revenue, after paying the tax, but he would pay an additional price for all the commodities he consumed, raw produce included.

His landlord, however, would be differently situated, he

---

[1] This subject is further discussed in a letter to Trower of 28 Jan. 1820, below, VIII, 153 ff.

would be benefited by the tax on his tenant's profits, as he
would be compensated for the additional price at which he
would purchase his manufactured commodities, if they rose in
price; and he would have the same money revenue, if in consequence of a rise in the value of money, commodities sold
at their former price. A tax on the profits of the farmer, is
not a tax proportioned to the gross produce of the land, but
to its net produce, after the payment of rent, wages, and all
other charges. As the cultivators of the different kinds of land,
No. 1, 2 and 3, employ precisely the same capitals, they will
get precisely the same profits, whatever may be the quantity
of gross produce, which one may obtain more than the other;
and consequently they will be all taxed alike. Suppose the
gross produce of the land of the quality No. 1 to be 180 qrs.,
that of No. 2, 170 qrs., and of No. 3, 160, and each to be taxed
10 quarters, the difference between the produce of No. 1, No. 2
and No. 3, after paying the tax, will be the same as before;
for if No. 1 be reduced to 170, No. 2 to 160, and No. 3 to
150 qrs.; the difference between 3 and 1 will be as before,
20 qrs.; and of No. 3 and No. 2, 10 qrs. If, after the tax, the
prices of corn and of every other commodity should remain
the same as before, money rent as well as corn rent, would
continue unaltered; but if the price of corn, and every other
commodity should rise in consequence of the tax, money rent
will also rise in the same proportion. If the price of corn were
4*l.* per quarter, the rent of No. 1 would be[1] 80*l.*, and that of
No. 2, 40*l.*; but if corn rose five per cent., or to 4*l.* 4*s.*, rent
would also rise five per cent., for twenty quarters of corn would
then be worth 84*l.*, and ten quarters 42*l.*[2]; so that in every
case the landlord will be unaffected by such a tax. A tax on

[1] Eds. 1-2 'would have been'.
[2] Eds. 1-2 'but if corn rose ten per cent., or to 4*l.* 8*s.*, rent would also rise ten per cent., for twenty quarters of corn would then be worth 88*l.*, and ten quarters 44*l.*'

the profits of stock always leaves corn rent unaltered, and therefore money rent varies with the price of corn; but a tax on raw produce, or tithes, never leaves corn rent unaltered, but generally leaves money rent the same as before. In another part of this work[1] I have observed, that if a land-tax of the same money amount, were laid on every kind of land in cultivation, without any allowance for difference of fertility, it would be very unequal in its operation, as it would be a profit to the landlord of the more fertile lands. It would raise the price of corn in proportion to the burden borne by the farmer of the worst land; but this additional price being obtained for the greater quantity of produce yielded by the better land, farmers of such land would be benefited during their leases, and afterwards, the advantage would go to the landlord in the form of an increase of rent. The effect of an equal tax on the *profits*[2] of the farmer is precisely the same; it raises the money rent of the landlords, if money retains the same value; but as the profits of all other trades are taxed as well as those of the farmer, and consequently the prices of all goods, as well as corn, are raised, the landlord loses as much by the increased money price of the goods and corn on which his rent is expended, as he gains by the rise of his rent. If money should rise in value, and all things should, after a tax on the profits of stock, fall to their former prices, rent also would be the same as before. The landlord would receive the same money rent, and would obtain all the commodities on which it was expended at their former price; so that under all circumstances he would continue untaxed.*

* That the profits of the farmer only should be taxed, and not the profits of any other capitalist, would be highly beneficial to landlords. It would, in fact, be a tax on the consumers of raw produce, partly for the benefit of the State, and partly for the benefit of landlords.[3]

[1] Above, p. 182.   [3] Eds. 1-2 do not contain this note.
[2] In eds. 1-2 not in italics.

This circumstance is curious. By taxing the profits of the farmer you do not burthen him more than if you exempted his profits from the tax, and the landlord has a decided interest that his tenants' profits should be taxed, as it is only on that condition that he himself continues really untaxed.[1]

A tax on the profits of capital[2] would also affect the stock-holder, if all commodities were to rise in proportion to the tax, although his dividends continued untaxed[3]; but if, from the alteration in the value of money, all commodities were to sink to their former price, the stock-holder would pay nothing towards the tax; he would purchase all his commodities at the same price, but would still receive the same money dividend.

If it be agreed, that by taxing the profits of one manu-facturer only, the price of his goods would rise, to put him on an equality with all other manufacturers; and that by taxing the profits of two manufacturers, the prices of two descriptions of goods must rise, I do not see how it can be disputed, that by taxing the profits of all manufacturers, the prices of all goods would rise, provided the mine which supplied us with money, were in this country, and continued untaxed.[4] But as money, or the standard of money, is a commodity imported from abroad, the prices of all goods could not rise; for such an effect could not take place without an additional quantity of money,*

* On further consideration, I doubt whether any more money would be required to circulate the same quantity of commodities, if their prices be raised by taxation, and not by difficulty of production. Suppose 100,000 quarters of corn to be sold in a certain district, and in a certain time, at 4*l.* per quarter, and that in consequence of a direct tax of 8*s.* per quarter, corn rises to 4*l.* 8*s.*, the same quantity of money, I think, and no more, would be required to circulate this corn at the increased price. If I before purchased 11 quarters at 4*l.*, and in consequence of the tax am obliged to reduce my consumption to 10 quarters, I shall not

[1] Ed. 1 does not contain this para-graph.
[2] Eds. 1-2 'of stock'.
[3] Eds. 1-2 do not contain ', al-though his dividends continued untaxed'.
[4] Ed. 1 reads 'were in the country taxed.'

which could not be obtained in exchange for dear goods, as was shewn in page 104. If, however, such a rise could take place, it could not be permanent, for it would have a powerful influence on foreign trade. In return for commodities imported, those dear goods could not be exported, and therefore we should for a time continue to buy, although we ceased to sell; and should export money, or bullion, till the relative prices of commodities were nearly the same as before. It appears to me absolutely certain, that a well regulated tax on profits, would ultimately restore commodities both of home and foreign manufacture, to the same money price which they bore before the tax was imposed.

As taxes on raw produce, tithes, taxes on wages, and on the necessaries of the labourer, will, by raising wages, lower profits, they will all, though not in an equal degree, be attended with the same effects.

The discovery of machinery, which materially improves home manufactures, always tends to raise the relative value of money, and therefore to encourage its importation. All taxation, all increased impediments, either to the manufacturer, or the grower of commodities, tend, on the contrary, to lower the relative value of money, and therefore to encourage its exportation.

require more money, for in all cases I shall pay 44*l.* for my corn. The public would, in fact, consume one-eleventh less, and this quantity would be consumed by Government. The money necessary to purchase it, would be derived from the 8*s.* per quarter, to be received from the farmers in the shape of a tax, but the amount levied would at the same time be paid to them for their corn; therefore the tax is in fact a tax in kind, and does not make it necessary that any more money should be used, or, if any, so little, that the quantity may be safely neglected.[1]

[1] Eds. 1-2 do not contain this note. Cp. above, p. 169, n. On Ricardo's change of view on this subject, see 'A Note on Prices and Taxation', below, IV, 319 ff.

CHAPTER XVI

TAXES ON WAGES

TAXES on wages will raise wages, and therefore will diminish
the rate of the profits of stock. We have already seen that a tax
on necessaries will raise their prices, and will be followed by
a rise of wages. The only difference between a tax on necessaries, and a tax on wages is, that the former will necessarily
be accompanied by a rise in the price of necessaries, but the
latter will not; towards a tax on wages, consequently, neither
the stock-holder, the landlord, nor any other class but the
employers of labour will contribute. A tax on wages is wholly
a tax on profits, a tax on necessaries is partly a tax on profits,
and partly a tax on rich consumers. The ultimate effects which
will result from such taxes then, are precisely the same as those
which result from a direct tax on profits.

"The wages of the inferior classes of workmen," says Adam
Smith, "I have endeavoured to shew in the first book, are every
where necessarily regulated by two different circumstances; the
demand for labour, and the ordinary or average price of provisions. The demand for labour, according as it happens to be
either increasing, stationary, or declining, or to require an increasing, stationary, or declining population, regulates the subsistence of the labourer, and determines in what degree it shall
be either liberal, moderate, or scanty. The *ordinary or average*
price of provisions determines the quantity of money which
must be paid to the workman, in order to enable him, one year
with another, to purchase this liberal, moderate, or scanty subsistence. While the demand for labour, and the price of provisions, therefore, remain the same, a direct tax upon the wages

of labour can have no other effect than to raise them somewhat higher than the tax."[1]

To the proposition, as it is here advanced by Dr. Smith, Mr. Buchanan offers two objections. First, he denies that the money wages of labour are regulated by the price of provisions; and secondly, he denies that a tax on the wages of labour would raise the price of labour. On the first point, Mr. Buchanan's argument is as follows, page 59[2]: "The wages of labour, it has already been remarked, consist not in money, but in what money purchases, namely, provisions and other necessaries; and the allowance of the labourer out of the common stock, will always be in proportion to the supply. Where provisions are *cheap and abundant*, his share will be the larger; and where they are *scarce and dear*, it will be the less. His wages will always give him his just share, and they cannot give him more. It is an opinion, indeed, adopted by Dr. Smith and most other writers, that the money price of labour is regulated by the money price of provisions, and that when provisions rise in price, wages rise in proportion. But it is clear that the price of labour has no necessary connexion with the price of food, since it depends entirely on the supply of labourers compared with the demand. Besides, it is to be observed, that the high price of provisions is a certain indication of a deficient supply, and arises in the natural course of things, for the purpose of retarding the consumption. A smaller supply of food, shared among the same number of consumers, will evidently leave a smaller portion to each, and the labourer must bear his share of the common want. To distribute this burden equally, and to prevent the labourer from consuming subsistence so freely as before, the price rises. But wages it seems must rise along

---

[1] Bk. v, ch. ii, pt. ii, art. iii; vol. II, p. 348. Ricardo's italics.
[2] Buchanan's ed. of the *Wealth of Nations*, vol. IV, *Observations*. Ricardo's italics.

with it, that he may still use the same quantity of a scarcer commodity; and thus nature is represented as counteracting her own purposes: first, raising the price of food, to diminish the consumption, and afterwards, raising wages to give the labourer the same supply as before."

In this argument of Mr. Buchanan, there appears to me to be a great mixture of truth and error. Because a high price of provisions is sometimes occasioned by a deficient supply, Mr. Buchanan assumes it as a certain indication of deficient[1] supply. He attributes to one cause exclusively, that which may arise from many. It is undoubtedly true, that in the case of a deficient supply, a smaller quantity will be shared among the same number of consumers, and a smaller portion will fall to each. To distribute this privation equally, and to prevent the labourer from consuming subsistence so freely as before, the price rises. It must, therefore, be conceded to Mr. Buchanan, that any rise in the price of provisions, occasioned by a deficient supply, will not necessarily raise the money wages of labour, as the consumption must be retarded; which can only be effected by diminishing the power of the consumers to purchase. But, because the price of provisions is raised by a deficient supply, we are by no means warranted in concluding, as Mr. Buchanan appears to do, that there may not be an abundant supply, with a high price; not a high price with regard to money only, but with regard to all other things.

The natural price of commodities, which always ultimately governs their market price, depends on the facility of production; but the quantity produced is not in proportion to that facility. Although the lands, which are now taken into cultivation, are much inferior to the lands in cultivation three centuries ago, and, therefore, the difficulty of production is increased, who can entertain any doubt, but that the quantity produced

---

[1] Ed. 1 'of a deficient'.

now, very far exceeds the quantity then produced? Not only
is a high price compatible with an increased supply, but it rarely
fails to accompany it. If, then, in consequence of taxation, or
of difficulty of production, the price of provisions be raised,
and the quantity be not diminished, the money wages of labour
will rise; for, as Mr. Buchanan has justly observed, "The wages
of labour consist not in money, but in what money purchases,
namely, provisions and other necessaries; and the allowance
of the labourer out of the common stock, will always be in
proportion to the supply."

With respect to the second point, whether a tax on the wages
of labour would raise the price of labour, Mr. Buchanan says,
"After the labourer has received the fair recompense of his
labour, how can he have recourse on his employer, for what
he is afterwards compelled to pay away in taxes? There is no
law or principle in human affairs to warrant such a conclusion.
After the labourer has received his wages, they are in his own
keeping, and he must, as far as he is able, bear the burthen of
whatever exactions he may ever afterwards be exposed to: for
he has clearly no way of compelling those to reimburse him,
who have already paid him the fair price of his work."[1]
Mr. Buchanan has quoted, with great approbation, the following able passage from Mr. Malthus's work on population[2],
which appears to me completely to answer his objection. "The
price of labour, when left to find its natural level, is a most
important political barometer, expressing the relation between
the supply of provisions, and the demand for them, between
the quantity to be consumed, and the number of consumers;
and, taken on the average, independently of accidental circumstances, it further expresses, clearly, the wants of the society
respecting population; that is, whatever may be the number

[1] Buchanan's ed. of the *Wealth of*   [2] Ed. 3 has 'Work on Popula-
Nations, vol. III, p. 338, note.   tion'.

of children to a marriage necessary to maintain exactly the present population, the price of labour will be just sufficient to support this number, or be above it, or below it, according to the state of the real funds, for the maintenance of labour, whether stationary, progressive, or retrograde. Instead, however, of considering it in this light, we consider it as something which we may raise or depress at pleasure, something which depends principally on his Majesty's justices of the peace. When an advance in the price of provisions already expresses that the demand is too great for the supply, in order to put the labourer in the same condition as before, we raise the price of labour, that is, we increase the demand, and are then much surprised, that the price of provisions continues rising. In this, we act much in the same manner, as if, when the quicksilver in the common weather glass, stood at *stormy*, we were to raise it by some forcible pressure to settled fair, and then be greatly astonished that it continued raining."[1]

"The price of labour will express, clearly, the wants of the society respecting population;" it will be just sufficient to support the population, which at that time the state of the funds for the maintenance of labourers, requires. If the labourer's wages were before only adequate to supply the requisite population, they will, after the tax, be inadequate to that supply, for he will not have the same funds to expend on his family. Labour will, therefore, rise, because the demand continues, and it is only by raising the price, that the supply is not checked.

Nothing is more common, than to see hats or malt rise when taxed; they rise because the requisite supply would not be afforded if they did not rise: so with labour, when wages are taxed, its price rises, because, if it did not, the requisite population would not be kept up. Does not Mr. Buchanan allow all

---

[1] Quoted by Buchanan (*ib.* vol. IV, pp. 62–3) from *Essay on Population*, 3rd ed., 1806, vol. II, pp. 165–6.

that is contended for, when he says, that "were he (the labourer) indeed reduced to a bare allowance of necessaries, he would then suffer no further abatement of his wages, as he could not on such conditions continue his race?"[1] Suppose the circumstances of the country to be such, that the lowest labourers are not only called upon to continue their race, but to increase it; their wages would be[2] regulated accordingly. Can they multiply in the degree required[3], if a tax takes from them a part of their wages, and reduces them to bare necessaries?

It is undoubtedly true, that a taxed commodity will not rise in proportion to the tax, if the demand for it diminish[4], and if the quantity cannot be reduced. If metallic money were in general use, its value would not for a considerable time be increased by a tax, in proportion to the amount of the tax, because at a higher price, the demand would be diminished, and the quantity would not be diminished; and unquestionably the same cause frequently influences the wages of labour; the number of labourers cannot be rapidly increased or diminished in proportion to the increase or diminution of the fund which is to employ them; but in the case supposed, there is no necessary diminution of demand for labour, and if diminished, the demand does not abate in proportion to the tax. Mr. Buchanan forgets that the fund raised by the tax, is employed by Government in maintaining labourers, unproductive indeed, but still labourers. If labour were not to rise when wages are taxed, there would be a great increase in the competition for labour, because the owners of capital, who would have nothing to pay towards such a tax, would have the same funds for employing labour; whilst the Government who received the tax would

---

[1] Buchanan's ed. of the *Wealth of Nations*, vol. III, p. 338, note.
[2] Eds. 1-2 'would have been'.
[3] Eds. 1-2 do not contain 'in the degree required'.
[4] Ed. 1 'for it will diminish'.

have an additional fund for the same purpose. Government and the people thus become competitors, and the consequence of their competition is a rise in the price of labour. The same number of men only will be employed, but they will be employed at additional wages.

If the tax had been laid at once on the people of capital[1], their fund for the maintenance of labour would have been diminished in the very same degree that the fund of Government for that purpose had been increased; and therefore there would have been no rise in wages; for though there would be the same demand, there would not be the same competition. If when the tax were levied, Government at once exported the produce of it as a subsidy to a foreign State, and if therefore these funds were devoted to the maintenance of foreign, and not of English labourers, such as soldiers, sailors, &c. &c.; then, indeed, there would be a diminished demand for labour, and wages might not increase, although they were taxed; but the same thing would happen if the tax had been laid on consumable commodities, on the profits of stock, or if in any other manner the same sum had been raised to supply this subsidy: less labour could be employed at home. In one case wages are prevented from rising, in the other they must absolutely fall. But suppose the amount of a tax on wages were, after being raised on the labourers, paid gratuitously to their employers, it would increase their money fund for the maintenance of labour, but it would not increase either commodities or labour. It would consequently increase the competition amongst the employers of labour, and the tax would be ultimately attended with no loss either to master or labourer. The master would pay an increased price for labour; the addition which the labourer received would be paid as a tax to government, and would be again returned to the masters. It must, however, not be for-

[1] Eds. 1-2 do not contain 'of capital'.

gotten, that the produce of taxes[1] is generally wastefully expended, they are always obtained at the expense of the people's comforts and enjoyments, and commonly either diminish capital or retard its accumulation. By diminishing capital they tend to diminish the real fund destined for the maintenance of labour; and therefore to diminish the real demand for it. Taxes then, generally, as far as they impair the real capital of the country, diminish the demand for labour, and therefore it is a probable, but not a necessary, nor a peculiar consequence of a tax on wages, that though wages would rise, they would not rise by a sum precisely equal to the tax.

Adam Smith, as we have seen,[2] has fully allowed that the effect of a tax on wages, would be to raise wages by a sum at least equal to the tax, and would be finally, if not immediately, paid by the employer of labour. Thus far we fully agree; but we essentially differ in our views of the subsequent operation of such a tax.

"A direct tax upon the wages of labour, therefore," says Adam Smith, "though the labourer might perhaps pay it out of his hand, could not properly be said to be even advanced by him; at least if the demand for labour and the average price of provisions remained the same after the tax as before it. In all such cases, not only the tax but something more than the tax, would in reality be advanced by the person who immediately employed him. The final payment would in different cases fall upon different persons. The rise which such a tax might occasion in the wages of manufacturing labour, would be advanced by the master manufacturer, *who would be entitled and obliged to charge it with a profit, upon the price of his goods*.[3] The rise

---

[1] Ed. 1 in place of the next three lines reads 'is often wastefully expended, and that by diminishing capital they tend' etc.
[2] Above, pp. 215–16.
[3] Adam Smith continues 'The final payment of this rise of wages, therefore, together with the additional profit of the master manufacturer, would fall upon the consumer.'

which such a tax might occasion in country labour, would be advanced by the farmer, who, in order to maintain the same number of labourers as before, would be obliged to employ a greater capital. In order to get back this greater capital, *together with the ordinary profits of stock*, it would be necessary that he should retain a larger portion, or what comes to the same thing, the price of a larger portion, of the produce of the land, and consequently that he should pay less rent to the landlord. The final payment of this rise of wages would in this case fall upon the landlord, *together with the additional profits of the farmer who had advanced it*. In all cases a direct tax upon the wages of labour must, in the long run, occasion both a greater reduction in the rent of land, and a greater rise in the price of manufactured goods, than would have followed, from the proper assessment of a sum equal to the produce of the tax, partly upon the rent of land, and partly upon consumable commodities." Vol. iii. p. 337.[1] In this passage it is asserted that the additional wages paid by farmers will ultimately fall on the landlords, who will receive a diminished rent; but that the additional wages paid by manufacturers will occasion a rise in the price of manufactured goods, and will therefore fall on the consumers of those commodities.

Now, suppose a society to consist of landlords, manufacturers, farmers and labourers,[2] the labourers, it is agreed, would be recompensed for the tax;—but by whom?—who would pay that portion which did not fall on the landlords?— the manufacturers could pay no part of it; for if the price of their commodities should rise in proportion to the additional wages they paid, they would be in a better situation after than before the tax. If the clothier, the hatter, the shoe-maker, &c., should be each able to raise the price of their goods 10 per

---

[1] The reference is to Buchanan's ed.; in Cannan's ed., vol. ii, p. 349. There are several inaccuracies in the quotation, and the italics are Ricardo's.

[2] Eds. 1-2 have a full stop here.

cent.,—supposing 10 per cent. to recompense them completely for the additional wages they paid,—if, as Adam Smith says, "they would be entitled and obliged to charge the additional wages *with a profit* upon the price of their goods," they could each consume as much as before of each other's goods, and therefore they would pay nothing towards the tax. If the clothier paid more for his hats and shoes, he would receive more for his cloth, and if the hatter paid more for his cloth and shoes, he would receive more for his hats. All manufactured commodities then would be bought by them with as much advantage as before, and inasmuch as corn would not be raised in price which is Dr. Smith's supposition[1] whilst they had an additional sum to lay out upon its purchase, they would be benefited, and not injured by such a tax.

If then neither the labourers nor the manufacturers would contribute towards such a tax; if the farmers would be also recompensed by a fall of rent, landlords alone must not only bear its whole weight, but they must also contribute to the increased gains of the manufacturers. To do this, however, they should consume all the manufactured commodities in the country, for the additional price charged on the whole mass is little more than the tax originally imposed on the labourers in manufactures.

Now it will not be disputed that the clothier, the hatter, and all other manufacturers, are consumers of each other's goods[2]; it will not be disputed that labourers of all descriptions consume soap, cloth, shoes, candles, and various other commodities; it is therefore impossible that the whole weight of these taxes should fall on landlords only.

But if the labourers pay no part of the tax, and yet manufactured commodities rise in price, wages must rise, not only

[1] Ed. 1 does not contain 'which is Dr. Smith's supposition'. [2] Misprinted 'good' in ed. 3.

to compensate them for the tax, but for the increased price of manufactured necessaries, which, as far as it affects agricultural labour, will be a new cause for the fall of rent; and, as far as it affects manufacturing labour, for a further rise in the price of goods. This rise in the price of goods will again operate on wages, and the action and re-action first of wages on goods, and then of goods on wages, will be extended without any assignable limits. The arguments by which this theory is supported, lead to such absurd conclusions, that it may at once be seen that the principle is wholly indefensible.

All the effects which are produced on the profits of stock and the wages of labour, by a rise of rent and a rise of necessaries, in the natural progress of society, and increasing difficulty of production, will equally follow from[1] a rise of wages in consequence of taxation; and, therefore, the enjoyments of the labourer, as well as those of his employers, will be curtailed by the tax; and not by this tax particularly, but by every[2] other which should raise an equal amount[3], as they would all tend to diminish the fund destined for the maintenance of labour.

The error of Adam Smith proceeds in the first place from supposing, that all taxes paid by the farmer must necessarily fall on the landlord, in the shape of a deduction from rent. On this subject, I have explained myself most fully,[4] and I trust that it has been shewn, to the satisfaction of the reader, that since much capital is employed on the land which pays no rent, and since it is the result obtained by this capital which regulates the price of raw produce, no deduction can be made from rent; and, consequently, either no remuneration will be made to the farmer for a tax on wages, or if made, it must be made by an addition to the price of raw produce.

[1] Eds. 1-2 'be produced by' in place of 'equally follow from'.
[2] Eds. 1-2 'any' in place of 'every'.
[3] Ed. 1 does not contain the remainder of this sentence.
[4] Above, pp. 183-4.

If taxes press unequally on the farmer, he will be enabled to raise the price of raw produce, to place himself on a level with those who carry on other trades; but a tax on wages, which would not affect him more than it would affect any other trade, could not be removed or compensated by a high price of raw produce; for the same reason which should induce him to raise the price of corn, namely, to remunerate himself for the tax, would induce the clothier to raise the price of cloth, the shoemaker, hatter, and upholsterer, to raise the price of shoes, hats, and furniture.

If they could all raise the price of their goods, so as to remunerate themselves, with a profit, for the tax; as they are all consumers of each other's commodities, it is obvious that the tax could never be paid; for who would be the contributors if all were compensated?

I hope, then, that I have succeeded in shewing, that any tax which shall have the effect of raising wages, will be paid by a diminution of profits, and, therefore, that a tax on wages is in fact a tax on profits.

This principle of the division of the produce of labour and capital between wages and profits, which I have attempted to establish, appears to me so certain, that excepting in the immediate effects, I should think it of little importance whether the profits of stock, or the wages of labour, were taxed. By taxing the profits of stock, you would probably alter the rate at which the funds for the maintenance of labour increase, and wages would be disproportioned to the state of that fund, by being too high. By taxing wages, the reward paid to the labourer would also be disproportioned to the state of that fund, by being too low. In the one case by a fall, and in the other by a rise in money wages, the natural equilibrium between profits and wages would be restored. A tax on wages, then, does not fall on the landlord, but it falls on the profits

of stock: it does not "entitle and oblige the master manufacturer to charge it with a profit on the prices of his goods,"
for he will be unable to increase their price, and therefore he
must himself wholly and without compensation pay such a
tax.*

If the effect of taxes on wages be such as I have described,
they do not merit the censure cast upon them by Dr. Smith.
He observes of such taxes, "These, and some other taxes of
the same kind, by raising the price of labour, are said to have
ruined the greater part of the manufactures of Holland. Similar
taxes, though not quite so heavy, take place in the Milanese,
in the states of Genoa, in the duchy of Modena, in the duchies
of Parma, Placentia, and Guastalla, and in the ecclesiastical
states. A French author of some note, has proposed to reform
the finances of his country, by substituting in the room of other
taxes [1], this most ruinous of all taxes. 'There is nothing so
absurd,' says Cicero, 'which has not sometimes been asserted
by some philosophers.'" [2] And in another place he says: "taxes
upon necessaries, by raising the wages of labour, necessarily
tend to raise the price of all manufactures, and consequently
to diminish the extent of their sale and consumption." [3] They
would not merit this censure, even if Dr. Smith's principle
were correct, that such taxes would enhance the prices of manufactured commodities; for such an effect could be only temporary, and would subject us to no disadvantage in our foreign

---

* M. Say appears to have imbibed the general opinion on this subject.
Speaking of corn, he says, "thence it results, that its price influences
the price of *all* other commodities. A farmer, a manufacturer, or a merchant, employs a certain number of workmen, who all have occasion to
consume a certain quantity of corn. If the price of corn rises, he is obliged
to raise, in an equal proportion, the price of his productions." Vol. i.
p. 255.

[1] Adam Smith says 'of the greater part of other taxes'.

[2] Bk. v, ch. ii, pt. ii, art. iv; vol. II, pp. 359–60.

[3] *ib.* vol. II, p. 357.

trade. If any cause should raise the price of a few manufactured commodities, it would prevent or check their exportation; but if the same cause operated generally on all, the effect would be merely nominal, and would neither interfere with their relative value, nor in any degree diminish the stimulus to a trade of barter, which all commerce, both foreign and domestic, really is.

I have already attempted to shew, that when any cause raises the prices of all commodities[1], the effects are nearly similar to a fall in the value of money. If money falls in value, all commodities rise in price; and if the effect is confined to one country, it will affect its foreign commerce in the same way as a high price of commodities caused by general taxation;[2] and, therefore, in examining the effects of a low value of money confined to one country, we are also examining the effects of a high price of commodities confined to one country. Indeed, Adam Smith was fully aware of the resemblance between these two cases, and consistently maintained that the low value of money, or, as he calls it, of silver in Spain, in consequence of the prohibition against its exportation, was very highly prejudicial to the manufactures and foreign commerce of Spain. "But that degradation in the value of silver, which being the effect either of the peculiar situation, or of the political institutions of a particular country, takes place only in that country, is a matter of very great consequence, which, far from tending to make any body really richer, tends to make every body really poorer. *The rise in the money price of all commodities, which is in this case peculiar to that country,*[3] tends to discourage more or less every sort of industry which is carried on within it, and to enable foreign nations, by furnishing almost all sorts of goods for a smaller quantity of silver than its own workmen can afford to

---

[1] Ed. 1 'of all commodities in general'.

[2] Above, pp. 168–72.

[3] Not in italics in ed. 1, or in the *Wealth of Nations*.

do, to undersell them not only in the foreign, but even in the home market." Vol. ii. page 278.[1]

One, and I think the only one, of the disadvantages of a low value of silver in a country, proceeding from a forced abundance, has been ably explained by Dr. Smith. If the trade in gold and silver were free, "the gold and silver which would go abroad, would not go abroad for nothing, but would bring back an equal value of goods of some kind or another. Those goods, too, would not be all matters of mere luxury and expense, to be consumed by idle people, who produce nothing in return for their consumption. As the real wealth and revenue of idle people would not be augmented by this extraordinary exportation of gold and silver, so would neither their consumption be augmented[2] by it. Those goods would, probably the greater part of them, and certainly some part of them, consist in materials, tools, and provisions, for the employment and maintenance of industrious people, who would reproduce with a profit, the full value of their consumption. A part of the dead stock of the society would thus be turned into active stock, and would put into motion a greater quantity of industry than had been employed before."[3]

By not allowing a free trade in the precious metals when the prices of commodities are raised, either by taxation, or by the influx of the precious metals, you prevent a part of the dead stock of the society from being turned into active stock—you prevent a greater quantity of industry from being employed. But this is the whole amount of the evil; an evil never felt by those countries where the exportation of silver is either allowed or connived at.

The exchanges between countries are at par only, whilst they

[1] The reference is to Buchanan's ed.; in Cannan's ed., vol. II, pp. 12–13.

[2] Adam Smith says 'much augmented'.

[3] Bk. IV, ch. v; vol. II, pp. 14–15.

have precisely that quantity of currency which in the actual
situation of things they should have to carry on the circulation
of their commodities. If the trade in the precious metals were
perfectly free, and money could be exported without any expense whatever, the exchanges could be no otherwise in every
country than at par. If the trade in the precious metals were
perfectly free, if they were generally used in circulation, even
with the expenses of transporting them, the exchange could
never in any of them deviate more from par, than by these
expenses. These principles, I believe, are now no where disputed. If a country used paper money, not exchangeable for
specie, and, therefore, not regulated by any fixed standard, the
exchanges in that country might deviate from par, in the same
proportion as[1] its money might be multiplied beyond that
quantity which would have been allotted to it by general commerce, if the trade in money had been free, and the precious
metals had been used, either for money, or for the standard
of money.

If by the general operations of commerce, 10 millions of
pounds sterling, of a known weight and fineness of bullion,
should be the portion of England, and 10 millions of paper
pounds were substituted, no effect would be produced on the
exchange; but if by the abuse of the power of issuing paper
money, 11 millions of pounds should be employed in the circulation, the exchange would be 9 per cent. against England; if
12 millions were employed, the exchange would be 16 per cent.;
and if 20 millions, the exchange would be 50 per cent. against
England. To produce this effect it is not, however, necessary
that paper money should be employed: any cause which retains
in circulation a greater quantity of pounds than would have
circulated, if commerce had been free, and the precious metals

---

[1] Ed. 1 'might deviate as much from par, as'; ed. 2 (owing to an im- perfect correction) 'might deviate as from par, in the same proportion as'.

of a known weight and fineness had been used, either for money, or for the standard of money, would exactly produce the same effects. Suppose that by clipping the money, each pound did not contain the quantity of gold or silver which by law it should contain, a greater number of such pounds might be employed in the circulation, than if they were not clipped. If from each pound one tenth were taken away, 11 millions of such pounds might be used instead of 10; if two tenths were taken away, 12 millions might be employed; and if one half were taken away, 20 millions might not be found superfluous. If the latter sum were used instead of 10 millions, every commodity in England would be raised to double its former price, and the exchange would be 50 per cent. against England; but this would occasion no disturbance in foreign commerce, nor discourage the manufacture of any one commodity. If, for example, cloth rose in England from 20*l.* to 40*l.* per piece, we should just as freely export it after as before the rise, for a compensation of 50 per cent. would be made to the foreign purchaser in the exchange; so that with 20*l.* of his money, he could purchase a bill which would enable him to pay a debt of 40*l.* in England. In the same manner if he exported a commodity which cost 20*l.* at home, and which sold in England for 40*l.* he would only receive 20*l.*, for 40*l.* in England would only purchase a bill for 20*l.* on a foreign country. The same effects would follow from whatever cause 20 millions could be forced to perform the business of circulation in England, if 10 millions only were necessary. If so absurd a law, as the prohibition of the exportation of the precious metals, could be enforced, and the consequence of such prohibition were to force 11 millions of good pounds, fresh from the mint,[1] instead of 10, into circulation, the exchange would be 9 per cent. against England; if 12 millions, 16 per cent.; and if 20 millions, 50 per cent. against

[1] Ed. 1 does not contain 'of good pounds, fresh from the mint,'.

England. But no discouragement would be given to the manufactures of England; if home commodities sold at a high price
in England, so would foreign commodities; and whether they
were high or low would be of little importance to the foreign
exporter and importer, whilst he would, on the one hand, be
obliged to allow a compensation in the exchange when his
commodities sold at a dear rate, and would receive the same
compensation, when he was obliged to purchase English commodities at a high price. The sole disadvantage, then, which
could happen to a country from retaining, by prohibitory laws,
a greater quantity of gold and silver in circulation than would
otherwise remain there, would be the loss which it would
sustain from employing a portion of its capital unproductively,
instead of employing it productively. In the form of money
this capital is productive of no profit; in the form of materials,
machinery, and food, for which it might be exchanged, it would
be productive of revenue, and would add to the wealth and
the resources of the State. Thus then, I hope, I have satisfactorily proved, that a comparatively low price of the precious
metals, in consequence of taxation, or, in other words, a
generally high price of commodities, would be of no disadvantage to a State, as a part of the metals would be exported,
which, by raising their value, would again lower the prices
of commodities. And further, that if they were not exported,
if by prohibitory laws they could be retained in a country,
the effect on the exchange would counterbalance the effect
of high prices. If, then, taxes on necessaries and on wages
would not raise the prices of all commodities on which labour
was expended, they cannot be condemned on such grounds;
and moreover, even if the opinion given by Adam Smith,[1] that
they would have such an effect were well founded, they would
be in no degree injurious on that account. They would be

---

[1] Eds. 1-2 do not contain 'given by Adam Smith,'.

objectionable for no other reason than those which might be justly urged against taxes of any other description.

The landlords, as such, would be exempted from the burden of the tax; but as far as they directly employed labour in the expenditure of their revenues, by supporting gardeners, menial servants, &c. they would be subject to its operation.[1]

It is undoubtedly true, that "taxes upon luxuries have no tendency to raise the price of any other commodities, except that of the commodities taxed;" but it is not true, "that taxes upon necessaries, by raising the wages of labour, necessarily tend to raise the price of all manufactures." It is true, that "taxes upon luxuries are finally paid by the consumers of the commodities taxed, without any retribution. They fall indifferently upon every species of revenue, the wages of labour, the profits of stock, and the rent of land;" but it is not true, "that taxes upon necessaries, *so far as they affect the labouring poor*, are finally paid partly by landlords in the diminished rent of their lands, and partly by rich consumers, whether landlords or others, in the advanced price of manufactured goods;"[2] for, *so far as these taxes affect the labouring poor*, they will be almost wholly paid by the diminished profits of stock, a small part only being paid by the labourers themselves in the diminished demand for labour, which taxation of every kind has a tendency to produce.

It is from Dr. Smith's erroneous view of the effect of those taxes, that he has been led to the conclusion, that "the middling and superior ranks of people, if they understood their own interest, ought always to oppose all taxes upon the necessaries of life, as well as all direct taxes upon the wages of labour." This conclusion follows from his reasoning, "that the final

---

[1] Eds. 1-2 contain neither this paragraph nor the last sentence of the previous paragraph, beginning 'They would be'.

[2] Bk. v, ch. ii, pt. ii, art. iv; vol. ii, p. 357. The passages quoted are almost consecutive.

payment of both one and the other falls altogether upon themselves, and always with a considerable overcharge. They fall heaviest upon the landlords,* who always pay in a double capacity; in that of landlords, by the reduction of their rent, and in that of rich consumers, by the increase of their expense. The observation of Sir Matthew Decker,[1] that certain taxes, are in the price of certain goods, sometimes repeated and accumulated four or five times, is perfectly just with regard to taxes upon the necessaries of life. In the price of leather, for example, you must pay, not only for the tax upon the leather of your own shoes, but for a part of that upon those of the shoemaker and the tanner. You must pay, too, for the tax upon the salt, upon the soap, and upon the candles, which those workmen consume while employed in your service, and for the tax upon the leather, which the salt-maker, the soap-maker, and the candle-maker consume, while employed in their service."[2]

Now as Dr. Smith does not contend that the tanner, the salt-maker, the soap-maker, and the candle-maker, will either of them be benefited by the tax on leather, salt, soap, and candles; and as it is certain, that Government will receive no more than the tax imposed, it is impossible to conceive, that more can be paid by the public upon whomsoever the tax may fall. The rich consumers may, and indeed will, pay for the poor consumer, but they will pay no more than the whole amount of the tax; and it is not in the nature of things, that "the tax should be repeated and accumulated four or five times."

A system of taxation may be defective; more may be raised from the people, than what finds its way into the coffers of the State, as a part, in consequence of its effect on prices, may

---

* So far from this being true, they would scarcely affect the landlords and stockholder.[3]

[1] *An Essay on the Causes of the Decline of the Foreign Trade*, London, 1744, p. 17.

[2] Bk. v, ch. ii, pt. ii, art. iv; vol. II, p. 357.
[3] Eds. 1-2 do not contain this note.

possibly be received by those who are benefited by the peculiar mode in which taxes are laid. Such taxes are pernicious, and should not be encouraged; for it may be laid down as a principle, that when taxes operate justly, they conform to the first of Dr. Smith's maxims, and raise from the people as little as possible beyond what enters into the public treasury of the State. M. Say says, "others offer plans of finance, and propose means for filling the coffers of the sovereign, without any charge to his subjects. But unless a plan of finance is of the nature of a commercial undertaking, it cannot give to[1] Government more than it takes away, either from individuals or from Government itself, under some other form. Something cannot be made out of nothing, by the stroke of a wand. In whatever way an operation may be disguised, whatever forms we may constrain a value to take, whatever metamorphosis we may make it undergo, we can only have a value by creating it, or by taking it from others. The very best of all plans of finance is to spend little, and the best of all taxes is, that which is the least in amount."[2]

Dr. Smith uniformly, and I think justly, contends, that the labouring classes cannot materially contribute to the burdens of the State. A tax on necessaries, or on wages, will therefore be shifted from the poor to the rich: if then the meaning of Dr. Smith is, "that certain taxes are in the price of certain goods sometimes repeated, and accumulated four or five times," for the purpose only of accomplishing this end, namely, the transference of the tax from the poor to the rich, they cannot be liable to censure on that account.

Suppose the just share of the taxes of a rich consumer to be 100*l.* and that he would pay it directly, if the tax were laid on income, on wine, or on any other luxury; he would suffer no

---

[1] Eds. 1-2 do not contain 'to'.　　　[2] *Traité d'Economie politique*, 2nd ed., 1814, vol. II, p. 298.

injury if by the taxation of necessaries, he should be only called
upon for the payment of 25*l*., as far as his own consumption
of necessaries, and that of his family was concerned, but should
be required to repeat this tax three times, by paying an additional price for other commodities to remunerate the labourers,
or their employers, for the tax which they have been called
upon to advance. Even in that case the reasoning is inconclu-
sive: for if there be no more paid than what is required by
Government; of what importance can it be to the rich consumer, whether he pay the tax directly, by paying an increased
price for an object of luxury, or indirectly, by paying an increased price for the necessaries and other commodities he consumes? If more be not paid by the people, than what is received by Government, the rich consumer will only pay his
equitable share; if more is paid, Adam Smith should have stated
by whom it is received[1], but his whole argument is founded
in error, for the prices of commodities would not be raised by
such taxes.

M. Say does not appear to me to have consistently adhered
to the obvious principle, which I have quoted from his able
work; for in the next page, speaking of taxation, he says,
"When it is pushed too far, it produces this lamentable effect,
it deprives the contributor of a portion of his riches, without
enriching the State. This is what we may comprehend, if we
consider that every man's power of consuming, whether productively or not, is limited by his income. He cannot then be
deprived of a part of his income, without being obliged proportionally to reduce his consumption. Hence arises a diminution of demand for those goods, which he no longer consumes,
and particularly for those on which the tax is imposed. From
this diminution of demand, there results a diminution of
production, and consequently of taxable commodities. The

---

[1] Ed. 1 does not contain the remainder of this sentence.

contributor then will lose a portion of his enjoyments; the producer a portion of his profits; and the treasury, a portion of its receipts."[1]

M. Say instances the tax on salt in France, previous to the revolution; which, he says, diminished the production of salt by one half.[2] If, however, less salt was consumed, less capital was employed in producing it; and, therefore, though the producer would obtain less profit[3] on the production of salt, he would obtain more on the production of other things. If a tax, however burdensome it may be, falls on revenue, and not on capital, it does not diminish demand, it only alters the nature of it. It enables Government to consume as much of the produce of the land and labour of the country, as was before consumed by the individuals who contribute to the tax, an evil sufficiently great without overcharging it[4]. If my income is 1000*l.* per annum, and I am called upon for 100*l.* per annum for a tax, I shall only be able to demand nine tenths of the quantity of goods, which I before consumed, but I enable Government to demand the other tenth. If the commodity taxed be corn, it is not necessary that my demand for corn should diminish, as I may prefer to pay 100*l.* per annum more for my corn, and to the same amount abate in my demand for wine, furniture, or any other luxury.* Less capital will consequently be employed in the wine or upholstery trade, but more will be employed in manufacturing those commodities, on which the taxes levied by Government will be expended.

* M. Say says, that "the tax added to the price of a commodity, raises its price. Every increase in the price of a commodity, necessarily reduces the number of those who are able to purchase it, or at least the quantity they will consume of it." This is by no means a necessary consequence. I do not believe, that if bread were taxed, the consumption of bread would be diminished, more than if cloth, wine, or soap were taxed.

[1] *Traité*, 1814, vol. ii, p. 300.
[2] *ib.* vol. ii, p. 300, note.
[3] Ed. 1 'profits'.

[4] Ed. 1 does not contain ', an evil sufficiently great without overcharging it'.

M. Say says[1] that M. Turgot, by reducing the market dues on fish (*les droits d'entrée et de halle sur la marée*) in Paris one half, did not diminish the amount of their produce, and that consequently, the consumption of fish must have doubled. He infers from this, that the profits of the fisherman and those engaged in the trade, must also have doubled, and that the income of the country must have increased, by the whole amount of these increased profits; and by giving a stimulus to accumulation, must have increased the resources of the State.*

Without calling in question the policy, which dictated this alteration of the tax, I have my doubts,[2] whether it gave any great stimulus to accumulation. If the profits of the fisherman and others engaged in the trade, were doubled in consequence of more fish being consumed, capital and labour must have been withdrawn from other occupations to engage them in this particular trade. But in those occupations capital and labour were productive of profits, which must have been given up when they were withdrawn. The ability of the country to accumulate, was only increased by the difference between the profits obtained in the business in which the capital was newly engaged, and those obtained in that from which it was withdrawn.

Whether taxes be taken from revenue or capital, they diminish the taxable commodities of the State. If I cease to expend 100*l.* on wine, because by paying a tax of that amount I have enabled

---

* The following remark of the same author appears to me equally erroneous: "When a high duty is laid on cotton, the production of all those goods of which cotton is the basis is diminished. If the total value added to cotton in its various manufactures, in a particular country, amounted to 100 millions of francs per annum, and the effect of the tax was, to diminish the consumption one half, then the tax would deprive that country every year of 50 millions of francs, in addition to the sum received by Government." Vol. ii. p. 314.

[1] *Traité d'Economie politique*, 1814, vol. II, pp. 301–2.

[2] Ed. 1 'I may be permitted to doubt'.

Government to expend 100*l.* instead of expending it myself, one hundred pounds worth of goods are necessarily withdrawn from the list of taxable commodities. If the revenue of the individuals of a country be 10 millions, they will have at least 10 millions worth of taxable commodities. If by taxing some, one million be transferred to the disposal of Government, their revenue will still be nominally 10 millions, but they will remain with only nine millions worth of taxable commodities. There are no circumstances under which taxation does not abridge the enjoyments of those on whom the taxes ultimately fall, and no means by which those enjoyments can again be extended, but the accumulation of new revenue.

Taxation can never be so equally applied, as to operate in the same proportion on the value of all commodities, and still to preserve them at the same relative value. It frequently operates very differently from the intention of the legislature, by its indirect effects. We have already seen,[1] that the effect of a direct tax on corn and raw produce, is, if money be also produced in the country, to raise the price of all commodities, in proportion as raw produce enters into their composition, and thereby to destroy the natural relation which previously existed between them. Another indirect effect is, that it raises wages, and lowers the rate of profits; and we have also seen, in another part of this work,[2] that the effect of a rise of wages, and a fall of profits, is to lower the money prices of those commodities which are produced in a greater degree by the employment of fixed capital.

That a commodity, when taxed, can no longer be so profitably exported, is so well understood, that a drawback is frequently allowed on its exportation, and a duty laid on its importation. If these drawbacks and duties be accurately laid,

---

[1] Above, pp. 159 and 169.   [2] Above, pp. 62–3 (ed. 1) and p. 46 (ed. 3).

not only on the commodities themselves, but on all which they may indirectly affect, then, indeed, there will be no disturbance in the value of the precious metals. Since we could as readily export a commodity after being taxed as before, and since no peculiar facility would be given to importation, the precious metals would not, more than before, enter into the list of exportable commodities.

Of all commodities, none are perhaps so proper for taxation, as those which, either by the aid of nature or art, are produced with peculiar facility. With respect to foreign countries, such commodities may be classed under the head of those which are not regulated in their price by the quantity of labour bestowed, but rather by the caprice, the tastes, and the power of the purchasers. If England had more productive tin mines than other countries, or if, from superior machinery or fuel, she had peculiar facilities in manufacturing cotton goods, the prices of tin, and of cotton goods, would still in England be regulated by the comparative quantity of labour and capital required to produce them, and the competition of our merchants would make them very little dearer to the foreign consumer. Our advantage in the production of these commodities might be so decided, that probably they could bear a very great additional price in the foreign market, without very materially diminishing their consumption. This price they never could attain, whilst competition was free at home, by any other means but by a tax on their exportation. This tax would fall wholly on foreign consumers, and part of the expenses of the Government of England would be defrayed, by a tax on the land and labour of other countries. The tax on tea, which at present is paid by the people of England, and goes to aid the expenses of the Government of England, might, if laid in China, on the exportation of the tea, be diverted to the payment of the expenses of the Government of China.

Taxes on luxuries have some advantage over taxes on necessaries. They are generally paid from income, and therefore do not diminish the productive capital of the country. If wine were much raised in price in consequence of taxation, it is probable that a man would rather forego the enjoyments of wine, than make any important encroachments on his capital, to be enabled to purchase it. They are so identified with price, that the contributor is hardly aware that he is paying a tax. But they have also their disadvantages. First, they never reach capital, and on some extraordinary occasions it may be expedient that even capital should contribute towards the public exigencies; and secondly, there is no certainty as to the amount of the tax, for it may not reach even income. A man intent on saving, will exempt himself from a tax on wine, by giving up the use of it. The income of the country may be undiminished, and yet the State may be unable to raise a shilling by the tax.

Whatever habit has rendered delightful, will be relinquished with reluctance, and will continue to be consumed notwithstanding a very heavy tax; but this reluctance has its limits, and experience every day demonstrates that an increase in the nominal amount of taxation, often diminishes the produce. One man will continue to drink the same quantity of wine, though the price of every bottle should be raised three shillings, who would yet relinquish the use of wine rather than pay four. Another will be content to pay four, yet refuse to pay five shillings. The same may be said of other taxes on luxuries: many would pay a tax of 5*l.* for the enjoyment which a horse affords, who would not pay 10*l.* or 20*l.* It is not because they cannot pay more, that they give up the use of wine and of horses, but because they will not pay more. Every man has some standard in his own mind by which he estimates the value of his enjoyments, but that standard is as various as the human character. A country whose financial situation has become extremely artificial, by the mischievous policy of accumulating a large national debt, and a consequently enormous taxation, is particularly exposed to the inconvenience attendant on this mode of raising taxes. After visiting with a tax the whole round of luxuries; after laying horses, carriages, wine, servants, and all the other enjoyments of the rich, under contribution;[1] a minister is induced to have recourse to more direct taxes, such as income and property taxes, neglecting the golden maxim of M. Say, "that the very best of all plans of finance is to spend little, and the best of all taxes is that which is the least in amount."[2]

---

[1] Ed. 1, from here to the end of the chapter, reads: 'a minister is disposed to conclude that the country is arrived at the maximum of taxation, because by increasing the rate, he cannot increase the amount of any one of these taxes. But in this conclusion he will not be always correct, for it is very possible that such a country could bear a very great addition to its burdens without infringing on the integrity of its capital.' This passage was altered because in McCulloch's opinion it held out 'an apology to ministers for taxation'; see Ricardo's letter, below, VII, 337–8,

[2] Quoted above, p. 235.

CHAPTER XVII

TAXES ON OTHER COMMODITIES
THAN RAW PRODUCE

ON the same principle that a tax on corn would raise the price of corn, a tax on any other commodity would raise the price of that commodity. If the commodity did not rise by a sum equal to the tax, it would not give the same profit to the producer which he had before, and he would remove his capital to some other employment.

The taxing of all commodities, whether they be necessaries or luxuries, will, while money remains at an unaltered value, raise their prices by a sum at least equal to the tax.* A tax on the manufactured necessaries of the labourer would have the same effect on wages as a tax on corn, which differs from other necessaries only by being the first and most important on the list; and it would produce precisely the same effects on the profits of stock and foreign trade. But a tax on luxuries would

* It is observed by M. Say, "that a manufacturer is not enabled to make the consumer pay the whole tax levied on his commodity, because its increased price will diminish its consumption." Should this be the case, should the consumption be diminished, will not the supply also speedily be diminished? Why should the manufacturer continue in the trade, if his profits are below the general level? M. Say appears here also to have forgotten the doctrine which he elsewhere supports, "that the cost of production determines the price, below which commodities cannot fall for any length of time, because production would be then either suspended or diminished."—Vol. ii. p. 26.

"The tax in this case falls then partly on the consumer who is obliged to give more for the commodity taxed, and partly on the producer, who, after deducting the tax, will receive less. The public treasury will be benefited by what the purchaser pays in addition, and also by the sacrifice which the producer is obliged to make of a part of his profits. It is the effort of gunpowder, which acts at the same time on the bullet which it projects, and on the gun which it causes to recoil."—Vol. ii. p. 333.

have no other effect than to raise their price. It would fall wholly on the consumer, and could neither increase wages nor lower profits.

Taxes which are levied on a country for the purpose of supporting war, or for the ordinary expenses of the State, and which are chiefly devoted to the support of unproductive labourers, are taken from the productive industry of the country; and every saving which can be made from such expenses will be generally added to the income, if not to the capital of the contributors. When, for the expenses of a year's war, twenty millions are raised by means of a loan, it is the twenty millions which are withdrawn from the productive capital of the nation. The million per annum which is raised by taxes to pay the interest of this loan, is merely transferred from those who pay it to those who receive it, from the contributor to the tax, to the national creditor. The real expense is the twenty millions, and not the interest which must be paid for it.* Whether the interest be or be not paid, the country will neither be richer nor poorer. Government might at once have required the twenty millions in the shape of taxes; in

* "Melon says,[1] that the debts of a nation are debts due from the right hand to the left, by which the body is not weakened. It is true that the general wealth is not diminished by the payment of the interest on arrears of the debt: The dividends are a value which passes from the hand of the contributor to the national creditor: Whether it be the national creditor or the contributor who accumulates or consumes it, is, I agree, of little importance to the society; but the principal of the debt—what has become of that? It exists no more. The consumption which has followed the loan has annihilated a capital which will never yield any further revenue. The society is deprived not of the amount of interest, since that passes from one hand to the other, but of the revenue from a destroyed capital. This capital, if it had been employed productively by him who lent it to the State, would equally have yielded him an income, but that income would have been derived from a real production, and would not have been furnished from the pocket of a fellow citizen."—*Say*, vol. ii. p. 357. This is both conceived and expressed in the true spirit of the science.

[1] *Essai politique sur le commerce*, 'nouvelle édition', 1761, p. 296.

which case it would not have been necessary to raise annual taxes to the amount of a million. This, however, would not have changed the nature of the transaction. An individual instead of being called upon to pay 100*l*. per annum, might have been obliged to pay 2000*l*. once for all. It might also have suited his convenience rather to borrow this 2000*l*., and to pay 100*l*. per annum for interest to the lender, than to spare the larger sum from his own funds. In one case it is a private transaction between A and B, in the other Government guarantees to B the payment of interest[1] to be equally paid by A. If the transaction had been of a private nature, no public record would be kept of it, and it would be a matter of comparative indifference to the country whether A faithfully performed his contract to B, or unjustly retained the 100*l*. per annum in his own possession. The country would have a general interest in the faithful performance of a contract, but with respect to the national wealth, it would have no other interest than whether A or B would make this 100*l*. most productive; but on this question it would neither have the right nor the ability to decide. It might be possible, that if A retained it for his own use, he might squander it unprofitably, and if it were paid to B, he might add it to his capital, and employ it productively. And the converse would also be possible; B might squander it, and A might employ it productively. With a view to wealth only, it might be equally or more desirable that A should or should not pay it; but the claims of justice and good faith, a greater utility, are not to be compelled to yield to those of a less; and accordingly, if the State were called upon to interfere, the courts of justice would oblige A to perform his contract. A debt guaranteed by the nation, differs in no respect from the above transaction. Justice and good faith demand that the interest of the national debt should continue to be

---

[1] Ed. 1 'of the interest'.

paid, and that those who have advanced their capitals for the general benefit, should not be required to forego their equitable claims, on the plea of expediency.

But independently of this consideration, it is by no means certain, that political utility would gain any thing by the sacrifice of political integrity; it does by no means follow, that the party exonerated from the payment of the interest of the national debt would employ it more productively than those to whom indisputably it is due. By cancelling the national debt, one man's income might be raised from 1000*l.* to 1500*l.*, but another man's would be lowered from 1500*l.* to 1000*l.* These two men's incomes now amount to 2500*l.*, they would amount to no more then. If it be the object of Government to raise taxes, there would be precisely the same taxable capital and income in one case, as in the other. It is not, then, by the payment of the interest on the national debt, that a country is distressed, nor is it by the exoneration from payment that it can be relieved. It is only by saving from income, and retrenching in expenditure, that the national capital can be increased; and neither the income would be increased, nor the expenditure diminished by the annihilation of the national debt. It is by the profuse expenditure of Government, and of individuals, and by loans, that the[1] country is impoverished; every measure, therefore, which is calculated to promote public and private economy[2], will relieve the public distress; but it is error and delusion to suppose, that a real national difficulty can be removed, by shifting it from the shoulders of one class of the community, who justly ought to bear it, to the shoulders of another class, who, upon every principle of equity, ought to bear no more than their share.[3]

---

[1] Eds. 1-2 'a' in place of 'the'.
[2] Eds. 1-2 spell 'œconomy'.

[3] In ed. 1 this and the three subsequent paragraphs are joined together.

From what I have said, it must not be inferred that I consider the system of borrowing as the best calculated to defray the extraordinary expenses of the State. It is a system which tends to make us less thrifty—to blind us to our real situation. If the expenses of a war be 40 millions per annum, and the share which a man would have to contribute towards that annual expense were 100*l.*, he would endeavour, on being at once called upon for his portion, to save speedily the 100*l.* from his income. By the system of loans, he is called upon to pay only the interest of this 100*l.*, or 5*l.* per annum, and considers that he does enough by saving this 5*l.* from his expenditure, and then deludes himself with the belief, that he is as rich as before. The whole nation, by reasoning and acting in this manner, save only the interest of 40 millions, or two millions; and thus, not only lose all the interest or profit which 40 millions of capital, employed productively, would afford, but also 38 millions, the difference between their savings and expenditure. If, as I before observed, each man had to make his own loan, and contribute his full proportion to the exigencies of the State, as soon as the war ceased, taxation would cease, and we should immediately fall into a natural state of prices. Out of his private funds, A might have to pay to B interest for the money he borrowed of him during the war, to enable him to pay his quota of the expense; but with this the nation would have no concern.

A country which has accumulated a large debt, is placed in a most artificial situation; and although the amount of taxes, and the increased price of labour, may not, and I believe does not, place it under any other disadvantage with respect to foreign countries, except the unavoidable one of paying those taxes, yet it becomes the interest of every contributor to withdraw his shoulder from the burthen, and to shift this payment from himself to another; and the temptation to remove himself

and his capital to another country, where he will be exempted
from such burthens, becomes at last irresistible, and overcomes
the natural reluctance which every man feels to quit the place
of his birth, and the scene of his early associations. A country
which has involved itself in the difficulties attending this artificial system, would act wisely by ransoming itself from them,
at the sacrifice of any portion of its property which might be
necessary to redeem its debt. That which is wise in an individual,
is wise also in a nation. A man who has 10,000*l.*, paying him
an income of 500*l.*, out of which he has to pay 100*l.* per annum
towards the interest of the debt, is really worth only 8000*l.*,
and would be equally rich, whether he continued to pay 100*l.*
per annum, or at once, and for only once, sacrificed 2000*l.* But
where, it is asked, would be the purchaser of the property which
he must sell to obtain this 2000*l.*? the answer is plain: the
national creditor, who is to receive this 2000*l.*, will want an
investment for his money, and will be disposed either to lend
it to the landholder, or manufacturer, or to purchase from them
a part of the property of which they have to dispose. To such
a payment[1] the stockholders themselves would largely contribute. This scheme[2] has been often recommended,[3] but we
have, I fear, neither wisdom enough, nor virtue enough, to
adopt it. It must, however, be admitted, that during peace,
our unceasing efforts should be directed towards paying off
that part of the debt which has been contracted during war;
and that no temptation of relief, no desire of escape from
present, and I hope temporary distresses, should induce us to
relax in our attention to that great object.

No sinking fund can be efficient for the purpose of diminishing
the debt, if it be not derived from the excess of the public

---

[1] Ed. 1 'To such an effect'.
[2] Ed. 1 'Such a scheme'.

[3] It was first proposed by Archibald
Hutcheson in 1714; see below, V,
41, n. 1.

revenue over the public expenditure. It is to be regretted, that the sinking fund in this country is only such in name; for there is no excess of revenue above expenditure. It ought, by economy, to be made what it is professed to be, a really efficient fund for the payment of the debt. If, on the breaking out of any future war, we shall not have very considerably reduced our debt, one of two things must happen, either the whole expenses of that war must be defrayed by taxes raised from year to year, or we must, at the end of that war, if not before, submit to a national bankruptcy; not that we shall be unable to bear any large additions to the debt; it would be difficult to set limits to the powers of a great nation; but assuredly there are limits to the price, which in the form of perpetual taxation, individuals will submit to pay for the privilege merely of living in their native country.*

When a commodity is at a monopoly price, it is at the very highest price at which the consumers are willing to purchase it. Commodities are only at a monopoly price, when by no possible device their quantity can be augmented; and when therefore, the competition is wholly on one side—amongst the buyers. The monopoly price of one period may be much lower or higher than the monopoly price of another, because the com-

---

* "Credit, in general, is good, as it allows capitals to leave those hands where they are not usefully employed, to pass into those where they will be made productive: it diverts a capital from an employment useful only to the capitalist, such as an investment in the public funds, to make it productive in the hands of industry. It facilitates the employments of all capitals, and leaves none unemployed."—Economie Politique, p. 463. 2 Vol. 4th Edition.—This must be an oversight of M. Say. The capital of the stockholder can never be made productive—it is, in fact, no capital. If he were to sell his stock, and employ the capital he obtained for it, productively, he could only do so by detaching the capital of the buyer of his stock from a productive employment.[1]

[1] Eds. 1-2 do not contain this note. Say's reference to 'the public funds' appears first in his 4th ed., 1819; the passage was altered in the 5th ed., 1826, in a way that avoids Ricardo's objection.

petition amongst the purchasers must depend on their wealth, and their tastes and caprices. Those peculiar wines, which are produced in very limited quantity, and those works of art, which from their excellence or rarity, have acquired a fanciful value, will be exchanged for a very different quantity of the produce of ordinary labour, according as the society is rich or poor, as it possesses an abundance or scarcity of such produce, or as it may be in a rude or polished state. The exchangeable value therefore of a commodity which is at a monopoly price, is no where regulated by the cost of production.

Raw produce is not at a monopoly price, because the market price of barley and wheat is as much regulated by their cost of production, as the market price of cloth and linen. The only difference is this, that one portion of the capital employed in agriculture regulates the price of corn, namely, that portion which pays no rent; whereas, in the production of manufactured commodities, every portion of capital is employed with the same results; and as no portion pays rent, every portion is equally a regulator of price: corn, and other raw produce, can be augmented, too, in quantity, by the employment of more capital on the land, and therefore they are not at a monopoly price. There is competition among the sellers, as well as amongst the buyers. This is not the case in the production of those rare wines, and those valuable specimens of art, of which we have been speaking; their quantity cannot be increased, and their price is limited only by the extent of the power and will of the purchasers. The rent of these vineyards may be raised beyond any moderately assignable limits, because no other land being able to produce such wines, none can be brought into competition with them.

The corn and raw produce of a country may, indeed, for a time sell at a monopoly price; but they can do so permanently only when no more capital can be profitably employed on the

lands, and when, therefore, their produce cannot be increased.
At such time, every portion of land in cultivation, and every
portion of capital employed on the land will yield a rent, differing, indeed, in proportion to the difference in the return. At such
a time too, any tax which may be imposed on the farmer, will fall
on rent, and not on the consumer. He cannot raise the price of
his corn, because, by the supposition, it is already at the highest
price at which the purchasers will or can buy it. He will not be
satisfied with a lower rate of profits, than that obtained by
other capitalists, and, therefore, his only alternative will be to
obtain a reduction of rent, or to quit his employment.

Mr. Buchanan considers corn and raw produce as at a
monopoly price, because they yield a rent: all commodities
which yield a rent, he supposes must be at a monopoly price;
and thence he infers, that all taxes on raw produce would fall
on the landlord, and not on the consumer. "The price of
corn," he says, "which always affords a rent, being in no respect
influenced by the expenses of its production, those expenses
must be paid out of the rent; and when they rise or fall, therefore, the consequence is not a higher or lower price, but a
higher or a lower rent. In this view, all taxes on farm servants,
horses, or the implements of agriculture, are in reality land-
taxes; the burden falling on the farmer during the currency of
his lease, and on the landlord, when the lease comes to be
renewed. In like manner all those improved implements of
husbandry which save expense to the farmer, such as machines
for threshing and reaping, whatever gives him easier access to
the market, such as good roads, canals and bridges, though they
lessen the original cost of corn, do not lessen its market price.
Whatever is saved by those improvements, therefore, belongs
to the landlord as part of his rent."[1]

It is evident that if we yield to Mr. Buchanan the basis on

[1] Buchanan's ed. of *Wealth of Nations*, vol. IV, *Observations*, pp. 37–8.

which his argument is built, namely, that the price of corn always yields a rent, all the consequences which he contends for would follow of course. Taxes on the farmer would then fall not on the consumer but on rent; and all improvements in husbandry would increase rent: but I hope I have made it sufficiently clear, that until a country is cultivated in every part, and up to the highest degree, there is always a portion of capital employed on the land which yields no rent, and that it is this portion of capital, the result of which, as in manufactures, is divided between profits and wages that regulates the price of corn. The price of corn, then, which does not afford a rent, being influenced by the expenses of its production, those expenses cannot be paid out of rent. The consequence therefore of those expenses increasing, is a higher price, and not a lower rent.*

It is remarkable that both Adam Smith and Mr. Buchanan, who entirely agree that taxes on raw produce, a land-tax, and tithes, all fall on the rent of land, and not on the consumers of raw produce, should nevertheless admit that taxes on malt would fall on the consumer of beer, and not on the rent of the landlord. Adam Smith's argument is so able a statement of the view which I take of the subject of the tax on malt, and every other tax on raw produce, that I cannot refrain from offering it to the attention of the reader.

"The rent and profits of barley land must always be nearly equal to those of other equally fertile, and equally well cultivated land. If they were less, some part of the barley land would soon be turned to some other purpose; and if they were

---

* "Manufacturing industry increases its produce in proportion to the demand, and the price falls; *but the produce of land cannot be so increased*; and a high price is still necessary to prevent the consumption from exceeding the supply." *Buchanan*, vol. iv. p. 40. Is it possible that Mr. Buchanan can seriously assert, that the produce of the land cannot be increased, if the demand increases?

greater, more land would soon be turned to the raising of barley. When the ordinary price of any particular produce of land is at what may be called a monopoly price, a tax upon it necessarily reduces the rent and profit* of the land which grows it. A tax upon the produce of those precious vineyards, of which the wine falls so much short of the effectual demand, that its price is always above the natural proportion to that of¹ other equally fertile, and equally well cultivated land, would necessarily reduce the rent and profit* of those vineyards. The price of the wines being already the highest that could be got for the quantity commonly sent to market, it could not be raised higher without diminishing that quantity; and the quantity could not be diminished without still greater loss, because the lands could not be turned to any other equally valuable produce. The whole weight of the tax, therefore, would fall upon the rent and profit*; properly upon the *rent* of the vineyard." "But the ordinary price of barley has never been a monopoly price; and the rent and profit of barley land have never been above their natural proportion to those of other equally fertile and equally well cultivated land. The different taxes which have been imposed upon malt, beer, and ale, *have never lowered the price of barley*; have never reduced the rent and profit* of barley land. The price of malt to the brewer, has constantly risen in proportion to the taxes imposed upon it; and those taxes, together with the different duties upon beer and ale, have constantly either raised the price, or, what comes to the same thing, reduced the quality of those commodities to the consumer. The final payment of those taxes has fallen

---

* I wish the word "Profit" had been omitted. Dr. Smith must suppose the profits of the tenants of these precious vineyards to be above the general rate of profits. If they were not, they would not pay the tax, unless they could shift it either to the landlord or consumer.

¹ Adam Smith says 'of the produce of'.

constantly upon the consumer, and not upon the producer."[1]
On this passage Mr. Buchanan remarks, "A duty on malt never
could reduce the price of barley, because, unless as much could
be made of barley by malting it as by selling it unmalted, the
quantity required would not be brought to market. It is clear,
therefore, that the price of malt must rise in proportion to the
tax imposed on it, as the demand could not otherwise be supplied. The price of barley, however, is just as much a monopoly
price as that of sugar; they both yield a rent, and the market
price of both has equally lost all connexion with the original
cost."[2]

It appears then to be the opinion of Mr. Buchanan, that a
tax on malt would raise the price of malt, but that a tax on the
barley from which malt is made, would not raise the price of
barley; and, therefore, if malt is taxed, the tax will be paid by
the consumer; if barley is taxed, it will be paid by the landlord,
as he will receive a diminished rent. According to Mr. Buchanan
then, barley is at a monopoly price, at the highest price which
the purchasers are willing to give for it; but malt made of
barley is not at a monopoly price, and consequently it can be
raised in proportion to the taxes that may be imposed upon it.
This opinion of Mr. Buchanan of the effects of a tax on malt
appears to me to be in direct contradiction to the opinion he
has given of a similar tax, a tax on bread. "A tax on bread will
be ultimately paid, not by a rise of price, but by a reduction
of rent."* If a tax on malt would raise the price of beer, a tax
on bread must raise the price of bread.

The following argument of M. Say is founded on the same
views as Mr. Buchanan's: "The quantity of wine or corn which
a piece of land will produce, will remain nearly the same, what-

* Vol. iii. p. 355.

[1] Bk. v, ch. ii, pt. ii, art. iv; vol. II,   [2] Buchanan's ed. of the *Wealth of*
pp. 376–7.   *Nations*, vol. III, p. 386, note.

ever may be the tax with which it is charged. The tax may take away a half, or even three-fourths of its net produce, or of its rent if you please, yet the land would nevertheless be cultivated for the half or the quarter not absorbed by the tax. The rent, that is to say the landlord's share, would merely be somewhat lower. The reason of this will be perceived, if we consider, that in the case supposed, the quantity of produce obtained from the land, and sent to market, will remain nevertheless the same. On the other hand the motives on which the demand for the produce is founded, continue also the same.

"Now, if the quantity of produce supplied, and the quantity demanded, necessarily continue the same, notwithstanding the establishment or the increase of the tax, the price of that produce will not vary; and if the price do not vary, the consumer will not pay the smallest portion of this tax.

"Will it be said that the farmer, he who furnishes labour and capital, will, jointly with the landlord, bear the burden of this tax? certainly not; because the circumstance of the tax has not diminished the number of farms to be let, nor increased the number of farmers. Since in this instance also the supply and demand remain the same, the rent of farms must also remain the same. The example of the manufacturer of salt, who can only make the consumers pay a portion of the tax, and that of the landlord who cannot reimburse himself in the smallest degree, prove the error of those who maintain, in opposition to the economists, that all taxes fall ultimately on the consumer."—Vol. ii. p. 338.

If the tax "took away half, or even three-fourths of the net produce of the land," and the price of produce did not rise, how could those farmers obtain the usual profits of stock who paid very moderate rents, having that quality of land which required a much larger proportion of labour to obtain a given result, than land of a more fertile quality? If the whole rent were remitted, they would still obtain lower profits than those in other trades, and would therefore not continue to cultivate their land, unless they could raise the price of its produce. If the tax fell on the farmers, there would be fewer farmers disposed to hire farms; if it fell on the landlord, many farms would not be let at all, for they would afford no rent. But from what fund would those pay the tax who produce corn without paying any rent? It is quite clear that the tax must fall on the consumer. How would such land, as M. Say describes in the following passage, pay a tax of one-half or three-fourths of its produce?

"We see in Scotland poor lands thus cultivated by the proprietor, and which could be cultivated by no other person. Thus too, we see in the interior provinces of the United States vast and fertile lands, the revenue of which, alone, would not be sufficient for the maintenance of the proprietor. These lands are cultivated nevertheless, but it must be by the proprietor himself, or, in other ,words, he must add to the rent, which is little or nothing, the profits of his capital and industry, to enable him to live in competence. It is well known that land, though cultivated, yields no revenue to the landlord when no farmer will be willing to pay a rent for it: which is a proof that such land will give only the profits of the capital, and of the industry necessary for its cultivation."—*Say*, Vol. ii. p. 127.

CHAPTER XVIII

POOR RATES

WE have seen that taxes on raw produce, and on the profits of the farmer, will fall on the consumer of raw produce; since unless he had the power of remunerating himself by an increase of price, the tax would reduce his profits below the general level of profits, and would urge him to remove his capital to some other trade. We have seen too, that he could not, by deducting it from his rent, transfer the tax to his landlord; because that farmer who paid no rent, would, equally with the cultivator of better land, be subject to the tax, whether it were laid on raw produce, or on the profits of the farmer. I have also attempted to shew, that if a tax were general, and affected equally all profits, whether manufacturing or agricultural, it would not operate either on the price of goods or raw produce, but would be immediately, as well as ultimately, paid by the producers. A tax on rent, it has been observed, would fall on the landlord only, and could not by any means be made to devolve on the tenant.

The poor rate is a tax which partakes of the nature of all these taxes, and under different circumstances falls on the consumer of raw produce and goods, on the profits of stock, and on the rent of land. It is a tax which falls with peculiar weight on the profits of the farmer, and therefore may be considered as affecting the price of raw produce. According to the degree in which it bears on manufacturing and agricultural profits equally, it will be a general tax on the profits of stock, and will occasion no alteration in the price of raw produce and manufactures. In proportion to the farmer's inability to remunerate himself, by raising the price of raw produce, for that portion of the tax which peculiarly affects him, it will be a tax on rent,

and will be paid by the landlord. To know, then, the operation
of the poor rate at any particular time, we must ascertain
whether at that time it affects in an equal or unequal degree
the profits of the farmer and manufacturer; and also whether
the circumstances be such as to afford to the farmer the power
of raising the price of raw produce.

The poor rates are professed to be levied on the farmer in
proportion to his rent; and accordingly, the farmer who paid
a very small rent, or no rent at all, should pay little or no tax.
If this were true, poor rates, as far as they are paid by the
agricultural class, would entirely fall on the landlord, and could
not be shifted to the consumer of raw produce. But I believe
that it[1] is not true; the poor rate is not levied according to the
rent which a farmer actually pays to his landlord; it is proportioned to the annual value of his land, whether that annual
value be given to it by the capital of the landlord or of the
tenant.

If two farmers rented land of two different qualities in the
same parish, the one paying a rent of 100*l.* per annum for 50
acres of the most fertile land, and the other the same sum of
100*l.* for 1000 acres of the least fertile land, they would pay
the same amount of poor rates, if neither of them attempted
to improve the land; but if the farmer of the poor land, pre-
suming on a very long lease, should be induced, at a great
expense, to improve the productive powers of his land, by
manuring, draining, fencing, &c., he would contribute to the
poor rates, not in proportion to the actual rent paid to the
landlord, but to the actual annual value of the land. The rate
might equal or exceed the rent; but whether it did or not,
no part of this rate would be paid by the landlord. It would
have been previously calculated upon by the tenant; and if the
price of produce were not sufficient to compensate him for all

---

[1] Ed. 1 does not contain 'it'.

his expenses, together with this additional charge for poor rates, his improvements would not have been undertaken. It is evident, then, that the tax in this case is paid by the consumer; for if there had been no rate, the same improvements would have been undertaken, and the usual and general rate of profits would have been obtained on the stock employed, with a lower price of corn.

Nor would it make the slightest difference in this question, if the landlord had made these improvements himself, and had in consequence raised his rent from 100*l.* to 500*l.*; the rate would be equally charged to the consumer; for whether the landlord[1] should expend a large sum of money on his land, would depend on the rent, or what is called rent, which he would receive as a remuneration for it; and this again would depend on the price of corn, or other raw produce, being sufficiently high not only to cover this additional rent, but also the rate to which the land would be subject. If[2] at the same time all manufacturing capital contributed to the poor rates, in the same proportion as the capital expended by the farmer or landlord in improving the land, then it would no longer be a partial tax on the profits of the farmer's or landlord's capital, but a tax on the capital of all producers; and, therefore, it could no longer be shifted either on the consumer of raw produce or on the landlord. The farmer's profits would feel the effect of the rate no more than those of the manufacturer; and the former could not, any more than the latter, plead it as a reason for an advance in the price of his commodity. It is not the absolute, but the relative fall of profits, which prevents capital from being employed in any particular trade: it is the difference of profit which sends capital from one employment to another.

[1] Ed. 1 'he' instead of 'the land-lord'. [2] Ed. 1 'But if'.

It must be acknowledged, however, that in the actual state of the poor rates, a much larger amount falls on the farmer than on the manufacturer, in proportion to their respective profits; the farmer being rated according to the actual productions which he obtains, the manufacturer only according to the value of the buildings in which he works, without any regard to the value of the machinery, labour, or stock which he may employ. From this circumstance it follows, that the farmer will be enabled to raise the price of his produce by this whole difference. For since the tax falls unequally, and peculiarly on his profits, he would have less motive to devote his capital to the land, than to employ it in some other trade, were not the price of raw produce raised.[1] If, on the contrary, the rate had fallen with greater weight on the manufacturer than on the farmer, he would have been enabled to raise the price of his goods by the amount of the difference, for the same reason that the farmer under similar circumstances could raise the price of raw produce. In a society, therefore, which is extending its agriculture, when poor rates fall with peculiar weight on the land, they will be paid partly by the employers of capital in a diminution of the profits of stock, and partly by the consumer of raw produce in its increased price. In such a state of things, the tax may, under some circumstances, be even advantageous rather than injurious to landlords; for if the tax paid by the cultivator of the worst land, be higher in proportion to the quantity of produce obtained, than that paid by the farmers of the more fertile lands, the rise in the price of corn, which will extend to all corn, will more than compensate the latter for the tax. This advantage will remain with them during the continuance of their leases, but it will afterwards be transferred to their landlords. This, then, would be the effect of poor rates in an advancing society; but in a

[1] Ed. 1 'unless the price of raw produce were raised.'

stationary, or in a retrograde country, so far as capital could not be withdrawn from the land, if a further rate were levied for the support of the poor, that part of it which fell on agriculture would be paid, during the current leases, by the farmers; but, at the expiration of those leases, it would almost wholly fall on the landlords. The farmer, who, during his former lease, had expended his capital in improving his land, if it were still in his own hands would be rated for this new tax according to the new value which the land had acquired by its improvement, and this amount he would be obliged to pay during his lease, although his profits might thereby be reduced below the general rate of profits; for the capital which he has expended may be so incorporated with the land, that it cannot be removed from it. If, indeed, he, or his landlord, (should it have been expended by him) were able to remove this capital, and thereby reduce the annual value of the land, the rate would proportionably fall, and as the produce would at the same time be diminished, its price would rise; he would be compensated for the tax, by charging it to the consumer, and no part would fall on rent; but this is impossible, at least with respect to some proportion of the capital, and consequently in that proportion the tax will be paid by the farmers during their leases, and by landlords at their expiration. This additional tax, if it fell with peculiar severity on manufacturers, which it does not, would,[1] under such circumstances, be added to the price of their goods; for there can be no reason why their profits should be reduced below the general rate of profits, when their capitals might be easily removed to agriculture. *

* In a former part of this work,[2] I have noticed the difference between rent, properly so called, and the remuneration paid to the landlord under that name, for the advantages which the expenditure of his capital has

[1] Eds. 1-2 'This additional tax, as far as it fell unequally on manufacturers, would'.

[2] Above, p. 67.

procured to his tenant; but I did not perhaps sufficiently distinguish the difference which would arise from the different modes in which this capital might be applied. As a part of this capital, when once expended in the improvement of a farm, is inseparably amalgamated with the land, and tends to increase its productive powers, the remuneration paid to the landlord for its use is strictly of the nature of rent, and is subject to all the laws of rent. Whether the improvement be made at the expense of the landlord or the tenant, it will not be undertaken in the first instance, unless there is a strong probability that the return will at least be equal to the profit that can be made by the disposition of any other equal capital; but when once made, the return obtained will ever after be wholly of the nature of rent, and will be subject to all the variations of rent. Some of these expenses, however, only give advantages to the land for a limited period, and do not add permanently to its productive powers: being bestowed on buildings, and other perishable improvements, they require to be constantly renewed, and therefore do not obtain for the landlord any permanent addition to his real rent.

CHAPTER XIX

ON SUDDEN CHANGES IN THE CHANNELS OF TRADE

A GREAT manufacturing country is peculiarly exposed to temporary reverses and contingencies, produced by the removal of capital from one employment to another. The demands for the produce of agriculture are uniform, they are not under the influence of fashion, prejudice, or caprice. To sustain life, food is necessary, and the demand for food must continue in all ages, and in all countries. It is different with manufactures; the demand for any particular manufactured commodity, is subject not only to the wants, but to the tastes and caprice of the purchasers. A new tax too may destroy the comparative advantage which a country before possessed in the manufacture of a particular commodity; or the effects of war may so raise the freight and insurance on its conveyance, that it can no longer enter into competition with the home manufacture of the country to which it was before exported. In all such cases, considerable distress, and no doubt some loss, will be experienced by those who are engaged in the manufacture of such commodities; and it will be felt not only at the time of the change, but through the whole interval during which they are removing their capitals, and the labour which they can command, from one employment to another.

Nor will distress be experienced in that country alone where such difficulties originate, but in the countries to which its commodities were before exported. No country can long import, unless it also exports, or can long export unless it also imports. If, then, any circumstance should occur, which should permanently prevent a country from importing the usual amount

of foreign commodities, it will necessarily diminish the manufacture of some of those commodities which were usually
exported; and although the total value of the productions of
the country will probably be but little altered, since the same
capital will be employed, yet they will not be equally abundant
and cheap; and considerable distress will be experienced through
the change of employments. If by the employment of 10,000*l.*
in the manufacture of cotton goods for exportation, we imported annually 3000 pair of silk stockings of the value of
2000*l.*, and by the interruption of foreign trade we should be
obliged to withdraw this capital from the manufacture of cotton,
and employ it ourselves in the manufacture of stockings, we
should still obtain stockings of the value of 2000*l.* provided
no part of the capital were destroyed; but instead of having
3000 pair, we might only have 2500. In the removal of the
capital from the cotton to the stocking trade, much distress
might be experienced, but it would not considerably impair
the value of the national property, although it might lessen
the quantity of our annual productions.*

* "Commerce enables us to obtain a commodity in the place where
it is to be found, and to convey it to another where it is to be consumed;
it therefore gives us the power of increasing the value of the commodity,
by the whole difference between its price in the first of these places, and
its price in the second." M. Say, p. 458, vol. ii. True, but how is this
additional value given to it? By adding to the cost of production, first,
the expenses of conveyance; secondly, the profit on the advances of
capital made by the merchant. The commodity is only more valuable,
for the same reasons that every other commodity may become more
valuable, because more labour is expended on its production and conveyance, before it is purchased by the consumer. This must not be mentioned as one of the advantages of commerce. When the subject is more
closely examined, it will be found that the whole benefits of commerce
resolve themselves into the means which it gives us of acquiring, not more
valuable objects, but more useful ones.[1]

[1] Eds. 1-2 do not contain this note.   but the passage was already in
The reference is to the 4th ed., 1819,   the 2nd ed. of Say, 1814, vol. II,
of Say's *Traité d'Économie politique*,   pp. 437-8.

The commencement of war after a long peace, or of peace after a long war, generally produces considerable distress in trade. It changes in a great degree the nature of the employments to which the respective capitals of countries were before devoted; and during the interval while they are settling in the situations which new circumstances have made the most beneficial, much fixed capital is unemployed, perhaps wholly lost, and labourers are without full employment. The duration of this distress will be longer or shorter according to the strength of that disinclination, which most men feel to abandon that employment of their capital to which they have long been accustomed. It is often protracted too by the restrictions and prohibitions, to which the absurd jealousies which prevail between the different States of the commercial commonwealth give rise.

The distress which proceeds from a revulsion of trade, is often mistaken for that which accompanies a diminution of the national capital, and a retrograde state of society; and it would perhaps be difficult to point out any marks by which they may be accurately distinguished.

When, however, such distress immediately accompanies a change from war to peace, our knowledge of the existence of such a cause will make it reasonable to believe, that the funds for the maintenance of labour have rather been diverted from their usual channel, than materially impaired, and that after temporary suffering, the nation will again advance in prosperity. It must be remembered too that the retrograde condition is always an unnatural state of society. Man from youth grows to manhood, then decays, and dies; but this is not the progress of nations. When arrived to a state of the greatest vigour, their further advance may indeed be arrested, but their natural tendency is to continue for ages, to sustain undiminished their wealth, and their population.

In rich and powerful countries, where large capitals are invested in machinery, more distress will be experienced from a revulsion in trade, than in poorer countries where there is proportionally a much smaller amount of fixed, and a much larger amount of circulating capital, and where consequently more work is done by the labour of men. It is not so difficult to withdraw a circulating as a fixed capital, from any employment in which it may be engaged. It is often impossible to divert the machinery which may have been erected for one manufacture, to the purposes of another; but the clothing, the food, and the lodging of the labourer in one employment may be devoted to the support of the labourer in another; or the same labourer may receive the same food, clothing and lodging, whilst his employment is changed. This, however, is an evil to which a rich nation must submit; and it would not be more reasonable to complain of it, than it would be in a rich merchant to lament that his ship was exposed to the dangers of the sea, whilst his poor neighbour's cottage was safe from all such hazard.

From contingencies of this kind, though in an inferior degree, even agriculture is not exempted. War, which in a commercial country, interrupts the commerce of States, frequently prevents the exportation of corn from countries where it can be produced with little cost, to others not so favourably situated. Under such circumstances an unusual quantity of capital is drawn to agriculture, and the country which before imported becomes independent of foreign aid. At the termination of the war, the obstacles to importation are removed, and a competition destructive to the home-grower commences, from which he is unable to withdraw, without the sacrifice of a great part of his capital. The best policy of the State would be, to lay a tax, decreasing in amount from time to time, on the importation of foreign corn, for a limited number of years, in order to afford to the home-grower an opportunity to withdraw his capital gradually from the land.* In so doing, the country might not be making the most advantageous distribution of its capital, but the temporary tax to which it was subjected, would be for the advantage of a particular class, the distribution of whose capital was highly useful in procuring a supply of food when importation was stopped. If such exertions in a period of emergency were followed by risk of ruin on the termination of the difficulty, capital would shun such an employment. Besides the usual profits of stock, farmers would expect to be compensated for the risk which they incurred of a sudden influx of corn; and, therefore, the price to the consumer, at the seasons when he most required a supply, would be enhanced, not only by the superior cost of growing corn at home, but also by the insurance which he

---

* In the last volume to the supplement of the Encyclopædia Britannica,[1] article "Corn Laws and Trade," are the following excellent suggestions and observations: "If we shall at any future period, think of retracing our steps, in order to give time to withdraw capital from the cultivation of our poor soils, and to invest it in more lucrative employments, a gradually diminishing scale of duties may be adopted. The price at which foreign grain should be admitted duty free, may be made to decrease from 80s. its present limit, by 4s. or 5s. per quarter annually, till it reaches 50s. when the ports could safely be thrown open, and the restrictive system be for ever abolished. When this happy event shall have taken place, it will be no longer necessary to force nature. The capital and enterprise of the country will be turned into those departments of industry in which our physical situation, national character, or political institutions, fit us to excel. The corn of Poland, and the raw cotton of Carolina, will be exchanged for the wares of Birmingham, and the muslins of Glasgow. The genuine commercial spirit, that which permanently secures the prosperity of nations, is altogether inconsistent with the dark and shallow policy of monopoly. The nations of the earth are like provinces of the same kingdom—a free and unfettered intercourse is alike productive of general and of local advantage." The whole article is well worthy of attention; it is very instructive, is ably written, and shews that the author is completely master of the subject.[2]

---

[1] Vol. III, p. 363.
[2] Ed. 1 does not contain this note. It was added in ed. 2 with another (below, p. 318) at the request of

McCulloch, who was the author of the *Encyclopædia* article; see McCulloch's letter, below, VII, 354.

would have to pay, in the price, for the peculiar risk to which
this employment of capital was exposed. Notwithstanding,
then, that it would be more productive of wealth to the country,
at whatever sacrifice of capital it might be done, to allow the
importation of cheap corn, it would, perhaps, be advisable to
charge it with a duty for a few years.

In examining the question of rent, we found, that with every
increase in the supply of corn, and with the consequent fall
of its price, capital would be withdrawn from the poorer land;
and land of a better description, which would then pay no rent,
would become the standard by which the natural price of corn
would be regulated. At 4*l.* per quarter, land of an inferior
quality, which may be designated by No. 6, might be cultivated; at 3*l.* 10*s.* No. 5; at 3*l.* No. 4, and so on. If corn, in
consequence of permanent abundance, fell to 3*l.* 10*s.*, the capital
employed on No. 6 would cease to be employed; for it was
only when corn was at 4*l.* that it could obtain the general profits,
even without paying rent: it would, therefore, be withdrawn
to manufacture those commodities with which all the corn
grown on No. 6 would be purchased and imported. In this
employment it would necessarily be more productive to its
owner, or it would not be withdrawn from the other; for if
he could not obtain more corn by purchasing it with a commodity which he manufactured, than he got from the land for
which he paid no rent, its price could not be under 4*l.*[1]

It has, however, been said,[2] that capital cannot be withdrawn

---

[1] Eds. 1-2 read 'for if he could
obtain more corn by growing it on
land for which he paid no rent,
than by manufacturing a commodity with which he purchased
it, its price could not be under 4*l.*'
[2] The allusion is to W. Jacob who,
attacking a passage of Ricardo's
Essay on Profits (below, IV, 32),

had remarked that 'the capital invested in the poorer lands *cannot* be
withdrawn', adding: 'Every man
who has been ten miles from the
Royal Exchange, knows that deep
ploughing, cleaning, manuring,
liming, and draining...form the
capital thus expended' (*A Letter to
Samuel Whitbread*, 1815, p. 34).

from the land; that it takes the form of expenses, which cannot be recovered, such as manuring, fencing, draining, &c., which are necessarily inseparable from the land. This is in some degree true; but that capital which consists of cattle, sheep, hay and corn ricks, carts, &c. may be withdrawn; and it always becomes a matter of calculation, whether these shall continue to be employed on the land, notwithstanding the low price of corn, or whether they shall be sold, and their value transferred to another employment.

Suppose, however, the fact to be as stated, and that no part of the capital could be withdrawn*; the farmer would continue to raise corn, and precisely the same quantity too, at whatever price it might sell; for it could not be his interest to produce less, and if he did not so employ his capital, he would obtain from it no return whatever. Corn could not be imported, because he would sell it lower than 3l. 10s. rather than not sell it at all, and by the supposition the importer could not sell it under that price. Although then the farmers, who

---

* Whatever capital becomes fixed on the land, must necessarily be the landlord's, and not the tenants, at the expiration of the lease. Whatever compensation the landlord may receive for this capital, on re-letting his land, will appear in the form of rent; but no rent will be paid, if, with a given capital, more corn can be obtained from abroad, than can be grown on this land at home. If the circumstances of the society should require corn to be imported, and 1000 quarters can be obtained by the employment of a given capital, and if this land, with the employment of the same capital, will yield 1100 quarters, 100 quarters will necessarily go to rent; but if 1200 can be got from abroad, then this land will go out of cultivation, for it will not then yield even the general rate of profit. But this is no disadvantage, however great the capital may have been, that had been expended on the land. Such capital is spent with a view to augment the produce—that, it should be remembered, is the end; of what importance then can it be to the society, whether half its capital be sunk in value, or even annihilated, if they obtain a greater annual quantity of production? Those who deplore the loss of capital in this case, are for sacrificing the end to the means.[1]

[1] Eds. 1-2 do not contain this note. Cp. Ricardo's reply to Brougham's speech of 30 May 1820, below, V, 85-6.

cultivated land of this quality, would undoubtedly be injured by the fall in the exchangeable value of the commodity which they produced,—how would the country be affected? We should have precisely the same quantity of every commodity produced, but raw produce and corn would sell at a much cheaper price. The capital of a country consists of its commodities, and as these would be the same as before, reproduction would go on at the same rate. This low price of corn would however only afford the usual profits of stock to the land, No. 5, which would then pay no rent, and the rent of all better land would fall: wages would also fall, and profits would rise.

However low the price of corn might fall; if capital could not be removed from the land, and the demand did not increase, no importation would take place; for the same quantity as before would be produced at home. Although there would be a different division of the produce, and some classes would be benefited, and others injured, the aggregate of production would be precisely the same, and the nation collectively would neither be richer nor poorer.

But there is this advantage always resulting from a relatively low price of corn,—that the division of the actual production is more likely to increase the fund for the maintenance of labour, inasmuch as more will be allotted, under the name of profit, to the productive class, a less under the name rent, to the unproductive class.

This is true, even if the capital cannot be withdrawn from the land, and must be employed there, or not be employed at all: but if great part of the capital can[1] be withdrawn, as it evidently could, it will be only withdrawn, when it will yield more to the owner by being withdrawn than by being suffered to remain where it was; it will only be withdrawn then, when it can elsewhere be employed more productively both for the

---

[1] Ed. 1 'could'.

owner and the public. He consents to sink that part of his capital which cannot be separated from the land, because with that part which he can take away, he can obtain a greater value, and a greater quantity of raw produce, than by not sinking this part of the capital. His case is precisely similar to that of a man who has erected machinery in his manufactory at a great expense, machinery which is afterwards so much improved upon by more modern inventions, that the commodities manufactured by him very much sink in value. It would be entirely a matter of calculation with him whether he should abandon the old machinery, and erect the more perfect, *losing all the value of the old*, or continue to avail himself of its comparatively feeble powers. Who, under such circumstances, would exhort him to forego the use of the better machinery, because it would deteriorate or annihilate the value of the old? Yet this is the argument of those who would wish us to prohibit the importation of corn, because it will deteriorate or annihilate that part of the capital of the farmer which is for ever sunk in land. They do not see that the end of all commerce is to increase production, and that by increasing production, though you may occasion partial loss, you increase the general happiness. To be consistent, they should endeavour to arrest all improvements in agriculture and manufactures, and all inventions of machinery; for though these contribute to general abundance, and therefore to the general happiness, they never fail, at the moment of their introduction, to deteriorate or annihilate the value of[1] a part of the existing capital of farmers and manufacturers.[2]*

* Among the most able of the publications, on the impolicy of restricting the Importation of Corn, may be classed Major Torrens' Essay on the External Corn Trade. His arguments appear to me to be unanswered, and to be unanswerable.[3]

[1] Ed. 1 does not contain 'the value of'.

[2] Cp. the similar arguments in *Essay on Profits*, below, IV, 33, 41.

[3] Ed. 1 does not contain this note. On its origin see above, p. 97, n. 6.

Agriculture, like all other trades, and particularly in a commercial country, is subject to a reaction, which, in an opposite direction, succeeds the action of a strong stimulus. Thus, when war interrupts the importation of corn, its consequent high price attracts capital to the land, from the large profits which such an employment of it affords; this will probably cause more capital to be employed, and more raw produce to be brought to market than the demands of the country require. In such case, the price of corn will fall from the effects of a glut, and much agricultural distress will be produced, till the average supply is brought to a level with the average demand.

CHAPTER XX

VALUE AND RICHES, THEIR
DISTINCTIVE PROPERTIES

"A MAN is rich or poor," says Adam Smith, "according to the degree in which he can afford to enjoy the necessaries, conveniences, and amusements of human life."[1]

Value, then, essentially differs from riches, for value depends not on abundance, but on the difficulty or facility of production. The labour of a million of men in manufactures, will always produce the same value, but will not always produce the same riches. By the invention of machinery, by improvements in skill, by a better division of labour, or by the discovery of new markets, where more advantageous exchanges may be made, a million of men may produce double, or treble the amount of riches, of "necessaries, conveniences, and amusements," in one state of society, that they could produce in another, but they will not on that account add any thing to value; for every thing rises or falls in value, in proportion to the facility or difficulty of producing it, or, in other words, in proportion to the quantity of labour employed on its production. Suppose with a given capital, the labour of a certain number of men produced 1000 pair of stockings, and that by inventions in machinery, the same number of men can produce 2000 pair, or that they can continue to produce 1000 pair, and can produce besides 500 hats; then the value of the 2000 pair of stockings, or of the 1000 pair of stockings, and 500 hats, will be neither more nor less than that of the 1000 pair of stockings before the introduction of machinery; for they will

[1] Bk. 1, ch. v; vol. 1, p. 32.

be the produce of the same quantity of labour. But the value of the general mass of commodities will nevertheless be diminished; for, although the value of the increased quantity produced, in consequence of the improvement, will be the same exactly as the value would have been of the less quantity that would have been produced, had no improvement taken place, an effect is also produced on the portion of goods still unconsumed, which were manufactured previously to the improvement; the value of those goods will be reduced, inasmuch as they must fall to the level, quantity for quantity, of the goods produced under all the advantages of the improvement: and the society will, notwithstanding the increased quantity of commodities[1], notwithstanding its augmented riches, and its augmented means of enjoyment, have a less amount of value. By constantly increasing the facility of production, we constantly diminish the value of some of the commodities before produced, though by the same means we not only add to the national riches, but also to the power of future production. Many of the errors in political economy have arisen from errors on this subject, from considering an increase of riches, and an increase of value, as meaning the same thing, and from unfounded notions as to what constituted a standard measure of value. One man considers money as a standard of value, and a nation grows richer or poorer, according to him, in proportion as its commodities of all kinds can exchange for more or less money. Others represent money as a very convenient medium for the purpose of barter, but not as a proper measure by which to estimate the value of other things; the real measure of value according to them, is corn,* and a country is rich or poor, according as

* Adam Smith says, "that the difference between the real and the nominal price of commodities and labour, is not a matter of mere speculation, but may sometimes be of considerable use in practice."[2] I agree

[1] Ed. 1 'of its commodities'.   Smith says 'the distinction', not
[2] Bk. I, ch. v; vol. I, p. 35. Adam   'the difference'.

its commodities will exchange for more or less corn.* There
are others again, who consider a country rich or poor, according to the quantity of labour that it can purchase.[1] But
why should gold, or corn, or labour, be the standard measure
of value, more than coals or iron?—more than cloth, soap,
candles, and the other necessaries of the labourer?—why, in
short, should any commodity, or all commodities together, be
the standard, when such a standard is itself subject to fluctuations in value? Corn, as well as gold, may from difficulty or
facility of production, vary 10, 20, or 30 per cent., relatively
to other things; why should we always say, that it is those
other things which have varied, and not the corn? That commodity is alone invariable, which at all times requires the same
sacrifice of toil and labour to produce it. Of such a commodity
we have no knowledge, but we may hypothetically argue and
speak about it, as if we had; and may improve our knowledge
of the science, by shewing distinctly the absolute inapplica-
bility of all the standards which have been hitherto adopted.[2]
But supposing either of these to be a correct standard of value,
still it would not be a standard of riches, for riches do not
depend on value. A man is rich or poor, according to the
abundance of necessaries and luxuries which he can command;
and whether the exchangeable value of these for money, for

with him; but the real price of labour and commodities, is no more to
be ascertained by their price in goods, Adam Smith's real measure, than
by their price in gold and silver, his nominal measure. The labourer is
only paid a really high price for his labour, when his wages will purchase
the produce of a great deal of labour.

* In vol. i. p. 108, M. Say infers, that silver is now of the same value,
as in the reign of Louis XIV. "because the same quantity of silver will
buy the same quantity of corn."

[1] In eds. 1-2 the note on Say is
attached here instead of two lines
above.
[2] These observations on an invariable standard of value should
have been altered in ed. 3 to agree
with the changes introduced in
Chapter I; see above, p. 17, n. 3
and cp. p. 43 ff.

corn, or for labour, be high or low, they will equally contribute to the enjoyment of their possessor. It is through confounding the ideas of value and wealth, or riches that it has been asserted, that by diminishing the quantity of commodities, that is to say of the necessaries, conveniences, and enjoyments of human life, riches may be increased. If value were the measure of riches, this could not be denied, because by scarcity the value of commodities is raised; but if Adam Smith be correct, if riches consist in necessaries and enjoyments, then they cannot be increased by a diminution of quantity.

It is true, that the man in possession of a scarce commodity is richer, if by means of it he can command more of the necessaries and enjoyments of human life; but as the general stock out of which each man's riches are drawn, is diminished in quantity, by all that any individual takes from it, other men's shares must necessarily be reduced in proportion as this favoured individual is able to appropriate a greater quantity to himself.

Let water become scarce, says Lord Lauderdale,[1] and be exclusively possessed by an individual, and you will increase his riches, because water will then have value; and if wealth be the aggregate of individual riches, you will by the same means also increase wealth. You undoubtedly will increase the riches of this individual, but inasmuch as the farmer must sell a part of his corn, the shoemaker a part of his shoes, and all men give up a portion of their possessions for the sole purpose of supplying themselves with water, which they before had for nothing, they are poorer by the whole quantity of commodities which they are obliged to devote to this purpose, and the proprietor of water is benefited precisely by the amount of their loss. The same quantity of water, and the same quantity

[1] *An Inquiry into the Nature and Origin of Public Wealth, and into the Means and Causes of its Increase,* Edinburgh, 1804, p. 44.

of commodities, are enjoyed by the whole society, but they are differently distributed. This is, however, supposing rather a monopoly of water than a scarcity of it. If it should be scarce, then the riches of the country and of individuals would be actually diminished, inasmuch as it would be deprived of a portion of one of its enjoyments. The farmer would not only have less corn to exchange for the other commodities which might be necessary or desirable to him, but he, and every other individual, would be abridged in the enjoyment of one of the most essential of their comforts. Not only would there be a different distribution of riches, but an actual loss of wealth.

It may be said, then, of two countries possessing precisely the same quantity of all the necessaries and comforts of life, that they are equally rich, but the value of their respective riches would depend on the comparative facility or difficulty with which they were produced. For if an improved piece of machinery should enable us to make two pair of stockings, instead of one, without additional labour, double the quantity would be given in exchange for a yard of cloth. If a similar improvement be made in the manufacture of cloth, stockings and cloth will exchange in the same proportions as before, but they will both have fallen in value; for in exchanging them for hats, for gold, or other commodities in general, twice the former quantity must be given. Extend the improvement to the production of gold, and every other commodity; and they will all regain their former proportions. There will be double the quantity of commodities annually produced in the country, and therefore the wealth of the country will be doubled, but this wealth will not have increased in value.

Although Adam Smith has given the correct description of riches, which I have more than once noticed, he afterwards explains them differently, and says, "that a man must be rich or poor according to the quantity of labour which he can afford to purchase.''[1] Now, this description differs essentially from the other, and is certainly incorrect; for, suppose the mines were to become more productive, so that gold and silver fell in value, from the greater facility of their production; or that velvets were to be manufactured with so much less labour than before, that they fell to half their former value; the riches of all those who purchased those commodities would be increased; one man might increase the quantity of his plate, another might buy double the quantity of velvet; but with the possession of this additional plate and velvet, they could employ no more labour than before; because, as the exchangeable value of velvet and of plate would be lowered, they must part with proportionally more of these species of riches to purchase a day's labour. Riches, then, cannot be estimated by the quantity of labour which they can purchase.

From what has been said, it will be seen that the wealth of a country may be increased in two ways: it may be increased by employing a greater portion of revenue in the maintenance of productive labour,—which will not only add to the quantity, but to the value of the mass of commodities; or it may be increased, without employing any additional quantity of labour, by making the same quantity more productive,—which will add to the abundance, but not to the value of commodities.

In the first case, a country would not only become rich, but the value of its riches would increase. It would become rich by parsimony; by diminishing its expenditure on objects of luxury and enjoyment; and employing those savings in reproduction.

In the second case, there will not necessarily be either any diminished expenditure on luxuries and enjoyments, or any increased quantity of productive labour employed, but with the same labour more would be produced; wealth would in-

---

[1] Bk. I, ch. v; vol. I, p. 32.

crease, but not value. Of these two modes of increasing wealth, the last must be preferred, since it produces the same effect without the privation and diminution of enjoyments, which can never fail to accompany the first mode. Capital is that part of the wealth of a country which is employed with a view to future production, and may be increased in the same manner as wealth. An additional capital will be equally efficacious in the production of future wealth, whether it be obtained from improvements in skill and machinery, or from using more revenue reproductively; for wealth always depends on the quantity of commodities produced, without any regard to the facility with which the instruments employed in production may have been procured. A certain quantity of clothes and provisions will maintain and employ the same number of men, and will therefore procure the same quantity of work to be done, whether they be produced by the labour of 100 or 200[1] men; but they will be of twice the value if 200 have been employed on their production.[2]

M. Say, notwithstanding the corrections he has made in the fourth and last edition of his work, "Traité d'Economie Politique," appears to me to have been singularly unfortunate in his definition of riches and value. He considers these two

---

[1] Ed. 1 'or of 200'.

[2] Eds. 1-2 in place of the five paragraphs that follow in the text (ending p. 285) read:

'M. Say appears to me to have been singularly unfortunate in his definition of riches and value in the first chapter of his excellent work: the following is the substance of his reasoning: riches, he observes, consist only of things which have a value in themselves: riches are great, when the sum of the values of which they are composed is great. They are small when the sum of their values is small. Two things having an equal value, are riches of equal amount. They are of equal value, when by general consent they are freely exchanged for each other. Now, if mankind attach value to a thing, it is on account of the *uses* to which it is applicable. This faculty, which certain things have, of satisfying the various wants of mankind, I call utility. To create objects that have a value of any kind is to create riches, since the utility of things is the first foundation of their value, and it is terms as synonymous, and that a man is rich in proportion as he increases the value of his possessions, and is enabled to command an abundance of commodities. "The value of incomes is then increased," he observes, "if they can procure, it does not signify by what means, a greater quantity of products." According to M. Say, if the difficulty of producing cloth were to double, and consequently cloth was to exchange for double the quantity of the commodities for which it exchanged before, it would be doubled in value, to which I give my fullest assent; but if there were any peculiar facility in producing the commodities, and no increased difficulty in producing cloth, and cloth should in consequence exchange as before for double the

the value of things which constitutes riches. But we do not create objects: all we can do is to reproduce matter under another form—we can give it utility. Production then is a creation, not of matter but of utility, and it is measured by the value arising from the utility of the object produced. The utility of any object, according to general estimation, is pointed out by the quantity of other commodities for which it will exchange. This valuation, arising from the general estimate formed by society, constitutes what Adam Smith calls value in exchange; what Turgot calls appreciable value; and what we may more briefly designate by the term *value*.

'Thus far M. Say, but in his account of value and riches he has confounded two things which ought always to be kept separate, and which are called by Adam Smith, value in use and value in exchange. If by an improved machine I can, with the same quantity of labour, make two pair of stockings instead of one, I in no way impair the *utility* of one pair of stockings, though I diminish their value. If then I had precisely the same quantity of coats, shoes, stockings, and all other things, as before, I should have precisely the same quantity of useful objects, and should therefore be equally rich, if utility were the measure of riches; but I should have a less amount of value, for my stockings would be of only half their former value. Utility then is not the measure of exchangeable value.

'If we ask M. Say in what riches consist, he tells us in the possession of objects having value. If we then ask him what he means by value, he tells us that things are valuable in proportion as they possess utility. If again we ask him to explain to us by what means we are to judge of the utility of objects, he answers, by their value. Thus then the measure of value is utility, and the measure of utility is value.'

These references are to Say's *Traité d'Économie politique*, 2nd ed., 1814; those in the text of ed. 3 are to Say's 4th. ed., 1819.

quantity of commodities, M. Say would still say that cloth had doubled in value, whereas according to my view of the subject, he should say, that cloth retained its former value, and those particular commodities had fallen to half their former value. Must not M. Say be inconsistent with himself when he says, that by facility of production, two sacks of corn may be produced by the same means that one was produced before, and that each sack will therefore fall to half its former value, and yet maintain that the clothier who exchanges his cloth for two sacks of corn, will obtain double the value he before obtained, when he could only get one sack in exchange for his cloth. If two sacks be of the value that one was of before, he evidently obtains the same value and no more,—he gets, indeed, double the quantity of riches—double the quantity of utility—double the quantity of what Adam Smith calls value in use, but not double the quantity of value, and therefore M. Say cannot be right in considering value, riches, and utility to be synonymous. Indeed, there are many parts of M. Say's work to which I can confidently refer in support of the doctrine which I maintain, respecting the essential difference between value and riches, although it must be confessed that there are also various other passages in which a contrary doctrine is maintained. These passages I cannot reconcile, and I point them out by putting them in opposition to each other, that M. Say may, if he should do me the honour to notice these observations in any future edition of his work, give such explanations of his views as may remove the difficulty, which many others, as well as myself, feel in our endeavours to expound them.

1. In the exchange of two products, we only in fact exchange the productive services which have served to create them............p. 504.
2. There is no real dearness but that which arises from the cost of production. A thing really dear, is that which costs, much in producing.........................497.[1]
3. The value of all the productive services that must be consumed to create a product, constitute the cost of production of that product......505.

4. It is utility which determines the demand for a commodity, but it is the cost of its production which limits the extent of its demand. When its utility does not elevate its value to the level of the cost of production, the thing is not worth what it cost; it is a proof that the productive services might be employed to create a commodity of a superior value. The possessors of productive funds, that is to say, those who have the disposal of labour, of capital or land, are perpetually occupied in comparing the cost of production with the value of the things produced, or which comes to the same thing, in comparing the value of different commodities with each other; because the cost of production is nothing else but the value of productive services, consumed in forming a production; and the value of a

5. The value of incomes is then increased, if they can procure (it does not signify by what means,) a greater quantity of products.[2]
6. Price is the measure of the value of things, and their value is the measure of their utility. 2 Vol.[3]........p. 4.

7. Exchanges made freely, shew at the time, in the place, and in the state of society in which we are, the value which men attach to the things exchanged. ....466.
8. To produce, is to create value, by giving or increasing the utility of a thing, and thereby establishing a demand for it, which is the first cause of its value. Vol. 2............487.
9. Utility being created, constitutes a product. The exchangeable value which results, is only the measure of this utility, the measure of the production which has taken place....490.
10. The utility which people of a particular country find in a product, can no otherwise be appreciated than by the price which they give for it.......................502.
11. This price, is the measure of the utility, which it has in the judgment of men; of the satisfaction which they derive from consuming it, because they would not prefer consuming this utility, if for the price which it cost they could acquire a utility which would give them more satisfaction....................506.

[1] Should be p. 457.

[2] p. 497, note.
[3] Should be vol. 1.

productive service is nothing else than the value of the commodity, which is the result. The value of a commodity, the value of a productive service, the value of the cost of production are all, then, similar values when every thing is left to its natural course.[1]

12. The quantity of all other commodities which a person can immediately obtain in exchange for the commodity of which he wishes to dispose, is at all times a value not to be disputed. Vol. 2. ......4.[2]

If there is no real dearness but that which arises from cost of production, (*see* 2.) how can a commodity be said to rise in value, (*see* 5.) if its cost of production be not increased? and merely because it will exchange for more of a cheap commodity—for more of a commodity the cost of production of which has diminished? When I give 2000 times more cloth for a pound of gold than I give for a pound of iron, does it prove that I attach 2000 times more utility to gold than I do to iron? certainly not; it proves only as admitted by M. Say, (*see* 4.) that the cost of production of gold is 2000 times greater than the cost of production of iron. If the cost of production of the two metals were the same, I should give the same price for them; but if utility were the measure of value, it is probable I should give more for the iron. It is the competition of the producers "who are perpetually employed in comparing the cost of production with the value of the thing produced," (*see* 4.) which regulates the value of different commodities. If, then, I give one shilling for a loaf, and 21 shillings for a guinea, it is no proof that this in my estimation is the comparative measure of their utility.

In No. 4, M. Say maintains with scarcely any variation, the doctrine which I hold concerning value. In his productive services, he includes the services rendered by land, capital, and labour; in mine I include only capital and labour, and wholly

---

[1] pp. 507–8.

[2] These quotations are from Say's 4th ed., 1819; they are all, except 6 and 12, to be found in the 'Épitome des principes de l'économie politique' which concludes vol. II.

exclude land. Our difference proceeds from the different view which we take of rent: I always consider it as the result of a partial monopoly, never really regulating price, but rather as the effect of it. If all rent were relinquished by landlords, I am of opinion, that the commodities produced on the land would be no cheaper, because there is always a portion of the same commodities produced on land, for which no rent is or can be paid, as the surplus produce is only sufficient to pay the profits of stock.

To conclude, although no one is more disposed than I am to estimate highly the advantage which results to all classes of consumers, from the real abundance and cheapness of commodities, I cannot agree with M. Say, in estimating the value of a commodity, by the abundance of other commodities for which it will exchange; I am of the opinion of a very distinguished writer, M. Destutt de Tracy, who says, that "To measure any one thing is to compare it with a determinate quantity of that same thing which we take for a standard of comparison, for unity. To measure, then to ascertain a length, a weight, a value, is to find how many times they contain metres, grammes, francs, in a word, unities of the same description."[1] A franc is not a measure of value for any thing, but for a quantity of the same metal of which francs are made, unless francs, and the thing to be measured, can be referred to some other measure which is common to both. This, I think, they can be, for they are both the result of labour; and, therefore, labour is a common measure, by which their real as well as their relative value may be estimated. This also, I am happy to say, appears to be M. Destutt de Tracy's opinion.* He says,

* Elemens d'Ideologie, Vol. iv. p. 99.[2]—In this work M. de Tracy has given a useful and an able treatise on the general principles of Political

[1] *Élémens d'idéologie, Première partie. Idéologie proprement dite,* 'par A. L. C. Destutt-Tracy, Sénateur', 2nd ed., Paris, Courcier, 1804, p. 187.

[2] *Élémens d'idéologie, IVe et V^e parties. Traité de la volonté et de ses effets,* 'par le Cte Destutt de Tracy, Pair de France', Paris, Courcier, 1815, pp. 99–100.

"as it is certain that our physical and moral faculties are alone our original riches, the employment of those faculties, labour of some kind, is our only original treasure, and that it is always from this employment, that all those things are created which we call riches, those which are the most necessary, as well as those which are the most purely agreeable. It is certain too, that all those things only represent the labour which has created them, and if they have a value, or even two distinct values, they can only derive them from that of the labour from which they emanate."[1]

M. Say, in speaking of the excellences and imperfections of the great work of Adam Smith, imputes to him, as an error, that "he attributes to the labour of man alone, the power of producing value. A more correct analysis shews us that value is owing to the action of labour, or rather the industry of man, combined with the action of those agents which nature supplies, and with that of capital. His ignorance of this principle prevented him from establishing the true theory of the influence of machinery in the production of riches."[2]

In contradiction to the opinion of Adam Smith, M. Say, in the fourth chapter, speaks of the value which is given to commodities by natural agents, such as the sun, the air, the pressure of the atmosphere, &c., which are sometimes substituted for the labour of man, and sometimes concur with him in producing.† But these natural agents, though they add greatly to *value in use*, never add exchangeable value, of which M. Say

Economy, and I am sorry to be obliged to add, that he supports, by his authority, the definitions which M. Say has given of the words "value," "riches," and "utility."[3]

    † "The first man who knew how to soften metals by fire, is not the creator of the value which that process adds to the melted metal. That

[1] Here end the five paragraphs inserted in ed. 3 (cp. above, p. 279, n. 2).

[2] *Traité d'Économie politique*, 2nd ed., 1814, vol. I, pp. li–lii.

[3] Eds. 1-2 do not contain this note.

is speaking, to a commodity: as soon as by the aid of machinery, or by the knowledge of natural philosophy, you oblige natural agents to do the work which was before done by man, the exchangeable value of such work falls accordingly. If ten men turned a corn mill, and it be discovered that by the assistance of wind, or of water, the labour of these ten men may be spared, the flour which is the produce partly[1] of the work performed by the mill, would immediately fall in value, in proportion to the quantity of labour saved; and the society would be richer by the commodities which the labour of the ten men could produce, the funds destined for their maintenance being in no degree impaired. M. Say constantly overlooks the essential difference that there is between value in use, and value in exchange.[2]

M. Say accuses Dr. Smith of having overlooked the value which is given to commodities by natural agents, and by machinery, because he considered that the value of all things was derived from the labour of man; but it does not appear

value is the result of the physical action of fire added to the industry and capital of those who availed themselves of this knowledge."

"From this error Smith has drawn this false result, that the value of all productions represents the recent or former labour of man, *or, in other words, that riches are nothing else but accumulated labour; from which, by a second consequence, equally false, labour is the sole measure of riches, or of the value of productions.*"* The inferences with which M. Say concludes are his own, and not Dr. Smith's; they are correct if no distinction be made between value and riches, and in this passage M. Say makes none[3]: but though Adam Smith, who defined riches to consist in the abundance of necessaries, conveniences[4] and enjoyments of human life, would have allowed that machines and natural agents might very greatly add to the riches of a country, he would not have allowed that they add any thing to the value of those riches.[5]

* Chap. iv. p. 31.

[1] Eds. 1-2 do not contain 'partly'.
[2] Ed. 1 does not contain this sentence.
[3] Eds. 1-2 do not contain ', and in

this passage M. Say makes none'.
[4] Misprinted 'convenience' in eds. 2-3.
[5] Eds. 1-2 'to value in exchange.'

to me, that this charge is made out; for Adam Smith no where undervalues the services which these natural agents and machinery perform for us, but he very justly distinguishes the nature of the value which they add to commodities—they are serviceable to us, by increasing the abundance of productions, by making men richer, by adding to value in use; but as they perform their work gratuitously, as nothing is paid for the use of air, of heat, and of water, the assistance which they afford us, adds nothing to value in exchange.[1]

---

[1] Eds. 1-2 have here an additional passage:

'In the first chapter of the second book, M. Say himself gives a similar statement of value, for he says that "utility is the foundation of value, that commodities are only desirable, because they are in some way useful, but that their value depends not on their utility, not on the degree in which they are desired, but on the quantity of labour necessary to procure them." "The utility of a commodity thus understood, makes it an object of man's desire, makes him wish for it, and establishes a demand for it. When to obtain a thing, it is sufficient to desire it, it may be considered as an article of natural wealth, given to man in an unlimited quantity, and which he enjoys, without purchasing it by any sacrifice; such are the air, water, the light of the sun. If he obtained in this manner all the objects of his wants and desires, he would be infinitely rich: he would be in want of nothing. But unfortunately this is not the case; the greater part of the things which are convenient and agreeable to him, as well as those which are indispensably necessary in the social state, for which man seems to be specifically formed, are not given to him gratuitously; they could only exist by the exertion of certain labour, the employment of a certain capital, and, in many cases, by the use of land. These are obstacles in the way of gratuitous enjoyment; obstacles from which result a real expense of production; because we are obliged to pay for the assistance of these agents of production." "It is only when this utility has thus been communicated to a thing (viz. by industry, capital, and land,) that it is a production, *and that it has a value*. It is its utility which is the foundation of the demand for it, *but the sacrifices, and the charges necessary to obtain it, or in other words, its price*, limits the extent of this demand." [*Traité d'Économie politique*, 2nd ed., 1814, vol. II, pp. 3, 4. The first passage is a free summary, not a quotation.]

'The confusion which arises from confounding the terms "value" and "riches" will best be seen in the following passages. (M. Say, *Catechisme d'Economie Politique*, p. 99.) His pupil observes: "You have said, besides, that the riches of a society were composed of the sum total of the values which it possessed; it appears to me to follow, that the fall of one production, of stockings for example, by diminishing the sum total of the value belonging to the society, diminishes the mass of its riches;" to which the following answer is given: "the *sum* of the society's riches will not fall on that account. Two pair of stockings are produced instead of one; and two pair at three francs, are equally valuable with one pair at six francs. The income of the society remains the same, because the manufacturer has gained as much on two pair at three francs, as he gained on one pair at six francs." Thus far M. Say, though incorrect, is at least consistent. If value be the measure of riches, the society is equally rich, because the value of all its commodities is the same as before. But now for his inference. "But when the income remains the same, and productions fall in price, the society is really enriched. If the same fall took place in all commodities at the same time, which is not absolutely impossible, the society by procuring at half their former price, all the objects of its consumption, without having lost any portion of its income, would really be twice as rich as before,

and could purchase twice the quantity of goods."

'In the first passage we are told, that if every thing fell to half its value, from abundance, the society would be equally rich, because there would be double the quantity of commodities at half their former value, or in other words there would be the same value. But in the last passage we are informed, that by doubling the quantity of commodities, although the value of each commodity should be diminished one half, and therefore the value of all the commodities together be precisely the same as before, yet the society would be twice as rich as before. In the first case riches are estimated by the amount of value: in the second, they are estimated by the abundance of commodities contributing to human enjoyments. M. Say further says, "that a man is infinitely rich without valuables, if he can for nothing obtain all the objects he desires["]; yet in another place we are told, "that riches consist, not in the product itself, for it is not riches if it have not value, but in its value." Vol. ii, p. 2.'

On the changes introduced in this chapter in ed. 3, see letter to McCulloch of 4 Dec. 1820, below, VIII, 315.

CHAPTER XXI

EFFECTS OF ACCUMULATION ON PROFITS AND INTEREST

FROM the account which has been given of the profits of stock, it will appear, that no accumulation of capital will permanently lower profits, unless there be some permanent cause for the rise of wages. If the funds for the maintenance of labour were doubled, trebled, or quadrupled, there would not long be any difficulty in procuring the requisite number of hands, to be employed by those funds; but owing to the increasing difficulty of making constant additions to the food of the country, funds of the same value would probably not maintain the same quantity of labour. If the necessaries of the workman could be constantly increased with the same facility, there could be no permanent alteration in the rate of profits or wages, to whatever amount capital might be accumulated. Adam Smith, however, uniformly ascribes the fall of profits to accumulation of capital, and to the competition which will result from it, without ever adverting to the increasing difficulty of providing food for the additional number of labourers which the additional capital will employ. "The increase of stock," he says, "which raises wages, tends to lower profit. When the stocks of many rich merchants are turned into the same trade, their mutual competition naturally tends to lower its profit; and when there is a like increase of stock in all the different trades carried on in the same society, the same competition must produce the same effect in all."[1] Adam Smith speaks here of a rise of wages, but it is of a temporary rise, proceeding from increased funds before the population is increased; and he does not appear to see, that at

[1] Bk. 1, ch. ix; vol. 1, p. 89.

the same time that capital is increased, the work to be effected by capital, is increased in the same proportion. M. Say has, however, most satisfactorily shewn, that there is no amount of capital which may not be employed in a country, because demand is only limited by production. No man produces, but with a view to consume or sell, and he never sells, but with an intention to purchase some other commodity, which may be immediately useful to him, or which may contribute to future production. By producing, then, he necessarily becomes either the consumer of his own goods, or the purchaser and consumer of the goods of some other person. It is not to be supposed that he should, for any length of time, be ill-informed of the commodities which he can most advantageously produce, to attain the object which he has in view, namely, the possession of other goods; and, therefore, it is not probable that he will continually produce a commodity for which there is no demand.*

There cannot, then, be accumulated in a country any amount of capital which cannot be employed productively, until wages rise so high in consequence of the rise of necessaries, and so little consequently remains for the profits of stock, that the motive for accumulation ceases.† While the profits of stock are high, men will have a motive to accumulate. Whilst a man has

* Adam Smith speaks of Holland, as affording an instance of the fall of profits from the accumulation of capital, and from every employment being consequently overcharged. "The Government there borrow at 2 per cent., and private people of good credit, at 3 per cent."[1] But it should be remembered, that Holland was obliged to import almost all the corn which she consumed, and by imposing heavy taxes on the necessaries of the labourer, she further raised the wages of labour. These facts will sufficiently account for the low rate of profits and interest in Holland.

† Is the following quite consistent with M. Say's principle? "The more disposable capitals are abundant in proportion to the extent of employment for them, the more will the rate of interest on loans of capital fall."— Vol. ii. p. 108. If capital to any extent can be employed by a country, how can it be said to be abundant, compared with the extent of employment for it?

[1] Bk. i, ch. ix; vol. i, p. 93.

any wished-for gratification unsupplied, he will have a demand for more commodities; and it will be an effectual demand while he has any new value to offer in exchange for them. If ten thousand pounds were given to a man having 100,000*l.* per annum, he would not lock it up in a chest, but would either increase his expenses by 10,000*l.*; employ it himself productively, or lend it to some other person for that purpose; in either case, demand would be increased, although it would be for different objects. If he increased his expenses, his effectual demand might probably be for buildings, furniture, or some such enjoyment. If he employed his 10,000*l.* productively, his effectual demand would be for food, clothing, and raw material, which might set new labourers to work; but still it would be demand.*

Productions are always bought by productions, or by

---

* Adam Smith says, that "When the produce of any particular branch of industry exceeds what the demand of the country requires, the surplus must be sent abroad, and exchanged for something for which there is a demand at home. *Without such exportation, a part of the productive labour of the country must cease, and the value of its annual produce diminish.* The land and labour of Great Britain produce generally more corn, woollens, and hardware, than the demand of the home market requires. The surplus part of them, therefore, must be sent abroad, and exchanged for something for which there is a demand at home. It is only by means of such exportation, that this surplus can acquire a value sufficient to compensate the labour and expense of producing it."[1] One would be led to think by the above passage, that Adam Smith concluded we were under some necessity of producing a surplus of corn, woollen goods, and hardware, and that the capital which produced them could not be otherwise employed. It is, however, always a matter of choice in what way a capital shall be employed, and therefore there can never, for any length of time, be a surplus of any commodity; for if there were, it would fall below its natural price, and capital would be removed to some more profitable employment. No writer has more satisfactorily and ably shewn than Dr. Smith, the tendency of capital to move from employments in which the goods produced do not repay by their price the whole expenses, including the ordinary profits, of producing and bringing them to market.*

* See Chap. X. Book I.

[1] Bk. II, ch. v; vol. I, p. 352. The italics are Ricardo's.

services;[1] money is only the medium by which the exchange is effected. Too much of a particular commodity may be produced, of which there may be such a glut in the market, as not to repay the capital expended on it; but this cannot be the case with respect to all commodities; the demand for corn is limited by the mouths which are to eat it, for shoes and coats by the persons who are to wear them; but though a community, or a part of a community, may have as much corn, and as many hats and shoes, as it is able or may wish to consume, the same cannot be said of every commodity produced by nature or by art. Some would consume more wine, if they had the ability to procure it. Others having enough of wine, would wish to increase the quantity or improve the quality of their furniture. Others might wish to ornament their grounds, or to enlarge their houses. The wish to do all or some of these is implanted in every man's breast; nothing is required but the means, and nothing can afford the means, but an increase of production. If I had food and necessaries at my disposal, I should not be long in want of workmen who would put me in possession of some of the objects most useful or most desirable to me.

Whether these increased productions, and the consequent demand which they occasion, shall or shall not lower profits, depends solely on the rise of wages; and the rise of wages, excepting for a limited period, on the facility of producing the food and necessaries of the labourer. I say excepting for a limited period, because no point is better established, than that the supply of labourers will always ultimately be in proportion to the means of supporting them.

There is only one case, and that will be temporary, in which the accumulation of capital with a low price of food may be attended with a fall of profits; and that is, when the funds for the maintenance of labour increase much more rapidly than

[1] Ed. 1 does not contain 'or by services;'.

population;—wages will then be high, and profits low. If every man were to forego the use of luxuries, and be intent only on accumulation, a quantity of necessaries might be produced, for which there could not be any immediate consumption. Of commodities so limited in number, there might undoubtedly be an universal glut, and consequently there might neither be demand for an additional quantity of such commodities, nor profits on the employment of more capital. If men ceased to consume, they would cease to produce. This admission does not impugn the general principle. In such a country as England, for example, it is difficult to suppose that there can be any disposition to devote the whole capital and labour of the country to the production of necessaries only.

When merchants engage their capitals in foreign trade, or in the carrying trade, it is always from choice, and never from necessity: it is because in that trade their profits will be somewhat greater than in the home trade.

Adam Smith has justly observed "that the desire of food is limited in every man by the narrow capacity of the human stomach, but the desire of the conveniences and ornaments of building, dress, equipage, and household furniture, seems to have no limit or certain boundary."[1] Nature then has necessarily limited the amount of capital which can at any one time be profitably engaged in agriculture, but she has placed no limits to the amount of capital that may be employed in procuring "the conveniences and ornaments" of life. To procure these gratifications in the greatest abundance is the object in view, and it is only because foreign trade, or the carrying trade, will accomplish it better, that men engage in them in preference to manufacturing the commodities required, or a substitute for them, at home. If, however, from peculiar circumstances, we were precluded from engaging capital in foreign trade, or in the

---

[1] Bk. i, ch. xi, pt. ii; vol. i, p. 165.

carrying trade, we should, though with less advantage, employ it at home; and while there is no limit to the desire of "conveniences, ornaments of building, dress, equipage, and household furniture," there can be no limit to the capital that may be employed in procuring them, except that which bounds our power to maintain the workmen who are to produce them.

Adam Smith, however, speaks of the carrying trade as one, not of choice, but of necessity; as if the capital engaged in it would be inert if not so employed, as if the capital in the home trade could overflow, if not confined to a limited amount. He says, "when the capital stock of any country is increased to such a degree, *that it cannot be all employed in supplying the consumption, and supporting the productive labour of that particular country*, the surplus part of it naturally disgorges itself into the carrying trade, and is employed in performing the same offices to other countries."[1]

"About ninety-six thousand hogsheads of tobacco are annually purchased with a part of the surplus produce of British industry. But the demand of Great Britain does not require, perhaps, more than fourteen thousand. If the remaining eighty-two thousand, therefore, could not be sent abroad *and exchanged for something more in demand at home*, the importation of them would[2] cease immediately, *and with it the productive labour of all the*[3] *inhabitants of Great Britain, who are at present employed in preparing the goods with which these eighty-two thousand hogsheads are annually purchased*."[4] But could not this portion of the productive labour of Great Britain be employed in preparing some other sort of goods, with which something more in demand at home might be purchased? And if it could not,

---

[1] Bk. II, ch. v; vol. I, p. 353. The italics are Ricardo's in this and the following quotations.
[2] Adam Smith says 'must', not 'would'. There are other minor inaccuracies in this and the following quotations.
[3] Adam Smith says 'those'.
[4] Bk. II, ch. v; vol. I, p. 352.

might we not employ this productive labour, though with less advantage, in making those goods in demand at home, or at least some substitute for them? If we wanted velvets, might we not attempt to make velvets; and if we could not succeed, might we not make more cloth, or some other object desirable to us?

We manufacture commodities, and with them buy goods abroad, because we can obtain a greater quantity than we could make at home. Deprive us of this trade, and we immediately manufacture again for ourselves. But this opinion of Adam Smith is at variance with all his general doctrines on this subject. "If a foreign country can supply us with a commodity cheaper than we ourselves can make it, better buy it of them with some part of the produce of our own industry, employed in a way in which we have some advantage. *The general industry of the country being always in proportion to the capital which employs it,* will not thereby be diminished,[1] but only left to find out the way in which it can be employed with the greatest advantage."[2]

Again. "Those, therefore, who have the command of more food than they themselves can consume, are always willing to exchange the surplus, or, what is the same thing, the price of it, for gratifications of another kind. What is over and above satisfying the limited desire, is given for the amusement of those desires which cannot be satisfied, but seem to be altogether endless. The poor, in order to obtain food, exert themselves to gratify those fancies of the rich; and to obtain it more certainly, they vie with one another in the cheapness and perfection of their work. The number of workmen increases with the increasing quantity of food, or with the growing improvement and cultivation of the lands; and as the nature of their business admits of the utmost subdivisions of labours, the quantity of materials which they can work up increases in a much greater

---

[1] Ricardo omits here a few words not pertinent to the issue.   [2] Bk. IV, ch. ii; vol. I, p. 422.

proportion than their numbers. Hence arises a demand for every sort of material which human invention can employ, either usefully or ornamentally, in building, dress, equipage, or household furniture; for the fossils and minerals contained in the bowels of the earth, the precious metals, and the precious stones."[1]

It follows then from these admissions that there is no limit to demand—no limit to the employment of capital while it yields any profit, and that however abundant capital may become, there is no other adequate reason for a fall of profit but a rise of wages, and further it may be added, that the only adequate and permanent cause for the rise of wages is the increasing difficulty of providing food and necessaries for the increasing number of workmen.[2]

Adam Smith has justly observed, that it is extremely difficult to determine the rate of the profits of stock. "Profit is so fluctuating, that even in a particular trade, and much more in trades in general, it would be difficult to state the average rate of it. To judge of what it may have been formerly, or in remote periods of time, with any degree of precision must be altogether impossible." Yet since it is evident that much will be given for the use of money, when much can be made by it, he suggests that "the market rate of interest will lead us to form some notion of the rate of profits, and the history of the progress of interest afford us that of the progress of profits."[3] Undoubtedly if the market rate of interest could be accurately known for any considerable period, we should have a tolerably correct criterion, by which to estimate the progress of profits.

But in all countries, from mistaken notions of policy, the State has interfered to prevent a fair and free market rate of

[1] Bk. 1, ch. xi, pt. ii; vol. 1, p. 165.
[2] Ed. 1 does not contain this paragraph.
[3] These two passages, although in inverted commas, are not quotations, but free summaries. See Bk. 1, ch. ix; vol. 1, pp. 89–90.

interest, by imposing heavy and ruinous penalties on all those who shall take more than the rate fixed by law. In all countries probably these laws are evaded, but records give us little information on this head, and point out rather the legal and fixed rate, than the market rate of interest. During the present war, Exchequer and Navy Bills have been frequently[1] at so high a discount, as to afford the purchasers of them 7, 8 per cent., or a greater rate of interest for their money. Loans have been raised by Government at an interest exceeding 6 per cent. and individuals have been frequently obliged, by indirect means, to pay more than 10 per cent. for the interest of money; yet during this same period the legal rate of interest has been uniformly at 5 per cent. Little dependence for information then can be placed on that which is the fixed and legal rate of interest, when we find it may differ so considerably from the market rate. Adam Smith informs us,[2] that from the 37th of Henry VIII. to 21st of James I. 10 per cent. continued to be the legal rate of interest. Soon after the Restoration, it was reduced to 6 per cent., and by the 12th of Anne, to 5 per cent. He thinks the legal rate followed, and did not precede the market rate of interest. Before the American war, Government borrowed at 3 per cent., and the people of credit in the capital, and in many other parts of the kingdom at 3½, 4, and 4½ per cent.

The rate of interest, though ultimately and permanently governed by the rate of profit, is however subject to temporary variations from other causes. With every fluctuation in the quantity and value of money, the prices of commodities naturally vary. They vary also, as we have already shewn, from the alteration in the proportion of supply to demand, although there should not be either greater facility or difficulty of production. When the market prices of goods fall from an abundant supply, from a diminished demand, or from a rise in the value

[1] Eds. 1-2 'have frequently been'.   [2] Bk. i, ch. ix; vol. i, pp. 90–91.

of money, a manufacturer naturally accumulates an unusual quantity of finished goods, being unwilling to sell them at very depressed prices. To meet his ordinary payments, for which he used to depend on the sale of his goods, he now endeavours to borrow on credit, and is often obliged to give an increased rate of interest. This, however, is but of temporary duration; for either the manufacturer's expectations were well grounded, and the market price of his commodities rises, or he discovers that there is a permanently diminished demand, and he no longer resists the course of affairs: prices fall, and money and interest regain their real value. If by the discovery of a new mine, by the abuses of banking, or by any other cause, the quantity of money be greatly increased, its ultimate effect is to raise the prices of commodities in proportion to the increased quantity of money; but there is probably always an interval, during which some effect is produced on the rate of interest.

The price of funded property is not a steady criterion by which to judge of the rate of interest. In time of war, the stock market is so loaded by the continual loans of Government, that the price of stock has not time to settle at its fair level, before a new operation of funding takes place, or it is affected by anticipation of political events. In time of peace, on the contrary, the operations of the sinking fund, the unwillingness, which a particular class of persons feel to divert their funds to any other employment than that to which they have been accustomed, which they think secure, and in which their dividends are paid with the utmost regularity, elevates the price of stock, and consequently depresses the rate of interest on these securities below the general market rate. It is observable too, that for different securities, Government pays very different rates of interest. Whilst 100*l.* capital in 5 per cent. stock is selling for 95*l.*, an exchequer bill of 100*l.*, will be sometimes selling for 100*l.* 5*s.*, for which exchequer bill, no more interest

will be annually paid than 4*l*. 11*s*. 3*d*.: one of these securities
pays to a purchaser at the above prices, an interest of more than
5¼ per cent., the other but little more than 4¼; a certain quantity
of these exchequer bills is required as a safe and marketable
investment for bankers; if they were increased much beyond
this demand, they would probably be as much depreciated as
the 5 per cent. stock. A stock paying 3 per cent. per annum will
always sell at a proportionally greater price than stock paying
5 per cent., for the capital debt of neither can be discharged but
at par, or 100*l*. money for 100*l*. stock. The market rate of
interest may fall to 4 per cent., and Government would then
pay the holder of 5 per cent. stock at par, unless he consented
to take 4 per cent. or some diminished rate of interest under
5 per cent.: they would have no advantage from so paying the
holder of 3 per cent. stock, till the market rate of interest had
fallen below 3 per cent. per annum. To pay the interest on the
national debt, large sums of money are withdrawn from circulation four times in the year for a few days. These demands for
money being only temporary, seldom affect prices; they are
generally surmounted by the payment of a large rate of
interest.*

* "All kinds of public loans," observes M. Say, "are attended with the
inconvenience of withdrawing capital, or portions of capital, from productive employments, to devote them to consumption; and when they
take place in a country, *the Government of which does not inspire much
confidence*, they have the further inconvenience of raising the interest of
capital. Who would lend at 5 per cent. per annum to agriculture, to manufacturers, and to commerce, when a borrower may be found ready to pay
an interest of 7 or 8 per cent.? That sort of income, which is called profit
of stock, would rise then at the expense of the consumer. Consumption
would be reduced by the rise in the price of produce; and the other productive services would be less in demand, less well paid. The whole nation,
capitalists excepted, would be the sufferers from such a state of things."[1]
To the question: "who would lend money to farmers, manufacturers,
and merchants, at 5 per cent. per annum, when another borrower, having

[1] *Traité d'Économie politique*, 2nd ed., 1814, vol. II, p. 360. The italics
are Ricardo's.

little credit, would give 7 or 8?" I reply, that every prudent and reasonable man would. Because the rate of interest is 7 or 8 per cent. there, where the lender runs extraordinary risk, is this any reason that it should be equally high in those places where they are secured from such risks? M. Say allows, that the rate of interest depends on the rate of profits; but it does not therefore follow, that the rate of profits depends on the rate of interest. One is the cause, the other the effect, and it is impossible for any circumstances to make them change places.

CHAPTER XXII

BOUNTIES ON EXPORTATION, AND
PROHIBITIONS OF IMPORTATION

A BOUNTY on the exportation of corn tends to lower its price
to the foreign consumer, but it has no permanent effect on its
price in the home market.

Suppose that to afford the usual and general profits of stock,
the price of corn should in England be 4*l.* per quarter; it could
not then be exported to foreign countries where it sold for
3*l.* 15*s.* per quarter. But if a bounty of 10*s.* per quarter were
given on exportation, it could be sold in the foreign market at
3*l.* 10*s.*, and consequently the same profit would be afforded to
the corn grower, whether he sold it at 3*l.* 10*s.* in the foreign, or
at 4*l.* in the home market.

A bounty then, which should lower the price of British corn
in the foreign country, below the cost of producing corn in that
country, would naturally extend the demand for British, and
diminish the demand for their own corn. This extension of
demand for British corn could not fail to raise its price for a
time in the home market, and during that time to prevent also
its falling so low in the foreign market as the bounty has a
tendency to effect. But the causes which would thus operate on
the market price of corn in England would produce no effect
whatever on its natural price, or its real cost of production. To
grow corn would neither require more labour nor more capital,
and, consequently, if the profits of the farmer's stock were
before only equal to the profits of the stock of other traders,
they will, after the rise of price, be considerably above them.
By raising the profits of the farmer's stock, the bounty will
operate as an encouragement to agriculture, and capital will be

withdrawn from manufactures to be employed on the land, till the enlarged demand for the foreign market has been supplied, when the price of corn will again fall in the home market to its natural and necessary price, and profits will be again at their ordinary and accustomed level. The increased supply of grain operating on the foreign market, will also lower its price in the country to which it is exported, and will thereby restrict the profits of the exporter to the lowest rate at which he can afford to trade.

The ultimate effect then of a bounty on the exportation of corn, is not to raise or to lower the price in the home market, but to lower the price of corn to the foreign consumer—to the whole extent of the bounty, if the price of corn had not before been lower in the foreign, than in the home market—and in a less degree, if the price in the home had been above the price in the foreign market.

A writer in the fifth vol. of the Edinburgh Review,[1] on the subject of a bounty on the exportation of corn, has very clearly pointed out its effects on the foreign and home demand. He has also justly remarked, that it would not fail to give encouragement to agriculture in the exporting country; but he appears to have imbibed the common error which has misled Dr. Smith,[2] and, I believe, most other writers on this subject. He supposes, because the price of corn ultimately regulates wages, that therefore it will regulate the price of all other commodities. He says that the bounty, "by raising the profits of farming, will operate as an encouragement to husbandry; by raising the price of corn to the consumers at home, it will diminish for the time their power of purchasing this necessary of life, and thus abridge their real wealth. It is evident, however, that this last effect must be temporary: the wages of the labouring consumers had

[1] October 1804, Art. xv, p. 190ff.   [2] See below, p. 307.
(by Francis Horner).

been adjusted before by competition, and the same principle will adjust them again to the same rate, by raising the money price of labour, *and, through that, of other commodities, to the money price of corn.* The bounty upon exportation, therefore, will ultimately raise the money price of corn in the home market; not directly, however, but through the medium of an extended demand in the foreign market, and a consequent enhancement of the real price at home: *and this rise of the money price, when it has once been communicated to other commodities, will of course become fixed.*"[1]

If, however, I have succeeded in shewing that it is not the rise in the money wages of labour which raises the price of commodities, but that such rise always affects profits, it will follow that the prices of commodities would not rise in consequence of a bounty.

But a temporary rise in the price of corn, produced by an increased demand from abroad, would have no effect on the money price of labour.[2] The rise of corn is occasioned by a competition for that supply which was before exclusively appropriated to the home market. By raising profits, additional capital is employed in agriculture, and the increased supply is obtained; but till it be obtained, the high price is absolutely necessary to proportion the consumption to the supply, which would be counteracted by a rise of wages. The rise of corn is the consequence of its scarcity, and is the means by which the demand of the home purchasers is diminished. If wages were increased, the competition would increase, and a further rise of the price of corn would become necessary. In this account of the effects of a bounty, nothing has been supposed to occur to raise the natural price of corn, by which its market price is ultimately governed; for it has not been supposed, that any additional labour would be required on the land to insure a given pro-

[1] p. 197. The italics are Ricardo's.   [2] Eds. 1-2 'money price of wages.'

duction, and this alone can raise its[1] natural price. If the natural price of cloth were 20*s.* per yard, a great increase in the foreign demand might raise the price to 25*s.*, or more, but the profits which would then be made by the clothier would not fail to attract capital in that direction, and although the demand should be doubled, trebled, or quadrupled, the supply would ultimately be obtained, and cloth would fall to its natural price of 20*s.* So, in the supply of corn, although we should export 2, 3, or 800,000 quarters annually, it would ultimately be produced at its natural price, which never varies, unless a different quantity of labour becomes necessary to production.

Perhaps in no part of Adam Smith's justly celebrated work, are his conclusions more liable to objection, than in the chapter on bounties.[2] In the first place, he speaks of corn as of a commodity of which the production cannot be increased, in consequence of a bounty on exportation; he supposes invariably, that it acts only on the quantity actually produced, and is no stimulus to further production. "In years of plenty," he says, "by occasioning an extraordinary exportation, it necessarily keeps up the price of corn in the home market above what it would naturally fall to. In years of scarcity, though the bounty is frequently suspended, yet the great exportation which it occasions in years of plenty, must frequently hinder, more or less, the plenty of one year from relieving the scarcity of another. Both in the years of plenty and in years of scarcity, therefore, the bounty necessarily tends to raise the money price of corn somewhat higher than it otherwise would be in the home market."*[3]

* In another place he says, that "whatever extension of the foreign market can be occasioned by the bounty, must, in every particular year, be altogether at the expense of the home market; as every bushel of corn

---

[1] Eds. 1-2 do not contain 'its'.
[2] Bk. IV, ch. v.

[3] *ib.* vol. II, p. 9. There are slight inaccuracies in this and the following quotations.

Adam Smith appears to have been fully aware, that the correctness of his argument entirely depended on the fact, whether the increase "of the money price of corn, by rendering that commodity more profitable to the farmer, would not necessarily encourage its production."

"I answer," he says, "that this might be the case, if the effect of the bounty was to raise the real price of corn, or to enable the farmer, with an equal quantity of it, to maintain a greater number of labourers in the same manner, whether liberal, moderate, or scanty, as other labourers are commonly maintained in his neighbourhood."[1]

If nothing were consumed by the labourer but corn, and if the portion which he received was the very lowest which his sustenance required, there might be some ground for supposing, that the quantity paid to the labourer could, under no circumstances, be reduced,—but the money wages of labour sometimes do not rise at all, and never rise in proportion to the rise in the

which is exported by means of the bounty, and which would not have been exported without the bounty, would have remained in the home market to increase the consumption, and to lower the price of that commodity. The corn bounty, it is to be observed, as well as every other bounty upon exportation, imposes two different taxes upon the people: first, the tax which they are obliged to contribute, in order to pay the bounty; and, secondly, the tax which arises from the advanced price of the commodity in the home market, and which, as the whole body of the people are purchasers of corn, must, in this particular commodity, be paid by the whole body of the people. In this particular commodity, therefore, this second tax is by much the heaviest of the two." "For every five shillings, therefore, which they contribute to the payment of the first tax, they must contribute six pounds four shillings to the payment of the second." "The extraordinary exportation of corn, therefore, occasioned by the bounty, not only in every particular year diminishes the home, just as much as it extends the foreign market and consumption; but, by restraining the population and industry of the country, its final tendency is to stunt and restrain the gradual extension of the home market, and thereby, in the long run, rather to diminish than to augment the whole market and consumption of corn."[2]

[1] Bk. IV, ch. v; vol. II, p. 11.   [2] *ib.* vol. II, pp. 10–11.

money price of corn, because corn, though an important part, is only a part of the consumption of the labourer. If half his wages were expended on corn, and the other half on soap, candles, fuel, tea, sugar, clothing, &c., commodities on which no rise is supposed to take place, it is evident that he would be quite as well paid with a bushel and a half of wheat, when it was 16s. a bushel, as he was with two bushels, when the price was 8s. per bushel; or with 24s. in money, as he was before with 16s. His wages would rise only 50 per cent. though corn rose 100 per cent.; and, consequently, there would be sufficient motive to divert more capital to the land, if profits on other trades continued the same as before. But such a rise of wages would also induce manufacturers to withdraw their capitals from manufactures, to employ them on the land; for whilst the farmer increased the price of his commodity 100 per cent., and his wages only 50 per cent., the manufacturer would be obliged also to raise wages 50 per cent., whilst he had no compensation whatever, in the rise of his manufactured commodity, for this increased charge of production; capital would consequently flow from manufactures to agriculture, till the supply would again lower the price of corn to 8s. per bushel, and wages to 16s. per week; when the manufacturer would obtain the same profits as the farmer, and the tide of capital would cease to set in either direction. This is in fact the mode in which the cultivation of corn is always extended, and the increased wants of the market supplied. The funds for the maintenance of labour increase, and wages are raised. The comfortable situation of the labourer induces him to marry—population increases, and the demand for corn raises its price relatively to other things— more capital is profitably employed on agriculture, and continues to flow towards it, till the supply is equal to the demand, when the price again falls, and agricultural and manufacturing profits are again brought to a level.

But whether wages were stationary after the rise in the price of corn, or advanced moderately, or enormously, is of no importance to this question, for wages are paid by the manufacturer as well as by the farmer, and, therefore, in this respect they must be equally affected by a rise in the price of corn. But they are unequally affected in their profits, inasmuch as the farmer sells his commodity at an advanced price, while the manufacturer sells his for the same price as before. It is, however, the inequality of profit, which is always the inducement to remove capital from one employment to another; and, therefore, more corn would be produced, and fewer commodities manufactured. Manufactures would not rise, because fewer would be¹ manufactured, for a supply of them would be obtained in exchange for the exported corn.

A bounty, if it raises the price of corn, either raises it in comparison with the price of other commodities, or it does not. If the affirmative be true, it is impossible to deny the greater profits of the farmer, and the temptation to the removal of capital, till its price is again lowered by an abundant supply. If it does not raise it in comparison with other commodities, where is the injury to the home consumer, beyond the inconvenience of paying the tax? If the manufacturer pays a greater price for his corn, he is compensated by the greater price at which he sells his commodity, with which his corn is ultimately purchased.

The error of Adam Smith proceeds precisely from the same source as that of the writer in the Edinburgh Review; for they both think "that the money price of corn regulates that of all other home-made commodities."* "It regulates," says Adam Smith, "the money price of labour, which must always be such as to enable the labourer to purchase a quantity of corn suffi-

---

* The same opinion is held by M. Say.—Vol. ii. p. 335.

¹ Eds. 1-2 'were' in place of 'would be'.

cient to maintain him and his family, either in the liberal, moderate, or scanty manner, in which the advancing, stationary, or declining circumstances of the society oblige his employers to maintain him.[1] By regulating the money price of all the other parts of the rude produce of land, it regulates that of the materials of almost all manufactures. By regulating the money price of labour, it regulates that of manufacturing art and industry; and by regulating both, it regulates that of the complete manufacture. *The money price of labour, and of every thing that is the produce either of land and[2] labour, must necessarily rise or fall in proportion to the money price of corn.*"[3]

This opinion of Adam Smith, I have before attempted to refute.[4] In considering a rise in the price of commodities as a necessary consequence of a rise in the price of corn, he reasons as though there were no other fund from which the increased charge could be paid. He has wholly neglected the consideration of profits, the diminution of which forms that fund, without raising the price of commodities. If this opinion of Dr. Smith were well founded, profits could never really fall, whatever accumulation of capital there might be. If, when wages rose, the farmer could raise the price of his corn, and the clothier, the hatter, the shoemaker, and every other manufacturer, could also raise the price of their goods in proportion to the advance, although estimated in money they might be all raised, they would continue to bear the same value relatively to each other. Each of these trades could command the same quantity as before of the goods of the others, which, since it is goods, and not money, which constitute wealth, is the only circumstance that could be of importance to them; and the whole rise in the price of raw produce and of goods, would be injurious to no other

---

[1] Ricardo omits here a paragraph of Adam Smith's text.
[2] Adam Smith says 'or'.

[3] Bk. IV, ch. V; vol. II, pp. 11–12. The italics are Ricardo's.
[4] Above, pp. 28 ff. and 54 ff.

persons but to those whose property consisted of gold and
silver, or whose annual income was paid in a contributed quantity of those metals, whether in the form of bullion or of money.
Suppose the use of money to be wholly laid aside, and all trade
to be carried on by barter. Under such circumstances, could
corn rise in exchangeable value with other things? If it could,
then it is not true that the value of corn regulates the value of
all other commodities; for to do that, it should not vary in
relative value to them. If it could not, then it must be maintained, that whether corn be obtained on rich, or on poor land,
with much labour, or with little, with the aid of machinery, or
without, it would always exchange for an equal quantity of all
other commodities.

I cannot, however, but remark that, though Adam Smith's
general doctrines correspond with this which I have just quoted,
yet in one part of his work he appears to have given a correct
account of the nature of value. "The proportion between the
value of gold and silver, and that of goods of any other kind,
DEPENDS IN ALL CASES,[1]" he says, "*upon the proportion between
the quantity of labour which is necessary in order to bring a certain
quantity of gold and silver to market, and that which is necessary
to bring thither a certain quantity of any other sort of goods.*"[2]
Does he not here fully acknowledge that if any increase takes
place in the quantity of labour, required to bring one sort of
goods to market, whilst no such increase takes place in bringing
another sort thither, the first sort[3] will rise in relative value? If
no more labour than before be required to bring either cloth or
gold[4] to market, they will not vary in relative value, but if more
labour be required to bring corn and shoes to market, will not

---

[1] In eds. 1-2 the last four words are in italics.
[2] Bk. II, ch. ii; vol. I, pp. 311–12. The quotation is abridged, and the italics are Ricardo's.
[3] Ed. 1 'those goods' in place of 'the first sort'.
[4] Ed. 1 'If no more labour be re-quired to bring cloth and gold'.

corn and shoes rise in value relatively to cloth, and money made of gold?

Adam Smith again considers that the effect of the bounty is to cause a partial degradation in the value of money. "That degradation," says he, "in the value of silver, which is the effect of the fertility of the mines, and which operates equally, or very nearly equally, through the greater part of the commercial world, is a matter of very little consequence to any particular country. The consequent rise of all money prices, though it does not make those who receive them really richer, does not make them really poorer. A service of plate becomes really cheaper, and every thing else remains precisely of the same real value as before." This observation is most correct.

"But that degradation in the value of silver, which being the effect either of the peculiar situation, or of the political institutions of a particular country, takes place only in that country, is a matter of very great consequence, which, far from tending to make any body really richer, tends to make every body really poorer. The rise in the money price of all commodities, which is in this case peculiar to that country, tends to discourage more or less every sort of industry which is carried on within it, and to enable foreign nations, by furnishing almost all sorts of goods for a smaller quantity of silver than its own workmen can afford to do, to undersell them, not only in the foreign, but even in the home market."[1]

I have elsewhere[2] attempted to shew that a partial degradation in the value of money, which shall affect both agricultural produce, and manufactured commodities, cannot possibly be permanent. To say that money is partially degraded, in this sense, is to say that all commodities are at a high price; but

---

[1] Bk. IV, ch. V; vol. II, pp. 12–13.   [2] Above, pp. 168–72 and cp. p. 228.

while gold and silver are at liberty to make purchases in the cheapest market, they will be exported for the cheaper goods of other countries, and the reduction of their quantity, will increase their value at home; commodities will regain their usual level, and those fitted for foreign markets will be exported, as before.

A bounty, therefore, cannot, I think, be objected to on this ground.

If then, a bounty raises the price of corn in comparison with all other things, the farmer will be benefited, and more land will be cultivated; but if the bounty do not raise the value of corn relatively to other things, then no other inconvenience will attend it, than that of paying the bounty; one which I neither wish to conceal nor underrate.

Dr. Smith states, that "by establishing high duties on the importation, and bounties on the exportation of corn, the country gentlemen seemed to have imitated the conduct of the manufacturers." By the same means, both had endeavoured to raise the value of their commodities. "They did not, perhaps, attend to the great and essential difference which nature has established between corn, and almost every other sort of goods. When by either of the above means, you enable our manufacturers to sell their goods for somewhat a better price than they otherwise could get for them, you raise not only the nominal, but the real price of those goods. You increase not only the nominal, but the real profit, the real wealth and revenue of those manufacturers—you really encourage those manufactures. But when, by the like institutions, you raise the nominal or money price of corn, you do not raise its real value, you do not increase the real wealth of our farmers or country gentlemen, you do not encourage the growth of corn. The nature of things has stamped upon corn a real value, which cannot be altered by merely altering its money price. Through the world in general, that value is equal to the quantity of labour which it can maintain."[1]

I have already attempted to shew,[2] that the market price of corn would, under an increased demand from the effects of a bounty, exceed its natural price, till the requisite additional supply was obtained, and that then it would again fall to its natural price. But the natural price of corn is not so fixed as the natural price of commodities; because, with any great additional demand for corn, land of a worse quality must be taken into cultivation, on which more labour will be required to produce a given quantity, and the natural price of corn will[3] be raised. By a continued bounty, therefore, on the exportation of corn, there would be created a tendency to a permanent rise in the price of corn, and this, as I have shewn elsewhere,* never fails to raise rent. Country gentlemen, then, have not only a temporary but a permanent interest in prohibitions of the importation of corn, and in bounties on its exportation; but manufacturers have no permanent interest in establishing high duties on the importation, and bounties[4] on the exportation of commodities; their interest is wholly temporary.

A bounty on the exportation of manufactures will, undoubtedly, as Dr. Smith contends, raise for a time[5] the market price of manufactures, but it will not raise their natural price. The labour of 200 men will produce double the quantity of these goods that 100 could produce before; and, consequently, when the requisite quantity of capital was employed in supplying the requisite quantity of manufactures, they would again fall to their natural price, and all advantage from a high market

* See Chapter on Rent.

[1] Bk. IV, ch. v; vol. II, pp. 16–17. A very free quotation, with several omissions.
[2] Above, p. 301.
[3] Ed. 1 'would'.

[4] Eds. 1-2 'a bounty' in place of 'establishing high duties on the importation, and bounties'.
[5] Eds. 1-2 do not contain 'for a time'.

price would cease.[1] It is, then, only during the interval after the
rise in the market price of commodities, and till[2] the additional
supply is obtained, that the manufacturers will enjoy high
profits; for as soon as prices had subsided, their profits would
sink to the general level.

Instead of agreeing, therefore, with Adam Smith, that the
country gentlemen had not so great an interest in prohibiting
the importation of corn, as the manufacturer had in prohibiting
the importation of manufactured goods, I contend, that they
have a much superior interest; for their advantage is permanent,
while that of the manufacturer is only temporary. Dr. Smith
observes, that nature has established a great and essential
difference between corn and other goods, but the proper inference from that circumstance is directly the reverse of that
which he draws from it; for it is on account of this difference
that rent is created, and that country gentlemen have an interest
in the rise of the natural price of corn. Instead of comparing
the interest of the manufacturer with the interest of the country
gentleman, Dr. Smith should have compared it with the interest
of the farmer, which is very distinct from that of his landlord.
Manufacturers have no interest in the rise of the natural price
of their commodities, nor have farmers any interest in the rise
of the natural price of corn, or other raw produce, though both
these classes are benefited while the market price of their productions exceeds[3] their natural price. On the contrary, landlords
have a most decided interest in the rise of the natural price of
corn; for the rise of rent is the inevitable consequence of the
difficulty of producing raw produce, without which its natural
price could not rise. Now, as bounties on exportation and prohibitions of the importation of corn increase the demand, and

---

[1] Eds. 1-2 do not contain ', and all
advantage from a high market price
would cease'.

[2] Eds. 1-2 'before' in place of 'till'.

[3] Misprinted 'exceed' in ed. 3.

drive us to the cultivation of poorer lands, they necessarily occasion an increased difficulty of production.

The sole effect of high duties on the importation either of manufactures or of corn, or of a bounty on their exportation, is[1] to divert a portion of capital to an employment, which it would not naturally seek. It causes a pernicious distribution of the general funds of the society—it bribes a manufacturer to commence or continue in a comparatively less profitable employment. It is the worst species of taxation, for it does not give to the foreign country all that it takes away from the home country, the balance of loss being made up by the less advantageous distribution of the general capital. Thus, if the price of corn is in England 4*l.* and in France 3*l.* 15*s.* a bounty of 10*s.* will ultimately reduce it to 3*l.* 10*s.* in France, and maintain it at the same price of 4*l.* in England. For every quarter exported, England pays a tax of 10*s.* For every quarter imported into France, France gains only 5*s.*, so that the value of 5*s.* per quarter is absolutely lost to the world, by such a distribution of its funds as to cause diminished production, probably not of corn, but of some other object of necessity or enjoyment.

Mr. Buchanan appears to have seen the fallacy of Dr. Smith's arguments respecting bounties, and on the last passage which I have quoted, very judiciously remarks: "In asserting that nature has stamped a real value on corn, which cannot be altered by merely altering its money price, Dr. Smith confounds its value in use with its value in exchange. A bushel of wheat will not feed more people during scarcity than during plenty; but a bushel of wheat will exchange for a greater quantity of luxuries and conveniences when it is scarce, than when it is abundant; and the landed proprietors, who have a surplus of food to dispose of, will, therefore, in times of scarcity, be richer men; they

---

[1] Eds. 1-2 'The sole effect of the bounty either on the exportation of manufactures, or of corn, is'.

will exchange their surplus for a greater value of other enjoyments, than when corn is in greater plenty. It is vain to argue,
therefore, that if the bounty occasions a forced exportation of
corn, it will not also occasion a real rise of price."[1] The whole
of Mr. Buchanan's arguments on this part of the subject of
bounties, appear to me to be perfectly clear and satisfactory.

Mr. Buchanan, however, has not, I think, any more than
Dr. Smith, or the writer in the Edinburgh Review, correct
opinions as to the influence of a rise in the price of labour on
manufactured commodities. From his peculiar views, which
I have elsewhere noticed,[2] he thinks that the price of labour has
no connexion with the price of corn, and, therefore, that the
real value of corn might and would rise without affecting the
price of labour; but if labour were affected, he would maintain
with Adam Smith and the writer in the Edinburgh Review, that
the price of manufactured commodities would also rise; and
then I do not see how he would distinguish such a rise of corn,
from a fall in the value of money, or how he could come to any
other conclusion than that of Dr. Smith. In a note to page 276,
vol. i.[3] of the Wealth of Nations, Mr. Buchanan observes, "but
the price of corn does not regulate the money price of all the
other parts of the rude produce of land. It regulates the price
neither of metals, nor of various other useful substances, such
as coals, wood, stones, &c.; *and as it does not regulate the price
of labour, it does not regulate the price of manufactures*; so that the
bounty, in so far as it raises the price of corn, is undoubtedly
a real benefit to the farmer. It is not on this ground, therefore,
that its policy must be argued. Its encouragement to agriculture, by raising the price of corn, must be admitted; and the
question then comes to be, whether agriculture ought to be
thus encouraged?"—It is then, according to Mr. Buchanan, a

---

[1] Buchanan's ed. of the *Wealth of*   [2] Above, p. 216.
Nations, vol. II, p. 287, note.   [3] Should be vol. ii.

real benefit to the farmer, because it does not raise the price of labour; but if it did, it would raise the price of all things in proportion, and then it would afford no particular encouragement to agriculture.

It must, however, be conceded, that the tendency of a bounty on the exportation of any commodity is to lower in a small degree the value of money. Whatever facilitates exportation, tends to accumulate money in a country; and, on the contrary, whatever impedes exportation, tends to diminish it. The general effect of taxation, by raising the prices of the commodities taxed, tends to diminish exportation, and, therefore, to check the influx of money; and on the same principle, a bounty encourages the influx of money. This is more fully explained in the general observations on taxation.[1]

The injurious effects of the mercantile system have been fully exposed by Dr. Smith;[2] the whole aim of that system was to raise the price of commodities, in the home market, by prohibiting foreign competition; but this system was no more injurious to the agricultural classes than to any other part of the community. By forcing capital into channels where it would not otherwise flow, it diminished the whole amount of commodities produced. The price, though permanently higher, was not sustained by scarcity, but by difficulty of production; and, therefore, though the sellers of such commodities sold them for a higher price, they did not sell them, after the requisite quantity of capital was employed in producing them, at higher profits.*

---

* M. Say supposes the advantage of the manufacturers at home to be more than temporary. "A government which absolutely prohibits the importation of certain foreign goods, establishes a monopoly *in favour of those* who produce such commodities at home, *against those* who consume them; in other words, those at home who produce them having the exclusive privilege of selling them, may elevate their price above the

[1] Above, pp. 168–72.   [2] Bk. IV, 'Of Systems of Political Œconomy'.

The manufacturers themselves, as consumers, had to pay an additional price for such commodities, and, therefore, it cannot be correctly said, that "the enhancement of price occasioned by both, (corporation laws and high duties on the importations of foreign commodities,) is every where finally paid by the landlords, farmers, and labourers of the country."[1]

It is the more necessary to make this remark, as in the present day the authority of Adam Smith is quoted by country gentlemen, for imposing similar high duties on the importation of foreign corn. Because the cost of production, and, therefore, the prices of various manufactured commodities, are raised to the consumer by one error in legislation, the country has been called upon, on the plea of justice, quietly to submit to fresh exactions. Because we all pay an additional price for our linen, muslin, and cottons, it is thought just that we should pay also an additional price for our corn. Because, in the general distribution of the labour of the world, we have prevented the greatest amount of productions from being obtained, by our portion of[2] that labour, in manufactured commodities, we should further punish ourselves by diminishing the productive powers of the general labour in the supply of raw produce. It would be much wiser to acknowledge the errors which a mistaken policy has induced us to adopt, and immediately to commence a

natural price; and the consumers at home, not being able to obtain them elsewhere, are obliged to purchase them at a higher price." Vol. i. p. 201.

But how can they permanently support the market price of their goods above the natural price, when every one of their fellow citizens is free to enter into the trade? They are guaranteed against foreign, but not against home competition. The real evil arising to the country from such monopolies, if they can be called by that name, lies, not in raising the market price of such goods, but in raising their real and natural price. By increasing the cost of production, a portion of the labour of the country is less productively employed.

[1] Bk. 1, ch. x; vol. 1, p. 129.   [2] Eds. 1-2 do not contain 'our portion of'.

gradual recurrence to the sound principles of an universally free trade.*

"I have already had occasion to remark," observes M. Say, "in speaking of what is improperly called the balance of trade, that if it suits a merchant better to export the precious metals to a foreign country than any other goods, it is also the interest of the State that he should export them, because the State only gains or loses through the channel of its citizens; and in what concerns foreign trade, that which best suits the individual, best suits also the State; therefore, by opposing obstacles to the exportation which individuals would be inclined to make of the precious metals, nothing more is done, than to force them to substitute some other commodity less profitable to themselves and to the State. It must, however, be remarked, that I say only *in what concerns foreign trade*; because the profits which merchants make by their dealings with their countrymen, as well as those which are made in the exclusive commerce with colonies, are not entirely gains for the State. In the trade between individuals of the same country, there is no other gain but the value of an utility produced; *que la valeur d'une utilité produite*."† Vol. i. p. 401. I cannot see the distinction here made between the profits of the home and foreign trade. The

* "A freedom of trade is alone wanted to guarantee a country like Britain, abounding in all the varied products of industry, in merchandise suited to the wants of every society, from the possibility of a scarcity. The nations of the earth are not condemned to throw the dice to determine which of them shall submit to famine. There is always abundance of food in the world. To enjoy a constant plenty, we have only to lay aside our prohibitions and restrictions, and cease to counteract the benevolent wisdom of Providence." Article, "Corn Laws and Trade." Supplement to Encyclopædia Britannica.[1]

† Are not the following passages contradictory to the one above quoted? "Besides, that home trade, though less noticed, (because it is in

[1] Ed. 1 does not contain this note. The author of the article was McCulloch; cp. above, p. 267.

object of all trade is to increase productions. If for the purchase
of a pipe of wine, I had it in my power to export bullion, which
was bought with the value of the produce of 100 days' labour,
but Government, by prohibiting the exportation of bullion,
should oblige me to purchase my wine with a commodity
bought with the value of the produce of 105 days' labour, the
produce of five days' labour is lost to me, and, through me, to
the State. But if these transactions took place between individuals, in different provinces of the same country, the same
advantage would accrue both to the individual, and, through
him, to the country; if he were unfettered in his choice of the
commodities, with which he made his purchases; and the same
disadvantage, if he were obliged by Government to purchase
with the least beneficial commodity. If a manufacturer could
work up with the same capital, more iron where coals are
plentiful, than he could where coals are scarce, the country
would be benefited by the difference. But if coals were no
where plentiful, and he imported iron, and could get this additional quantity, by the manufacture of a commodity, with the
same capital and labour, he would in like manner benefit his
country by the additional quantity of iron. In the 7th Chap.[1]
of this work, I have endeavoured to shew that all trade, whether
foreign or domestic, is beneficial, by increasing the quantity,
and not by increasing the value of productions. We shall have

a variety of hands) is the most considerable, it is also the most profitable.
The commodities exchanged in that trade are necessarily the productions
of the same country." Vol. i. p. 84.

"The English Government has not observed, that the most profitable
sales are those which a country makes to itself, because they cannot take
place, without two values being produced by the nation; the value which
is sold, and the value with which the purchase is made." Vol. i. p. 221.
I shall, in the 26th chapter, examine the soundness of this opinion.

[1] All eds. print '6th Chap.', which correctly denotes the chapter 'On
Foreign Trade' in ed. 1, but not in eds. 2-3 (cp. above, p. 10).

no greater value, whether we carry on the most beneficial home and foreign trade, or in consequence of being fettered by prohibitory laws, we are obliged to content ourselves with the least advantageous. The rate of profits, and the value produced, will be the same. The advantage always resolves itself into that which M. Say appears to confine to the home trade; in both cases there is no other gain but that of the value of an *utilité produite.*

CHAPTER XXIII

ON BOUNTIES ON PRODUCTION[1]

I T may not be uninstructive to consider the effects of a bounty on the *production* of raw produce and other commodities, with a view to observe the application of the principles which I have been endeavouring to establish, with regard to the profits of stock, the division of[2] the annual produce of the land and labour, and the relative prices of manufactures and raw produce. In the first place let us suppose that a tax was imposed on all commodities, for the purpose of raising a fund to be employed by Government, in giving a bounty on the *production* of corn. As no part of such a tax would be expended by Government, and as all that was received from one class of the people, would be returned to another, the nation collectively would neither be richer nor poorer, from such a tax and bounty. It would be readily allowed, that the tax on commodities by which the fund was created, would raise the price of the commodities taxed; all the consumers of those commodities, therefore, would contribute towards that fund; in other words, their natural or necessary price being raised, so would, too, their market price. But for the same reason that the natural price of those commodities would be raised, the natural price of corn would be lowered; before the bounty was paid on production, the farmers obtained as great a price for their corn as was necessary to repay them their rent and their expenses, and afford them the general rate of profits; after the bounty, they would receive more than that rate, unless the price of corn fell by a sum at least equal to the

[1] Ed. 3 misprints 'productions' here and in one of the running titles, but has 'production' in the Contents and in the other running titles.

[2] Eds. 1-2 do not contain 'the division of'.

bounty. The effect then of the tax and bounty, would be to raise the price of commodities in a degree equal to the tax levied on them, and to lower the price of corn by a sum equal to the bounty paid. It will be observed, too, that no permanent alteration could be made in the distribution of capital between agriculture and manufactures, because as there would be no alteration, either in the amount of capital or population, there would be precisely the same demand for bread and manufactures. The profits of the farmer would be no higher than the general level, after the fall in the price of corn; nor would the profits of the manufacturer be lower after the rise of manufactured goods; the bounty then would not occasion any more capital to be employed on the land in the production of corn, nor any less in the manufacture of goods. But how would the interest of the landlord be affected? On the same principles that a tax on raw produce would lower the corn rent of land, leaving the money rent unaltered, a bounty on production, which is directly the contrary of a tax, would raise corn rent, leaving the money rent unaltered.* With the same money rent the landlord would have a greater price to pay for his manufactured goods, and a less price for his corn; he would probably therefore be neither richer nor poorer.

Now, whether such a measure would have any operation on the wages of labour, would depend on the question, whether the labourer, in purchasing commodities, would pay as much towards the tax as he would receive from the effects of[1] the bounty, in the low price of his food. If these two quantities were equal, wages would continue unaltered; but if the commodities taxed were not those consumed by the labourer, his wages would fall, and his employer would be benefited by the difference. But this is no real advantage to his employer; it

* See p. 158.

[1] Eds. 1-2 do not contain 'the effects of'.

would indeed operate to increase the rate of his profits, as every fall of wages must do; but in proportion as the labourer contributed less to the fund from which the bounty was paid, and which, let it be remembered, must be raised, his employer must contribute more; in other words, he would contribute as much to the tax by his expenditure, as he would receive in the effects of the bounty and the higher rate of profits together. He obtains a higher rate of profits to requite him for his payment, not only of his own quota of the tax, but of his labourer's also; the remuneration which he receives for his labourer's quota, appears in diminished wages, or, which is the same thing, in increased profits; the remuneration for his own appears in the diminution in the price of the corn which he consumes, arising from the bounty.

Here it will be proper to remark the different effects produced on profits from an alteration in the real labour, or natural,[1] value of corn, and an alteration in the relative value of corn, from taxation and from bounties. If corn is lowered in price by an alteration in its labour price, not only will the rate of the profits of stock be altered,[2] but the condition of the capitalist will be improved. With greater profits, he will have no more to pay for the objects on which those profits are expended; which does not happen, as we have just seen, when the fall is occasioned artificially by a bounty. In the real fall in the value of corn, arising from less labour being required to produce one of the most important objects of man's consumption, labour is rendered more productive. With the same capital the same labour is employed, and an increase of productions is the result; not only then will the rate of profits be increased, but the condition

---

[1] Eds. 1–2 do not contain ', or natural,'.
[2] From here to the end of the next sentence eds. 1-2 read 'but the abso-lute profits also; which does not happen, as we have just seen, when the fall is occasioned artificially by a bounty.'

of him who obtains them will be improved[1]; not only will each capitalist have a greater money revenue, if he employs the same money capital, but also when that money is expended, it will procure him a greater sum of commodities; his enjoyments will be augmented. In the case of the bounty, to balance the advantage which he derives from the fall of one commodity, he has the disadvantage of paying a price more than proportionally high for another; he receives an increased rate of profits in order to enable him to pay this higher price; so that his real situation, though not deteriorated,[2] is in no way improved: though he gets a higher rate of profits, he has no greater command of the produce of the land and labour of the country. When the fall in the value of corn is brought about by natural causes, it is not counteracted by the rise of other commodities; on the contrary, they fall from the raw material falling from which they are made: but when the fall in corn is occasioned by artificial means, it is always counteracted by a real rise in the value of some other commodity, so that if corn be bought cheaper, other commodities are bought dearer.

This then is a further proof, that no particular disadvantage arises from taxes on necessaries, on account of their raising wages and lowering the rate of profits. Profits are indeed lowered, but only to the amount of the labourer's portion of the tax, which must at all events be paid either by his employer or by the consumer of the produce of the labourer's work. Whether you deduct 50l. per annum from the employer's revenue, or add 50l. to the prices of the commodities which he consumes, can be of no other consequence to him or to the community, than as it may equally affect all other classes. If it be added to the prices of the commodity, a miser may avoid the

[1] Eds. 1-2 'not only then will the rate of profits, but the absolute profits of stock be increased'.

[2] Eds. 1-2 do not contain ', though not deteriorated,'.

tax by not consuming; if it be indirectly deducted from every man's revenue, he cannot avoid paying his fair proportion of the public burthens.

A bounty on the production of corn then, would produce no real effect on the annual produce of the land and labour of the country, although it would make corn relatively cheap, and manufactures relatively dear. But suppose now that a contrary measure should be adopted, that a tax should be raised on corn for the purpose of affording a fund for a bounty on the production of commodities.

In such case, it is evident that corn would be dear, and commodities cheap; labour would continue at the same price if the labourer were as much benefited by the cheapness of commodities as he was injured by the dearness of corn; but if he were not, wages would rise, and profits would fall, while money rent would continue the same as before; profits would fall, because, as we have just explained, that would be the mode in which the labourer's share of the tax would be paid by the employers of labour. By the increase of wages the labourer would be compensated for the tax which he would pay in the increased price of corn; by not expending any part of his wages on the manufactured commodities, he would receive no part of the bounty; the bounty would be all received by the employers, and the tax would be partly paid by the employed; a remuneration would be made to the labourers, in the shape of wages, for this increased burden laid upon them, and thus the rate of profits would be reduced. In this case too there would be a complicated measure producing no national result whatever.

In considering this question, we have purposely left out of our consideration the effect of such a measure on foreign trade; we have rather been supposing the case of an insulated country, having no commercial connexion with other countries. We have seen that as the demand of the country for corn and commodities would be the same, whatever direction the bounty might take, there would be no temptation to remove capital from one employment to another: but this would no longer be the case if there were foreign commerce, and that commerce were free. By altering the relative value of commodities and corn, by producing so powerful an effect on their natural prices, we should be applying a strong stimulus to the exportation of those commodities whose natural prices were lowered, and an equal stimulus to the importation of those commodities whose natural prices were raised, and thus such a financial measure might entirely alter the natural distribution of employments; to the advantage indeed of the foreign countries, but ruinously to that in which so absurd a policy was adopted.

CHAPTER XXIV

DOCTRINE OF ADAM SMITH CONCERNING THE RENT OF LAND

"Such parts only of the produce of land," says Adam Smith, "can commonly be brought to market, of which the ordinary price is sufficient to replace the stock which must be employed in bringing them thither, together with its ordinary profits. If the ordinary price is more than this, the surplus part of it will naturally go to the rent of land. *If it is not more, though the commodity can[1] be brought to market, it can afford no rent to the landlord.* Whether the price is, or is not more, depends upon the demand."[2]

This passage would naturally lead the reader to conclude that its author could not have mistaken the nature of rent, and that he must have seen that the quality of land which the exigencies of society might require to be taken into cultivation, would depend on "*the ordinary price of its produce,*" *whether it were "sufficient to replace the stock, which must be employed in cultivating it, together with its ordinary profits.*"

But he had adopted the notion that "there were some parts of the produce of land for which the demand must always be such as to afford a greater price than what is sufficient to bring them to market;"[3] and he considered food as one of those parts.

He says, that "land, in almost any situation, produces a greater quantity of food than what is sufficient to maintain all the labour necessary for bringing it to market, in the most liberal way in which that labour is ever maintained. The surplus,

---

[1] Adam Smith says 'may'.
[2] Bk. I, ch. xi; vol. I, p. 146. The italics are Ricardo's.
[3] *ib.* vol. I, p. 146.

too, is always more than sufficient to replace the stock which employed that labour, together with its profits. Something, therefore, always remains for a rent to the landlord."[1]

But what proof does he give of this?—no other than the assertion that "the most desert moors in Norway and Scotland produce some sort of pasture for cattle, of which the milk and the increase are always more than sufficient, not only to maintain all the labour necessary for tending them, and to pay the ordinary profit to the farmer, or owner of the herd or flock, but to afford some small rent to the landlord."[2] Now of this I may be permitted to entertain a doubt; I believe that as yet in every country, from the rudest to the most refined, there is land of such a quality that it cannot yield a produce more than sufficiently valuable to replace the stock employed upon it, together with the profits ordinary and usual in that country. In America we all know that this is the case, and yet no one maintains that the principles which regulate rent, are different in that country and in Europe. But if it were true that England had so far advanced in cultivation, that at this time there were no lands remaining which did not afford a rent, it would be equally true, that there formerly must have been such lands; and that whether there be or not, is of no importance to this question, for it is the same thing if there be any capital employed in Great Britain on land which yields only the return of stock with its ordinary profits, whether it be employed on old or on new land. If a farmer agrees for land on a lease of seven or fourteen years, he may propose to employ on it a capital of 10,000*l.*, knowing that at the existing price of grain and raw produce, he can replace that part of his stock which he is obliged to expend, pay his rent, and obtain the general rate of profit. He will not employ 11,000*l.*, unless the last 1000*l.* can be employed so productively as to afford him the usual profits of stock. In his calculation,

---

[1] Bk. I, ch. xi, pt. i; vol. I, p. 147.   [2] *ib.* vol. I, pp. 147–8.

whether he shall employ it or not, he considers only whether
the price of raw produce is sufficient to replace his expenses and
profits, for he knows that he shall have no additional rent to
pay. Even at the expiration of his lease his rent will not be
raised; for if his landlord should require rent, because this additional 1000*l*. was employed, he would withdraw it; since by
employing it, he gets, by the supposition, only the ordinary
and usual profits which he may obtain by any other employment of stock; and, therefore, he cannot afford to pay rent for
it, unless the price of raw produce should further rise, or, which
is the same thing, unless the usual and general rate of profits
should fall.

If the comprehensive mind of Adam Smith had been directed
to this fact, he would not have maintained that rent forms one
of the component parts of the price of raw produce; for price is
every where regulated by the return obtained by this last portion
of capital, for which no rent whatever is paid. If he had adverted
to this principle, he would have made no distinction between
the law which regulates the rent of mines and the rent of land.

"Whether a coal mine, for example," he says, "can afford
any rent, depends partly upon its fertility, and partly upon its
situation. A mine of any kind may be said to be either fertile
or barren, according as the quantity of mineral which can be
brought from it by a certain quantity of labour, is greater or less
than what can be brought by an equal quantity from the greater
part of other mines of the same kind. Some coal mines, advantageously situated, cannot be wrought on account of their
barrenness. The produce does not pay the expense. They can
afford neither profit nor rent. There are some, of which the
produce is barely sufficient to pay the labour, and replace,
together with its ordinary profits, the stock employed in working
them. They afford some profit to the undertaker of the work,
but no rent to the landlord. They can be wrought advan-

tageously by nobody but the landlord, who being himself the undertaker of the work, gets the ordinary profit of the capital which he employs in it. Many coal mines in Scotland are wrought in this manner, and can be wrought in no other. The landlord will allow nobody else to work them without paying some rent, and nobody can afford to pay any.

"Other coal mines in the same country, sufficiently fertile, cannot be wrought on account of their situation. A quantity of mineral sufficient to defray the expense of working, could be brought from the mine by the ordinary, or even less than the ordinary quantity of labour; but in an inland country, thinly inhabited, and without either good roads or water-carriage, this quantity could not be sold."[1] The whole principle of rent is here admirably and perspicuously explained, but every word is as applicable to land as it is to mines; yet he affirms that "it is otherwise in estates above ground. The proportion[2], both of their produce and of their rent, is in proportion to their absolute, and not to their relative fertility."[3] But, suppose that there were no land which did not afford a rent; then, the amount of rent on the worst land would be in proportion to the excess of the value of the produce above the expenditure of capital and the ordinary profits of stock: the same principle would govern the rent of land of a somewhat better quality, or more favourably situated, and, therefore, the rent of this land would exceed the rent of that inferior to it, by the superior advantages which it possessed; the same might be said of that of the third quality, and so on to the very best. Is it not, then, as certain, that it is the relative fertility of the land, which determines the portion of the produce, which shall be paid for the rent of land, as it is that the relative fertility of mines, determines the portion of their produce, which shall be paid for the rent of mines?

[1] Bk. 1, ch. xi, pt. ii; vol. 1, pp. 165–6.

[2] Adam Smith says 'The value'.

[3] Bk. 1, ch. xi, pt. iii; vol. 1, p. 174.

After Adam Smith has declared that there are some mines which can only be worked by the owners, as they will afford only sufficient to defray the expense of working, together with the ordinary profits of the capital employed, we should expect that he would admit that it was these particular mines which regulated the price of the produce from all mines[1]. If the old mines are insufficient to supply the quantity of coal required, the price of coal will rise, and will continue rising till the owner of a new and inferior mine finds that he can obtain the usual profits of stock by working his mine. If his mine be tolerably fertile, the rise will not be great before it becomes his interest so to employ his capital; but if it be not tolerably fertile[2], it is evident that the price must continue to rise till it will afford him the means of paying his expenses, and obtaining the ordinary profits of stock. It appears, then, that it is always the least fertile mine which regulates the price of coal. Adam Smith, however, is of a different opinion: he observes, that "the most fertile coal mine, too, regulates the price of coals at all the other mines in its neighbourhood. Both the proprietor and the undertaker of the work find, the one that he can get a greater rent, the other, that he can get a greater profit, by somewhat underselling all their neighbours. Their neighbours are soon obliged to sell at the same price, though they cannot so well afford it, and though it always diminishes, and sometimes takes away altogether, both their rent and their profit. Some works are abandoned altogether; others can afford no rent, and can be wrought only by the proprietor."[3] If the demand for coal should be diminished, or if by new processes the quantity should be increased, the price would fall, and some mines would be abandoned; but in every case, the price must be sufficient to pay the expenses and

---

[1] Eds. 1-2 do not contain 'from all mines'.

[2] Eds. 1-2 'less productive' in place of 'not tolerably fertile'.

[3] Bk. 1, ch. xi, pt. ii; vol. 1, pp. 167–8.

profit of that mine which is worked without being charged with rent. It is, therefore, the least fertile mine which regulates price. Indeed, it is so stated in another place by Adam Smith himself, for he says, "The lowest price at which coals can be sold for any considerable time, is like that of all other commodities, the price which is barely sufficient to replace, together with its ordinary profits, the stock which must be employed in bringing them to market. At a coal mine for which the landlord can get no rent, but which he must either work himself, or let it alone all together, the price of coals must generally be nearly about this price."[1]

But the same circumstance, namely, the abundance and consequent cheapness of coals, from whatever cause it may arise, which would make it necessary to abandon those mines on which there was no rent, or a very moderate one, would, if there were the same abundance, and consequent cheapness of raw produce, render it necessary to abandon the cultivation of those lands for which either no rent was paid, or a very moderate one. If, for example, potatoes should become the general and common food of the people, as rice is in some countries, one fourth, or one half of the land now in cultivation, would probably be immediately abandoned; for if, as Adam Smith says, "an acre of potatoes will produce six thousand weight of solid nourishment, three times the quantity produced by the acre of wheat,"[2] there could not be for a considerable time such a multiplication of people, as to consume the quantity that might be raised on the land before employed for the cultivation of wheat; much land would consequently be abandoned, and rent would fall; and it would not be till the population had been doubled or trebled, that the same quantity of land could be in cultivation, and the rent paid for it as high as before.

Neither would any greater proportion of the gross produce

[1] Bk. I, ch. xi, pt. ii; vol. I, p. 168.   [2] ib. pt.i ; vol. I, p. 161.

be paid to the landlord, whether it consisted of potatoes, which would feed three hundred people, or of wheat, which would feed only one hundred; because, though the expenses of production would be very much diminished if the labourer's wages were chiefly regulated by the price of potatoes and not by the price of wheat, and though therefore the proportion of the whole gross produce, after paying the labourers, would be greatly increased, yet no part of that additional proportion would go to rent, but the whole invariably to profits,—profits being at all times raised as wages fall, and lowered as wages rise. Whether wheat or potatoes were cultivated, rent would be governed by the same principle—it would be always equal to the difference between the quantities of produce obtained with equal capitals, either on the same land or on land of different qualities; and, therefore, while lands of the same quality were cultivated, and there was no alteration in their relative fertility or advantages, rent would always bear the same proportion to the gross produce.

Adam Smith, however, maintains that the proportion which falls to the landlord would be increased by a diminished cost of production, and, therefore, that he would receive a larger share as well as a larger quantity, from an abundant than from a scanty produce. "A rice field," he says, "produces a much greater quantity of food than the most fertile corn field. Two crops in the year, from thirty to sixty bushels each, are said to be the ordinary produce of an acre. Though its cultivation, therefore, requires more labour, a much greater surplus remains after maintaining all that labour. In those rice countries, therefore, where rice is the common and favourite vegetable food of the people, and where the cultivators are chiefly maintained with it, *a greater share of this greater surplus should belong to the landlord than in corn countries.*"[1]

---

[1] Bk. i, ch. xi, pt. i; vol. i, p. 160. The italics are Ricardo's.

Mr. Buchanan also remarks, that "it is quite clear, that if any other produce which the land yielded more abundantly than corn, were to become the common food of the people, the rent of the landlord would be improved in proportion to its greater abundance."[1]

If potatoes were to become the common food of the people, there would be a long interval during which the landlords would suffer an enormous deduction of rent. They would not probably receive nearly so much of the sustenance of man as they now receive, while that sustenance would fall to a third of its present value. But all manufactured commodities, on which a part of the landlord's rent is expended, would suffer no other fall than that which proceeded from the fall in the raw material of which they were made, and which would arise only from the greater fertility of the land, which might then be devoted to its production.

When, from the progress of population, land of the same quality as before should be taken into cultivation,[2] the landlord would have not only the same proportion of the produce as before, but that proportion would also be of the same value as before. Rent then would be the same as before; profits, however, would be much higher, because the price of food, and consequently wages[3], would be much lower. High profits are favourable to the accumulation of capital. The demand for labour would further increase, and landlords would be permanently benefited by the increased demand for land.

Indeed, the very same lands might be cultivated much higher, when such an abundance of food could be produced from them, and consequently they would, in the progress of society, admit of much higher rents, and would sustain a much greater popu-

---

[1] Buchanan's ed. of the *Wealth of Nations*, vol. I, p. 266, note.
[2] Eds. 1-2 contain in addition 'to produce the food required, and the same number of men should be employed in producing it,'.
[3] Ed. 1 'consequently of wages'.

lation than before. This could not fail to be highly beneficial to landlords, and is consistent with the principle which this enquiry, I think, will not fail to establish; that all extraordinary profits are in their nature but of limited duration, as the whole surplus produce of the soil, after deducting from it only such moderate profits as are sufficient to encourage accumulation, must finally rest with the landlord.

With so low a price of labour as such an abundant produce would cause, not only would the lands already in cultivation yield a much greater quantity of produce, but they would admit of a great additional capital being employed on them, and a greater value to be drawn from them, and, at the same time, lands of a very inferior quality could be cultivated with high profits, to the great advantage of landlords, as well as to the whole class of consumers. The machine which produced the most important article of consumption would be improved, and would be well paid for according as its services were demanded. All the advantages would, in the first instance, be enjoyed by labourers, capitalists, and consumers; but with the progress of population, they would be gradually transferred to the proprietors of the soil.[1]

Independently of these improvements, in which the community have an immediate, and the landlords a remote interest, the interest[2] of the landlord is always opposed to that of the consumer and manufacturer. Corn can be permanently at an advanced price, only because additional labour is necessary to produce it; because its cost of production is increased. The same cause invariably raises rent, it is therefore for the interest of the landlord that the cost attending the production of corn should be increased. This, however, is not the interest of the consumer;

---

[1] Eds. 1-2 do not contain the last two paragraphs or the first two lines of the next. They were added to meet Malthus's criticism; see below,

II, 118 and cp. above, p. 81, n. 1.
[2] Eds. 1-2 begin this paragraph 'The interest'.

to him it is desirable that corn should be low relatively to money
and commodities, for it is always with commodities or money
that corn is purchased. Neither is it the interest of the manufacturer that corn should be at a high price, for the high price
of corn will occasion high wages, but will not raise the price
of his commodity. Not only, then, must more of his commodity, or, which comes to the same thing, the value of
more of his commodity, be given in exchange for the corn which
he himself consumes, but more must be given, or the value of
more, for wages to his workmen, for which he will receive no
remuneration. All classes, therefore, except the landlords, will
be injured by the increase in the price of corn. The dealings
between the landlord and the public are not like dealings in
trade, whereby both the seller and buyer may equally be said
to gain, but the loss is wholly on one side, and the gain wholly
on the other; and if corn could by importation be procured
cheaper, the loss in consequence of not importing is far greater
on one side, than the gain is on the other.

Adam Smith never makes any distinction between a low value
of money, and a high value of corn, and therefore infers, that
the interest of the landlord is not opposed to that of the rest of
the community. In the first case, money is low relatively to all
commodities; in the other, corn is high relatively to all. In the
first, corn and commodities continue at the same relative values;
in the second, corn is higher relatively to commodities as well
as money.

The following observation of Adam Smith is applicable to
a low value of money, but it is totally inapplicable to a high
value of corn. "If importation (of corn) was at all times free,
our farmers and country gentlemen would probably, one year
with another, get less money for their corn than they do at
present, when importation is at most times in effect prohibited;
but the money which they got would be of more value, *would*

buy more goods of all other kinds, and would employ more labour. Their real wealth, their real revenue, therefore, would be the same as at present, though it might be expressed by a smaller quantity of silver; and they would neither be disabled nor discouraged from cultivating corn as much as they do at present. On the contrary, as the rise in the real value of silver, in consequence of lowering the money price of corn, lowers somewhat the money price of all other commodities, it gives the industry of the country where it takes place, some advantage in all foreign markets, and thereby tends to encourage and increase that industry. But the extent of the home market for corn, must be in proportion to the general industry of the country where it grows, or to the number of those who produce something else,[1] to give in exchange for corn. But in every country the home market, as it is the nearest and most convenient, so is it likewise the greatest and most important market for corn. That rise in the real value of silver, therefore, which is the effect of lowering the average money price of corn, tends to enlarge the greatest and most important market for corn, and thereby to encourage, instead of discouraging, its growth."[2]

A high or low money price of corn, arising from the abundance and cheapness of gold and silver, is of no importance to the landlord, as every sort of produce would be equally affected, just as Adam Smith describes; but a relatively high price of corn is at all times greatly beneficial to the landlord[3]; for first, it gives him a greater quantity of corn for rent; and, secondly, for every equal measure of corn he will have a command, not only over a greater quantity of money, but over a greater quantity of every commodity which money can purchase.

[1] Ricardo here omits several words, which do not affect the sense.
[2] Bk. IV, ch. v; vol. II, p. 37.
[3] In eds. 1-2 the remainder of the paragraph reads ', as with the same quantity of corn it not only gives him a command over a greater quantity of money, but over a greater quantity of every commodity which money can purchase.'

CHAPTER XXV

ON COLONIAL TRADE

ADAM SMITH, in his observations on colonial trade, has shewn, most satisfactorily, the advantages of a free trade, and the injustice suffered by colonies, in being prevented by their mother countries, from selling their produce at the dearest market, and buying their manufactures and stores at the cheapest. He has shewn, that by permitting every country freely to exchange the produce of its industry when and where it pleases, the best distribution of the labour of the world will be effected, and the greatest abundance of the necessaries and enjoyments of human life will be secured.

He has attempted also to shew, that this freedom of commerce, which undoubtedly promotes the interest of the whole, promotes also that of each particular country; and that the narrow policy adopted in the countries of Europe respecting their colonies, is not less injurious to the mother countries themselves, than to the colonies whose interests are sacrificed.

"The monopoly of the colony trade," he says, "like all the other mean and malignant expedients of the mercantile system, depresses the industry of all other countries, but chiefly that of the colonies, without, in the least, increasing, but on the contrary diminishing, that of the country in whose favour it is established."[1]

This part of his subject, however, is not treated in so clear and convincing a manner as that in which he shews the injustice of this system towards the colony.

[1] Bk. IV, ch. vii, pt. iii; vol. II, p. 111.

It may, I think, be doubted whether[1] a mother country may not sometimes be benefited by the restraints to which she subjects her colonial possessions. Who can doubt, for example, that if England were the colony of France, the latter country would be benefited by a heavy bounty paid by England on the exportation of corn, cloth, or any other commodities? In examining the question of bounties, on the supposition of corn being at 4*l.* per quarter in this country, we saw,[2] that with a bounty of 10*s.* per quarter, on exportation in England, corn would have been reduced to 3*l.* 10*s.* in France. Now, if corn had previously been at 3*l.* 15*s.* per quarter in France, the French consumers would have been benefited by 5*s.* per quarter on all imported corn; if the natural price of corn in France were before 4*l.*, they would have gained the whole bounty of 10*s.* per quarter. France would thus be benefited by the loss sustained by England: she would not gain a part only of what England lost, but the whole.[3]

It may, however, be said, that a bounty on exportation is a measure of internal policy, and could not easily be imposed by the mother country.

If it would suit the interests of Jamaica and Holland to make an exchange of the commodities which they respectively produce, without the intervention of England, it is quite certain, that by their being prevented from so doing, the interests of Holland and Jamaica would suffer; but if Jamaica is obliged to send her goods to England, and there exchange them for Dutch goods, an English capital, or English agency, will be employed in a trade in which it would not otherwise be engaged. It is allured thither by a bounty, not paid by England, but by Holland and Jamaica.

[1] Eds. 1-2 begin this paragraph 'Without affirming or denying, that the actual practice of Europe with regard to their colonies is injurious to the mother countries, I may be permitted to doubt whether'.

[2] Above, p. 314.

[3] Ed. 1 'but in some cases the whole.'

That the loss sustained, through a disadvantageous distribution of labour in two countries, may be beneficial to one of them, while the other is made to suffer more than the loss actually belonging to such a distribution, has been stated by Adam Smith himself; which, if true, will at once prove that a measure, which may be greatly hurtful to a colony, may be partially beneficial to the mother country.

Speaking of treaties of commerce, he says, "When a nation binds itself by treaty, either to permit the entry of certain goods from one foreign country which it prohibits from all others, or to exempt the goods of one country from duties to which it subjects those of all others, the country, or at least the merchants and manufacturers of the country, whose commerce is so favoured, must necessarily derive great advantage from the treaty. Those merchants and manufacturers enjoy a sort of monopoly in the country, which is so indulgent to them. That country becomes a market, both more extensive and more advantageous for their goods; more extensive, because the goods of other nations, being either excluded or subjected to heavier duties, it takes off a greater quantity of them[1]; more advantageous, because the merchants of the favoured country, enjoying a sort of monopoly there, will often sell their goods for a better price than if exposed to the free competition of all other nations."[2]

Let the two nations, between which the commercial treaty is made, be the mother country and her colony, and Adam Smith, it is evident, admits, that a mother country may be benefited by oppressing her colony. It may, however, be again remarked, that unless the monopoly of the foreign market be in the hands of an exclusive company, no more will be paid for commodities by foreign purchasers than by home purchasers; the price which they will both pay will not differ greatly from their natural

[1] Adam Smith says 'of theirs'.   [2] Bk. IV, ch. vi; vol. II, p. 46.

price in the country where they are produced. England, for example, will, under ordinary circumstances, always be able to buy French goods, at the natural price of those goods in France, and France would have an equal privilege of buying English goods at their natural price in England. But at these prices, goods would be bought without a treaty. Of what advantage or disadvantage then is the treaty to either party?

The disadvantage of the treaty to the importing country would be this: it would bind her to purchase a commodity, from England for example, at the natural price of that commodity in England, when she might perhaps have bought it at the much lower natural price of some other country. It occasions then a disadvantageous distribution of the general capital, which falls chiefly on the country bound by its treaty to buy in the least productive market; but it gives no advantage to the seller on account of any supposed monopoly, for he is prevented by the competition of his own countrymen from selling his goods above their natural price; at which he would sell them, whether he exported them to France, Spain, or the West Indies, or sold them for home consumption.

In what then does the advantage of the stipulation in the treaty consist? It consists in this: these particular goods could not have been made in England for exportation, but for the privilege which she alone had of serving this particular market; for the competition of that country, where the natural price was lower, would have deprived her of all chance of selling those commodities. This, however, would have been of little importance, if England were quite secure that she could sell to the same amount any other goods which she might fabricate, either in the French market, or with equal advantage in any other. The object which England has in view, is, for example, to buy a quantity of French wines of the value of 5000*l.*—she desires then to sell goods somewhere by which she may get 5000*l.* for

this purpose. If France gives her a monopoly of the cloth
market, she will readily export cloth for this purpose; but if the
trade is free, the competition of other countries may prevent
the natural price of cloth in England from being sufficiently low
to enable her to get 5000*l.* by the sale of cloth, and to obtain the
usual profits by such an employment of her stock. The industry
of England must be employed, then, on some other commodity;
but there may be none of her productions which, at the existing
value of money, she can afford to sell at the natural price of
other countries. What is the consequence? The wine drinkers
of England, are still willing to give 5000*l.* for their wine, and
consequently 5000*l.* in money is exported to France for that
purpose. By this exportation of money its value is raised in
England, and lowered in other countries; and with it the *natural
price* of all commodities produced by British industry is also
lowered. The advance in the value of money[1] is the same thing
as the decline in the price of commodities. To obtain 5000*l.*,
British commodities may now be exported; for at their reduced
natural price they may now enter into competition with the
goods of other countries. More goods are sold, however, at the
low prices to obtain the 5000*l.* required, which, when obtained,
will not procure the same quantity of wine; because, whilst the
diminution of money in England has lowered the natural price
of goods there, the increase of money in France has raised the
natural price of goods and wine in France. Less wine, then, will
be imported into England, in exchange for its commodities,
when the trade is perfectly free, than when she is peculiarly
favoured by commercial treaties. The *rate* of profits, however,
will not have varied; money will have altered in relative value
in the two countries, and the advantage gained by France will
be the obtaining a greater quantity of English, in exchange for
a given quantity of French, goods, while the loss sustained by

[1] Ed. 1 'in the price of money'.

England will consist in obtaining a smaller quantity of French goods in exchange for a given quantity of those of England.

Foreign trade, then, whether fettered, encouraged, or free, will always continue, whatever may be the comparative difficulty of production in different countries; but it can only be regulated by altering the natural price, not the natural value, at which commodities can be produced in those countries, and that is effected by altering the distribution of the precious metals. This explanation confirms the opinion which I have elsewhere given,[1] that there is not a tax, a bounty, or a prohibition, on the importation or exportation of commodities, which does not occasion a different distribution of the precious metals, and which does not, therefore, every where alter both the natural and the market price of commodities.

It is evident, then, that the trade with a colony may be so regulated, that it shall at the same time be less beneficial to the colony, and more beneficial to the mother country, than a perfectly free trade. As it is disadvantageous to a single consumer to be restricted in his dealings to one particular shop, so is it disadvantageous for a nation of consumers to be obliged to purchase of one particular country. If the shop or the country afforded the goods required the cheapest, they would be secure of selling them without any such exclusive privilege; and if they did not sell cheaper, the general interest would require that they should not be encouraged to continue a trade which they could not carry on at an equal advantage with others. The shop, or the selling country, might lose by the change of employments, but the general benefit is never so fully secured, as by the most productive distribution of the general capital; that is to say, by an universally free trade.

An increase in the cost of production of a commodity, if it be an article of the first necessity, will not necessarily diminish its

[1] Above, pp. 141–2.

consumption; for although the general power of the purchasers to consume, is diminished by the rise of any one commodity, yet they may relinquish the consumption of some other commodity whose cost of production has not risen. In that case, the quantity supplied and the quantity demanded, will be the same as before[1]; the cost of production only will have increased, and yet the price will rise, and must rise, to place the profits of the producer of the enhanced commodity on a level with the profits derived from other trades.

M. Say acknowledges that the cost of production is the foundation of price, and yet in various parts of his book he maintains that price is regulated by the proportion which demand bears to supply. The real and ultimate regulator of the relative value of any two commodities, is the cost of their production, and not[2] the respective quantities which may be produced, nor the competition amongst the purchasers.

According to Adam Smith, the colony trade, by being one in which British capital only can be employed, has raised the rate of profits of all other trades; and as, in his opinion, high profits, as well as high wages, raise the prices of commodities, the monopoly of the colony trade has been, he thinks[3], injurious to the mother country; as it has diminished her power of selling manufactured commodities as cheap as other countries. He says, that "in consequence of the monopoly, the increase of the colony trade has not so much occasioned an addition to the trade which Great Britain had before, as a total change in its direction. Secondly, this monopoly has necessarily contributed to keep up the rate of profit in all the different branches of British trade, higher than it naturally would have been, had all nations been allowed a free trade to the British colonies." "But

---

[1] Ed. 1 'In that case, the quantity supplied will be in the same proportion to the demand as before'.

[2] Ed. 1 'neither' in place of 'not'.
[3] Ed. 1 'according to him' in place of 'he thinks'.

whatever raises in any country the ordinary rate of profit higher than it otherwise would be, necessarily subjects that country both to an absolute, and to a relative disadvantage in every branch of trade of which she has not the monopoly. It subjects her to an absolute disadvantage, because in such branches of trade, her merchants cannot get this greater profit without selling dearer than they otherwise would do, both the goods of foreign countries which they import into their own, and the goods of their own country which they export to foreign countries. Their own country must both buy dearer and sell dearer; must both buy less and sell less; must both enjoy less and produce less than she otherwise would do."

"Our merchants frequently complain of the high wages of British labour as the cause of their manufactures being undersold in foreign markets; but they are silent about the high profits of stock. They complain of the extravagant gain of other people, but they say nothing of their own. The high profits of British stock, however, may contribute towards raising the price of British manufacture in many cases as much, and in some perhaps more, than the high wages of British labour."[1]

I allow that the monopoly of the colony trade will change, and often prejudicially, the direction of capital; but from what I have already said on the subject of profits,[2] it will be seen that any change from one foreign trade to another, or from home to foreign trade, cannot, in my opinion, affect the rate of profits. The injury suffered will be what I have just described; there will be a worse distribution of the general capital and industry, and, therefore, less will be produced. The natural price of commodities will be raised, and, therefore, though the consumer will be able to purchase to the same money value, he will obtain a less quantity of commodities. It will be seen too, that if it

[1] Bk. IV, ch. vii, pt. iii; vol. II,   [2] Above, p. 133.
pp. 99–100.

even had the effect of raising profits, it would not occasion the least alteration in prices; prices being regulated neither by wages nor profits.

And does not Adam Smith agree in this opinion, when he says, that "the prices of commodities, or the value of gold and silver as compared wi⁺h commodities, depends upon the proportion between the *quantity of labour* which is necessary in order to bring a certain quantity of gold and silver to market, and that which is necessary to bring thither a certain quantity of any other sort of goods?"[1] That quantity will not be affected, whether profits be high or low, or wages low or high. How then can prices be raised by high profits?

[1] Bk. II, ch. ii; vol. I, pp. 311–12. This passage has been quoted above, p. 309; in neither case is the quotation verbally accurate.

CHAPTER XXVI

ON GROSS AND NET REVENUE

ADAM SMITH constantly magnifies the advantages which a
country derives from a large gross, rather than a large net
income. "In proportion as a greater share of the capital of a
country is employed in agriculture," he says, "the greater will
be the quantity of productive labour which it puts into motion
within the country; as will likewise be the value which its employment adds to the annual produce of the land and labour of
the society. After agriculture, the capital employed in manufactures puts into motion the greatest quantity of productive
labour, and adds the greatest value to the annual produce. That
which is employed in the trade of exportation has the least
effect of any of the three."*[1]

Granting, for a moment, that this were true; what would be
the advantage resulting to a country from the employment of
a great quantity of productive labour, if, whether it employed
that quantity or a smaller, its net rent and profits together would
be the same. The whole produce of the land and labour of every
country is divided into three portions: of these, one portion is
devoted to wages, another to profits, and the other to rent. It is
from the two last portions only, that any deductions can be

---

* M. Say is of the same opinion with Adam Smith: "The most productive employment of capital, for the country in general, after that on
the land, is that of manufactures and of home trade; because it puts in
activity an industry of which the profits are gained in the country, while
those capitals which are employed in foreign commerce, make the industry
and lands of all countries to be productive, without distinction.

"The employment of capital the least favourable to a nation, is that of
carrying the produce of one foreign country to another." *Say,* vol. ii.
p. 120.

[1] Bk. II, ch. v; vol. I, p. 346.

made for taxes, or for savings; the former, if moderate, constituting always the necessary expenses of production.* To an
individual with a capital of 20,000*l.*, whose profits were 2000*l.*
per annum, it would be a matter quite indifferent whether his
capital would employ a hundred or a thousand men, whether the
commodity produced sold for 10,000*l.*, or for 20,000*l.*, provided, in all cases, his profits were not diminished below 2000*l.*
Is not the real interest of the nation similar? Provided its net
real income, its rent and profits be the same, it is of no importance whether the nation consists of ten or of twelve millions
of inhabitants. Its power of supporting fleets and armies, and
all species of unproductive labour, must be in proportion to its
net, and not in proportion to its gross income. If five millions
of men could produce as much food and clothing as was necessary for ten millions, food and clothing for five millions would
be the net revenue. Would it be of any advantage to the country,
that to produce this same net revenue, seven millions of men
should be required, that is to say, that seven millions should be
employed to produce food and clothing sufficient for twelve
millions? The food and clothing of five millions would be still
the net revenue. The employing a greater number of men would
enable us neither to add a man to our army and navy, nor to
contribute one guinea more in taxes.

It is not on the grounds of any supposed advantage accruing
from a large population, or of the happiness that may be enjoyed by a greater number of human beings, that Adam Smith

* Perhaps this is expressed too strongly, as more is generally allotted
to the labourer under the name of wages, than the absolutely necessary
expenses of production. In that case a part of the net produce of the
country is received by the labourer, and may be saved or expended by him;
or it may enable him to contribute to the defence of the country.[1]

[1] Eds. 1-2 do not contain this note; pp. 222-3), had criticised the state-
Say, in a note to the French ed. ment in the text as too general.
of Ricardo's *Principles*, 1819 (vol. II,

supports the preference of that employment of capital, which gives motion to the greatest quantity of industry, but expressly on the ground of its increasing the power of the country* for he says, that "the riches, and, so far as power depends upon riches, the power of every country must always be in proportion to the value of its annual produce, the fund from which all taxes must ultimately be paid."[1] It must however be obvious, that the power of paying taxes, is in proportion to the net, and not in proportion to the gross, revenue.

In the distribution of employments amongst all countries, the capital of poorer nations will be naturally employed in those pursuits, wherein a great quantity of labour is supported at home, because in such countries the food and necessaries for an increasing population can be most easily procured. In rich countries, on the contrary, where food is dear, capital will naturally flow, when trade is free, into those occupations wherein the least quantity of labour is required to be maintained at home: such as the carrying trade, the distant foreign trade, and trades where expensive machinery is required; to trades[2] where profits are in proportion to the capital, and not in proportion to the quantity of labour employed.†

* M. Say has totally misunderstood me in supposing that I have considered as nothing, the happiness of so many human beings. I think the text sufficiently shews that I was confining my remarks to the particular grounds on which Adam Smith had rested it.[3]

† "It is fortunate that the natural course of things draws capital, not to those employments where the greatest profits are made, but to those where the[4] operation is most profitable to the community."—Vol. ii. p. 122. M. Say has not told us what those employments are, which, while they are the most profitable to the individual, are not the most profitable

[1] Bk. II, ch. v; vol. I, p. 351.
[2] Eds. 1-2 do not contain 'and trades where expensive machinery is required; to trades'.
[3] Eds. 1-2 do not contain this note. It refers to a note by Say in the French ed. of Ricardo's *Principles*

(vol. II, p. 224) where he argues that there is 'une plus grande masse de bonheur' in a population of seven millions than in one of five. Cp. *Notes on Malthus*, below, II, 382.
[4] Ed. 1 'their'.

Although I admit, that from the nature of rent, a given capital employed in agriculture, on any but the land last cultivated, puts in motion a greater quantity of labour than an equal capital employed in manufactures and trade, yet I cannot admit that there is any difference in the quantity of labour employed by a capital engaged in the home trade, and an equal capital engaged in the foreign trade.

"The capital which sends Scots manufactures to London, and brings back English corn and manufactures to Edinburgh," says Adam Smith, "necessarily replaces, by every such operation, two British capitals which had both been employed in the agriculture or manufactures of Great Britain.

"The capital employed in purchasing foreign goods for home consumption, when this purchase is made with the produce of domestic industry, replaces, too, by every such operation, two distinct capitals; but one of them only is employed in supporting domestic industry. The capital which sends British goods to Portugal, and brings back Portuguese goods to Great Britain, replaces, by every such operation, only one British capital, the other is a Portuguese one. Though the returns, therefore, of the foreign trade of consumption should be as quick as[1] the home trade, the capital employed in it will give but one half the encouragement to the industry or productive labour of the country."[2]

This argument appears to me to be fallacious; for though two capitals, one Portuguese and one English, be employed, as Dr. Smith supposes, still a capital will be employed in the foreign trade, double of what would be employed in the home trade.

to the State. If countries with limited capitals, but with abundance of fertile land, do not early engage in foreign trade, the reason is, because it is less profitable to individuals, and therefore also less profitable to the State.

[1] Adam Smith says 'as quick as those of'.

[2] Bk. II, ch. v; vol. I, p. 348.

Suppose that Scotland employs a capital of a thousand pounds in making linen, which she exchanges for the produce of a similar capital employed in making silks in England,[1] two thousand pounds, and a proportional quantity of labour will be employed by the two countries. Suppose now, that England discovers, that she can import more linen from Germany, for the silks which she before exported to Scotland, and that Scotland discovers that she can obtain more silks from France in return for her linen, than she before obtained from England, —will not England and Scotland immediately cease trading with each other, and will not the home trade of consumption be changed for a foreign trade of consumption? But although two additional capitals will enter into this trade, the capital of Germany and that of France, will not the same amount of Scotch and of English capital continue to be employed, and will it not give motion to the same quantity of industry as when it was engaged in the home trade?

[1] Eds. 1-2 have a full stop here.

CHAPTER XXVII

ON CURRENCY AND BANKS

So much[1] has already been written on currency, that of those who give their attention to such subjects, none but the prejudiced are ignorant of its true principles. I shall, therefore, take only a brief survey of some of the general laws which regulate its quantity and value.

Gold and silver, like all other commodities, are valuable only in proportion to the quantity of labour necessary to produce them, and bring them to market. Gold is about fifteen times dearer than silver, not because there is a greater demand for it, nor because the supply of silver is fifteen times greater than that of gold, but solely because fifteen times the quantity of labour is necessary to procure a given quantity of it.

The quantity of money that can be employed in a country must depend on its value: if gold alone were employed for the circulation of commodities, a quantity would be required, one fifteenth only of what would be necessary, if silver were made use of for the same purpose.

A circulation can never be so abundant as to overflow; for by diminishing its value, in the same proportion you will increase its quantity, and by increasing its value, diminish its quantity.[2]

[1] In ed. 1 the chapter opens 'It is not my intention to detain the reader by any long dissertation on the subject of money. So much'.

[2] In ed. 1 a note is attached here: '"The use of gold and silver then establishes in every place a certain necessity for these commodities; and when the country possesses the quantity necessary to satisfy this want, all that is further imported, not being in demand, is unfruitful in value, and of no use to its owners."—*Say*, vol. i. p. 187.

'In page 196, M. Say says, that supposing a country to require 1000 carriages, and to be possessed of 1500—all above 1000 would be useless; and thence he infers, that if it possesses more money than is *necessary*, the overplus will not be employed.'

While the State[1] coins money, and charges no seignorage, money will be of the same value as any other piece of the same metal of equal weight and fineness; but if the State charges a seignorage for coinage, the coined piece of money will generally exceed the value of the uncoined piece of metal by the whole seignorage charged, because it will require a greater quantity of labour, or, which is the same thing, the value of the produce of a greater quantity of labour, to procure it.

While the State alone coins, there can be no limit to this charge of seignorage; for by limiting the quantity of coin, it can be raised to any conceivable value.

It is on this principle that paper money circulates: the whole charge for paper money may be considered as seignorage. Though it has no intrinsic value, yet, by limiting its quantity, its value in exchange is as great as an equal denomination of coin, or of bullion in that coin. On the same principle, too, namely, by a limitation of its quantity, a debased coin would circulate at the value it should bear, if it were of the legal weight and fineness, and[2] not at the value of the quantity of metal which it actually contained. In the history of the British coinage, we find, accordingly, that the currency was never depreciated in the same proportion that it was debased; the reason of which was, that it never was increased in quantity,[3] in proportion to its diminished intrinsic[4] value.*

There is no point more important in issuing paper money, than to be fully impressed with the effects which follow from the principle of limitation of quantity. It will scarcely be believed fifty years hence, that Bank directors and ministers gravely contended in our times, both in parliament, and before

---

* Whatever I say of gold coin, is equally applicable to silver coin; but it is not necessary to mention both on every occasion.

[1] Eds. 1-2 'state', here and below.   [3] Eds. 1-2 'never was multiplied'.
[2] Eds. 1-2 do not contain 'and'.   [4] Ed. 1 does not contain 'intrinsic'.

committees of parliament, that the issues of notes by the Bank of
England, unchecked by any power in the holders of such notes,
to demand in exchange either specie, or bullion, had not, nor
could have any effect on the prices of commodities, bullion, or
foreign exchanges.[1]

After the establishment of Banks, the State has not the sole
power of coining or issuing money. The currency may as
effectually be increased by paper as by coin; so that if a State
were to debase its money, and limit its quantity, it could not
support its value, because the Banks would have an equal power
of adding to the whole quantity of circulation.

On these principles, it will be seen that it is not necessary that
paper money should be payable in specie to secure its value; it
is only necessary that its quantity should be regulated according
to the value of the metal which is declared to be the standard.
If the standard were gold of a given weight and fineness, paper
might be increased with every fall in the value of gold, or, which
is the same thing in its effects, with every rise in the price of
goods.

"By issuing too great a quantity of paper," says Dr. Smith,
"of which the excess was continually returning, in order to be
exchanged for gold and silver, the Bank of England was, for
many years together, obliged to coin gold to the extent of
between eight hundred thousand pounds and a million a year,
or at an average, about eight hundred and fifty thousand
pounds. For this great coinage, the Bank, in consequence of
the worn and degraded state into which the gold coin had
fallen a few years ago, was frequently obliged to purchase
bullion, at the high price of four pounds an ounce, which it soon
after issued in coin at 3*l.* 17*s.* 10½*d.* an ounce, losing in this

---

[1] Ed. 1 does not contain this paragraph. See McCulloch's advice to
'enlarge a little on the principle of
limitation' (below, VII, 353). For
the contention of the Bank Directors before the Bullion Committee
see below, III, 357, 373.

manner between two and a half and three per cent. upon the coinage of so very large a sum. Though the Bank, therefore, paid no seignorage, though the Government was properly at the expense of the coinage, this liberality of Government did not prevent altogether the expense of the Bank."[1]

On the principle above stated, it appears to me most clear, that by not re-issuing the paper thus brought in, the value of the whole currency, of the degraded as well as the new gold coin, would have been raised, when all demands on the Bank would have ceased.

Mr. Buchanan, however, is not of this opinion, for he says, "that the great expense to which the Bank was at this time exposed, was occasioned, not, as Dr. Smith seems to imagine, by any imprudent issue of paper, but by the debased state of the currency, and the consequent high price of bullion. The Bank, it will be observed, having no other way of procuring[2] guineas but by sending bullion to the Mint to be coined, was always forced to issue new coined guineas, in exchange for its returned notes; and when the currency was generally deficient in weight, and the price of bullion high in proportion, it became profitable to draw these heavy guineas from the Bank in exchange for its paper; to convert them into bullion, and to sell them with a profit for Bank paper, to be again returned to the Bank for a new supply of guineas, which were again melted and sold. To this drain of specie, the Bank must always be exposed while the

---

[1] Bk. II, ch. ii; vol. I, p. 285.

[2] In ed. 1 a note is attached here:

"'In the transactions of Government with individuals, and in those of individuals between themselves, a piece of money is never received, whatever denomination may be given to it, but at its intrinsic value, increased by the value of the utility which the impression it bears has added to it."—*Say*, vol. i. p. 327.

"'Money is so little a mark of value, that if the pieces of money lose a part of their value by friction, from use, or by the knavery of the clippers of money, all goods rise in price in proportion to the alteration which they have experienced; and if Government orders a recoinage, and restores each piece to its legal weight and fineness, goods will fall to their former price; if they have not been exposed to variations from other causes."—*Say*, vol. i. p. 346.'

currency is deficient in weight, as both an easy and a certain profit then arises from the constant interchange of paper for specie. It may be remarked, however, that to whatever inconvenience and expense the Bank was then exposed by the drain of its specie, it never was imagined necessary to rescind the obligation to pay money for its notes."[1]

Mr. Buchanan evidently thinks that the whole currency must, necessarily, be brought down to the level of the value of the debased pieces; but, surely, by a diminution of the quantity of the currency, the whole that remains can be elevated to the value of the best pieces.

Dr. Smith appears to have forgotten his own principle, in his argument on colony currency. Instead of ascribing the depreciation of that paper to its too great abundance, he asks whether, allowing the colony security to be perfectly good, a hundred pounds, payable fifteen years hence, would be equally valuable with a hundred pounds to be paid immediately?[2] I answer yes, if it be not too abundant.

Experience, however, shews, that neither a State nor a Bank ever have had the unrestricted power of issuing paper money, without abusing that power: in all States, therefore, the issue of paper money ought to be under some check and controul[3]; and none seems so proper for that purpose, as that of subjecting the issuers of paper money to the obligation of paying their notes, either in gold coin or bullion.

[4 "To secure the public* against any other variations in the

* This, and the following paragraphs, to the close of the bracket, p. 361, is extracted from a Pamphlet entitled "Proposals for an Economical and Secure Currency,"[5] published by the author[6] in the year 1816.

[1] Buchanan's ed. of the *Wealth of Nations*, vol. I, pp. 477–8, note.
[2] Bk. II, ch. ii; vol. I, p. 309.
[3] Eds. 1-2 'control'.
[4] The square brackets in this case re Ricardo's. The quotation is not contained in ed. 1 and was inserted at McCulloch's suggestion; see below, VII, 353.
[5] Below, IV, 66–70.
[6] Ed. 2 does not contain 'by the author'.

value of currency than those to which the standard itself is subject, and, at the same time, to carry on the circulation with a medium the least expensive, is to attain the most perfect state to which a currency can be brought, and we should possess all these advantages by subjecting the Bank to the delivery of uncoined gold or silver at the Mint standard and price, in exchange for their notes, instead of the delivery of guineas; by which means paper would never fall below the value of bullion, without being followed by a reduction of its quantity. To prevent the rise of paper above the value of bullion, the Bank should be also obliged to give their paper in exchange for standard gold at the price of 3*l.* 17*s.* per ounce. Not to give too much trouble to the Bank, the quantity of gold to be demanded in exchange for paper at the Mint price of 3*l.* 17*s.* 10½*d.*, or the quantity to be sold to the Bank at 3*l.* 17*s.*, should never be less than twenty ounces. In other words, the Bank should be obliged to purchase any quantity of gold that was offered them, not less than twenty ounces, at 3*l.* 17*s.** per ounce, and to sell any quantity that might be demanded at 3*l.* 17*s.* 10½*d.* While they have the power of regulating the quantity of their paper, there is no possible inconvenience that could result to them from such a regulation.

"The most perfect liberty should be given, at the same time to export or import every description of bullion. These transactions in bullion would be very few in number, if the Bank regulated their loans and issues of paper by the criterion which I have so often mentioned, namely, the price of standard

---

* The price of 3*l.* 17*s.* here mentioned, is, of course, an arbitrary price. There might be good reason, perhaps, for fixing it either a little above, or a little below. In naming 3*l.* 17*s.* I wish only to elucidate the principle. The price ought to be so fixed as to make it the interest of the seller of gold rather to sell it to the Bank, than to carry it to the Mint to be coined.

The same remark applies to the specified quantity of twenty ounces. There might be good reason for making it ten or thirty.

bullion, without attending to the absolute quantity of paper in circulation.

"The object which I have in view would be in a great measure attained, if the Bank were obliged to deliver uncoined bullion, in exchange for their notes, at the Mint price and standard; though they were not under the necessity of purchasing any quantity of bullion offered them at the prices to be fixed, particularly if the Mint were to continue open to the public for the coinage of money: for that regulation is merely suggested, to prevent the value of money from varying from the value of bullion more than the trifling difference between the prices at which the Bank should buy and sell, and which would be an approximation to that uniformity in its value, which is acknowledged to be so desirable.

"If the Bank capriciously limited the quantity of their paper, they would raise its value; and gold might appear to fall below the limits at which I propose the Bank should purchase. Gold, in that case, might be carried to the Mint, and the money returned from thence, being added to the circulation, would have the effect of lowering its value, and making it again conform to the standard; but it would neither be done so safely, so economically, nor so expeditiously, as by the means which I have proposed; against which the Bank can have no objection to offer, as it is for their interest to furnish the circulation with paper, rather than oblige others to furnish it with coin.

"Under such a system, and with a currency so regulated, the Bank would never be liable to any embarrassments whatever, excepting on those extraordinary occasions, when a general panic seizes the country, and when every one is desirous of possessing the precious metals as the most convenient mode of realizing or concealing his property. Against such panics, Banks have no security, *on any system*; from their very nature they are subject to them, as at no time can there be in a Bank, or in a country, so much specie or bullion as the monied individuals of such country have a right to demand. Should every man withdraw his balance from his banker on the same day, many times the quantity of Bank notes now in circulation would be insufficient to answer such a demand. A panic of this kind was the cause of the crisis in 1797; and not, as has been supposed, the large advances which the Bank had then made to Government. Neither the Bank nor Government were at that time to blame; it was the contagion of the unfounded fears of the timid part of the community, which occasioned the run on the Bank, and it would equally have taken place if they had not made any advances to Government, and had possessed twice their present capital. If the Bank had continued paying in cash, probably the panic would have subsided before their coin had been exhausted.

"With the known opinion of the Bank directors, as to the rule for issuing paper money, they may be said to have exercised their powers without any great indiscretion. It is evident that they have followed their own principle with extreme caution. In the present state of the law, they have the power, without any control whatever, of increasing or reducing the circulation in any degree they may think proper: a power which should neither be intrusted to the State itself, nor to any body in it; as there can be no security for the uniformity in the value of the currency, when its augmentation or diminution depends solely on the will of the issuers. That the Bank have the power of reducing the circulation to the very narrowest limits will not be denied, even by those who agree in opinion with the directors, that they have not the power of adding indefinitely to its quantity. Though I am fully assured, that it is both against the interest and the wish of the Bank to exercise this power to the detriment of the public, yet, when I contemplate the evil consequences which might ensue from a sudden and great reduction of the circulation, as well as from a great addition to it, I cannot but deprecate the facility with which the State has armed the Bank with so formidable a prerogative.

"The inconvenience to which country banks were subjected before the restriction on cash payments, must, at times, have been very great. At all periods of alarm, or of expected alarm, they must have been under the necessity of providing themselves with guineas, that they might be prepared for every exigency which might occur. Guineas, on these occasions, were obtained at the Bank in exchange for the larger notes, and were conveyed by some confidential agent, at expense and risk, to the country bank. After performing the offices to which they were destined, they found their way again to London, and in all probability were again lodged in the Bank, provided they had not suffered such a loss of weight, as to reduce them below the legal standard.

"If the plan now proposed, of paying Bank notes in bullion, be adopted, it would be necessary either to extend the same privilege to country banks, or to make Bank notes, a legal tender, in which latter case, there would be no alteration in the law respecting country banks, as they would be required, precisely as they now are, to pay their notes, when demanded, in Bank of England notes.

"The saving which would take place, from not submitting the guineas to the loss of weight, from the friction which they must undergo in their repeated journeys, as well as of the expences of conveyance, would be considerable; but by far the greatest advantage would result from the permanent supply of the country, as well as of the London circulation, as far as the smaller payments are concerned, being provided in the very cheap medium, paper, instead of the very valuable medium, gold; thereby enabling the country to derive all the profit which may be obtained by the productive employment of a capital to that amount. We should surely not be justified in rejecting so decided a benefit, unless some specific inconvenience could be pointed out as likely to follow from adopting the cheaper medium."][1]

A currency is in its most perfect state when it consists wholly of paper money, but of paper money of an equal value with the gold which it professes to represent. The use of paper instead of gold, substitutes the cheapest in place of the most expensive medium, and enables the country, without loss to any individual, to exchange all the gold which it before used for this purpose, for raw materials, utensils, and food; by the use of which, both its wealth and its enjoyments are increased.

In a national point of view, it is of no importance whether the issuers of this well regulated paper money be the Government or a Bank, it will, on the whole, be equally productive of riches, whether it be issued by one or by the other; but it is not so with respect to the interest of individuals. In a country where the market rate of interest is 7 per cent., and where the State requires for a particular expense 70,000*l.* per annum, it is a question of importance to the individuals of that country, whether they must be taxed to pay this 70,000*l.* per annum, or whether they could raise it without taxes. Suppose that a million of money should be required to fit out an expedition. If the State issued a million of paper, and displaced a million of coin, the expedition would be fitted out without any charge to the people; but if a Bank issued a million of paper, and lent it to Government at 7 per cent., thereby displacing a million of coin, the country would be charged with a continual tax of 70,000*l.* per annum: the people would pay the tax, the Bank would receive it, and the society would in either case be as wealthy as before; the expedition would have been really fitted out by the improvement of our system, by rendering capital of

---

[1] The square brackets in this case are Ricardo's; see above p. 356.

the value of a million productive in the form of commodities, instead of letting it remain unproductive in the form of coin; but the advantage would always be in favour of the issuers of paper; and as the State represents the people, the people would have saved the tax, if they, and not the Bank, had issued this million.

I have already observed, that if there were perfect security that the power of issuing paper money would not be abused, it would be of no importance with respect to the riches of the country collectively, by whom it was issued; and I have now shewn that the public would have a direct interest that the issuers should be the State, and not a company of merchants or bankers. The danger, however, is, that this power would be more likely to be abused, if in the hands of Government, than if in the hands of a banking company. A company would, it is said, be more under the control of law, and although it might be their interest to extend their issues beyond the bounds of discretion, they would be limited and checked by the power which individuals would have of calling for bullion or specie. It is argued that the same check would not be long respected, if Government had the privilege of issuing money; that they would be too apt to consider present convenience, rather than future security, and might, therefore, on the alleged grounds of expediency, be too much inclined to remove the checks, by which the amount of their issues was controlled.

Under an arbitrary Government, this objection would have great force; but, in a free country, with an enlightened legislature, the power of issuing paper money, under the requisite checks of convertibility at the will of the holder, might be safely lodged in the hands of commissioners appointed for that special purpose, and they might be made totally independent of the control of ministers.

The sinking fund is managed by commissioners, responsible

only to parliament, and the investment of the money entrusted to their charge, proceeds with the utmost regularity; what reason can there be to doubt that the issues of paper money might be regulated with equal fidelity, if placed under similar management?

It may be said, that although the advantage accruing to the State, and, therefore, to the public, from issuing paper money, is sufficiently manifest, as it would exchange a portion of the national debt, on which interest is paid by the public, into a debt bearing no interest; yet it would be disadvantageous to commerce, as it would preclude the merchants from borrowing money, and getting their bills discounted, the method in which Bank paper is partly issued.

This, however, is to suppose that money could not be borrowed, if the Bank did not lend it, and that the market rate of interest and profit depends on the amount[1] of the issues of money, and on the channel through which it is issued. But as a country would have no deficiency of cloth, of wine, or any other commodity, if they had the means of paying for it, in the same manner neither would there be any deficiency of money to be lent, if the borrowers offered good security, and were willing to pay the market rate of interest for it.

In another part of this work,[2] I have endeavoured to shew, that the real value of a commodity is regulated, not by the accidental advantages which may be enjoyed by some of its producers, but by the real difficulties encountered by that producer who is least favoured. It is so with respect to the interest for money; it is not regulated by the rate at which the Bank will lend, whether it be 5, 4, or 3 per cent., but by the rate of profits which can be made by the employment of capital, and which is totally independent of the quantity, or of the value of money. Whether a Bank lent one million, ten millions, or a hundred

---

[1] Ed. 1 'amounts'.   [2] Above, p. 73.

millions, they would not permanently alter the market rate of interest; they would alter only the value of the money which they thus issued. In one case, 10 or 20 times more money might be required to carry on the same business, than what might be required in the other. The applications to the Bank for money, then, depend on the comparison between the rate of profits that may be made by the employment of it, and the rate at which they are willing to lend it. If they charge less than the market rate of interest, there is no amount of money which they might not lend,—if they charge more than that rate, none but spend-thrifts and prodigals would be found to borrow of them. We accordingly find, that when the market rate of interest exceeds the rate of 5 per cent. at which the Bank uniformly lend, the discount office is besieged with applicants for money; and, on the contrary, when the market rate is even temporarily under 5 per cent., the clerks of that office have no employment.

The reason, then, why for the last twenty years, the Bank is said to have given so much aid to commerce, by assisting the merchants with money, is, because they have, during that whole period, lent money below the market rate of interest; below that rate at which the merchants could have borrowed else-where; but, I confess, that to me this seems rather an objection to their establishment, than an argument in favour of it.

What should we say of an establishment which should regularly supply half the clothiers with wool[1] under the market price? Of what benefit would it be to the community? It would not extend our trade, because the wool would equally have been bought if they had charged the market price for it. It would not lower the price of cloth to the consumer, because the price, as I have said before, would be regulated by the cost of its pro-duction to those who were the least favoured. Its sole effect, then, would be, to swell the profits of a part of the clothiers

---

[1] Eds. 1-2 'with their wool'.

beyond the general and common rate of profits. The establishment would be deprived of its fair profits, and another part of the community would be in the same degree benefited. Now this is precisely the effect of our banking establishments; a rate of interest is fixed by the law below that at which it can be borrowed in the market, and at this rate the Bank are required to lend, or not to lend at all. From the nature of their establishment, they have large funds which they can only dispose of in this way; and a part of the traders of the country are unfairly, and, for the country, unprofitably benefited, by being enabled to supply themselves with an instrument of trade, at a less charge than those who must be influenced only by market price.

The whole business, which the whole community can carry on, depends on the quantity of its[1] capital, that is, of its raw material, machinery, food, vessels, &c. employed in production. After a well regulated paper money is established, these can neither be increased nor diminished by the operations of banking. If, then, the State were to issue the paper money of the country, although it should never discount a bill, or lend one shilling to the public, there would be no alteration in the amount of trade; for we should have the same quantity of raw materials, of machinery, food, and ships; and it is probable, too, that the same amount of money might be lent, not always[2] at 5 per cent. indeed, a rate fixed by law, when that might be under the market rate,[3] but at 6, 7, or 8 per cent., the result of the fair competition in the market between the lenders and the borrowers.

Adam Smith speaks[4] of the advantages derived by merchants from the superiority of the Scotch mode of affording accommodation to trade, over the English mode, by means of cash

[1] Eds. 1-2 do not contain 'its'.
[2] Eds. 1-2 do not contain 'always'.
[3] Eds. 1-2 do not contain 'when that might be under the market rate,'.
[4] Bk. II, ch. ii; vol. I, pp. 280-3.

accounts. These cash accounts are credits given by the Scotch banker to his customers, in addition to the bills which he discounts for them; but, as the banker, in proportion as he advances money, and sends it into circulation in one way, is debarred from issuing so much in the other, it is difficult to perceive in what the advantage consists. If the whole circulation will bear only one million of paper, one million only will be circulated; and it can be of no real importance either to the banker or merchant, whether the whole be issued in discounting bills, or a part be so issued, and the remainder be issued by means of these cash accounts.

It may perhaps be necessary to say a few words on the subject of the two metals, gold and silver, which are employed in currency, particularly as this question appears to perplex, in many people's minds, the plain and simple principles of currency. "In England," says Dr. Smith, "gold was not considered as a legal tender for a long time after it was coined into money. The proportion between the values of gold and silver money was not fixed by any public law or proclamation, but was left to be settled by the market. If a debtor offered payment in gold, the creditor might either reject such payment altogether, or accept of it at such a valuation of the gold, as he and his debtor could agree upon."[1]

In this state of things it is evident that a guinea might sometimes pass for 22s. or more, and sometimes for 18s. or less, depending entirely on the alteration in the relative market value of gold and silver. All the variations, too, in the value of gold, as well as in the value of silver, would be rated in the gold coin, —it would appear as if silver was invariable, and as if[2] gold only was subject to rise and[3] fall. Thus, although a guinea passed for 22s. instead of 18s., gold might not have varied in

[1] Bk. I, ch. v; vol. I, p. 41.   [3] Ed. I 'or' in place of 'and'.
[2] Ed. I 'that' in place of 'as if'.

value; the variation might have been wholly confined to the silver, and therefore 22s. might have been of no more value than 18s. were before. And, on the contrary, the whole variation might have been in the gold: a guinea, which was worth 18s., might have risen to the value of 22s.

If now we suppose this silver currency to be debased by clipping, and also increased in quantity, a guinea might pass for 30s.; for the silver in 30s. of such debased money might be of no more value than the gold in one guinea. By restoring the silver currency to its Mint value, silver money would rise: but it would appear as if gold fell, for a guinea would probably be of no more value than 21 of such good shillings.

If now gold be also made a legal tender, and every debtor be at liberty to discharge a debt by the payment of 420 shillings, or twenty guineas for every 21l. that he owes, he will pay in one or the other according as he can most cheaply discharge his debt. If with five quarters of wheat he can procure as much gold bullion as the Mint will coin into twenty guineas, and for the same wheat as much silver bullion as the Mint will coin for him into 430 shillings, he will prefer paying in silver, because he would be a gainer of ten shillings by so paying his debt. But if, on the contrary, he could obtain with this wheat as much gold as would be coined into twenty guineas and a half, and as much silver only as would coin into 420 shillings, he would naturally prefer paying his debt in gold. If the quantity of gold which he could procure could be coined only into twenty guineas, and the quantity of silver into 420 shillings, it would be a matter of perfect indifference to him in which money, silver or gold, it was that he paid his debt. It is not then a matter of chance; it is not because gold is better fitted for carrying on the circulation of a rich country, that gold is ever preferred for the purpose of paying debts; but, simply, because it is the interest of the debtor so to pay them.

During a long period previous to 1797, the year of the restriction on the Bank payments in coin, gold was so cheap, compared with silver, that it suited the Bank of England, and all other debtors, to purchase gold in the market, and not silver, for the purpose of carrying it to the Mint to be coined, as they could in that coined metal more cheaply discharge their debts. The silver currency was, during a great part of this period, very much debased; but it existed in a degree of scarcity, and, therefore, on the principle which I have before explained, it never sunk in its current value. Though so debased, it was still the interest of debtors to pay in the gold coin. If, indeed, the quantity of this debased silver coin had been enormously great, or if the Mint had issued such debased pieces, it might have been the interest of debtors to pay in this debased money; but its quantity was limited, and it sustained its value, and, therefore, gold was in practice the real standard of currency.

That it was so, is no where denied; but it has been contended, that it was made so by the law, which declared that silver should not be a legal tender for any debt exceeding 25*l*., unless by weight, according to the Mint standard.

But this law did not prevent any debtor from paying his[1] debt, however large its amount, in silver currency fresh from the Mint; that the debtor did not pay in this metal, was not a matter of chance, nor a matter of compulsion, but wholly the effect of choice; it did not suit him to take silver to the Mint, it did suit him to take gold thither. It is probable, that if the quantity of this debased silver in circulation had been enormously great, and also a legal tender, that a guinea would have been again worth thirty shillings; but it would have been the debased shilling that would have fallen in value, and not the guinea that had risen.

It appears, then, that whilst each of the two metals was

---

[1] Ed. 1 'any' in place of 'his'.

equally a legal tender for debts of any amount, we were subject to a constant change in the principal standard measure of value. It would sometimes be gold, sometimes silver, depending entirely on the variations in the relative value of the two metals; and at such times the metal, which was not the standard, would be melted, and withdrawn from circulation, as its value would be greater in bullion than in coin. This was an inconvenience, which it was highly desirable should be remedied; but so slow is the progress of improvement, that although it had been unanswerably demonstrated by Mr. Locke,[1] and had been noticed by all writers on the subject of money since his day, a better system was never adopted till the session of Parliament, 1816[2], when it was enacted that gold only should be a legal tender for any sum exceeding forty[3] shillings.

Dr. Smith does not appear to have been quite aware of the effect of employing two metals as currency, and both a legal tender for debts of any amount; for he says, that "in reality, during the continuance of any one regulated proportion between the respective values of the different metals in coin, the value of the most precious metal regulates the value of the whole coin."[4] Because gold was in his day the medium in which it suited debtors to pay their debts, he thought that it had some inherent quality by which it did then, and always would regulate the value of silver coin.

On the reformation of the gold coin in 1774, a new guinea fresh from the Mint, would exchange for only twenty-one

---

[1] *Further Considerations Concerning Raising the Value of Money*, 1695, p. 20.

[2] Eds. 1-2 'the last session of Parliament'.

[3] Ed. 1 in the text reads 'twenty-one'; in the *Errata* 'forty-two'. 'A guinea' had been the suggestion of Adam Smith (*Wealth of Nations*,

vol. 1, p. 46) and of Lord Liverpool (see below, III, 67, n. 1); 'two guineas' was the Government proposal made on 30 May 1816 (*Hansard*, XXXIV, 958); '40s.' was enacted later in the same year (56 Geo. III, c. 68).

[4] Bk. 1, ch. v; vol. 1, p. 43.

debased shillings; but in the reign of King William, when the silver coin was in precisely the same condition, a guinea also new and fresh from the Mint would exchange for thirty shillings. On this Mr. Buchanan observes, "here, then, is a most singular fact, of which the common theories of currency offer no account; the guinea exchanging at one time for thirty shillings, its intrinsic worth in a debased silver currency, and afterwards the same guinea exchanged for only twenty-one of those debased shillings. It is clear that some great change must have intervened in the state of the currency between these two different periods, of which Dr. Smith's hypothesis offers no explanation."[1]

It appears to me, that the difficulty may be very simply solved, by referring this different state of the value of the guinea at the two periods mentioned, to the different *quantities* of debased silver currency in circulation. In King William's reign gold was not a legal tender; it passed only at a conventional value. All the large payments were probably made in silver, particularly as paper currency, and the operations of banking, were then little understood. The quantity of this debased silver money exceeded the quantity of silver money, which would have been maintained in circulation, if nothing but undebased money had been in use; and, consequently, it was depreciated as well as debased. But in the succeeding period when gold was a legal tender, when Bank notes also were used in effecting payments, the quantity of debased silver money did not exceed the quantity of silver coin fresh from the Mint, which would have circulated if there had been no debased silver money; hence, though the money was debased, it was not depreciated. Mr. Buchanan's explanation is somewhat different; he thinks that a subsidiary currency is not liable to depreciation, but that the main currency is. In King William's reign silver was the

[1] Buchanan's ed. of the *Wealth of Nations*, vol. 1, p. 65, note.

main currency, and hence was liable to depreciation. In 1774 it
was a subsidiary currency, and, therefore, maintained its value.
Depreciation, however, does not depend on a currency being
the subsidiary or the main currency, it depends wholly on its
being in excess of quantity. *

To a moderate seignorage on the coinage of money there
cannot be much objection, particularly on that currency which
is to effect the smaller payments. Money is generally enhanced
in value to the full amount of the seignorage, and, therefore, it

---

* It has lately been contended in parliament by Lord Lauderdale,[1] that,
with the existing Mint regulation, the Bank could not pay their notes in
specie, because the relative value of the two metals is such, that it would
be for the interest of all debtors to pay their debts with silver and not with
gold coin, while the law gives a power to all the creditors of the Bank to
demand gold in exchange for Bank notes. This gold, his Lordship thinks,
could be profitably exported, and if so, he contends[2] that the Bank, to keep
a supply, will[3] be obliged to buy gold constantly at a premium, and sell
it at par. If every other debtor could pay in silver, Lord Lauderdale would
be right; but he cannot do so if his debt exceed 40s. This, then, would
limit the amount of silver coin in circulation, (if Government had not
reserved to itself the power to stop the coinage of that metal whenever
they might think it expedient,)[4] because if too much silver were coined,
it would sink in relative value to gold, and no man would accept it in
payment for a debt exceeding 40 shillings, unless a compensation were
made for its lower value. To pay a debt of 100l., one hundred sovereigns,
or Bank notes to the amount of 100l. would be necessary, but 105l., in
silver coin might be required, if there were too much silver in circulation[5].
There are, then, two checks against an excessive quantity of silver coin;
first, the direct check which Government may at any time interpose to
prevent more from being coined; secondly, no motive of interest would
lead any one to take silver to the Mint, if he might do so,[6] for if it were
coined, it would not pass current at its Mint, but only[7] at its market value.[8]

---

[1] See Lord Lauderdale's Protest
against the rejection of his amendment to the Bank Restriction Continuance Bill, of 27 May 1818, in
Journals of the House of Lords, 1817–
1818, p. 698. Cp. below, VIII, 3.
[2] Ed. 2 does not contain 'if so, he
contends'.
[3] Ed. 2 'would'.

[4] In ed. 2 this clause is not in
brackets.
[5] Ed. 2 does not contain', if there
were too much silver in circulation'.
[6] Ed. 2 does not contain 'if he
might do so,'.
[7] Ed. 2 does not contain 'only'.
[8] Ed. 1 does not contain this note.

is a tax which in no way affects those who pay it, while the quantity of money is not in excess. It must, however, be re-marked, that in a country where a paper currency is established, although the issuers of such paper should be liable to pay it in specie on the demand of the holder, still, both their notes and the coin might be depreciated to the full amount of the seignorage on that coin, which is alone the legal tender, before the check, which limits the circulation of paper, would operate. If the seignorage of[1] gold coin were 5 per cent. for instance, the cur-rency, by an abundant issue of Bank-notes, might be really depreciated 5 per cent. before it would be the interest of the holders to demand coin for the purpose of melting it into bullion; a depreciation to which we should never be exposed, if either there was no seignorage on the gold coin; or, if a seignorage were allowed, the holders of Bank-notes might de-mand bullion, and not coin, in exchange for them, at the Mint price of $3l.$ $17s.$ $10\frac{1}{2}d.$ Unless, then, the Bank should be obliged to pay their notes in bullion or coin, at the will of the holder, the late law which allows a seignorage of 6 per cent., or four-pence per oz., on the silver coin, but which directs that gold shall be coined by the Mint without any charge whatever, is perhaps the most proper, as it will most[2] effectually prevent any unnecessary variation of the currency.[3]

---

[1] Ed. 1 'on'.

[2] Eds. 1-2 'more'.

[3] In ed. 1 a note is attached here:

'M. Say recommends that the seignorage should vary according to the quantity of business that the mint might be called upon to per-form.

'"Government should not coin the bullion of individuals except on payment, not only of the expenses, but also of the profits of coining.

This profit might be carried to a considerable height, in consequence of the exclusive privilege of coin-ing; but it must vary according to the circumstances of the mint, and the quantity required for circula-tion."—Vol. i. p. 380.

'Such a regulation would be ex-tremely pernicious, and would ex-pose us to considerable and unne-cessary variation in the bullion value of the currency.'

CHAPTER XXVIII

ON THE COMPARATIVE VALUE OF

GOLD, CORN, AND LABOUR,

IN RICH AND[1] POOR COUNTRIES

"GOLD and silver, like all other commodities," says Adam Smith, "naturally seek the market where the best price is given for them; and the best price is commonly given for every thing in the country which can best afford it. Labour, it must be remembered, is the ultimate price which is paid for every thing; and in countries where labour is equally well rewarded, the money price of labour will be in proportion to that of the subsistence of the labourer. But gold and silver will naturally exchange for a greater quantity of subsistence in a rich than in a poor country; in a country which abounds with subsistence, than in one which is but indifferently supplied with it."[2]

But corn is a commodity, as well as gold, silver, and other things; if all commodities, therefore, have a high exchangeable value in a rich country, corn must not be excepted; and hence we might correctly say, that corn exchanged for a great deal of money, because it was dear, and that money, too, exchanged for a great deal of corn, because that also was dear; which is to assert that corn is dear and cheap at the same time. No point in political economy can be better established, than that a rich country is prevented from increasing in population, in the same ratio as a poor country, by the progressive difficulty of providing food. That difficulty must necessarily raise the relative price of food, and give encouragement to its importation. How then can money, or gold and silver, exchange for more corn in rich, than in poor countries? It is only in rich countries, where

---

[1] Eds. 1-2 repeat 'in'.   [2] Bk. 1, ch. xi, pt. iii; vol. 1, p. 189.

corn is dear, that landholders induce the legislature to prohibit the importation of corn. Who ever heard of a law to prevent the importation of raw produce in America or Poland?—Nature has effectually precluded its importation by the comparative facility of its production in those countries.

How, then, can it be true, that "if you except corn, and such other vegetables, as are raised altogether by human industry, all other sorts of rude produce—cattle, poultry, game of all kinds, the useful fossils and minerals of the earth, &c., naturally grow dearer as the society advances."[1] Why should corn and vegetables alone be excepted? Dr. Smith's error throughout his whole work, lies in supposing that the value of corn is constant; that though the value of all other things may, the value of corn never can be raised. Corn, according to him, is always of the same value because it will always feed the same number of people. In the same manner it might be said, that cloth is always of the same value, because it will always make the same number of coats. What can value have to do with the power of feeding and clothing?

Corn, like every other commodity, has in every country its natural price, viz. that price which is necessary to its production, and without which it could not be cultivated: it is this price which governs its market price, and which determines the expediency of exporting it to foreign countries. If the importation of corn were prohibited in England, its natural price might rise to 6*l.* per quarter in England, whilst it was only at half that price in France. If at this time, the prohibition of importation were removed, corn would fall in the English market, not to a price between 6*l.* and 3*l.*, but ultimately and permanently to the natural price of France, the price at which it could be furnished to the English market, and afford the usual and ordinary profits of stock in France; and it would remain at this price, whether

[1] Bk. I, ch. xi, pt. iii; vol. I, p. 216.

England consumed a hundred thousand, or a million of quarters. If the demand of England were for the latter quantity, it is probable that, owing to the necessity under which France would be, of having recourse to land of a worse quality, to furnish this large supply, the natural price would rise in France; and this would of course affect also the price of corn in England. All that I contend for is, that it is the natural price of commodities in the exporting country, which ultimately regulates the prices at which they shall be sold, if they are not the objects of monopoly, in the importing country.

But Dr. Smith, who has so ably supported the doctrine of the natural price of commodities ultimately regulating their market price, has supposed a case in which he thinks that the market price would not be regulated either by the natural price of the exporting or of the importing country. "Diminish the real opulence either of Holland, or the territory of Genoa," he says, "while the number of their inhabitants remains the same; diminish their power of supplying themselves from distant countries, and the price of corn, instead of sinking with that diminution in the quantity of their silver which must necessarily accompany this declension, either as its cause or as its effect, will rise to the price of a famine."[1]

To me it appears, that the very reverse would take place: the diminished power of the Dutch or Genoese to purchase generally, might depress the price of corn for a time below its natural price in the country from which it was exported, as well as in the countries in which it was imported; but it is quite impossible that it could ever raise it above that price. It is only by increasing the opulence of the Dutch or Genoese, that you could increase the demand, and raise the price of corn above its former price; and that would take place only for a very limited time, unless new difficulties should arise in obtaining the supply.

[1] Bk. I, ch. xi, pt. iii; vol. I, p. 190.

Dr. Smith further observes on this subject: "When we are in want of necessaries, we must part with all superfluities, of which the value, as it rises in times of opulence and prosperity, so it sinks in times of poverty and distress." This is undoubtedly true; but he continues, "it is otherwise with necessaries. Their real price, the quantity of labour which they can purchase or command, rises in times of poverty and distress, and sinks in times of opulence and prosperity, which are always times of great abundance, for they could not otherwise be times of opulence and prosperity. Corn is a necessary, silver is only a superfluity."[1]

Two propositions are here advanced, which have no connexion with each other; one, that under the circumstances supposed, corn would command more labour, which is not disputed; the other, that corn would sell at a higher money price, that it would exchange for more silver; this I contend to be erroneous. It might be true, if corn were at the same time scarce—if the usual supply had not been furnished. But in this case it is abundant; it is not pretended that a less quantity than usual is imported, or that more is required. To purchase corn, the Dutch or Genoese want money, and to obtain this money, they are obliged to sell their superfluities. It is the market value and price of these superfluities which falls, and money appears to rise as compared with them. But this will not tend to increase the demand for corn, nor to lower the value of money, the only two causes which can raise the price of corn. Money, from a want of credit, and from other causes, may be in great demand, and consequently dear, comparatively with corn; but on no just principle can it be maintained, that under such circumstances money would be cheap, and therefore, that the price of corn would rise.

When we speak of the high or low value of gold, silver, or any other commodity in different countries, we should always

[1] Bk. I, ch. xi, pt. iii; vol. I, p. 191.

mention some medium in which we are estimating them, or no idea can be attached to the proposition. Thus, when gold is said to be dearer in England than in Spain, if no commodity is mentioned, what notion does the assertion convey? If corn, olives, oil, wine, and wool, be at a cheaper price in Spain than in England; estimated in those commodities, gold is dearer in Spain. If, again, hardware, sugar, cloth, &c. be at a lower price in England than in Spain, then, estimated in those commodities, gold is dearer in England. Thus gold appears dearer or cheaper in Spain, as the fancy of the observer may fix on the medium by which he estimates its value. Adam Smith, having stamped corn and labour as an universal measure of value, would naturally estimate the comparative value of gold by the quantity of those two objects for which it would exchange: and, accordingly, when he speaks of the comparative value of gold in two countries, I understand him to mean its value estimated in corn and labour.

But we have seen, that, estimated in corn, gold may be of very different value in two countries. I have endeavoured to shew that it will be low in rich countries, and high in poor countries; Adam Smith is of a different opinion: he thinks that the value of gold, estimated in corn, is highest in rich countries. But without further examining which of these opinions is correct, either of them is sufficient to shew, that gold will not necessarily be lower in those countries which are in possession of the mines, though this is a proposition maintained by Adam Smith. Suppose England to be possessed of the mines, and Adam Smith's opinion, that gold is of the greatest value in rich countries, to be correct: although gold would naturally flow from England to all other countries in exchange for their *goods*, it would not follow that gold was necessarily lower in England, as compared with corn and labour, than in those countries. In another place, however, Adam Smith speaks of the precious metals being necessarily lower in Spain and Portugal, than in other parts of Europe, because those countries happen to be almost the exclusive possessors of the mines which produce them. "Poland, where the feudal system still continues to take place, is at this day as beggarly a country as it was before the discovery of America. *The money price of corn, however, has risen;* THE REAL VALUE OF THE PRECIOUS METALS HAS FALLEN in Poland, in the same manner as in other parts of Europe. Their quantity, therefore, must have increased there as in other places, *and nearly in the same proportion to the annual produce of the land and labour.* This increase of the quantity of those metals, however, has not, it seems, increased that annual produce; has neither improved the manufactures and agriculture of the country, nor mended the circumstances of its inhabitants. Spain and Portugal, the countries which possess the mines, are, after Poland, perhaps, the two most beggarly countries in Europe. The value of the precious metals, however, *must be lower in Spain and Portugal* than in any other parts of Europe,[1] loaded, not only with a freight and insurance, but with the expense of smuggling, their exportation being either prohibited, or subjected to a duty. *In proportion to the annual produce of the land and labour, therefore, their quantity must be greater in* those countries than in any other part of Europe: those countries, however, are poorer than the greater part of Europe. Though the feudal system has been abolished in Spain and Portugal, it has not been succeeded by a much better."[2]

Dr. Smith's argument appears to me to be this: Gold, when estimated in corn, is cheaper in Spain than in other countries, and the proof of this is, not that corn is given by other countries to Spain for gold, but that cloth, sugar, hardware, are by those countries given in exchange for that metal.

---

[1] Ricardo omits here 'as they come from those countries to all other parts of Europe'.

[2] Bk. I, ch. xi, pt. iii; vol. I, p. 238. The italics are Ricardo's.

CHAPTER XXIX

TAXES PAID BY THE PRODUCER

MONS. SAY[1] greatly magnifies the inconveniences which result if a tax on a manufactured commodity is levied at an early, rather than at a late period of its manufacture. The manufacturers, he observes,[2] through whose hands the commodity may successively pass, must employ greater funds in consequence of having to advance the tax, which is often attended with considerable difficulty to a manufacturer of very limited capital and credit. To this observation no objection can be made.

Another inconvenience on which he dwells[3] is, that in consequence of the advance of the tax, the profits on the advance also must be charged to the consumer, and that this additional tax is one from which the treasury derives no advantage.

In this latter objection I cannot agree with M. Say. The State, we will suppose, wants to raise *immediately* 1000*l.* and levies it on a manufacturer, who will not, for a twelvemonth, be able to charge it to the consumer on his finished commodity. In consequence of such delay, he is obliged to charge for his commodity an additional price, not only of 1000*l.*, the amount of the tax, but probably of 1100*l.*, 100*l.* being for interest on the 1000*l.* advanced. But in return for this additional 100*l.* paid by the consumer, he has a real benefit, inasmuch as his payment of the tax which Government required immediately, and which he must finally pay, has been postponed for a year; an opportunity, therefore, has been afforded to him of lending to the manu-

---

[1] Eds. 1-2 'M. SAY'.

[2] *Traité d'Économie politique,* 2nd ed., 1814, vol. II, p. 342.

[3] *ib.* vol. II, pp. 342-3.

facturer, who had occasion for it, the 1000*l.* at 10 per cent., or at any other rate of interest which might be agreed upon. Eleven hundred pounds payable at the end of one year, when money is at 10 per cent. interest, is of no more value than 1000*l.* to be paid immediately. If Government delayed receiving the tax for one year till the manufacture of the commodity was completed, it would, perhaps, be obliged to issue an Exchequer bill bearing interest, and it would pay as much for interest as the consumer would save in price, excepting, indeed, that portion of the price which the manufacturer might be enabled in consequence of the tax, to add to his own real gains. If for the interest of the Exchequer bill, Government would have paid 5 per cent., a tax of 50*l.* is saved by not issuing it. If the manufacturer borrowed the additional capital at 5 per cent., and charged the consumer 10 per cent., he also will have gained 5 per cent. on his advance over and above his usual profits, so that the manufacturer and Government together gain, or save, precisely the sum which the consumer pays.

M. Simonde, in his excellent work, *De la Richesse Commerciale,* following the same line of argument as M. Say, has calculated [1] that a tax of 4000 francs, paid originally by a manufacturer, whose profits were at the moderate rate of 10 per cent., would, if the commodity manufactured, only passed through the hands of five different persons, be raised to the consumer to the sum of 6734 francs. This calculation proceeds on the supposition, that he who first advanced the tax, would receive from the next manufacturer 4400 francs, and he again from the next, 4840 francs; so that at each step 10 per cent. on its value would be added to it. This is to suppose that the value of the tax would be accumulating at compound interest; not at the rate of 10 per

[1] J. C. L. Simonde, *De la Richesse commerciale, ou Principes d'Économie politique, appliqués à la législation du commerce,* Genève, Paschoud, 1803, vol. II, pp. 43–6. When this work was published, the author had not yet adopted the name Sismondi.

cent. per annum, but at an absolute rate of 10 per cent. at every step of its progress. This opinion of M. de Simonde would be correct, if five years elapsed between the first advance of the tax, and the sale of the taxed commodity to the consumer; but if one year only elapsed, a remuneration of 400 francs, instead of 2734, would give a profit at the rate of 10 per cent. per annum, to all who had contributed to the advance of the tax, whether the commodity had passed through the hands of five manufacturers or fifty.

CHAPTER XXX

ON THE INFLUENCE OF DEMAND AND
SUPPLY ON PRICES

I⊤ is the cost of production which must ultimately regulate the
price of commodities, and not, as has been often said, the proportion between the supply and demand: the proportion between supply and demand may, indeed, for a time, affect the
market value of a commodity, until it is supplied in greater or
less abundance, according as the demand may have increased or
diminished; but this effect will be only of temporary duration.

Diminish the cost of production of hats, and their price will
ultimately fall to their new natural price, although the demand
should be doubled, trebled, or quadrupled. Diminish the cost
of subsistence of men, by diminishing the natural price of the
food and clothing, by which life is sustained, and wages will
ultimately fall, notwithstanding that the demand for labourers
may very greatly increase.

The opinion that the price of commodities depends solely
on the proportion of supply to demand, or demand to supply,
has become almost an axiom in political economy, and has been
the source of much error in that science. It is this opinion which
has made Mr. Buchanan maintain that wages are not influenced
by a rise or fall in the price of provisions, but solely by the
demand and supply of labour; and that a tax on the wages of
labour would not raise wages, because it would not alter the
proportion of the demand of labourers to the supply.[1]

The demand for a commodity cannot be said to increase, if
no additional quantity of it be purchased or consumed; and yet,
under such circumstances, its money value may rise. Thus, if

[1] See above p. 216.

the value of money were to fall, the price of every commodity would rise, for each of the competitors would be willing to spend[1] more money than before on its purchase; but though its price rose 10 or 20 per cent. if no more were bought than before, it would not, I apprehend, be admissible to say, that the variation in the price of the commodity was caused by the increased demand for it. Its natural price, its money cost of production, would be really altered by the altered value of money; and without any increase of demand, the price of the commodity would be naturally adjusted to that new value.

"We have seen," says M. Say, "that the cost of production determines the lowest price to which things can fall: the price below which they cannot remain for any length of time, because production would then be either entirely stopped or diminished." Vol. ii. p. 26.

He afterwards says, that the demand for gold having increased in a still greater proportion than the supply, since the discovery of the mines, "its price in goods, instead of falling in the proportion of ten to one, fell only in the proportion of four to one;"[2] that is to say, instead of falling in proportion as its natural price had fallen, fell in proportion as the supply exceeded the demand.*—"*The value of every commodity rises always in a direct ratio to the demand, and in an inverse ratio to the supply.*"[3]

* ["]If, with the quantity of gold and silver which actually exists, these metals only served for the manufacture of utensils and ornaments, they would be abundant, and would be much cheaper than they are at present: in other words, in exchanging them for any other species of goods, we should be obliged to give proportionally a greater quantity of them. But as a large quantity of these metals is used for money, and as this portion is used for no other purpose, there remains less to be employed in furniture and jewellery; now this scarcity adds to their value.["]—*Say*, vol. i.[4] p. 316. See also note to p. 78.

[1] Ed. 1 'to give', corrected in *Errata*.
[2] Vol. ii, p. 18.
[3] Vol. ii, p. 395.
[4] Misprinted 'vol. ii' in ed. 3.

The same opinion is expressed by the Earl of Lauderdale.

"With respect to the variations in value, of which every thing valuable is susceptible, if we could for a moment suppose that any substance possessed intrinsic and fixed value, so as to render an assumed quantity of it constantly, under all circumstances, of an equal value, then the degree of value of all things, ascertained by such a fixed standard, would vary according to the proportion *betwixt the quantity of them*, and the demand for them, and every commodity would, of course, be subject to a variation in its value, from four different circumstances:

1. "It would be subject to an increase of its value, from a diminution of its quantity.

2. "To a diminution of its value, from an augmentation of its quantity.

3. "It might suffer an augmentation in its value, from the circumstance of an increased demand.

4. "Its value might be diminished by a failure of demand.

"As it will, however, clearly appear that no commodity can possess fixed and intrinsic value, so as to qualify it for a measure of the value of other commodities, mankind are induced to select, as a practical measure of value, that which appears the least liable to any of these four sources of variations, *which are the sole causes of alteration of value.*

"When, in common language, therefore, we express the *value* of any commodity, it may vary at one period from what it is at another, in consequence of eight different contingencies:

1. "From the four circumstances above stated, in relation to the commodity of which we mean to express the value.

2. "From the same four circumstances, in relation to the commodity we have adopted as a measure of value."*

This is true of monopolized commodities, and indeed of the market price of all other commodities for a limited period. If

* An Inquiry into the Nature and Origin of Public Wealth, page 13.

the demand for hats should be doubled, the price would immediately rise, but that rise would be only temporary, unless the cost of production of hats, or their natural price, were raised. If the natural price of bread should fall 50 per cent. from some great discovery in the science of agriculture, the demand would not greatly increase, for no man would desire more than would satisfy his wants, and as the demand would not increase, neither would the supply; for a commodity is not supplied merely because it can be produced, but because there is a demand for it. Here, then, we have a case where the supply and demand have scarcely varied, or if they have increased, they have increased in the same proportion; and yet the price of bread will have fallen 50 per cent. at a time, too, when the value of money had continued invariable.

Commodities which are monopolized, either by an individual, or by a company, vary according to the law which Lord Lauderdale has laid down: they fall in proportion as the sellers augment their quantity, and rise in proportion to the eagerness of the buyers to purchase them; their price has no necessary connexion with their natural value: but the prices of commodities, which are subject to competition, and whose quantity may be increased in any moderate degree, will ultimately depend, not on the state of demand and supply, but on the increased or diminished cost of their production.

CHAPTER XXXI

ON MACHINERY[1]

In the present chapter I shall enter into some enquiry respecting the influence of machinery on the interests of the different classes of society, a subject of great importance, and one which appears never to have been investigated in a manner to lead to any certain or satisfactory results. It is more incumbent on me to declare my opinion on this question, because they have, on further reflection, undergone a considerable change; and although I am not aware that I have ever published any thing respecting machinery which it is necessary for me to retract, yet I have in other ways[2] given my support to doctrines which I now think erroneous; it, therefore, becomes a duty in me to submit my present views to examination, with my reasons for entertaining them.

Ever since I first turned my attention to questions of political economy, I have been of opinion, that such an application of machinery to any branch of production, as should have the effect of saving labour, was a general good, accompanied only with that portion of inconvenience which in most cases attends the removal of capital and labour from one employment to another. It appeared to me, that provided the landlords had the same money rents, they would be benefited by the reduction in the prices of some of the commodities on which those rents were expended, and which reduction of price could not fail to be the consequence of the employment of machinery. The capitalist, I thought, was eventually benefited precisely in the

---

[1] Eds. 1-2 do not contain this chapter.

[2] Perhaps an allusion to his own speech on Owen's plan on 16 Dec. 1819; see below, V, 30.

same manner. He, indeed, who made the discovery of the machine, or who first usefully applied it, would enjoy an additional advantage, by making great profits for a time; but, in proportion as the machine came into general use, the price of the commodity produced, would, from the effects of competition, sink to its cost of production, when the capitalist would get the same money profits as before, and he would only participate in the general advantage, as a consumer, by being enabled, with the same money revenue, to command an additional quantity of comforts and enjoyments. The class of labourers also, I thought, was equally benefited by the use of machinery, as they would have the means of buying more commodities with the same money wages, and I thought that no reduction of wages would take place, because the capitalist would have the power of demanding and employing the same quantity of labour as before, although he might be under the necessity of employing it in the production of a new, or at any rate of a different commodity. If, by improved machinery, with the employment of the same quantity of labour, the quantity of stockings could be quadrupled, and the demand for stockings were only doubled, some labourers would necessarily be discharged from the stocking trade; but as the capital which employed them was still in being, and as it was the interest of those who had it to employ it productively, it appeared to me that it would be employed on the production of some other commodity, useful to the society, for which there could not fail to be a demand; for I was, and am, deeply impressed with the truth of the observation of Adam Smith, that "the desire for food is limited in every man, by the narrow capacity of the human stomach, but the desire of the conveniences, and ornaments of building, dress, equipage and household furniture, seems to have no limit or certain boundary."[1] As, then, it appeared to me that there would be

[1] Also quoted above, p. 293.

the same demand for labour as before, and that wages would be no lower, I thought that the labouring class would, equally with the other classes, participate in the advantage, from the general cheapness of commodities arising from the use of machinery.

These were my opinions, and they continue unaltered, as far as regards the landlord and the capitalist; but I am convinced, that the substitution of machinery for human labour, is often very injurious to the interests of the class of labourers.

My mistake arose from the supposition, that whenever the net income of a society increased, its gross income would also increase; I now, however, see reason to be satisfied that the one fund, from which landlords and capitalists derive their revenue, may increase, while the other, that upon which the labouring class mainly depend, may diminish, and therefore it follows, if I am right, that the same cause which may increase the net revenue of the country, may at the same time render the population redundant, and deteriorate the condition of the labourer.

A capitalist we will suppose employs a capital of the value of 20,000*l.* and that he carries on the joint business of a farmer, and a manufacturer of necessaries. We will further suppose, that 7000*l.* of this capital is invested in fixed capital, viz. in buildings, implements, &c. &c. and that the remaining 13,000*l.* is employed as circulating capital in the support of labour. Let us suppose, too, that profits are 10 per cent., and consequently that the capitalist's capital is every year put into its original state of efficiency, and yields a profit of 2000*l.*

Each year the capitalist begins his operations, by having food and necessaries in his possession of the value of 13,000*l.*, all of which he sells in the course of the year to his own workmen for that sum of money, and, during the same period, he pays them the like amount of money for wages: at the end of the year they replace in his possession food and necessaries of the value of 15,000*l.*, 2000*l.* of which he consumes himself, or disposes of as may best suit his pleasure and gratification. As far as these products are concerned, the gross produce for that year is 15,000*l.*, and the net produce 2000*l.* Suppose now, that the following year the capitalist employs half his men in constructing a machine, and the other half in producing food and necessaries as usual. During that year he would pay the sum of 13,000*l.* in wages as usual, and would sell food and necessaries to the same amount to his workmen; but what would be the case the following year?

While the machine was being made, only one-half of the usual quantity of food and necessaries would be obtained, and they would be only one-half the value of the quantity which was produced before. The machine would be worth 7500*l.*, and the food and necessaries 7500*l.*, and, therefore, the capital of the capitalist would be as great as before; for he would have besides these two values, his fixed capital worth 7000*l.*, making in the whole 20,000*l.* capital, and 2000*l.* profit. After deducting this latter sum for his own expenses, he would have a no greater circulating capital than 5500*l.* with which to carry on his subsequent operations; and, therefore, his means of employing labour, would be reduced in the proportion of 13,000*l.* to 5500*l.*, and, consequently, all the labour which was before employed by 7500*l.*, would become redundant.

The reduced quantity of labour which the capitalist can employ, must, indeed, with the assistance of the machine, and after deductions for its repairs, produce a value equal to 7500*l.*, it must replace the circulating capital with a profit of 2000*l.* on the whole capital; but if this be done, if the net income be not diminished, of what importance is it to the capitalist, whether the gross income be of the value of 3000*l.*, of 10,000*l.*, or of 15,000*l.*?

In this case, then, although the net produce will not be diminished in value, although its power of purchasing commodities may be greatly increased, the gross produce will have fallen from a value of 15,000*l.* to a value of 7500*l.*, and as the power of supporting a population, and employing labour, depends always on the gross produce of a nation, and not on its net produce, there will necessarily be a diminution in the demand for labour, population will become redundant, and the situation of the labouring classes will be that of distress and poverty.

As, however, the power of saving from revenue to add to capital, must depend on the efficiency of the net revenue, to satisfy the wants of the capitalist, it could not fail to follow from the reduction in the price of commodities consequent on the introduction of machinery, that with the same wants he would have increased means of saving,—increased facility of transferring revenue into capital. But with every increase of capital he would employ more labourers; and, therefore, a portion of the people thrown out of work in the first instance, would be subsequently employed; and if the increased production, in consequence of the employment of the machine, was so great as to afford, in the shape of net produce, as great a quantity of food and necessaries as existed before in the form of gross produce, there would be the same ability to employ the whole population, and, therefore, there would not necessarily be any redundancy of people.

All I wish to prove, is, that the discovery and use of machinery may be attended with a diminution of gross produce; and whenever that is the case, it will be injurious to the labouring class, as some of their number will be thrown out of employment, and population will become redundant, compared with the funds which are to employ it.

The case which I have supposed, is the most simple that I could select; but it would make no difference in the result, if we supposed that the machinery was applied to the trade of any manufacturer,—that of a clothier, for example, or of a cotton manufacturer. If in the trade of a clothier, less cloth would be produced after the introduction of machinery; for a part of that quantity which is disposed of for the purpose of paying a large body of workmen, would not be required by their employer. In consequence of using the machine, it would be necessary for him to reproduce a value, only equal to the value consumed, together with the profits on the whole capital. 7500*l.* might do this as effectually as 15,000*l.* did before, the case differing in no respect from the former instance. It may be said, however, that the demand for cloth would be as great as before, and it may be asked from whence would this supply come? But by whom would the cloth be demanded? By the farmers and the other producers of necessaries, who employed their capitals in producing these necessaries as a means of obtaining cloth: they gave corn and necessaries to the clothier for cloth, and he bestowed them on his workmen for the cloth which their work afforded him.

This trade would now cease; the clothier would not want the food and clothing, having fewer men to employ and having less cloth to dispose of. The farmers and others, who only produced necessaries as means to an end, could no longer obtain cloth by such an application of their capitals, and, therefore, they would either themselves employ their capitals in producing cloth, or would lend them to others, in order that the commodity really wanted might be furnished; and that for which no one had the means of paying, or for which there was no demand, might cease to be produced. This, then, leads us to the same result; the demand for labour would diminish, and the commodities necessary to the support of labour would not be produced in the same abundance.

If these views be correct, it follows, 1st. That the discovery, and useful application of machinery, always leads to the increase of the net produce of the country, although it may not, and will not, after an inconsiderable interval, increase the value of that net produce.

2dly. That an increase of the net produce of a country is compatible with a diminution of the gross produce, and that the motives for employing machinery are always sufficient to insure its employment, if it will increase the net produce, although it may, and frequently must, diminish both the quantity of the gross produce, and its value.

3dly. That the opinion entertained by the labouring class, that the employment of machinery is frequently detrimental to their interests, is not founded on prejudice and error, but is conformable to the correct principles of political economy.

4thly. That if the improved means of production, in consequence of the use of machinery, should increase the net produce of a country in a degree so great as not to diminish the gross produce, (I mean always quantity of commodities and not value,) then the situation of all classes will be improved. The landlord and capitalist will benefit, not by an increase of rent and profit, but by the advantages resulting from the expenditure of the same rent, and profit, on commodities, very considerably reduced in value, while the situation of the labouring classes will also be considerably improved; 1st, from the increased demand for menial servants; 2dly, from the stimulus to savings from revenue, which such an abundant net produce will afford; and 3dly, from the low price of all articles of consumption on which their wages will be expended.

Independently of the consideration of the discovery and use of machinery, to which our attention has been just directed, the labouring class have no small interest in the manner in which the net income of the country is expended, although it should, in all cases, be expended for the gratification and enjoyments of those who are fairly entitled to it.

If a landlord, or a capitalist, expends his revenue in the manner of an ancient baron, in the support of a great number of retainers, or menial servants, he will give employment to much more labour, than if he expended it on fine clothes, or costly furniture; on carriages, on horses, or in the purchase of any other luxuries.

In both cases the net revenue would be the same, and so would be the gross revenue, but the former would be realised in different commodities. If my revenue were 10,000*l.*, the same quantity nearly of productive labour would be employed, whether I realised it in fine clothes and costly furniture, &c. &c. or in a quantity of food and clothing of the same value. If, however, I realised my revenue in the first set of commodities, no more labour would be *consequently* employed:—I should enjoy my furniture and my clothes, and there would be an end of them; but if I realised my revenue in food and clothing, and my desire was to employ menial servants, all those whom I could so employ with my revenue of 10,000*l.*, or with the food and clothing which it would purchase, would be to be added to the former demand for labourers, and this addition would take place only because I chose this mode of expending my revenue. As the labourers, then, are interested in the demand for labour, they must naturally desire that as much of the revenue as possible should be diverted from expenditure on luxuries, to be expended in the support of menial servants.

In the same manner, a country engaged in war, and which is under the necessity of maintaining large fleets and armies, employs a great many more men than will be employed when the war terminates, and the annual expenses which it brings with it, cease.

If I were not called upon for a tax of 500*l.* during the war, and which is expended on men in the situations of soldiers and sailors, I might probably expend that portion of my income on furniture, clothes, books, &c. &c. and whether it was expended in the one way or in the other, there would be the same quantity of labour employed in production; for the food and clothing of the soldier and sailor would require the same amount of industry to produce it as the more luxurious commodities; but in the case of the war, there would be the additional demand for men as soldiers and sailors; and, consequently, a war which is supported out of the revenue, and not from the capital of a country, is favourable to the increase of population.

At the termination of the war, when part of my revenue reverts to me, and is employed as before in the purchase of wine, furniture, or other luxuries, the population which it before supported, and which the war called into existence, will become redundant, and by its effect on the rest of the population, and its competition with it for employment, will sink the value of wages, and very materially deteriorate the condition of the labouring classes.

There is one other case that should be noticed of the possibility of an increase in the amount of the net revenue of a country, and even of its gross revenue, with a diminution of demand for labour, and that is, when the labour of horses is substituted for that of man. If I employed one hundred men on my farm, and if I found that the food bestowed on fifty of those men, could be diverted to the support of horses, and afford me a greater return of raw produce, after allowing for the interest of the capital which the purchase of the horses would absorb, it would be advantageous to me to substitute the horses for the men, and I should accordingly do so; but this would not be for the interest of the men, and unless the income I obtained, was so much increased as to enable me to employ the men as well as the horses, it is evident that the population would become redundant, and the labourers' condition would sink in the general scale. It is evident he could not, under any circumstances, be employed in agriculture; but if the produce of the land were increased by the substitution of horses for men, he might be employed in manufactures, or as a menial servant.

The statements which I have made will not, I hope, lead to the inference that machinery should not be encouraged. To elucidate the principle, I have been supposing, that improved machinery is *suddenly* discovered, and extensively used; but the truth is, that these discoveries are gradual, and rather operate in determining the employment of the capital which is saved and accumulated, than in diverting capital from its actual employment.

With every increase of capital and population, food will generally rise, on account of its being more difficult to produce. The consequence of a rise of food will be a rise of wages, and every rise of wages will have a tendency to determine the saved capital in a greater proportion than before to the employment of machinery. Machinery and labour are in constant competition, and the former can frequently not be employed until labour rises.

In America and many other countries, where the food of man is easily provided, there is not nearly such great temptation to employ machinery as in England, where food is high, and costs much labour for its production. The same cause that raises labour, does not raise the value of machines, and, therefore, with every augmentation of capital, a greater proportion of it is employed on machinery. The demand for labour will continue to increase with an increase of capital, but not in proportion to its increase; the ratio will necessarily be a diminishing ratio.*

* "The demand for labour depends on the increasing of circulating, and not of fixed capital. Were it true that the proportion between these two sorts of capital is the same at all times, and in all countries, then, indeed, it follows that the number of labourers employed is in proportion to the wealth of the State. But such a position has not the semblance of prob-

I have before observed, too, that the increase of net incomes, estimated in commodities, which is always the consequence of improved machinery, will lead to new savings and accumulations. These savings, it must be remembered are annual, and must soon create a fund, much greater than the gross revenue, originally lost by the discovery of the machine, when the demand for labour will be as great as before, and the situation of the people will be still further improved by the increased savings which the increased net revenue will still enable them to make.

The employment of machinery could never be safely discouraged in a State, for if a capital is not allowed to get the greatest net revenue that the use of machinery will afford here, it will be carried abroad, and this must be a much more serious discouragement to the demand for labour, than the most extensive employment of machinery; for, while a capital is employed in this country, it must create a demand for some labour; machinery cannot be worked without the assistance of men, it

ability. As arts are cultivated, and civilization is extended, fixed capital bears a larger and larger proportion to circulating capital. The amount of fixed capital employed in the production of a piece of British muslin is at least a hundred, probably a thousand times greater than that employed in the production of a similar piece of Indian muslin. And the proportion of circulating capital employed is a hundred or a thousand times less. It is easy to conceive that, under certain circumstances, the whole of the annual savings of an industrious people might be added to fixed capital, in which case they would have no effect in increasing the demand for labour."

Barton, "On the Condition of the Labouring Classes of Society,"[1] page 16.

It is not easy, I think, to conceive that under any circumstances, an increase of capital should not be followed by an increased demand for labour; the most that can be said is, that the demand will be in a diminishing ratio. Mr. Barton, in the above publication, has, I think, taken a correct view of some of the effects of an increasing amount of fixed capital on the condition of the labouring classes. His Essay contains much valuable information.

[1] *Observations on the Circumstances which Influence the Condition of the Labouring Classes of Society*, by John Barton, London, Arch, 1817.

cannot be made but with the contribution of their labour. By investing part of a capital in improved machinery, there will be a diminution in the progressive demand for labour; by exporting it to another country, the demand will be wholly annihilated.

The prices of commodities, too, are regulated by their cost of production. By employing improved machinery, the cost of production of commodities is reduced, and, consequently, you can afford to sell them in foreign markets at a cheaper price. If, however, you were to reject the use of machinery, while all other countries encouraged it, you would be obliged to export your money, in exchange for foreign goods, till you sunk the natural prices of your goods to the prices of other countries. In making your exchanges with those countries, you might give a commodity which cost two days labour, here, for a commodity which cost one, abroad, and this disadvantageous exchange would be the consequence of your own act, for the commodity which you export, and which cost you two days labour, would have cost you only one if you had not rejected the use of machinery, the services of which your neighbours had more wisely appropriated to themselves.

CHAPTER XXXII

MR. MALTHUS'S OPINIONS ON RENT

ALTHOUGH the nature of rent has in the former pages of this work been treated on at some length; yet I consider myself bound to notice some opinions on the subject, which appear to me erroneous, and which are the more important, as they are found in the writings of one, to whom, of all men of the present day, some branches of economical science are the most indebted. Of Mr. Malthus's Essay on Population, I am happy in the opportunity here afforded me of expressing my admiration. The assaults of the opponents of this great work have only served to prove its strength; and I am persuaded that its just reputation will spread with the cultivation of that science of which it is so eminent an ornament. Mr. Malthus, too, has satisfactorily explained the principles of rent, and shewed that it rises or falls in proportion to the relative advantages, either of fertility or situation, of the different lands in cultivation, and has thereby thrown much light on many difficult points connected with the subject of rent, which were before either unknown, or very imperfectly understood; yet he appears to me to have fallen into some errors, which his authority makes it the more necessary, whilst his characteristic candour renders it less unpleasing to notice. One of these errors lies in supposing rent to be a clear gain and a new creation of riches.

I do not assent to all the opinions of Mr. Buchanan concerning rent; but with those expressed in the following passage, quoted from his work by Mr. Malthus, I fully agree; and, therefore, I must dissent from Mr. Malthus's comment on them.

"In this view it (rent) can form no general addition to the stock of the community, as the neat surplus in question is nothing more than a revenue transferred from one class to another; and from the mere circumstance of its thus changing hands, it is clear that no fund can arise, out of which to pay taxes. The revenue which pays for the produce of the land, exists already in the hands of those who purchase that produce; and, if the price of subsistence were lower, it would still remain in their hands, where it would be just as available for taxation as when, by a higher price, it is transferred to the landed proprietor."[1]

After various observations on the difference between raw produce and manufactured commodities, Mr. Malthus asks, "Is it possible then, with M. de Sismondi,[2] to regard rent as the sole produce of labour, which has a value purely nominal, and the mere result of that augmentation of price which a seller obtains in consequence of a peculiar privilege; or, with Mr. Buchanan, to consider it as no addition to the national wealth, but merely a transfer of value, advantageous only to the landlords, and proportionably *injurious* to the consumers?"*

I have already expressed my opinion on this subject in treating of rent,[3] and have now only further to add, that rent is a creation of value, as I understand that word, but not a creation of wealth. If the price of corn, from the difficulty of producing any portion of it, should rise from 4*l*. to 5*l*. per quarter, a million of quarters will be of the value of 5,000,000*l*. instead of 4,000,000*l*., and as this corn will exchange not only for more money, but for more of every other commodity, the possessors will have a greater amount of value; and as no one else will, in consequence, have a less, the society altogether will be possessed of greater value, and in that sense rent is a creation of value. But this value is so far nominal, that it adds nothing to the

* An Inquiry into the Nature and Progress of Rent, p. 15.

[1] Buchanan's ed. of the *Wealth of Nations*, vol. III, p. 272, note; quoted by Malthus in *An Inquiry into...Rent*, 1815, p. 7.

[2] *De la Richesse commerciale*, 1803, vol. I, p. 49; cp. above, p. 380, n.

[3] Above, pp. 75–7.

wealth, that is to say,[1] the necessaries, conveniences, and enjoyments of the society. We should have precisely the same quantity, and no more of commodities, and the same million quarters of corn as before; but the effect of its being rated at 5*l.* per quarter, instead of 4*l.*, would be to transfer a portion of the value of the corn and commodities from their former possessors to the landlords. Rent then is a creation of value, but not a creation of wealth; it adds nothing to the resources of a country, it does not enable it to maintain fleets and armies; for the country would have a greater disposable fund if its land were of a better quality, and it could employ the same capital without generating a rent.

It must then be admitted that Mr. Sismondi and Mr. Buchanan, for both their opinions are substantially the same, were correct, when they considered rent as a value purely nominal, and as forming no addition to the national wealth, but merely as a transfer of value, advantageous only to the landlords, and proportionably injurious to the consumer.[2]

In another part of Mr. Malthus's "Inquiry" he observes,[3] "that the immediate cause of rent is obviously the excess of price above the cost of production at which raw produce sells in the market;" and in another place he says,[4] "that the causes of the high price of raw produce may be stated to be three:—

"First, and mainly, that quality of the earth, by which it can be made to yield a greater portion of the necessaries of life than is required for the maintenance of the persons employed on the land.

"2dly. That quality peculiar to the necessaries of life, of being able to create their own demand, or to raise up a number of demanders in proportion to the quantity of necessaries produced.

---

[1] Eds. 1-2 repeat here 'to'.
[2] Ed. 1 does not contain this paragraph. Cp. below, II, 116, where Ricardo defends this statement against Malthus's criticism.
[3] *Inquiry into...Rent*, p. 2.
[4] *ib.* p. 8.

"And 3dly. The comparative scarcity of the most fertile land." In speaking of the high price of corn, Mr. Malthus evidently does not mean the price per quarter or per bushel, but rather the excess of price for which the whole produce will sell, above the cost of its production, including always in the term "cost of its[1] production," profits as well as wages. One hundred and fifty quarters of corn at 3*l.* 10*s.* per quarter, would yield a larger rent to the landlord than 100 quarters at 4*l.*, provided the cost of production were in both cases the same.

High price, if the expression be used in this sense, cannot then be called a *cause* of rent; it cannot be said "that the immediate cause of rent is obviously the excess of price above the cost of production, at which raw produce sells in the market," for that excess is itself rent. Rent, Mr. Malthus has defined to be "that portion of the value of the whole produce which remains to the owner of the land, after all the outgoings belonging to its cultivation, of whatever kind, have been paid, including the profits of the capital employed, estimated according to the usual and ordinary rate of the profits of agricultural stock at the time being."[2] Now whatever sum this excess may sell for, is money rent; it is what Mr. Malthus means by "the excess of price above the cost of production at which raw produce sells in the market;" and, therefore, in an inquiry into the causes which may elevate the price of raw produce, compared with the cost of production, we are inquiring into the causes which may elevate rent.

In reference to the first cause which Mr. Malthus has assigned for the rise of rent, namely, "that quality of the earth by which it can be made to yield a greater portion of the necessaries of life than is required for the maintenance of the persons employed on the land," he makes the following observations[3]: "We still

[1] Eds. 1-2 do not contain 'its'.
[2] *Inquiry into...Rent*, pp. 1-2.
[3] Ed. 1 reads 'In reference to the first cause of the rise of rent, Mr. Malthus has the following observations'.

want to know why the consumption and supply are such as to make the price so greatly exceed the cost of production, and the main cause is evidently the *fertility* of the earth in producing the necessaries of life. Diminish this plenty, diminish the fertility of the soil, and the excess will diminish; diminish it still further, and it will disappear."[1] True, the excess of necessaries will diminish and disappear, but that is not the question. The question is, whether the excess of their price above the cost of their production will diminish and disappear, for it is on this that money rent[2] depends. Is Mr. Malthus warranted in his inference, that because the excess of quantity will diminish and disappear, therefore "the cause of the *high price* of the necessaries of life above the cost of production is to be found in their abundance, rather than in their scarcity; and is not only essentially different from the high price occasioned by artificial monopolies, but from the high price of those peculiar products of the earth, not connected with food, which may be called natural and necessary monopolies?"[3]

Are there no circumstances under which the fertility of the land, and the plenty of its produce may be diminished, without occasioning a diminished excess of its price above the cost of production, that is to say, a diminished rent? If there are, Mr. Malthus's proposition is much too universal; for he appears to me to state it as a general principle, true under all circumstances, that rent will rise with the increased fertility of the land, and will fall with its diminished fertility.

Mr. Malthus would undoubtedly be right, if, of any given farm,[4] in proportion as the land yielded abundantly, a greater share of the whole produce were paid to the landlord; but the contrary is the fact: when no other but the most fertile land is in

---

[1] *Inquiry into...Rent*, p. 13.
[2] Ed. 1 'rent money', corrected in *Errata*.
[3] *ib.* p. 13. Ricardo's italics.
[4] Eds. 1-2 do not contain 'of any given farm,'. Cp. above, p. 83, n.

cultivation, the landlord has the smallest proportion[1] of the whole produce, as well as the smallest value, and it is only when inferior lands are required to feed an augmenting population, that both the landlord's share of the whole produce, and the value he receives, progressively increase.

Suppose that the demand is for a million of quarters of corn, and that they are the produce of the land actually in cultivation. Now, suppose the fertility of all the land to be so diminished, that the very same lands will yield only 900,000 quarters. The demand being for a million of quarters, the price of corn would rise, and recourse must necessarily be had to land of an inferior quality sooner than if the superior land had continued to produce a million of quarters. But it is this necessity of taking inferior land into cultivation which is the cause of the rise of rent[2], and will elevate it, although the quantity of corn received by the landlord, be reduced in quantity. Rent, it must be remembered, is not in proportion to the absolute fertility of the land in cultivation, but in proportion to its relative fertility. Whatever cause may drive capital to inferior land, must elevate rent on the superior land[3]; the cause of rent being, as stated by Mr. Malthus in his third proposition, "the comparative scarcity of the most fertile land." The price of corn will naturally rise with the difficulty of producing the last portions of it, and the value of the whole quantity produced on a particular farm will be increased, although its quantity be diminished[4]; but as the cost of production will not increase on the more fertile land[5], as wages and profits taken together will continue always of the same

---

[1] Eds. 1-2 'share' in place of 'proportion'.
[2] Eds. 1-2 do not contain the remainder of this sentence, to 'in quantity.'
[3] Eds. 1-2 do not contain 'on the superior land'.

[4] Eds. 1-2 do not contain the last two lines beginning 'and the value of the whole quantity'.
[5] Eds. 1-2 do not contain 'on the more fertile land'.

value*, it is evident that the excess of price above the cost of production, or, in other words, rent must rise with the diminished fertility of the land, unless it is counteracted by a great reduction of capital, population, and demand. It does not appear then, that Mr. Malthus's proposition is correct: rent does not immediately and necessarily rise or fall with the increased or diminished fertility of the land; but its increased fertility renders it capable of paying at some future time an augmented rent. Land possessed of very little fertility can never bear any rent; land of moderate fertility may be made, as population increases, to bear a moderate rent; and land of great fertility a high rent; but it is one thing to be able to bear a high rent, and another thing actually to pay it. Rent may be lower in a country where lands are exceedingly fertile than in a country where they yield a moderate return, it being in proportion rather to relative than absolute fertility—to the value of the produce, and not to its abundance.†

Mr. Malthus supposes that the rent on land yielding those peculiar products of the earth which may be called natural and

* See page 115[1], where I have endeavoured to shew, that whatever facility or difficulty there may be in the production of corn; wages and profits together will be of the same value. When wages rise, it is always at the expense of profits, and when they fall, profits always rise.

† Mr. Malthus has observed in a late publication,[2] that I have misunderstood him in this passage, as he did not mean to say, that rent immediately and necessarily rises and falls with the increased or diminished fertility of the land. If so, I certainly did misunderstand him. Mr. Malthus's words are, "Diminish this plenty, diminish the fertility of the soil, and the excess (rent) will diminish; diminish it still further, and it will disappear."[3] Mr. Malthus does not state his proposition conditionally, but absolutely. I contended against what I understood him to maintain, that a diminution of the fertility of the soil was incompatible with an increase of rent.[4]

[1] Ed. 1 'page 124' (*i.e.* p. 115, above) ed. 2 'page 124' (*i.e.* p. 120, above), ed. 3 'page 120' (*i.e.* p. 120, above); the trouble was due to failure to adjust the reference to the pagination of ed. 2.

[2] *Principles of Political Economy*, below, II, 121, n. and cp. Ricardo's Note 59.

[3] Quoted above, p. 402.

[4] Eds. 1-2 do not contain this footnote.

necessary monopolies, is regulated by a principle essentially different from that which regulates the rent of land that yields the necessaries of life. He thinks that it is the scarcity of the products of the first which is the cause of a high rent, but that it is the abundance of the latter, which produces the same effect.

This distinction does not appear to me to be well founded; for you would as surely raise the rent of land yielding scarce wines, as the rent of corn land, by increasing the abundance of its produce, if, at the same time, the demand for this peculiar commodity increased; and without a similar increase of demand, an abundant supply of corn would lower instead of raise[1] the rent of corn land. Whatever the nature of the land may be, high rent must·depend on the high price of the produce; but, given the high price, rent must be high in proportion to abundance and not to scarcity.[2]

We are under no necessity of producing permanently any greater quantity of a commodity than that which is demanded. If by accident any greater quantity were produced, it would fall below its natural price, and therefore would not pay the cost of

---

[1] Ed. 2 'raising'.

[2] Ed. 1, in place of the last two paragraphs, reads: 'Mr. Malthus says, that the "cause of the excess of price of the necessaries of life above the cost of production, is to be found in their abundance rather than their scarcity, and is essentially different from the high price of those peculiar products of the earth, not connected with food, which may be called natural and necessary monopolies."

'In what are they essentially different? Would not the abundance of those peculiar products of the earth cause a rise of rent, if the demand for them at the same time increased? and can rent ever rise, whatever the commodity produced may be, from abundance merely, and without an increase of demand?

'The second cause of rent mentioned by Mr. Malthus, namely, "that quality peculiar to the necessaries of life, of being able to create their own demand, or to raise up a number of demanders in proportion to the quantity of necessaries produced," does not appear to me to be any way essential to it. It is not the abundance of necessaries which raises up demanders, but the abundance of demanders which raises up necessaries.' The passages from Malthus are also quoted above, p. 402 and p. 400.

production, including in that cost[1] the usual and ordinary profits of stock: thus the supply would be checked till it conformed to the demand, and the market price rose to the natural price.

Mr. Malthus appears to me to be too much inclined to think that population is only increased by the previous provision of food,—"that it is food that creates its own demand,"—that it is by first providing food, that encouragement is given to marriage, instead of considering that the general progress of population is affected by the increase of capital, the consequent demand for labour, and the rise of wages; and that the production of food is but the effect of that demand.

It is by giving the workman[2] more money, or any other commodity in which wages are paid, and which has not fallen in value, that his situation is improved. The increase of population, and the increase of food will generally be the effect, but not the necessary effect of high wages. The amended condition of the labourer, in consequence of the increased value which is paid him, does not necessarily oblige him to marry and take upon himself the charge of a family—he will, in all probability,[3] employ a portion of his increased wages in furnishing himself abundantly with food and necessaries,—but with the remainder he may, if it please him, purchase any commodities that may contribute to his enjoyments—chairs,[4] tables, and hardware; or[5] better clothes, sugar, and tobacco. His increased wages then will be attended with no other effect than an increased demand for some of those commodities; and as the race of labourers will not be materially increased, his wages will continue permanently

---

[1] Eds. 1-2 'together with' in place of 'including in that cost'.
[2] Misprinted 'workmen' in ed. 3.
[3] Ed. 2 does not contain ', in all probability,'.
[4] In place of the last four lines, beginning 'he will, in all probability', ed. 1 reads 'he may, if it please him, exchange his increased wages for any commodities that may contribute to his enjoyments—for chairs,' etc.
[5] Ed. 1 has in addition 'for'.

high. But although this might be the consequence of high wages, yet so great are the delights of domestic society, that in practice it is invariably found that an increase of population follows the amended condition of the labourer; and it is only because it does so, that, with the trifling exception already mentioned,[1] a new and increased demand arises for food. This demand then is the effect of an increase of capital and[2] population, but not the cause—it is only because the expenditure of the people takes this direction, that the market price of necessaries exceeds the natural price, and that the quantity of food required is produced; and it is because the number of people is increased, that wages again fall.

What motive can a farmer have to produce more corn than is actually demanded, when the consequence would be a depression of its market price below its natural price, and consequently a privation to him of a portion of his profits, by reducing them below the general rate? "If," says Mr. Malthus, "the necessaries of life, the most important products of land, had not the property of creating an increase of demand proportioned to their increased quantity, such increased quantity would occasion a fall in their exchangeable value.* However abundant might be the produce of the country[3], its population might remain stationary; and this abundance without a proportionate demand, and with a very high corn price of labour, which would naturally take place under these circumstances, might reduce the price of raw produce, like the price of manufactures, to the cost of production."[4]

* Of what increased quantity does Mr. Malthus speak? Who is to produce it? Who can have any motive to produce it, before any demand exists for an additional quantity?

[1] Ed. 1 does not contain ', with the trifling exception already mentioned,'.

[2] Eds. 1-2 do not contain 'capital and'.

[3] Eds. 1-2 'a country'.

[4] *Inquiry into...Rent*, pp. 9–10.

Might reduce the price of raw produce to the cost of production.[1] Is it ever for any length of time either above or below this price? Does not Mr. Malthus himself, state it never to be so? "I hope," he says, "to be excused for dwelling a little, and presenting to the reader, in various forms, the doctrine, that corn, in reference to the quantity [2] *actually produced*, is sold at its necessary price, like manufactures, because I consider it as a truth of the highest importance, which has been overlooked by the economists, by Adam Smith, and all those writers, who have represented raw produce as selling always at a monopoly price."[3]

"Every extensive country may thus be considered as possessing a gradation of machines for the production of corn and raw materials, including in this gradation not only all the various qualities of poor land, of which every territory has generally an abundance, but the inferior machinery which may be said to be employed when good land is further and further forced for additional produce. As the price of raw produce continues to rise, these inferior machines are successively called into action; and as the price of raw produce continues to fall, they are successively thrown out of action. The illustration here used, serves to shew, at once, the *necessity of the actual price of corn to the actual produce*, and the different effect which would attend a great reduction in the price of any particular manufacture, and a great reduction in the price of raw produce."*

* Inquiry, &c.[4] "In all progressive countries, the average price of corn is never higher than what is necessary to continue the average increase of produce." Observations, p. 21.[5]

"In the employment of fresh capital upon the land, to provide for the wants of an increasing population, whether this fresh capital is employed in bringing more land under the plough, or improving land already in

---

[1] In eds. 1-2 this sentence is in inverted commas and is followed by a question mark.
[2] Malthus italicizes also '*quantity*'.

[3] *Inquiry into...Rent*, p. 39.
[4] pp. 38-9. Ricardo's italics.
[5] Malthus's *Observations on the Effects of the Corn Laws*, ed. 3, 1815.

How are these passages to be reconciled to that which affirms, that if the necessaries of life had not the property of creating an increase of demand proportioned to their increased quantity, the abundant quantity produced would then, and then only, reduce the price of raw produce to the cost of production? If corn is never under its natural price, it is never more abundant than the actual population require it to be for their own consumption; no store can be laid up for the consumption of others; it can never then by its cheapness and abundance be a stimulus to population. In proportion as corn can be produced cheaply, the increased wages of the labourers will have more power to maintain families. In America, population increases rapidly, because food can be produced at a cheap price, and not because an abundant supply has been previously provided. In Europe population increases comparatively slowly, because food cannot be produced at a cheap value. In the usual and ordinary course of things, the demand for all commodities precedes their supply. By saying, that corn would, like manufactures, sink to its price of production, if it could not raise up demanders, Mr. Malthus cannot mean that all rent would be absorbed; for he has himself justly remarked, that if all rent were given up by the landlords, corn would not fall in price; rent being the effect, and not the cause of high price, and there being always one quality of land in cultivation which pays no rent whatever, the corn from which replaces by its price, only wages and profits.

cultivation, the main question always depends upon the expected returns of this capital; and no part of the gross profits can be diminished, without diminishing the motive to this mode of employing it. Every diminution of price, not fully and immediately balanced by a proportionate fall in all the necessary expenses of a farm, every tax on the land, every tax on farming stock, every tax on the necessaries of farmers, will tell in the computation; and if, after all these outgoings are allowed for, the price of the produce will not leave a fair remuneration for the capital employed, according to the general rate of profits, and a rent at least equal to the rent of the land in its former state, no sufficient motive can exist to undertake the projected improvement." Observations, p. 22.

In the following passage, Mr. Malthus has given an able exposition of the causes of the rise in the price of raw produce in rich and progressive countries, in every word of which I concur; but it appears to me to be at variance with some of the propositions maintained by him in[1] his Essay on Rent. "I have no hesitation in stating, that, independently of the irregularities in the currency of a country, and other temporary and accidental circumstances, the cause of the high comparative money price of corn is its high comparative *real price*,[2] or the greater quantity of capital and labour which must be employed to produce it; and that the reasons why the real price of corn is higher, and continually rising in countries which are already rich, and still advancing in prosperity and population, is to be found in the necessity of resorting constantly to poorer land, to machines which require a greater expenditure to work them, and which consequently occasion each fresh addition to the raw produce of the country to be purchased at a greater cost; in short, it is to be found in the important truth, that corn in a progressive country, is sold at a price necessary to yield the actual supply; and that, as this supply becomes more and more difficult, the price rises in proportion."[3]

The real price of a commodity is here properly stated to depend on the greater or less quantity of labour and capital (that is, accumulated labour) which must be employed to produce it. Real price does not, as[4] some have contended, depend on money value; nor, as others have said, on value relatively to corn, labour, or any other commodity taken singly, or to all commodities collectively; but, as Mr. Malthus justly says, "on the greater (or less) quantity of capital and labour which must be employed to produce it."

Among the causes of the rise of rent, Mr. Malthus mentions, "such an increase of population as will lower the wages of

---

[1] Ed. 1 'in some parts of'.
[2] Ricardo's italics.
[3] *Inquiry into...Rent*, pp. 40–1.
[4] Misprinted 'has' in ed. 3.

labour."[1] But if, as the wages of labour fall, the profits of stock rise, and they be together always of the same value,* no fall of wages can raise rent, for it will neither diminish the portion, nor the value of the portion of the produce which will be allotted to the farmer and labourer together; and, therefore, will not leave a larger portion, nor a larger value for the landlord. In proportion as less is appropriated for wages, more will be appropriated for profits, and *vice versâ*. This division will be settled by the farmer and his labourers, without any interference of the landlord; and, indeed, it is a matter in which he can have no interest, otherwise than as one division may be more favourable than another, to new accumulations, and to a further demand for land. If wages fell[2], profits, and not rent, would rise. If wages rose, profits, and not rent, would fall. The rise of rent and wages, and the fall of profits, are generally the inevitable effects of the same cause—the increasing demand for food, the increased quantity of labour required to produce it, and its consequently high price. If the landlord were to forego his whole rent, the labourers would not be in the least benefited. If it were possible for the labourers[3] to give up their whole wages, the landlords would derive no advantage from such a circumstance; but in both cases the farmer would receive and retain all which they relinquish[4]. It has been my endeavour to shew in this work, that a fall of wages would have no other effect than to raise profits. Every rise of profits is favourable to the accumulation of capital, and to the further increase of population, and therefore would, in all probability, ultimately lead to an increase of rent.[5]

* See p. 115[6].

---

[1] *Inquiry into…Rent*, p. 22.
[2] Eds. 1-2 'fall'.
[3] Eds. 1-2 'If the labourers were'.
[4] Eds. 1-2 'relinquished'.
[5] Eds. 1-2 do not contain this sentence, beginning 'Every rise'.

[6] Ed. 1 'p. 124' (*i.e.* p. 115, above), ed. 2 'p. 124' (*i.e.* p. 120, above), ed. 3 'p. 121' (*i.e.* p. 120, above). Cp. above, p. 404, n. 1.

Another cause of the rise of rent, according to Mr. Malthus, is "such agricultural improvements, or such increase of exertions, as will diminish the number of labourers necessary to produce a given effect."[1] To this passage I have the same objection that I had against that which speaks of the increased[2] fertility of land being the cause of an immediate rise of rent.[3] Both the improvement in agriculture, and the superior fertility will give to the land a capability of bearing at some future period a higher rent, because with the same price of food there will be a great additional quantity; but till the increase of population be[4] in the same proportion, the additional quantity of food would not be required, and, therefore, rents would be lowered and not raised. The quantity that could under the then existing circumstances be consumed, could be furnished[5] either with fewer hands, or with a less quantity of land, the price of raw produce would fall, and capital would be withdrawn from the land.* Nothing can raise rent, but a demand for new land of an inferior quality, or some cause which shall occasion an alteration in the relative fertility of the land already under cultivation.† Improvements in agriculture, and in the division of labour, are common to all land; they increase the absolute quantity of raw produce obtained from each, but probably do

---

* See p. 79[6], &c.

† It is not necessary to state, on every occasion, but it must be always understood, that the same results will follow, as far as regards the price of raw produce and the rise of rents, whether an additional capital of a given amount, be employed on new land, for which no rent is paid, or on land

---

[1] *Inquiry into...Rent*, p. 22.
[2] Ed. 2 does not contain 'increased'.
[3] See above, p. 400.
[4] Ed. 2 does not contain 'be'.
[5] In place of the sentences (beginning 'To this passage') which follow the quotation from Malthus, ed. 1 reads: 'This would not raise the value of the whole produce, and

would therefore not increase rent. It would rather have a contrary tendency, it would lower rent; for if in consequence of these improvements, the actual quantity of food required could be furnished' etc.
[6] Ed. 1 'p. 70' (*i.e.* p. 79, above), ed. 2 'p. 70' (*i.e.* p. 82, above), ed. 3 'p. 73' (*i.e.* p. 82, above). Cp. above, p. 404, n. 1.

not much disturb the relative proportions which before existed between them.

Mr. Malthus has justly commented on the error of Dr. Smith's argument, that corn is of so peculiar a nature, that its production cannot be encouraged by the same means that the production of all other commodities is encouraged. He observes,[1] "It is by no means intended to deny the powerful already in cultivation, if the produce obtained from both be precisely the same in quantity. See p. 72.[2]

M. Say, in his notes to the French translation of this work,[3] has endeavoured to shew that there is not at any time land in cultivation which does not pay a rent, and having satisfied himself on this point, he concludes that he has overturned all the conclusions which result from that doctrine. He infers, for example, that I am not correct in saying that taxes on corn, and other raw produce, by elevating their price, fall on the consumer, and do not fall on rent. He contends that such taxes must fall on rent.[4] But before M. Say can establish the correctness of[5] this inference, he must also shew that there is not any[6] capital employed on the land for which no rent is paid (see the beginning of this note, and pages 67 and 74 of the present work); now this he has not attempted to do. In no part of his notes has he refuted, or even noticed that important doctrine. By his note to page 182 of the second volume of the French edition, he does not appear to be aware that it has even[7] been advanced.[8]

[1] In place of the beginning of this paragraph ed. 1 reads: 'Mr. Malthus has justly commented on an error of Adam Smith, and says, "the substance of his (Dr. Smith's) argument is, that corn is of so peculiar a nature, that its real price cannot be raised by an increase of its money price; and that, as it is clearly an increase of real price alone, which can encourage its production, the rise of money price, occasioned by a bounty, can have no such effect." 'He continues:'.

[2] In Ed. 1 this paragraph reads: 'It is not necessary to state on every occasion, but it must be always understood, that the same effect will be produced by employing different, but equal portions of capital on the land already in cultivation, with different results. Rent is the difference of produce obtained with equal capitals, and with equal labour on the same, or on different qualities of land.'

[3] Ed. 2 has here in addition 'which I have only seen since this edition was in the press,'.

[4] In ed. 2 the last two sentences read 'He infers, for example, that I am not correct in saying that taxes on raw produce do not fall on rent, but by elevating the price of raw produce they fall on the consumer. He contends that they do fall on rent.'

[5] Ed. 2 does not contain 'the correctness of'.

[6] Ed. 2 'no' in place of 'not any'.

[7] Ed. 2 does not contain 'even'.

[8] Ed. 1 does not contain this paragraph.

influence of the price of corn upon the price of labour, on an average of a considerable number of years; but that this influence is not such as to prevent the movement of capital to, or from the land, which is the precise point in question, will be made sufficiently evident, by a short inquiry into the manner in which labour is paid, and brought into the market, and by a consideration of the consequences to which the assumption of Adam Smith's proposition would inevitably lead."*

Mr. Malthus then proceeds to shew, that demand and high price will as effectually encourage the production of raw produce, as the demand and high price of any other commodity will encourage its production. In this view it will be seen, from what I have said of the effects of bounties,[1] that I entirely concur. I have noticed the passage from Mr. Malthus's "Observations on the Corn Laws," for the purpose of shewing in what a different sense the term real price is used here,[2] and in his other pamphlet, entitled "Grounds of an Opinion", &c.[3] In this passage Mr. Malthus tells us, that "it is clearly an increase of real price alone which can encourage the production of corn,"[4] and, by real price, he evidently means the increase in its value relatively to all other things; or, in other words, the rise in its market above its natural price, or the cost of its production. If by real price this is what is meant, although I do not admit the propriety of thus naming it,[5] Mr. Malthus's opinion is undoubtedly correct; it is the rise in the market price of corn which alone encourages its production; for it may be laid down

* Observations on the Corn Laws, p. 4.[6]

[1] Above, p. 304 ff.
[2] This sentence should have been revised in eds. 2-3, which omit the relevant part of the quotation given in ed. 1; see above, p. 413, n. 1.
[3] *The Grounds of an Opinion on the Policy of Restricting the Importation of Foreign Corn*, 1815.

[4] *Observations*, 3rd ed. p. 4.
[5] Ed. 1 does not contain 'although I do not admit the propriety of thus naming it,'.
[6] Should be 'p. 5' in eds. 2-3, which omit the quotation from p. 4 given above, p. 413, n. 1.

as a principle uniformly true, that the only great[1] encouragement to the increased production of a commodity, is its market
value exceeding its natural or necessary value.

But this is not the meaning which Mr. Malthus, on other
occasions, attaches to the term, real price. In the Essay on Rent,[2]
Mr. Malthus says, by "the real growing price of corn, I mean
the real *quantity* of labour and capital, *which has been employed*
to produce the last additions which have been made to the
national produce." In another part he states[3] "the cause of the
high comparative real price of corn to be the greater *quantity* of
capital and labour, which must be *employed* to produce it."[*]
Suppose that in the foregoing passage we were to substitute this
definition of real price, would it not then run thus?—"It is
clearly the increase in the quantity of labour and capital which
must be employed to produce corn, which alone can encourage
its production." This would be to say, that it is clearly the rise
in the natural or necessary price of corn, which encourages its
production—a proposition which could not be maintained. It
is not the price at which corn can be produced, that has any influence on the quantity produced, but the price at which it can
be sold. It is in proportion to the degree of the difference of its
price above or below[4] the cost of production, that capital is

* Upon shewing this passage to Mr. Malthus, at the time when these
papers were going to the press, he observed, "that in these two instances
he had inadvertently used the term *real price*, instead of *cost of production*.["]
It will be seen, from what I have already said, that to me it appears, that in
these two instances he has used the term *real price* in its true and just ac-
ceptation, and that in the former case only it is incorrectly applied.[5]

[1] Eds. 1-2 do not contain 'great'.
[2] Not in the 'Essay on Rent', but
(as Ricardo had said in the preceding paragraph) in *Grounds of an
Opinion*, p. 21, n. Ricardo's italics.
[3] *Inquiry into…Rent*, p. 41. Malthus
actually says 'the cause of the high
comparative money price of corn is
its high comparative real price, or

the greater quantity of capital and
labour which must be employed to
produce it'. Ricardo quotes the
passage more accurately above,
p. 410 and below, p. 417.
[4] Eds. 1-2 'the degree of the excess
of its price above'.
[5] Cp. letter to Malthus of 26 March
1817, below, VII, 145.

attracted to, or repelled from the land. If that excess be such as to give to capital so employed, a greater than the general profit of stock, capital will go to the land; if less, it will be withdrawn from it.

It is not, then, by an alteration in the real price of corn that its production is encouraged, but by an alteration in its market price. It is not "because a greater quantity of capital and labour must be employed to produce it,"[1] (Mr. Malthus's just definition of real price,)[2] that more capital and labour are attracted to the land, but because the market price rises above this its real price, and, notwithstanding the increased charge, makes the cultivation of land the more profitable employment of capital.

Nothing can be more just than the following observations of Mr. Malthus, on Adam Smith's standard of value. "Adam Smith was evidently led into this train of argument, from his habit of considering *labour as the standard measure of value*, and corn as the measure of labour. But that corn is a very inaccurate measure of labour, the history of our own country will amply demonstrate; where labour, compared with corn, will be found to have experienced very great and striking variations, not only from year to year, but from century to century; and for ten, twenty, and thirty years together. *And that neither labour nor any other commodity can be an accurate measure of real value in exchange*, is now considered as one of the most incontrovertible doctrines of political economy; and, indeed, follows from the very definition of value in exchange."[3]

If neither corn nor labour are accurate measures of real value in exchange, which they clearly are not, what other commodity is?—certainly none. If, then, the expression, real price of commodities, have any meaning, it must be that which Mr. Malthus

---

[1] In ed. 3 by a misprint the inverted commas are closed at the end of the paragraph, instead of here.

[2] Eds. 1-2 do not enclose this phrase in brackets.

[3] *Observations*, 3rd ed., p. 12. Ricardo's italics here and below.

has stated in the Essay on Rent—it must be measured by the proportionate quantity of capital and labour necessary to produce them.

In Mr. Malthus's "Inquiry into the Nature of Rent," he says, "that, independently of irregularities in the currency of a country, and other temporary and accidental circumstances, the cause of the high comparative money price of corn, is its high comparative real price, *or the greater quantity of capital and labour which must be employed to produce it.*"*

This, I apprehend, is the correct account of all permanent variations in price, whether of corn or of any other commodity. A commodity can only permanently rise in price, either because a greater quantity of capital and labour must be employed to produce it, or because money has fallen in value; and, on the contrary, it can only fall in price, either because a less quantity of capital and labour may be employed to produce it, or because money has risen in value.

A variation arising from the latter of these[1] alternatives, an altered value of money, is common at once to all commodities; but a variation arising from the former cause, is confined to the particular commodity requiring more or less labour in its production. By allowing the free importation of corn, or by improvements in agriculture, raw produce would fall; but the price of no other commodity would be affected, except in proportion to the fall in the real value, or cost of production, of the raw produce, which entered into its composition.

Mr. Malthus, having acknowledged this principle, cannot, I think, consistently maintain that the whole money value of all the commodities in the country must sink exactly in proportion to the fall in the price of corn. If the corn consumed in the

* Page 40.

[1] Eds. 1-2 'the latter of either of these'.

country were of the value of ten millions per annum, and the manufactured and foreign commodities consumed were of the value of twenty millions, making altogether thirty millions, it would not be admissible to infer that the annual expenditure was reduced to 15 millions, because corn had fallen 50 per cent., or from 10 to 5 millions.

The value of the raw produce which entered into the composition of these manufactures might not, for example, exceed 20 per cent. of their whole value, and, therefore, the fall in the value of manufactured commodities, instead of being from 20 to 10 millions, would be only from 20 to 18 millions; and after the fall in the price of corn of 50 per cent., the whole amount of the annual expenditure, instead of falling from 30 to 15[1] millions, would fall from 30 to 23 millions.*

This, I say, would be their value, if you supposed it possible, that with such a cheap price of corn, no more corn and commodities would be consumed; but as all those who had employed capital in the production of corn on those lands which would no longer be cultivated, could employ it in the production of manufactured goods; and only a part of those manufactured goods would be given in exchange for foreign corn, as on any other supposition no advantage would be gained by importation, and low prices; we should have the additional value of all that quantity of manufactured goods which were so produced, and not exported to add to the above value, so that the real diminution, even in money value, of all the commodities in the country, corn included, would be equal only to the loss of

---

* Manufactures, indeed, could not fall in any such proportion, because, under the circumstances supposed, there would be a new distribution of the precious metals among the different countries. Our cheap commodities would be exported in exchange for corn and gold, till the accumulation of gold should lower its value, and raise the money price of commodities.

[1] Misprinted '25' in ed. 1.

the landlords, by the reduction of their rents, while the quantity of objects of enjoyment would be greatly increased.[1]

Instead of thus considering the effect of a fall in the value of raw produce; as Mr. Malthus was bound to do by his previous admission; he considers it as precisely the same thing as[2] a rise of 100 per cent. in the value of money, and, therefore, argues as if all commodities would sink to half their former price.

"During the twenty years beginning with 1794," he says, "and ending with 1813, the average price of British corn per quarter was about eighty-three shillings; during the ten years ending with 1813, ninety-two shillings; and during the last five years of the twenty, one hundred and eight shillings. In the course of these twenty years, the Government borrowed near five hundred millions of real capital; for which, on a rough average, exclusive of the sinking fund, it engaged to pay about five per cent. But if corn should fall to fifty shillings a quarter, and other commodities in proportion, instead of an interest of about five per cent., the Government would really pay an interest of seven, eight, nine, and for the last two hundred millions, ten per cent.

"To this extraordinary generosity towards the stockholders, I should be disposed to make no kind of objection, if it were not necessary to consider by whom it is to be paid; and a moment's reflection will shew us, that it can only be paid by the industrious classes of society, and the landlords; that is, by all those whose nominal income will vary with the variations in the measure of value. The nominal revenues of this part of the society, compared with the average of the last five years, will be diminished one half, and out of this nominally reduced income, they will have to pay the same nominal amount of taxes."*

* The Grounds of an Opinion, &c. page 36.[3]

[1] Eds. 1-2 do not contain this paragraph.
[2] Eds. 1-2 'with' in place of 'as'.
[3] Should be 39.

In the first place, I think, I have already shewn, that even the value of the gross income[1] of the whole country will not be diminished in the proportion for which Mr. Malthus here contends; it would not follow, that because corn fell fifty per cent., each man's gross[2] income would be reduced fifty per cent. in value*; his net income might be actually increased in value[3].

In the second place, I think the reader will agree with me, that the increased charge, if admitted, would not fall exclusively "on the landlords and the industrious classes of society:" the stockholder, by his expenditure, contributes his share to the support of the public burdens in the same way as the other classes of society. If, then, money became really more valuable, although he would receive a greater value, he would also pay a greater value in taxes, and, therefore, it cannot be true that the whole addition to the real value of the interest would be paid by "the landlords and the industrious classes."

The whole argument, however, of Mr. Malthus, is built on an infirm basis: it supposes, because the gross income of the country is diminished, that, therefore, the net income must also be diminished, in the same proportion. It has been one of the objects of this work to shew, that with every fall in the real value of necessaries, the wages of labour would fall, and that the profits of stock would rise—in other words, that of any given annual value a less portion would be paid to the labouring class, and a larger portion to those whose funds employed this class. Suppose the value of the commodities produced in a particular

---

* Mr. Malthus, in another part of the same work,[4] supposes commodities to vary 25 or 20 per cent. when corn varies $33\frac{1}{3}$.

---

[1] Eds. 1-2 'the nominal income' in place of 'even the value of the gross income'.

[2] Eds. 1-2 do not contain 'gross'.

[3] Eds. 1-2 do not contain ' ; his net income might be actually increased in value'.

[4] *Grounds of an Opinion*, p. 41.

manufacture to be 1000*l*., and to be divided between the master and his labourers, in the proportion of 800*l*. to labourers, and 200*l*. to the master; if the value of these commodities should fall to 900*l*., and 100*l*. be saved from the wages of labour, in consequence of the fall of necessaries, the net income of the masters would be in no degree impaired, and, therefore, he could with just as much facility pay the same amount of taxes, after, as before the reduction of price.*²

It is of importance to distinguish clearly between gross revenue and net revenue, for it is from the net revenue of a society that all taxes must be paid. Suppose that all the commodities in the country, all the corn, raw produce, manufactured goods, &c. which could be brought to market in the

* Of net produce and gross produce, M. Say speaks as follows: "The whole value produced is the gross produce; this value, after deducting from it the cost of production, is the net produce." Vol. II. p. 491. There can then be no net produce, because the cost of production, according to M. Say, consists of rent, wages, and profits. In page 508, he says, "The value of a product, the value of a productive service, the value of the cost of production, are all then similar values, whenever things are left to their natural course." Take a whole from a whole, and nothing remains.¹

¹ The references are to Say's 4th ed., 1819. Eds. 1-2 in place of this note have the following one: 'In Chap. XXVI. I have observed, that the real resources of a country, and its ability to pay taxes, depend on its net, and not on its gross income.' Ed. 1 reads 'Chap. 24.' in place of 'Chap. XXVI.', but in either case the reference is to the chapter 'On Gross and Net Revenue'.

² In place of the five paragraphs that follow in the text, ending on p. 425, ed. 1 and (unless otherwise stated) ed. 2 read: 'And that wages would fall as much as the mass of commodities, or rather that the net

income remaining to landlords, farmers, manufacturers, traders, and stockholders, the only real payers of taxes, would be as great as before, is very highly probable; for nothing would be even nominally lost to the society by the freest importation of corn, but that portion of rent of which the landlords would be deprived in consequence of the fall of raw produce.

'The difference between the value of corn and all other commodities sold in the country, before and after the importation of cheap corn, would be only equal to the fall of rent; because, independently of rent, course of the year, were of the value of 20 millions, and that in order to obtain this value, the labour of a certain number of men was necessary, and that the absolute necessaries of these labourers required an expenditure of 10 millions. I should say that the gross revenue of such society was 20 millions, and its net revenue 10 millions. It does not follow from this supposition, that the labourers should receive only 10 millions for their labour; they might receive 12, 14, or 15 millions, and in that case they would have 2, 4, or 5 millions of the net income. The rest would be divided between landlords and capitalists; but the whole net income would not exceed 10 millions. Suppose such a society paid 2 millions in taxes, its net income would be reduced to 8 millions.

Suppose now money to become more valuable by one-tenth, all commodities would fall, and the price of labour would fall, because the absolute necessaries of the labourer formed a part of those commodities, consequently the gross income would be reduced to 18 millions, and the net income to 9 millions. If the

the same quantity of labour would always produce the same value.

'The whole reduction which is made in wages, is a value actually added to the value of the net income before possessed by the society; whilst the only value which is taken from that net income is the value of that part of their rent of which the landlords will be deprived by a fall of raw produce. When we consider that the fall of produce acts upon a limited number of landlords [Ed. 2 'upon landlords only'], while it reduces the wages not only of those who are employed in agriculture, but of all those who are occupied in manufactures and commerce, it may well be doubted, whether the net revenue of the society would suffer any abatement whatever. [*Footnote:* 'This is on the supposition that money continued at the same value. In the last note, I have endeavoured to shew that money would not continue of the same value,—that it would fall, from increased importation; a fact which is much more favourable to my argument.']

'But, if it did, it must not be supposed that the ability to pay taxes will diminish in the same degree, as the money value, even of the net revenue. Suppose that my net revenue were diminished from 1000*l.* to 900*l.*; but that my taxes continued to be the same, to be 100*l.*: is it not probable that my taxes fell in the same proportion, and, instead of 2 millions, 1,800,000*l.* only were raised, the net income would be further reduced to 7,200,000*l.*, precisely of the same value as the 8 millions were before, and therefore the society would neither be losers nor gainers by such an event. But suppose that after the rise of money, 2 millions were raised for taxes as before, the society would be poorer by 200,000*l.* per annum, their taxes would be really raised one-ninth. To alter the money value of commodities, by altering the value of money, and yet to raise the same money amount by taxes, is then undoubtedly to increase the burthens of society.

But suppose of the 10 millions net revenue, the landlords received five millions as rent, and that by facility of production, or by the importation of corn, the necessary cost of that article in labour was reduced 1 million, rent would fall 1 million, and the prices of the mass of commodities would also fall to the same amount, but the net revenue would be just as great as before; the gross income would, it is true, be only 19 millions,

ability to pay this 100*l.* may be greater with the smaller than with the larger revenue? Commodities cannot fall so universally as Mr. Malthus supposes, without greatly benefiting the consumers, without enabling them with a much smaller money revenue to command more of the conveniences, necessaries, and luxuries of human life; and the question resolves itself into this— whether those who are in possession of the net revenue of the country will be benefited as much by the diminished price of commodities, as they will suffer by the greater real taxation. On which side the balance may preponderate, will depend on the proportion which taxes bear to the annual revenue; if it be enormously large, it may undoubtedly more than counterbalance the advantages from cheap necessaries; but I trust enough has been said, to shew, that Mr. Malthus has very greatly over-rated the loss to the tax-payers, from a fall in one of the most important necessaries of life; and that if they were not entirely remunerated for the real increase of taxes, by the fall of wages and increase of profits, they would be more than compensated, by the cheaper price of all objects on which their incomes were expended.'

and the necessary expenditure to obtain it 9 millions, but the net income would be 10 millions. Now suppose 2 millions raised in taxes on this diminished gross income, would the society altogether be richer or poorer? Richer, certainly; for after the payment of their taxes, they would have, as before, a clear income of 8 millions to bestow on the purchase of commodities, which had increased in quantity, and fallen in price, in the proportion of 20 to 19; not only then could the same taxation be endured, but greater, and yet the mass of the people be better provided with conveniences and necessaries.

If the net income of the society, after paying the same money taxation, be as great as before, and the class of landholders lose 1 million from a fall of rent, the other productive classes must have increased money incomes, notwithstanding the fall of prices. The capitalist will then be doubly benefited; the corn and butcher's meat consumed by himself and his family will be reduced in price; and the wages of his menial servants, of his gardeners, and labourers of all descriptions, will be also lowered. His horses and cattle will cost less, and be supported at a less expense. All the commodities in which raw produce enters as a principal part of their value, will fall. This aggregate amount of savings, made on the expenditure of income, at the same time that his money income is increased, will then be doubly beneficial to him, and will enable him not only to add to his enjoyments, but to bear additional taxes, if they should be required: his additional consumption of taxed commodities will much more than make up for the diminished demand of landlords, consequent on the reduction of their rents. The same observations apply to farmers and traders of every description.

But it may be said, that the capitalist's income will not be increased; that the million deducted from the landlord's rent, will be paid in additional wages to labourers! Be it so; this will make no difference in the argument: the situation of the society will be improved, and they will be able to bear the same money burthens with greater facility than before; it will only prove what is still more desirable, that the situation of another class, and by far the most important class in society, is the one which is chiefly benefited by the new distribution. All that they receive more than 9 millions, forms part of the net income of the country, and it cannot be expended without adding to its revenue, its happiness, or its power. Distribute then the net income as you please. Give a little more to one class, and a little less to another, yet you do not thereby diminish it; a greater amount of commodities will be still produced with the same labour, although the amount of the gross money value of such commodities will be diminished; but the net money income of the country, that fund from which taxes are paid and enjoyments procured, would be much more adequate, than before, to maintain the actual population, to afford it enjoyments and luxuries, and to support any given amount of taxation.[1]

That the stockholder is benefited by a great fall in the value of corn, cannot be doubted; but if no one else be injured, that is no reason why corn should be made dear: for the gains of the stockholder are national gains, and increase, as all other gains do, the real wealth and power of the country. If they are unjustly benefited, let the degree in which they are so, be accurately ascertained, and then it is for the legislature to devise a remedy; but no policy can be more unwise than to shut ourselves out from the great advantages arising from cheap corn, and abundant productions, merely because the stockholder would have an undue proportion of the increase.

To regulate the dividends on stock by the money value of

[1] Here end the five paragraphs not contained in eds. 1–2; see above, p. 421, n. 2.

corn, has never yet been attempted. If justice and good faith required such a regulation, a great debt is due to the old stock-holders; for they have been receiving the same money dividends for more than a century, although corn has, perhaps, been doubled or trebled in price.*

But it is a great mistake to suppose, that the situation of the stockholder will be more improved than that of the farmer, the manufacturer, and the other capitalists of the country; it will, in fact, be less improved.

The stockholder will undoubtedly receive the same money dividend, while not only the price of raw produce, and labour fell, but the prices of many other things into which raw produce entered as a component part. This, however, is an advantage, as I have just stated, which he would enjoy in common with all other persons who had the same money incomes to expend:— his money income would not be increased; that of the farmer, manufacturer and other employers of labour would, and conse-quently they would be doubly benefited.

It may be said, that although it may be true that capitalists would be benefited by a rise of profits, in consequence of a fall of wages, yet that their incomes would be diminished by the fall in the money value of their commodities. What is to lower them? Not any alteration in the value of money, for nothing has been supposed to occur to alter the value of money. Not

* Mr. M'Culloch, in an able publication, has very strongly contended for the justice of making the dividends on the national debt conform to the reduced value of corn. He is in favour of a free trade in corn, but he thinks it should be accompanied by a reduction of interest to the national creditor.[1]

[1] J. R. M'Culloch, *An Essay on the Question of Reducing the Interest on the National Debt; in which the Justice and Expediency of that Mea-sure are fully established*, Edinburgh, Brown and Black, 1816. Subse-quently M'Culloch repudiated and suppressed this publication; and in reprinting the *Principles* in his edition of Ricardo's *Works*, 1846, omitted this revealing footnote. See below, VII, 93, n. 2.

any diminution in the quantity of labour necessary to produce their commodities, for no such cause has operated, and if it did operate, would not lower money profits, though it might lower money prices. But the raw produce of which commodities are made, is supposed to have fallen in price, and, therefore, commodities will fall on that account. True, they will fall, but their fall will not be attended with any diminution in the money income of the producer. If he sell his commodity for less money, it is only because one of the materials from which it is made has fallen in value. If the clothier sell his cloth for 900*l.* instead of 1000*l.*, his income will not be less, if the wool from which it is made, has declined 100*l.* in value.[1]

Mr. Malthus says, "It is true, that the last additions to the agricultural produce of an improving country, are not attended with a large proportion of rent; and it is precisely this circumstance that may make it answer to a rich country to import some of its corn, if it can be secure of obtaining an equable supply. But in all cases the importation of foreign corn must fail to answer nationally, if it is not so much cheaper than the corn that can be grown at home, as to equal both the profits and the rent of the grain which it displaces." *Grounds, &c.* p. 36.

In this observation Mr. Malthus is quite correct; but imported corn *must* be always so much cheaper than the corn that can be grown at home, "as to equal both the profits and the rent of the grain which it displaces." If it were not, no advantage to any one could be obtained by importing it.[2]

As rent is the effect of the high price of corn, the loss of rent is the effect of a low price. Foreign corn never enters into competition with such home corn as affords a rent; the fall of price

---

[1] Eds. 1-2 do not contain the last three paragraphs beginning 'But it is'.

[2] Eds. 1-2 do not contain this paragraph; but for ed. 2 cp. below, p. 429, n. 1.

invariably affects the landlord till the whole of his rent is absorbed;—if it fall still more, the price will not afford even the common profits of stock; capital will then quit the land for some other employment, and the corn, which was before grown upon it, will then, and not till then, be imported. From the loss of rent, there will be a loss of value, of estimated money value, but, there will be a gain of wealth. The amount of the raw produce and other productions together will be increased; from the greater facility with which they are produced, they will, though augmented in quantity, be diminished in value.

Two men employ equal capitals—one in agriculture, the other in manufactures. That in agriculture produces a net annual value of 1200*l*. of which 1000*l*. is retained for profit, and 200*l*. is paid for rent; the other in manufactures produces only an annual value of 1000*l*. Suppose that by importation, the same quantity of corn which cost 1200*l*.[1] can be obtained for commodities which cost 950*l*., and that, in consequence, the capital employed in agriculture is diverted to manufactures, where it can produce a value of 1000*l*., the net revenue of the country will be of less value, it will be reduced from 2200*l*. to 2000*l*.; but there will not only be the same quantity of commodities and corn for its own consumption, but also as much addition to that quantity as 50*l*. would purchase, the difference between the value at which its manufactures were sold to the foreign country, and the value of the corn which was purchased from it.

Now this is precisely the question respecting the advantage of importing, or growing corn; it never can be imported till the quantity obtained from abroad by the employment of a given capital exceeds the quantity which the same capital will enable us to grow at home,—exceeds[2] not only that quantity which

[1] Ed. 1 does not contain 'which cost 1200*l*.'   [2] Ed. 2 does not contain 'exceeds'.

falls to the share of the farmer, but also that which is paid as rent to the landlord.[1]

Mr. Malthus says, "It has been justly observed by Adam Smith, that no equal quantity of productive labour employed in manufactures can ever occasion so great a reproduction as in agriculture."[2] If Adam Smith speaks of value, he is correct; but if he speaks of riches, which is the important point, he is mistaken; for he has himself defined riches to consist of the necessaries, conveniences, and enjoyments of human life. One set of necessaries and conveniences admits of no comparison with another set; value in use cannot be measured by any known standard; it is differently[3] estimated by different persons.

---

[1] Ed. 1 does not contain this paragraph. In ed. 2 it has an additional sentence at the end: 'Mr. Malthus may be quite sure therefore that no importation of foreign corn will ever take place "if it is not so much cheaper than the corn that can be grown at home, as to equal both the profits and the rent of the grain which it displaces."' The quotation is from *Grounds of an Opinion*, pp. 35–6.

[2] *Grounds of an Opinion*, p. 35. For the reference to Adam Smith, see above, p. 76.

[3] Since the present edition first appeared Mr Oswald St. Clair has pointed out that some copies of ed. 3 contain the alternative reading, 'variously'. This is clearly a correction intended to avoid the verbal repetition, and must have been made by Ricardo while the printing of the last sheet was in progress.

INDEX

A

ACCUMULATION of capital, effects of, [on the relative value of commodities, 22–25, 52–63. And][1,2] on profits and interest, 289–300.

Agriculture, effects of improvements in, on rents, 73–83. [Importance of them, 81, *note*.][3] Is affected by the distress proceeding from sudden revulsions of trade, 266–272. Agricultural improvements, no cause of the increase of rent, 412, 413.

B

Banks, establishment of, affects the sole power of the state in coining money, 354. Consequence of the Bank of England issuing too great a quantity of paper, 354–356. [That corporation can only be prevented from abusing its power of issuing paper money, by compelling it to pay its notes either in gold coin or bullion, 356–361.][2,3] The assistance given by the Bank of England to commerce, accounted for, 364, 365. See *Paper Currency*.

Bounties, on the exportation of corn, lower its price to the foreign consumer, 301–306. Effects of a bounty in raising the price of corn, illustrated, 307. Though such bounty may cause a partial degradation in the value of money, yet such degradation cannot be permanent, 310–311. Bounties on the exportation of manufactures raise their *market* but not their *natural* price, 312–314. The sole effect of bounty is to divert a portion of capital to an employment which it would not naturally seek, 314. Evils of such a system, 314–318. A bounty on the production of corn, will produce no real effect on the annual produce of the land and labour of the country, though it would make corn relatively cheap, and manufactures relatively dear, 321–325. But the effect of a tax on corn, in order to afford a fund for a bounty on the production of commodities, would be to enhance the price of corn, and render commodities cheap, 325, 326.

Buchanan (Mr.), observations of, on Adam Smith's doctrine of productive and unproductive labour, 76–77, *note*. [His examination of Smith's opinion concerning taxes upon the wages of labour, 216, 217. Remarks thereon, 217–235.][3] Remarks on his opinions respecting bounties on exportation, 315, 316.

C

Capital, [nature of, effects of the accumulation of, on the relative value of commodities investigated, 23.][1,2] Effects of, in a savage or infant state

F

G

H

I

L

M

Machinery, effects of, [in fixing the relative values of commodities, 58–63][1,2] [on labour, 16, 17. The author's *former* mistaken views of, 386–388. His present views substantiated by facts, that machinery is often injurious to the interests of labourers, 388–392. A *qualified* use of machinery vindicated, 395–397][3].

[*Malt*, observations on the tax upon, 252–254.][3]

Malthus (Mr.), examination of the opinions of, on rent, 398–409. The real cost of production regulates the price of commodities, 410, 414, 415. Increase of population no cause of the rise of rent, 410, 411, nor agricultural improvements, 412. His supposition, that net income is diminished, in proportion to a diminution of gross income, disproved, 419–422. Loss of rent, the effect of a low price of corn, 427.

Manufactures, improvement of, in any country, tends to alter the distribution of the precious metals among the nations of the world, 137–141. Manufacturers pay less poor-rate than farmers, 260, 261. The market price of manufactures, but not their natural price, raised by bounties on their exportation, 312, 313.

Mines, distinguished by their fertility or barrenness, 85, 86. Effect of discovering the rich mines of America on the price of the precious metals, 86. [Effect of improvements in the working of them on the value of money, 146.][3] Observations on the rent of mines, [85–87][3] [329–332][1,2].

Money, effects of the rise of the value of, on the price of commodities, 47–49. The rate of profit not affected by variations in the value of money, 50, 51. Different value of money in different countries accounted for, 141–143. The value of money, *generally*, diminished by improvements in the facility of working the mines of the precious metals, 146. [A fall in the value of money, raises the price of provisions, 164–168.][3] The demand for, regulated by its value, and its value by its quantity, 193. Low value of, in Spain, prejudicial to the commerce and manufactures of that country, 228. Observations on the rates of interest for money, 297, 298 [, 363, 364][1,2]. The value of, though partially degraded by a bounty on corn, yet not permanently degraded, 310, 311. The quantity of, employed in a country, dependant upon its value, 352. Effects of the state charging a seignorage on coining money, 353, 371, 372.

Monopoly price, observations on, 249–252. [Variation in value of monopolized commodities accounted for, 385.][3]

N

National Debt, observations on, 247–249.

[*Necessaries*, tax on, a cause of the high price of provisions, 168–172.][3]

Net Revenue, advantages of, unduly estimated by Adam Smith, 347, and by M. Say, *ibid. note*. Examination of their doctrines, 347–351. [The

* ['never' is omitted here, by a mistake, as is shown by the text, p. 105, line 4 from bottom.]